The English Riots of 2011

A Summer of Discontent

Edited by Daniel Briggs

The English Riots of 2011
A Summer of Discontent
Edited by Daniel Briggs

Published 2012 by
Waterside Press Ltd
Sherfield Gables
Sherfield on Loddon
Hook, Hampshire
United Kingdom RG27 0JG

Telephone +44(0)1256 882250
E-mail enquiries@watersidepress.co.uk
Online catalogue WatersidePress.co.uk

ISBN 978-1-904380-88-7 (Paperback)
ISBN 978-1-908162-20-5 (Kindle/Epub ebook)
ISBN 978-1-908162-21-2 (Adobe ebook)

Cover design © 2012 Waterside Press. Design by www.gibgob.com. Photograph of looters: © Tim Hales/AP/Press Association Images.

UK distributor Gardners Books, 1 Whittle Drive, Eastbourne, East Sussex, BN23 6QH. Tel: +44 (0)1323 521777; sales@gardners.com; www.gardners.com

North American distributor International Specialized Book Services (ISBS), 920 NE 58th Ave, Suite 300, Portland, Oregon, 97213-3786, USA. Tel: 1 800 944 6190 Fax 1 503 280 8832; orders@isbs.com; www.isbs.com

Cataloguing-In-Publication Data A catalogue record for this book can be obtained from the British Library.

Printed by MPG Books Group, Bodmin and King's Lynn.

e-book *The English Riots of 2011* is available as an ebook and also to subscribers of Myilibrary and Dawsonera (for ISBNs see above).

The English Riots of 2011

A Summer of Discontent

Edited by Daniel Briggs

⋙ **WATERSIDE** PRESS

CONTENTS

Acknowledgements   vii
About the Editor   viii

1. **Introduction**   9
   Daniel Briggs

2. **Frustrations, Urban Relations and Temptations:**   27
   Contextualising the English Riots
   Daniel Briggs

PART 1: RIOTING IN CONTEXT   43

3. **Everything Changes, Nothing Moves:**   45
   The Longue Durée of Social Anxieties about Youth Crime
   Geoffrey Pearson

4. **Riots in Retrospective:**   65
   Immigration and the Crisis of the 'Other'
   Steven Hirschler

5. **With the Benefit of Hindsight:**   91
   The Disturbances of August 2011 in Historical Context
   Tim Bateman

6. **Revisiting Brixton:**   111
   The War on Babylon 1981
   Sheldon Thomas

7. **More Police, Less Safety?**   127
   Policing as a Causal Factor in the Outbreak of Riots and Public Disturbances
   Axel Klein

PART 2: WHO, HOW AND WHY?_____ 147

8. **Gone Shopping:**   149
   Inarticulate Politics in the English Riots of 2011
   Simon Winlow and Steve Hall

9. **Policing the Riots:**   169
   New Social Media as Recruitment, Resistance, and Surveillance
   Stephanie Alice Baker

10. **Street Government:**   193
    The Role of the Urban Street Gang in the London Riots
    Simon Harding

11. **Reading the Riots Through Gender:**   215
    A Feminist Reflection on England's 2011 Riots
    Liz Kelly and Aisha K. Gill

PART 3: THE AFTERMATH _____ 235

12. **'There Are None Sicker Than the EDL':**   237
    Narratives of Racialisation and Resentment from Whitehall and Eltham, London
    Joel Busher

13. **From Words of Action to the Action of Words:**   257
    Politics, Post-riot Rhetoric and Contractual Governance
    Vicky Heap and Hannah Smithson

14. **Profiling the 'Rioters':**   279
    Findings from Manchester
    Rebecca Clarke

15. **Rurality and the Riots:**   303
From the Panel to the Village Pub
Steve Briggs

PART 4: THE WIDER PICTURE: SOCIAL CHANGE AND GLOBAL DISCONTENT _____ 327

16. **State-Sponsored Riot:**   329
Tales of Revolt and Crime in Egypt 2011
John Strawson

17. **'If You Won't Let Us Dream, Then We Won't Let You Sleep':** 347
Demarcation of Spaces and the Rise of the Spanish 15 M
Lorenzo Navarréte-Moreno, Celia Díaz-Catalán and Ricardo Zúñiga

18. **Post-Modern Greek Tragedy:**   361
Walking in the Steps of Thucydides in Athens
Daniel Briggs

19. **Concluding Thoughts**   381
Daniel Briggs

Index   403

ACKNOWLEDGEMENTS

My first thanks go to David Cameron whose speech branding the rioters' actions 'criminality, pure and simple' was the moment at which I decided to pursue this area as a form of social inquiry. I then have to thank the rioters who braved potential arrest to speak to me. Nadia Whitney and Jessica Lartey helped me with access to these people and Joyann Bannon assisted with interview transcriptions. Dan Hales of Barking and Dagenham Youth Offending Service assisted with discussions as well as numerous other court, probation and youth offending workers across London with whom I had informal discussions. A paper based on this data was published for a special issue of *Safer Communities* early in 2012 (see Vol 11(1)).

I was supported by Jo Sharrocks at Emerald Publishers and Professor Chris Fox and Dr Tim Bateman. The book evolved from the special issue and for that reason I extend immense gratitude to all the contributors for working hard within the publishing timeframe to assemble this collection within four months. Bryan Gibson, the Director of Waterside Press, was immensely enthusiastic about this project and has provided immeasurable support. Thanks to Dr. Joel Busher, Professor Simon Winlow and Dr. Stephanie Alice Baker for reading and commenting on several chapters and also to my father for reviewing my work.

I am grateful for the collegial companionship of John Strawson, Barry Heard, Dr. James Windle, Dr. John Morrison and Jennifer Schmidt-Petersen.

As always, appreciation and love go to those closest to me: they know who they are and they know what they did.

Daniel Briggs
August 2012

ABOUT THE EDITOR

Dr Daniel Briggs is a Reader in Criminology and Criminal Justice at the University of East London. He works with a range of social groups — from the most vulnerable to the most dangerous to the most misunderstood. His work takes him inside prisons, crack houses, mental health institutions, asylum-seeker institutions, hostels, care homes and hospices, and homeless services. His research interests include social exclusion, culture and deviance, and postmodern identities but more broadly he tends to research any social issues which are stigmatised, misunderstood and/or misrepresented. He has recently undertaken work in Spain on gypsies, youth risk behaviours while on holiday and the English riots of 2011. He is the author of *Crack Cocaine Users: High Society and Low Life in South London* (Routledge, 2011).

Descriptions of the other contributors to this work appear at the start of their individual chapters.

1

INTRODUCTION

Daniel Briggs

A glass smashes outside the train station and everyone turns around. There is caution and a collective nervousness. 'Is a riot breaking out?' people seem to be asking themselves. Numerous burly police officers guard each exit of the station, arms folded as if they mean business. No sign of the smaller, friendlier community support officers now. The hefty policemen talk about the violence which has brought London to its knees, looking around periodically, making image-driven evaluations of potential trouble-makers. They express particular interest in young people in groups of three or more. On the trains, the commuters frantically turn the newspaper pages, tut to themselves and shake their head every few seconds. 'What's wrong with these people?' one says to his friend who replies 'If it was me, I would just shoot the cunts'.

Field notes

This was the atmosphere at London Bridge overland station at the height of the violence and unrest during the English riots of August 2011. It was one of edgy anticipation. To the everyday person, such as the two people on the train in this exchange, the sequence of violence appeared to have evolved from nothing in a matter of days. Over the early August period in south and central London, I overheard similar conversations about the social unrest on trains, buses, in takeaways, gyms, parks and shopping malls. While some seemed a little understanding about protesting in the name of Mark Duggan's death, many others shrugged their shoulders and negatively moralised the behaviour. These people frowned on the defective people and their actions, and agreed that the state should punish them as harshly as possible. Indeed, such views were reflected in public opinion surveys conducted shortly after the riots. From 2,019 adults aged 18+, 88 per cent believed that the sentences on the 'rioters' and 'looters' were not tough enough, two thirds (69 per cent) felt that organized 'gangs' were the cause of the unrest, with significant numbers of the sample favouring water cannons (69 per cent), rubber bullets (54 per cent) and curfews (54 per cent) as future potential riots tactics. The survey also indicated significant sympathy with the police (75 per cent) (Optimum Research, 2011).

Perhaps they were entitled to feel outraged? It was estimated that 13,000 to 15,000 people 'rioted/looted' across English cities from 6th to 10th August 2011. Numerous people lost their businesses, family homes, had property damaged and, sadly, five people died. There were also financial costs. The disorder cost £50 million to police and £43.5 million to clean up. There was £300 million worth of damage to property and £80 million lost in business and sales. Insurance claims were estimated to reach £300 million and the figure thought to be lost in tourism revenue stood at £250 million. This amounts to around half a billion pounds (*Guardian* and LSE, 2011; Riots Communities and Victims Panel, 2012). However, many people didn't seem to know where to start when considering 'why' this all happened and the 'insanity' of the events raised complex causal questions that most of the media, the police and prominent politicians failed to address.

Unsurprisingly, public disapproval was quickly stoked up by media images and stories which were 'one-sided' in their depiction of the disorder. Over that week in early August, I followed the news with interest. First there were the victim testimonies, which preceded endless discussions of effective policing. There then followed debates about sentencing, and finally, the blame fell on the usual suspects—such as 'dysfunctional families', the 'underclass' and 'gangs'. No wonder the public thought 'gangs' were to blame. It was the silly season of August when news is flat but it became a 'story' dreamland for the media. The potential headliners were everywhere and the news stories were incessant: the next hotspot, the next victim. The Croydon family who watched their furniture business go up in flames; the moving figure of an old man trying to tidy up the ruins of his Do-It-Yourself (DIY) store in

Figure 1—Prime Minister David Cameron's Profile of the 'Rioters' and 'Looters'

According to David Cameron, the English 'rioter' and 'looter' are of the same breed; namely of the feral underclass type. These people, as Cameron would have it, are foreign to the hard-working, regular citizen and it is through poor life choices and lack of meritocratic initiative that they find themselves clinging to the margins of society. Some tend to laze around in their rundown council flats, watching Jeremy Kyle, only getting up to go to the chippy, to restock on cans of beer or to cash the social security benefit cheque. Some are also women who were irresponsible and sexually promiscuous when they were younger and have since had numerous children from different partners. There are also some who are violent, dodgy youths who wear hoodies, run 'gangs' and peddle drugs, seeking, where possible, to recruit young innocent children into their criminal networks—this group, Cameron would say, are especially dangerous and have been known to 'hang around' on street corners, doing nothing in particular apart from talking. Collectively, this strange group of people have limited capacity for the working world, have been excluded from school because they had 'special educational needs' or lacked the basic intellectual capacity, have wasted countless employment opportunities thereby exhausting numerous jobs, and perhaps also have 'mental health disorders' or 'substance misuse issues' which means they are a significant drain on the NHS and other social services. When they drift into the aesthetic beauty spots of the town centres they are a clear blemish to public life with their stained jogging trousers and cigarettes hanging, half-smoked from their lips. When they are not blighting public space with their unruly behaviours and vicious dogs, they are criminal opportunists: in a moment, taking advantage of an open window to invade a hard-working regular citizen's family home and steal their hard-earned treasures or stealthily profiting from a dozing security guard by smuggling some supermarket goods under their jackets. During the riots, these people came creeping out of the sink estate—otherwise known as Criminal Land—to enact their dark plans to raid places such as Currys and Greggs thus highlighting their inherent bad characteristics, and their savage-like, greedy tendencies to steal as much as they can carry while simultaneously causing immeasurable havoc on society.

north London; the brittle voice of an onlooker with her family, scared to come out of the house. By comparison, the commercial buildings, which represented the bulk of the targets (*Guardian* and LSE, 2011), were not getting half as much media coverage (Briggs, 2012). At one point, the BBC had a split screen with the flaming inferno of a building on one side and hooded gang youth on the other leaving the public to make the inextricable link that it was gangs who were up to no good (again!). This all seemed to make for a public unsympathetic and critical of the motives of the instigators.

Even more unsurprising were the senior politicians' statements which confined the behaviour to 'criminality, pure and simple', 'known offenders', 'gangs', the 'underclass' and/or 'other people' who came from 'other' areas to commit 'sick' acts (Briggs, 2012; Durkin, 2012). I was interested to learn about these people the politicians were describing: people who, by insinuation, no doubt had crime and violence pumping through their veins (see *Figure 1*). Collectively, politicians, media and police missed the glaring significance of a sinister commitment to consumerism (Bauman, 2011; Grover, 2011; Moxon, 2011; Varul, 2011) and predictably obfuscated the typical questions from the media which were directed at core issues of social mobility, racism, discrimination, and aggressive policing. Even austerity and inequality were sidelined from the political agenda as the discourse revolved in the main around some sort of bad characteristic of these people. Take this exchange from an interview with Kenneth Clarke, the Justice Secretary:[1]

> **Interviewer:** Looking at your department's statistics about 'who is doing the rioting', do you think there is a lost generation of young men who are frankly unsavable?

> **Kenneth Clarke:** There's obviously far too many of them. The danger is we're getting more of them. I remember riots 30 years ago [Brixton 1981], but these were very widespread [England 2011], very serious and the sheer casual criminality troubles me. You know, it was almost instantly, people were responding on their BlackBerry or mobile and turning out just to loot what they wanted. There was absolutely no undertone of anything except [pause] criminal people, just straight

---

1.   Interview video clip taken from ITV News, 15th September 2011.

away, going out to repeat crimes they had already been convicted of in the past. Quite outside the values of the ordinary, decent people in this country.

In this way, the politicians ratcheted-up public indignation by sternly renouncing the actions of the rioters and looters and appealing to the 'hard working, law abiding mainstream'. They also extended continuous sympathy for the victims and the affected communities, pledging immediate help and compensation for those areas worst hit. However, as I write, most of these communities still await recompense for their loss. Some communities spontaneously 'self-policed' and defended their interests, either as a result of a lack of confidence in the police to deal with matters or a lack of police presence in general (*Guardian* and LSE, 2011). The same communities even organized voluntary clear-up schemes across London each morning to deal with the post-riot mess. So that's the Big Society which David Cameron was talking about.

The first observation to make is that there was an immense misperception about the events of August 2011. Political rhetoric lambasted 'feral youth', 'gangs' and the 'underclass', strategically sidestepping over the role of consumerism in contemporary society and other well-documented, entrenched social problems. The news media depicted twisted versions of the events, and balanced reporting was absent, instead homing in on emotive victim testimonies and general panic. And as for the general public, aside perhaps from some of those living in affected communities, some didn't quite know what to think, but some of their discussions seemed to reflect political discourses that the 'gangs' were to blame and that to restore law and order, the 'criminals' needed harsh punishments. Let us briefly examine which areas were affected before considering the responses.

What Happened, Where?

The pockets of violence and disorder mainly occurred in urban cities across England, the worst of which affected London, Birmingham, Liverpool, Manchester and Nottingham.[2] Here are some brief details about these affected areas.

---

2. It is acknowledged that other cities and towns may have experienced disorder but for the purpose of this introduction I am only examining these cities. The order in which they are

London

Rioting and looting took place in London from Saturday 6th to Wednesday 10th August 2011; the longest period throughout the English riots. It is now mostly agreed that the killing of Mark Duggan triggered the unrest which followed across the country (*Chapter 2*). However, the disorder was recurrent in the same place on consecutive nights as disorder started in Tottenham on Saturday, evolving in Enfield, Brixton and Oxford Circus on Sunday, and Lewisham, Ealing, Croydon, Clapham on Monday, and East Ham and Woolwich on Tuesday.[3] The violence and disorder took the form of arson, criminal damage, looting, violent behaviour and clashes with police. Official statistics revealed that the average 'rioter' in London already had 15 convictions. By September 12th, 1715 offenders had been identified by the authorities in the capital; 462 had been found guilty and 315 sentenced. Among the convictions, most were for burglary (n=763), violent disorder (n=459) and theft (n=229) (Ministry of Justice, 2011).

Birmingham

Some indicate that the 'visibility of chaos' in cities such as London sparked off riots and looting in Birmingham (Spalek *et al*, 2012). There were varying levels of disorder which started on the 8th August and had desisted by 10th August. Despite some businesses anticipating trouble and boarding up their shops in the wake of what was going on in cities like Manchester and London, disorder and looting was generally confined to Birmingham High Street shops. Initial reports indicate that there was a standoff between some young people and the police in the city centre, and that as the numbers swelled. Looting was triggered when some of this group charged on a jeweller's shop. As other shops were sacked, the young crowd were joined by men in their 30s and 40s, white as well as Asian 'looters' and a significant number of women (Davies, 2012). The disorder in Birmingham was further marred by one particular notable event when, on the 10th of August, a car struck three young Asian shopkeepers who were defending their properties in the Aston area of North Birmingham. They died of their injuries. Post-riot

---

discussed does not represent the order in which disorder evolved in those areas.

3. These are just a few of the London locations which were affected by the disorder.

police statistics indicate that 75 per cent of those arrested in Birmingham already had previous convictions (West Midlands Police Authority, 2011).

Liverpool

Reports from Liverpool indicated that disorder started to evolve on Monday 8th August when 'mobs set fire to two vehicles' and the police presence which responded was met with around 150 youths who were pelting police vans with various objects. However, it is now evident that, in the main, stationary traffic continued to be the predominant targets on Tuesday 9th August although that second evening of rioting also saw crowds gather around Admiral Street police station to smash windows and set a nearby van on fire. On the same evening, disturbances also took place in nearby Birkenhead where 100 young people were reported to be sacking stationary cars. By comparison to other cities, the looting in Liverpool didn't seem to be as widespread.

Manchester

The social disorder in Greater Manchester began in Salford on Tuesday 9th August from the pursuit by Manchester Police of numerous individuals involved in criminal damage on a local housing estate. The police remained there and the crowd increased and this lead to violent confrontations into the looting of supermarkets and off licences (Jeffery and Jackson, 2012). However, disorder quickly developed into the mass systematic looting which then took place in Manchester City Centre two miles away. There were, however, further isolated incidents in the Trafford and Tameside boroughs. The nature of the crimes recorded in Greater Manchester reflected national data. The majority of individuals were convicted of some form of acquisitive offence including burglary (61 per cent); handling stolen goods (8 per cent); theft (5 per cent) or 'stealing from shops' (5 per cent) and most convictions were for activities on August 9th and 10th. Collectively, there were 110 individuals convicted and sentenced for involvement in the riots in Greater Manchester although another 700 were wanted by the authorities (see *Chapter 14*).

Nottingham

Disorder in Nottingham took place on Monday 8th and Tuesday 9th August and seemed to be predominantly directed at the police, stationary vehicles, and with some episodes of looting. On Monday, it was estimated that about 40 vehicles were damaged in a 'night of violence', motivated, Nottingham police claimed, by what took place in London over the weekend. Most events were confined to St Anne's, which has historically been a disadvantaged neighbourhood. Police foiled attempts to break into the local shopping precinct and other efforts were made to attack authority establishments the following evening when a local police station was 'firebombed' by rioters. By Friday 12th August, Nottinghamshire Police confirmed they had arrested 109 people of which 69 had been charged.

The Responses to the Events

Once the police had managed to wrestle back control of the streets, the state instigated all-out mobilisation of the criminal justice system (CJS). We shouldn't be too surprised that those punished felt the full force of the law, perhaps epitomised by the sentencing of two young men to four years in custody for threatening to incite disorder by organizing riots via Facebook (which didn't take place in the end). At the time of writing, more than 4,000 suspected rioters had been arrested nationally; nine out of ten of whom were already known to the police. More than 5,000 crimes were recorded in this very short period, which included 1,860 incidents of arson and criminal damage, 1,649 burglaries, 141 incidents of disorder and 366 incidents of violence against the person (Riots Communities and Victims Panel, 2012). There was also an increase in the use of custody and disproportionate sentencing (Briggs, 2012).

Aside from feeling the wrath of the criminal justice system, academics and experts, policymakers, practitioners and frontline workers got together to discuss how future disturbances could be prevented. There were familiar promises of improving police relations with the community, reconsideration of riot tactics and policing public order (see Benyon, 1984) but little strategic authority applied to solving the social symptoms which may have led to the problems. For example, the report compiled by the politically-backed Riots Communities and Victims Panel (2012: 13) proclaimed how 'plans should be put in place to deal with future disturbances'. In addition, it recommended that the police should reconsider future 'riot' tactics, before quickly sinking into recommendations which concerned the rebuilding of personal aspirations, individual resilience and tackling 'poor parenting'.

I attended several regional and local events in London which aimed to discuss what happened and consider ways to prevent further riots from occurring. One such event was run by London councils a month after the riots. At the table were mostly senior police officials, councillors, community safety managers, housing and health workers, youth offending workers and related professionals across London boroughs. The day I spent in this seminar typified the general lack of knowledge of: (a) how it all occurred, (b) the issues which aggravated further disorder; and (c) what to do to prevent it happening again. The seminar seemed to be much more about the police persuading other professionals of the 'threat of gangs' and an exercise to celebrate the 'glowing success' of existing interventions.

The second observation is that the main responses were predictable hardline, state-led punishments aiming to deter others from the same actions while also making an example of the 'criminals'. Perhaps, given the scale and unprecedented rapidity of spread of the disturbances, and the initial picture of an inadequate law enforcement response to maintain public order and protect people and property, this was not surprising. But even as the smoke cleared, there seemed to be little idea of how it started and what to do to prevent it occurring again. For example, one got the feeling that anyone who spoke up about delicate issues at that seminar was quickly hushed, with the political weight of 'consequence of actions', deterrence, and regulation of social media dominating. However, in the aftermath of the riots, some investigations began into how they arose.

A Clear Divide: In Pursuit of Reasons Why'

National, regional and local government quickly tried to explain the disorder by statistical profiling of the 'offenders' and their backgrounds, thereby confining their identities and motives to already-established public stereotypes about the sort of people who would normally be the culprits. Most, if not all, of this material takes a one-dimensional perspective on their motivations, thus rendering the protagonists' actions to the margins of 'background risk factors' — which doesn't give much idea about anything. In this vein, the offender profile has familiar underlying social characteristics; someone who was living in poverty and deprivation, lacking education, and who had numerous previous convictions. Typically:

> Young people appearing before the courts came disproportionately from areas with high levels of income deprivation as defined by the Income Deprivation Affecting Children Indices (IDACI) rankings for 2010 ... The Ministry of Justice also noted that 66 per cent of ten to 17-year-olds appearing before the courts for offences relating to the disorder, for whom data were available, had some form of special educational needs, compared with 21 per cent of all pupils in maintained secondary schools ... Over 76 per cent of those who have appeared before the courts for the disorder had previous cautions or convictions.

Ministry of Justice, 2011: 6-7

It seemed that the reporting quickly became an opportunity to look at how those who had been caught had failed at everything—their poor GCSE marks, their 'educational needs', their exclusion from school, their poverty and disadvantaged status, and therefore lower chance of employment (see House of Commons Home Affairs Select Committee, 2011). One report even suggested that because of these deficiencies, the 'rioters' and 'looters' 'have a lack of aspiration' (London Councils, 2011: 2). These accounts, as John Lea (2011) notes, tell us very little about who got involved and why they participated.

Independent research bodies/consultants were also involved in making sense of the disorder. An independent inquiry, the Riots Communities and Victims Panel, was set up by Prime Minister David Cameron. Their interim report found that young men, with previous convictions under the age of 25 were mostly involved in the English riots; 84 people, they note, had 50 or more previous convictions each. And it wasn't long before similar demographic profiling exercises were used to confirm the cohort's identity and their motives. The graphs highlight the 'rioters' defects such as special education needs, school truancy, school exclusion, that they were from low income areas, living in poverty, concluding that 'whilst these are striking statistics, the vast majority of people we spoke to (which were not rioters by the way) were clear that not having a good education or a job was an excuse to do wrong' (*Ibid.*, 11). Those without previous convictions, the interim report states, just made 'bad decisions'. This crude insight was a likely consequence of failing to consult with any of the perpetrators of the violence. In addition, the authors seemed surprised to learn about tensions between the police and urban communities and the number of young people 'who had no hopes for their future' (*Ibid.*, 7) — as if these things were something new and had somehow recently developed. The final report drew on 'poor parenting' as the source of the problems.

The few other studies on the issue to date do similar things: correlations are favoured which reduce an understanding to 'background risk factors'. Morrell *et al* (2011) do this in their study based on interviews with 206 young people; 133 of whom neither participated nor were involved in any capacity in the riots. Attempts are made to assign typologies for participation: young peoples' motivations are divided between personal factors (criminal history, experience of the police, attitudes to power and authority, job prospects and aspirations); family and community factors (family attitudes and behaviour, attachment to community); and societal factors (having a stake in the local area, youth provision, and poverty and materialism). This seems reasonable but the authors struggle to show how 'factors' interrelate: for example, 'a criminal history was a facilitating factor for involvement in rioting and looting' and 'experience of the police was a nudge factor'(*Ibid.*, 3). In short, the narratives from the interviews get dislocated in the separation of 'background, contributing factor'.

Perhaps the most robust analysis of the riots was undertaken by the *The Guardian* and the London School of Economics. This study seeks to understand the motivations of the rioters but also consider the role of social media and 'gangs'. Their interim report was based on interviews with 270 rioters across the country.[4] Importantly, unlike any other study to date, they interviewed a significant number who had not been caught/processed by the CJS. They found four fifths were male, and 29 per cent were juvenile (10-17), 49 per cent were aged 18-25 and 22 per cent 26 and above. In contrast to the suggestion that gangs were responsible, *The Guardian* and LSE indicated that gangs called a truce and united against the police. In opposition to

---

4.   London, Birmingham, Manchester, Salford Liverpool and Nottingham.

political beliefs, social media was downplayed as an instigator of the disorder but more the vehicle which made it happen. In the main, the instigators reflected anger and frustration at the police, especially through discriminatory practices such as the use of stop and search powers. However, the study also found that many rioters conceded to opportunism and looked to take advantage of a 'free-for-all' to obtain 'free stuff' when they saw law and order seemed to be absent.

Such analyses have also been supported by numerous academic articles published in the wake of the disorder. Unlike much of the governmental bulletins and independent research, sociological and criminological experts have been concerned with more nuanced commentaries on the riots by covering issues of race (Murji and Neal, 2011; Solomos, 2011), class (Scambler and Scambler, 2011), consumerism (Bauman, 2011; Grover, 2011; Moxon, 2011; Varul, 2011), the role of the 'crowd' in contexts of riots (Baker, 2012; Gorringe and Rosie, 2011), policing (Klein, 2012), politics (Angel, 2012) and its rhetoric (Briggs, 2012; Durkin, 2012; Heap and Smithson, 2012) and gender (Kelly and Gill, 2012). Collectively, these papers underlined that the riots represented deeper symptoms of unresolved, embedded social problems but also social changes which had started to spill over into our everyday lives.

The final observation to make is that state agencies, various official inquiries, and independent consultants and researchers were quick to consider demographics and 'background risk factors' as indices for participation in the riots. However, the way in which statistics and correlations were used removed most of the value and power of understanding real motivations and sidelined structural, situational and emotional considerations. More detailed and more balanced analyses, which have looked at the issue more objectively and without political sway, have come from sociological and criminological experts. They showed that the 'background risk or contributing factors' frequently overlap and that 'looting' and 'rioting' represented more complex social issues which warranted more detailed scrutiny. However, as we shall see, maybe some of these commentators may have made the wrong call on what the disorder represented.

Rationale For the Book

Most current research and analyses have challenged the specific issue of the rioters, their profiles and motivations. Equally, some have noted the political and social conditions for the disorder as well as the faults of the police. But we have been here before: we are familiar with the social ingredients for public disorder in contemporary England which have been simmering below the surface for some time. We knew where the finger would be pointed. And we knew the criminal justice system would come down hard on the protagonists. So what is new? What is different? Was this collective disorder 'political'? What contemporary theoretical explanations are available to us to make sense of it? If so, are they adequate enough?

It would be easy to assign an understanding of the riots to 'faulty young people', who are 'part of a gang' if we were to accept, at face value, the ideological position of the political elites and if we sat on our sofas shaking our heads at their deplorable behaviour. The official response has been predictably substandard and, unlike the Brixton riots in 1981, there will be no 'Scarman-like' figure to lead a public inquiry (Lea, 2011). *The Guardian* and LSE have led various discussion forums while the British Sociological Association (BSA) has published a series of sociological commentaries. Similarly, *Criminal Justice Matters* and the online forum Sociological Research Online quickly received numerous papers about the riots. However, there is also the danger that some of this work may fail to accurately comprehend what happened, perhaps over-politicising the riots, by confining it to issues of class and race without exploring it in its entirety, by using dated theoretical frameworks to rubber stamp what the disorder represented and/or by making these assumptions without any kind of robust qualitative/ethnographic analysis. Moreover, current analyses point only to the social disorder in this country when other countries have, and are experiencing, forms of public unrest and disorder: throughout the European Union, North Africa and in numerous Arab countries. Is what happened in England in 2011 similar to the unrest in these countries? In this book, I want to give greater consideration to these areas, but also to frame what took place in August 2011 across English cities in the context of global social change.

In September 2011, a month after the riots, I gave a paper at the conference 'Urban Unrest, Social Resentment and Justice' at York University where presentations were also delivered by Professor Tony Jefferson, Dr. Simon Winlow, Dr. Rowland Atkinson, Professor John Lea and Professor Simon Hallsworth and others. Shortly afterwards, I discussed the potential for the publication of a special edition of *Safer Communities* (published as Vol. 11, Issue 1 in 2012) with its editors, Professor Chris Fox and Dr Tim Bateman. They, along with help from the publishers Jo Sharrocks and Devon Blake at Emerald Publishers, helped me to collate a series of papers which sought to critically analyse the events (some of whom have taken forward their work in this book). This book therefore represents work which resulted from these two outputs as well as my own ethnographic work in London, the UK and in Athens, Greece.

Aims and Structure of the Book

The book draws together empirical and theoretical analyses, and personal commentaries with the aim to:

1. Provide a balanced commentary on the August 2011 riots which places in context the actions of those who took part;

2. Place these actions in their respective emotional, socio-structural, cultural, and historical theoretical frameworks as well as recognise their situational nuance;

3. Critically evaluate the response from the government and the CJS;

4. Consider what happened across English cities in 2011 against broader social changes such as: consumer society and the material force of ideology; wider, global issues of rising inequality; the failure of democratic governments in Western countries; economic market uncertainty; and oppressive state governance.

Following this introduction, the work begins with a chapter which considers why people participated in the disorder in London (*Chapter 2*), thereby acting as the springboard for more in-depth commentaries and analyses on what the riots may have represented. The book then divides into four parts.

Part I considers *Rioting in Context*. Early on in the disorder, assumptions were made that the unrest represented some sort of failed generation of feral youth. In *Chapter 3*, Geoffrey Pearson examines some of the cultural features of such accusations by discussing social anxieties which have historically surrounded young people. Using examples from riots in 1958 and 1981, Steven Hirschler discusses immigration controls and urban unrest while Tim Bateman explores the specific similarities and differences between unrest in 1981 and 2011. This section then offers a personal reflection from participation in previous riots in Brixton (Sheldon Thomas in *Chapter 6*) but also considers the common denominators which seem to feature in how contemporary rioting evolves — often through persistent, oppressive policing (Axel Klein in *Chapter 7*).

Part II offers a more detailed theoretical and empirical commentary on *Who, How and Why?: The English Riots of 2011*. Who was involved in the riots, in what capacity and why? The role of consumerism and ideology is considered (Simon Winlow and Steve Hall in *Chapter 8*) as well as social media (Stephanie Alice Baker in *Chapter 9*), 'gangs' (Simon Harding in *Chapter 10*) and gender (Liz Kelly and Aisha Gill in *Chapter 11*).

Part III examines *The Aftermath* to the riots by considering what it meant for certain social groups who were associated with the disorder — such as the English Defence League (EDL) (Joel Busher in *Chapter 12*). A discussion of contractual governance and its role in state responses (Vicky Heap and Hannah Smithson in *Chapter 13*) precedes a more detailed examination of how 'rioters' were processed through the criminal justice system in Manchester (Rebecca Clarke in *Chapter 14*), while *Chapter 15* applies a critique of the riots from a rural perspective (Steve Briggs).

Finally, **Part IV** examines *The Wider Picture: Social Change and Global Discontent* and considers the August 2011 riots against social protest in Egypt (John Stawson in *Chapter 16*), Spain (Lorenzo Navarréte-Moreno, Celia Díaz-Catalán and Ricardo Zúñiga in *Chapter 17*) and Greece (*Chapter 18*).

Concluding thoughts then follow. For now, let us consider how this all started.

References

Angel, H. (2012) 'Were the Riots Political?' in *Safer Communities Special Edition on the Riots*, Vol 11(1): 24-32.

Bauman, Z. (2011) 'The London Riots—On Consumerism Coming Home to Roost' cited online on 1st March 2012 at http://www.social-europe.eu/2011/08/the-london-riots-on-consumerism-coming-home-to-roost/

Benyon, J. (1984) *Scarman and After: Essays Reflecting on Lord Scarman's Report , The Riots and Their Aftermath*, London: Pergamon Press.

Briggs, D. (2012) 'What We Did When it Happened: A Timeline Analysis of the Social Disorder in London' in *Safer Communities Special Edition on the Riots*, Vol 11(1): 6-16.

Davies, T. (2012) 'Eyewitness, Birmingham, 4pm, Tuesday 9th August 2011' in *Criminal Justice Matters*, Vol 87 (1): 16-17.

Durkin, C. (2012) 'How 'Sick is Our Society' in *Safer Communities Special Edition on the Riots*, Vol 11(1): 50-53.

Gorringe, H. and Rosie, M. (2011) 'King Mob: Perceptions, Presumptions and Prescriptions about the Policing of the English Riots' in *Sociological Research Online*, Vol 16(4): 17.

Grover, C. (2011) 'Social Protest in 2011: Material and Cultural Aspects of Economic Inequalities' in *Sociological Research Online*, Vol 16(4): 18.

Heap, V. and Smithson, H. (2012) 'We've Got to be Touch, We've Got to be Robust, We've got to score a Clear Line Between Right and Wrong Right Through the Heart of this Country: Can and Should the Post-riot Rhetoric be Translated into Reality? in *Safer Communities Special Edition on the Riots*, Vol 11(1): 54-61.

House of Commons Home Affairs Committee (2011), *Policing Large Scale Disorder: Lessons from the Disturbances of 2011*, London: House of Commons.

Jeffery, B. and Jackson, W. (2012) 'The Pendleton Riot: A Political Sociology' in *Criminal Justice Matters*, Vol 87(1): 18-20.

Kelly, L. and Gill, A. (2012) 'Rotis Not Riots: A Feminist Dialogue of the Riots and their Aftermath' in *Safer Communities Special Edition on the Riots*, Vol 11(1): 24-32.

Klein, A. (2012) 'Policing as a Causal Factor—A Fresh View on Riots and Social Unrest' in *Safer Communities Special Edition on the riots*, Vol 11(1): 17-23.

Lea, J. (2011) 'Shock Horror: Rioters Cause Riots! Criminals Cause Crime', *British Society of Criminology Newsletter*, No. 69, Winter 2011.

London Councils (2011), London's Local Councils: Responding to the Riots and Promoting Safety,Resilient Communities, London: London Councils.

Ministry of Justice (2011), Statistical Bulletin on the Public Disorder of 6th-9th August 2011 cited online on 1st March 2012 at http://www.justice.gov.uk/publications/statistics-and-data/criminal-justice/public-disorder-august-11.htm

Moxon, D. (2011) 'Consumer Culture and the Riots of 2011' in *Sociological Research Online*, Vol 16(4): 19.

Murji, K. and Neal, S. (2011) 'Riots: Race and Politics in the 2011 Disorders' in *Sociological Research Online* 16(4): 24.Optimum Research (2011) *Reaction to the England Riots*, London: Optimum Research.

Riots Communities and Victims Panel (2012) *Five Days in August: An Interim Report on the 2011 English Riots*, London: Riots Communities and Victims Panel.

Scambler, G. and Scambler, A (2011) 'Underlying the Riots: The Invisible Politics of Class' in *Sociological Research Online*, Vol 16(4): 25.

Solomos, J. (2011) 'Race, Rumours and Riots: Past, Present and Future' in *Sociological Research Online*, Vol 16(4): 20.

Spalek, B., Isakjee, A. and Davies, T. (2012) 'Panic on the Streets of Birmingham? Struggles Over Space and belonging in the Revanchist City, in *Criminal Justice Matters*, Vol 87(1): 14-15.

Varul, M. Z. (2011) 'Veblen in the Inner city: On the Normality of Looting' in *Sociological Research Online* 16(4): 22.

West Midlands Police Authority (2011), Minutes from 'Special Meeting', 8 September, Midlands Art Centre, Birmingham.

2

FRUSTRATIONS, URBAN RELATIONS AND TEMPTATIONS:
CONTEXTUALISING THE ENGLISH RIOTS

Daniel Briggs

Introduction

In August 2011, England's cities experienced significant social disorder, resulting in violence and criminal damage. Unsurprisingly, politicians and police ascribed this unrest to the usual suspects—such as 'gangs', 'problem youth', 'dysfunctional families', and the 'feral underclass' while the media debates tended to revolve around the scale and severity of the violence, 'innocent victims', effective policing techniques and stiff sentencing practices. In a definitive speech, David Cameron, the British Prime Minister, branded the behaviour 'criminality, pure and simple'. At the time, balanced or accurate explanations for what was taking place were entirely absent; in particular, how and why the disorder developed and spread so quickly. In the months since, numerous commentators have tried to make sense of what happened and this is the principle aim of this chapter. Using empirical data gathered from 20 of those who participated in the riots,[1] I seek to place the events in context by showing why people may have participated in the disorder. I focus in this instance mostly on what happened in London and borrow on theoretical insights where the narratives indicate some association. This chapter shows that what took place in August 2011 does match the political rhetoric and media representations of the unrest and suggests that the events were

---

1. For more information on the methodological approaches see Briggs (2012b).

perhaps more complex—even in the wake of the subsequent analyses which followed. The chapter also acts as the 'springboard' for deeper discussion, in the chapters which follow, of the numerous social issues which were at play. I begin by discussing, what is considered to be, the 'trigger' event—the killing of Mark Duggan—before highlighting why people may have participated.

Frustrations and the 'Trigger': Mark Duggan's Death

Mark Duggan lived on the Broadwater Farm Estate in Tottenham, north London; an area with a history of tension between the black community and the police (*Chapter 1*). In the early evening of Thursday 4th August 2011, Duggan was shot and killed by the police after they stopped a cab in which he was a passenger. One police officer was also shot but survived. The way Duggan's death was reported on Thursday suggested that he was wanted by the police. It was also suggested that Duggan fired his gun first and that the police acted in response to the threat of his firearm (Angel, 2012). However, evidence now indicates Duggan was not armed when he was shot and that the policeman who was shot had been fired on by another officer (Laville, 2011). This exchange of gunfire did not go unnoticed. Both bystanders and some community members witnessed or heard quickly about the events via Facebook. Shawn, a friend of Duggan's, said:

> **Shawn:** The day Mark Duggan was killed, before the news went out, a friend put his picture on Facebook saying 'this picture speaks a thousand words' and it was a picture of the police standing over what looked like to be Mark Duggan. This was minutes after it [he was shot] took place, so someone had recorded it and put it online and this person was saying like 'looks like the police are trying to get their story straight'. The picture was posted on Facebook four minutes afterwards.

It seems attention to this event was quickly stimulated through online social media through Twitter and BlackBerry messenger ('BB' hereafter). However, the police failed to instigate any formal notification to the family; in fact, it was rumoured that Duggan's mother found out her son had died when she watched the news that evening.

Unfortunately, the police stalled the family's demands for clarity, and instead issued a statement suggesting that officers were fired upon by the 'suspect', Mark Duggan, before shooting back (Klein, 2012). Some in the local (and virtual) community found this difficult to believe having seen/read various posts about the event through social media. The following day, national and local news seemed contradictory; some media played upon images of a 'gangsta badboy' while others described him as a 'family man'. The latter seemed to be the view of local community members from the Broadwater Farm Estate who said Duggan was coming to terms with the death of someone close to him some weeks earlier. Local criticism quickly started to build against the police at the manner of the killing, because it was largely perceived as unjust. Nadine, a local resident in Tottenham, said:

> **Nadine:** On Friday the police was confusing it and that they [the police and Duggan] both fired but because of the Facebook, people in Tottenham knew he didn't discharge his gun or didn't believe that he discharged his gun. The police shot another officer and Mark Duggan already knew he was being followed [by the police] and put out a BB message. They [the local community] agreed that there would be protests on Saturday and we were all invited, my partner and my friend.

Unsatisfied with police action and lack of clarity on Duggan's death, a protest was arranged by the local Broadwater Farm residents. It was to take place on Saturday 6th August in an effort to gain transparency. Late that afternoon, around 300 people from the local community, including family and friends, gathered outside Tottenham Police Station after marching from Broadwater Farm Estate. The crowd said they wanted 'justice' for Mark Duggan's family and answers. Some like Dave and Dev — who remembered the riots which occurred in similar circumstances in Broadwater Farm in 1985 — participated in the protest, the potential injustice was not just about Duggan but about wider discrimination against the black community:

> **Dave:** For the black community, there was a message which was about treatment. A lot of black guys die in custody, a lot are poorly treated by the police but that message got lost. The peaceful demonstration was not getting through, it was getting lost in the fact that the 'look at these gangs, look at these blacks, gangs or whatever'. Lost.

29

Dev: Questions aren't being answered. So much frustration. They [the police] could have just come out and said 'we hear you and we are looking into it'. They could have nipped this in the bud. All the people wanted to know was that they wanted to be heard. It does look like there is something to cover up if the taxi driver suddenly isn't available.

Their views reflect what Reicher *et al* (2004: 561) note in the context of riots which: 'Groups have collective memories which can sometimes go back well beyond the experience or even the lifetime of any individual member'. The crowd gathered outside Tottenham Police Station started to get agitated when no senior police representative materialised to give transparency on the issue. By around 8 pm, there were reported confrontations with the police. From 8.30 pm until 10.30 pm, a double-decker bus was burnt out and police cars and buildings were vandalised and set alight. Then shops and businesses in the area started to get ransacked and looted.

When Mark Duggan was shot, the local community were unconvinced as to the reasons how and why it happened. They organized a protest at which the police failed to respond to their demands. These sequences of events are now widely believed to be the 'trigger' (Briggs, 2012b; Angel, 2012; Laville, 2011; Žižek, 2011), or as Moxon (2011) puts it, the 'initial moments' which led to the disorder that followed in London and around the country. They were, however, not the cause because, as we will see, it seems not all were engaging in acts of violence and criminal damage in the name of Mark Duggan's death.

From Protest to Provocation to Plunder: Urban Relations and Temptations

As the disorder was evolving in Tottenham, a lack of police presence seemed to attract others to the scene and some of those people seemed to have been encouraged through social media and news coverage of the disorder (*Guardian* and LSE, 2011). Yet those that came that Saturday evening, and in the days which followed to other areas of London and throughout England, did so with different agendas. The decision to participate, or turn up at least, it seems, was quite subjective and this was evident in the testimonies of those with whom I spoke. Some attached initial reasons to deep-rooted feelings of hate for the authorities (Klein, 2012; Morrell *et al*, 2011) and the government (Angel, 2012; Hatherley, 2011). Take Jamal for example. He is black, experiences life on a disadvantaged estate where there is almost no social mobility, a strong presences of 'gangs', drugs and crime, and habitual police harassment on people like him. He said to me it 'didn't take much' for him to decide to get involved in the disorder: although he downplayed his accumulation of free clobber, he seemed mostly upset that he couldn't get work and was treated like 'dirt' at the Job Centre—which was where he took out his anger:

> **Jamal:** I am no rude boy, no road boy, I carry no gun. I am not into rap music or being on road. I went to school but this government is making me think that the road is the only place for me because I have done everything they have asked of me. I have good GCSEs, A-levels, university 1ˢᵗ degree but there is nothing for me. Since graduating I have been a cleaner. There are no opportunities. Down the Job Centre, they treat me like dirt and accuse me of not trying but look at what I have achieved. I have been on the dole for so long and they tell me I need a job but I have no experience, and can't get it because no one is taking anyone on. Three guesses where I took my frustration out—Job Centre.

Research shows that others living in the area had also become the target for aggressive/restrictive social policies, law enforcement operations and broader social stigmatisation (*Guardian* and LSE, 2011). This did little for their inclusion—or shaming them into conformity (Grover, 2011)—but instead exacerbates their marginality, likely contributing to fragile feelings which were easily stimulated by gestures like incessant stop and search practices, police raids, etc. (Badiou, 2011; Lea, 2011; Young, 2007). This perhaps made them a population quite ready to counteract their structural position in an effort to send a message to those in charge who had been perpetuating their misery. In this conversation with Paul who claimed 'gang-affiliation', he reveals how local 'rival gangs' united against the police (see *Chapter 10*):

Paul: Obviously yeah there is serious rivalry between Tottenham and Hackney[2] and no one generally goes from one area to the other, there would be bloodshed. But on the riots, there was no gang war. The gangs was in the same area on Saturday night, came together against the police and I thought 'wow, it would have been nice if it had been a better situation but they are coming together for a cause they thought worth fighting for as a unit'. I was impressed, nah what I mean?

Dan: So even though there was beef [vendettas] between the gangs, they wanted to unite against something which was repressing them collectively.

Paul: Yeah, BB messages were sent out to cool it, saying like 'its not about a postcode war, it is 'us' against 'them' and 'forget our beef with each other and let's get the police'.

While most of the people I talked to saw little decisive action from the police (Hatherley, 2011; Klein, 2012; Newburn, 2011), some became fascinated with the revolving media images of the disorder (Body-Gendrot, 2011; *Guardian* and LSE, 2011); which made it easier for some just to turn up to see what was happening. This, some said, gave them some 'ideas' to make money. Some commentators would therefore suggest that their participation was almost 'senseless' in that there was little motivation other than they could (Žižek, 2011; *Chapter 8*).

This was perhaps the case for a group of three young men from East London. Their 'planned' operation for Sunday night looting quite quickly dissipated when they struck three designer shops followed by a Sainsbury's store, loading thousands of pounds worth of stolen goods into their car. They stashed the goods in a friend's garage and gave him a £2,000 cut of their profit. Overall, they made £20,000 between them which they split four ways. When I first met them in Stratford, one month after the disorder, their narratives were around 'hate for the police' and this, at the time, they said was largely their motivation. However, six months later after keeping in touch through Facebook, I had the opportunity to undertake a more focused interview. While the interview narratives point at hate for the police

---

2. These are two areas of London with 'gang' rivalries.

and criticism of the state, this time, however, they seemed less convincing, less sure of a reason:

Will: They [the police] shot him [Mark Duggan], killed him for no reason. You don't have to get shot for nothing.

Dan: Yes, but why then? Presumably you must hear of people getting hurt all the time or done over or whatever. I remember that conversation we had on Facebook about gangs and that.

Will: Probably because it was so close to home. It's a piss take, you know. How can police get away with shooting someone with no gun and get away with it and not go to prison? [pause] It's the police, man.

Dan: Right, I want everyone to chip in here because Will's doing all the work. I'm a little lost. Talk me through it in detail, from start to finish. Tell me as if I was from another planet and knew nothing about this.

Will: [To Craig] Tell him why you started rioting [nudges him and then sits back], tell him your part.

Craig: [Seriously] Right [sits forward as if to suggest his answer will be definitive], everyone started rioting so we started rioting. I just joined in.

[Steve laughs a little to himself]

Craig: We was smashing up shops [Steve sniggers], getting bits [looting], that boy was shot.

Will: Was it because he got shot?

Craig: [Looking a little vacant] Because he got shot. Police was covering it up. Shot for no reason.

Steve: I needed the money.

Note the general confusion which surrounds the narrative as they try to locate the essence of their behaviour. This dichotomy continues throughout their interview. In hindsight, it was difficult to see just how the significance of Mark Duggan's killing or the police oppression could have been at the centre of their intentions. When I pressed them on it, they seemed unconvinced at their own answers:

Dan: Ok, I am going to challenge you now. You say it is about the police [that you rioted] but you can't ignore how much you looted.

Steve: It's just that guy [Will]. Some people use it as an excuse. Like dese days, people haven't got much money as they had. I done it because I needed money. Like it's hard to explain. People wanted to get back at the police but at the same time get some bits.

Craig: Money for me was the main reason.

Steve: Like people was using the police as an excuse because no one wants to admit 'yeah I am a bit poor' or 'I need a bit of money because I am poor' but they do make an excuse that just because that boy died. When I saw everyone do it, I fought 'why can't I do that'. I felt a bit jealous. It was like everyone was out there, getting that money and I was sitting indoors.

Craig: Same here.

But 'money' was also not the clear motivation either because what they made from their designer-shop raids was legitimately reinvested back in some of the same shops they had looted — it went straight back into the consumer market. Furthermore, no money was saved or put towards any long-term cause, and if anything, had to be spent quickly.

In the absence of law enforcement, a few made arrangements to carry out more specific, targeted acts, which they argued, would be seen to be interpreted as 'part of the disorder' (Briggs, 2012b). On one evening of the riots in London, Stevie and 20 of his friends agreed to avenge some 'beef' they had with another youth in their area. They said they were not part of a gang *per se*, but just didn't like this person. They met up and torched his house, reasoning that the social disorder and chaos made it possible. Similarly, Wez, who said he used to 'roll with a crew' [gang], gives some insight into how some properties were avoided in the unrest while others were targeted on Saturday 6th and Sunday 7th:

> **Wez:** Like on my road there is a really popular chicken shop, like on a Friday night everyone is there. It is ram, bruv [very busy, man]. Then to the side, but not next door, there is a kebab shop. Proper nice kebabs, init. Now, the owners were called before the riots came that way and were told not to worry, init. But the businesses either side got torched or robbed. So I think there was some like loyalty in it because like the chicken shop looks out for us, but also there was this opportunity to settle beef, carry out revenge attacks and all the rest of it. But today is the best opportunity to burn down somewhere which we have beef with.

This suggests that there were different phases of the disorder which meant that the initial reasons for the unrest were not necessarily the same when it unfolded — people were in it for different reasons (Gorringe and Rosie, 2011; Sumner, 2011; Briggs, 2012b). For example, some testimonies also reflected a sense of disgust at the way in which the ruling classes had been robbing them, 'the poorer classes'. Harvey (2011) refers to this power imbalance as 'daylight robbery of the poor'. Some had watched news stories of various austerity cuts (such as the education maintenance allowance, youth provision, etc.) yet, at the same time, learned about banker bonus increases, MP's expense fiddles, and the FIFA[3] and phone hacking scandals (Angel, 2012; Badiou, 2011; Hatherley, 2011; Žižek, 2011). In fact, the words of those with whom I spoke seemed to reflect a real sense of disorientation especially given that, in their eyes, so many social institutions were rife with corruption, and concerned only with never-ending profiteering. Some participants in the riots therefore justified their actions by 'taking what was theirs' (Varul, 2011) since, they felt, those in power were doing similar things; thus a 'taking from' attitude is rationalised because access to the symbolisms of the

---

3. Fédération Internationale de Football Association.

good life are unavailable to them. Here, Jamie rationalises his looting of a commercial store that Saturday evening:

> **Jamie:** Basically, the government are stealing things all the time, so why can't we steal from them. It is justice. They can't say one thing and do another. When you did your election, you promised jobs, equality, benefits for families. I don't see anything like that in my area. There is no 'we' in the community. The government were talking about building a better community but how can you take away from the community and expect us to stump up for it when we are suffering as well. What is the point?

However, as we have seen in the example of Steve, Will and Craig, finger pointing at the police, the state or any kind of lived structural oppression feels like a smokescreen — it is not the whole story. It's true that inequality and injustice play some role, but the narratives were also heavily structured around a desire for consumption (Bauman, 2005, 2011; Žižek, 2011) — claiming the 'free stuff', as they saw it. This was also evident in the places which were looted as a result. While the media stories hinged on coverage of the 'innocent victims' who had been plagued by the 'criminals' (Briggs, 2012b), it was the designer boutiques, town centres, and main shopping precincts where chains such as Argos, Currys and J D Sports which were more widely targeted. The looters, it seems, unable or unwilling to strive for tokens of meritocratic recognition through education and work, went for the numerous symbols of consumer accolade which were now potentially available for retrieval (Bauman, 2011; Grover, 2011; Young, 2002). Indeed, Nadine's house party in Tottenham, full of family and friends that Saturday evening, emptied very quickly when the guests started to receive Facebook notifications and BB messages; of which were a mixture between offers for goods people had acquired and invitations to take part in the looting (Baker, 2012; see *Chapter 9*). Many, she said, left to claim 'free shit [stuff]'. Paul, who attended Saturday's events in Tottenham and claimed 'buff [nice] trainers', was feeling otherwise about getting involved in another night of 'rioting' and 'looting'; however, the pressure to participate and the promise of handsome rewards did not disappear on Sunday. His friend Shawn, although equally attracted by the booty, was drawn to potential participation for numerous reasons:

Paul: We was getting BB messages about the next destination, who has got this, if you want it, we can get it. There was like loads of adverts! I was with my mates and we was all getting similar messages of people getting stuff: 'This is what we have got', 'these are the goods if you are interested'; bags, trainers was a big one, paintings, computer things, games, clothes, anything really designer.

Shawn: I was getting messages as well but it wasn't all about tiefing [stealing]. Like if I was there, I would have got involved but not really with the looting but say if a police station was being done over, I would like get involved because I have bare [lots of] problems with the police. Anything to do with the police, I would have got involved.

In this way, participation was also fun and exciting (Katz, 1988; Spalek *et al*, 2011). However, what these testimonies confirm is that the 'rioters' seemed as concerned about their treatment by the authorities/state as they were about claiming free goods when the opportunity presented itself.

Discussion

This chapter has tried to frame the book in context and set the scene for the discussions which will ensue by presenting an account of what is considered to now represent the 'trigger' for the social disorder (Briggs, 2012b; Angel, 2012; Laville, 2011; Moxon, 2011; Žižek, 2011). While my colleagues will take forward some of these issues in greater depth in the chapters which follow, it is evident thus far that there was no one single explanation for the social unrest which took place in August 2011 (Briggs, 2012b; Gorringe, and Rosie, 2011; Lea, 2011); it was more than just 'criminality, pure and simple' (Harvey, 2011). What started off as a protest seemed to quickly turn into something else (Sumner, 2011): from declarations of frustrated urban relations to underlying narratives of consumer temptations—from protest to provocation to plunder.

Indeed, the chapter highlights perhaps predictable narratives of frustration; of mistreatment, discrimination, and social inequality (Badiou, 2011; Young, 2007). People in these communities, it seems, feel tired of watching successive governments continue to marginalise them and seek only to 'control' them while ratcheting-up law enforcement. Some say they are also tired of seeing people in powerful positions continue to cream off cash at their expense (Harvey, 2011; Varul, 2011). And while some protagonists of the English riots may be able to locate these injustices, they didn't seem to have articulated a critique of consumer capitalism (Harvey, 2011) or even their own participation in the market; and I don't think we can expect them to either (see Moxon, 2011). Some would say this instead represents a 'material force of ideology' (Žižek, 2011) which beckoned the 'disqualified consumers' to find ways to consume (Bauman, 2005, 2011). In this respect, rioting and looting could perhaps be considered 'senseless' in that it was the rioters trashing their own communities with little social motivation other than because they could.

So when people saw the law enforcement buffers were down (Hatherley, 2011; Hughes 2011; Klein, 2012; Newburn, 2011) when they watched the 'live violence' unfold or received phone calls or texts (Briggs, 2012a), the authorities weaknesses were exploited by social media. People quickly learnt of what was taking place — BB, Twitter and Facebook messages were posted of what was being targeted, what was available to loot, what people had got, and then followed the invitations — just like those described at Nadine's house party and between Steve, Will and Craig. Once the invitations started to travel across cyberspace, it became something subjective for the receiver. On the face of it, deep personal feelings of frustration with the authorities were apparent but below the surface, the narratives reveal a clear commitment to consumerism and quite calculated intentions to claim the prizes which they perhaps thought they were being starved of/wanted in any case. In this respect, it some became excited by the carnival of it all (Katz, 1988; Spalek *et al,* 2012), went along for a laugh or to see what was happening — perhaps to participate, witness (Morrell *et al,* 2011) or with no discernible rationale. Perhaps it was as Žižek (2011) states: a violent action demanding nothing. So if that is the case, what have people got to show for their participation?

References

Angel, H. (2012) 'Were the Riots Political?' in *Safer Communities Special Edition on the Riots*, Vol. 11(1): 24-32.

Badiou, A. (2011) 'Daily Humiliation' cited online on 1st March 2012 at http://www.versobooks.com/ blogs/681-alain-badiou-on-riots-and-racism-daily-humiliation.

Baker, S. A. (2012) 'From the Criminal Crowd to the "Mediated Crowd": The Impact of Social Media on the 2011 English Riots' in *Safer Communities Special Edition on the Riots*, Vol. 11(1): 40-49.

Bauman, Z. (2005) *Work, Consumerism and the New Poor*, New York: Open University Press.

Bauman, Z. (2011) 'The London Riots—On Consumerism Coming Home to Roost' cited online on 1st March 2012 at http://www.social-europe. eu/2011/08/the-london-riots-on-consumerism-coming-home-to-roost/

Body-Gendrot, S. (2011) 'Disorder in World Cities: Comparing Britain and France' cited online on 1st March 2012 at http://www.opendemocracy.net/ourkingdom/ sophie-body-gendrot/disorder-in-world-cities-comparing-britain-and-france?utm_source=feedblitz&utm_medium=FeedBlitzEmail&utm_ content=201210&utm_campaign=Nightly_2011-08-16%20 05:30

Briggs, D. (2012a) 'Editorial' in *Safer Communities Special Edition on the Riots*, Vol. 11(1): 3-5.

Briggs, D. (2012b) 'What We Did When It Happened: A Timeline analysis of the Social Disorder in London' in *Safer Communities Special Edition on the Riots*, Vol. 11(1): 6-16.

Gorringe, H. and Rosie, M. (2011) 'King Mob: Perceptions, Presumptions and Prescriptions about the Policing of the English Riots' in *Sociological Research Online*, Vol. 16(4).

Grover, C. (2011) 'Social Protest in 2011: Material and Cultural Aspects of Economic Inequalities' in *Sociological Research Online*, Vol. 16(4).

Guardian and LSE (2011) 'Reading the Riots: Investigating England's Summer of Disorder', London: *Guardian* and LSE.

Harvey, D. (2011) 'Feral Capitalism Hits the Streets' cited online on 1st March
2012 at http://davidharvey.org/2011/08/feral-capitalism-hits-the-streets/

Hatherley, O. (2011) 'Something Has Snapped, and It Has Been a Long Time
Coming' cited online on 1st March 2012 at http://www.versobooks.com/
blogs/660-something-has-snapped-and-it-has-been-a-long-time-coming.

House of Commons Home Affairs Committee (2011) *Policing Large Scale Disorder: Lessons From the Disturbances of 2011*, London: House of Commons.

Hughes, M. (2011) 'Riots spread because police lost control of the street report
finds' in *The Guardian*, Monday 19th December 2011.

Katz, J. (1988) *Seductions of Crime: Moral and Sensual Attractions in Doing Evil*,
New York: Basic Books.

Klein, A. (2012) 'Policing as a Causal Factor—A Fresh View on Riots and Social
Unrest' in *Safer Communities Special Edition on the Riots*, Vol. 11(1): 17-23.

Laville, S. (2011) 'Mark Duggan investigation plagued by 'inaccuracies' in *The
Guardian*, Thursday 24th November 2011.

Lea, J. (2011) 'Shock Horror: Rioters Cause Riots! Criminals Cause Crime', *British Society of Criminology Newsletter*, No.69, Winter 2011.

Morrell, G., Scott, S., McNeish, D. and Webster, S. (2011) *The August Riots in
England: Understanding the Involvement of Young People,* London: National
Centre for Social Research.

Moxon, D. (2011) 'Consumer Culture and the Riots of 2011' in *Sociological
Research Online*, Vol. 16(4): No page numbers.

Newburn, T. (2011) 'Cuts to Police Numbers' LSE Online Blog, cited online
on 1st March 2012 at http://blogs.lse.ac.uk/politicsandpolicy/2011/08/22/
police-relationship-conservatives/

Reicher, S., Stott, C., Cronin, P. and Adang, O. (2004) 'An Integrated Approach
to Crowd Psychology and Public Order Policing' in *Policing: An International Journal of Police Strategies & Management*, Vol. 27(4): 558–572.

Riley-Smith, B. (2011) 'Mark Duggan: Family Man, Gangsta or Both?' in *The
Week*, Monday 8th August 2011.

Spalek, B., Iskjee, A. and Davies, T. (2012) 'Panic on the Streets of Birmingham?
Struggles Over Space and Belonging in the Revanchist City' in *Criminal
Justice Matters,* Vol. 81(1):14-15.

Sumner, C. (2011) 'Riots, Aggravated Shopping and 30 years of Opportunism'. *CrimeTalk*. Online: cited online on 1st March 2012 at http://www.

crimetalk.org.uk/archive/section-list/38-frontpage-articles/427-riots-aggra-vated-shopping-and-30-years-of-opportunism-.html

Varul, M. Z. (2011) 'Veblen in the Inner city: On the Normality of Looting' in *Sociological Research Online* 16(4).

Young, J. (2002) 'Crime and Social Exclusion' in Maguire, M., Morgan, R. and Reiner, R. (Eds.) *The Oxford Handbook of Criminology*, 3rd edn. Oxford: Oxford University Press.

Young, J. (2007) *The Vertigo of Late Modernity*. London: Sage.

Žižek, S. (2011) 'Shoplifters of the World Unite' in *London Review of Books*, Friday 19th August 2011.

Part I

RIOTING IN CONTEXT

Geoffrey Pearson is Emeritus Professor of Criminology at Goldsmiths, University of London. His research interests concern crime, drugs, drug markets, youth studies and historical criminology. From 1998 to 2006 he was Editor-in-Chief of the *British Journal of Criminology*. He is the author of numerous books and articles, including *The Deviant Imagination* (Macmillan, 1975), *Working Class Youth Culture* (Routledge, 1976), *Hooligan: A History of Respectable Fears* (Macmillan, 1983), *Young People and Heroin* (Health Education Council and Gower, 1985), *The New Heroin Users* (Blackwell, 1987) and *Middle Market Drug Distribution (*Home Office, 2001).

3

EVERYTHING CHANGES, NOTHING MOVES:
THE LONGUE DURÉE OF SOCIAL ANXIETIES ABOUT YOUTH CRIME

Geoffrey Pearson

Introduction

While the riots of 2011 announced a new chapter in violent youth disorder Britain was already in the thick of a moral panic concerning its young people. Its constituent elements were gangs, shootings, stabbings, family dysfunction, lack of community cohesion, and the hovering background ambience of 'gangsta rap' music. Indeed, when interviewed about youth behaviour during the riots, Kenneth Clarke, the Justice Secretary, said that Britain had cultivated a 'lost generation' of young people. But really this worry was nothing new. As this chapter will show, there is a long history of social anxiety that finds its crystallising focus in a preoccupation with the rising youth generation, and the crime and violence for which it is responsible. History shows there is a common structure of preoccupations linking the past with the present—family breakdown, the declining influence of religion and education, lack of respect for authority, the erosion of community, the influence of demoralising popular entertainments—that are brought into play around quite different social and historical circumstances, which involve a profound historical amnesia and a deep cultural pessimism. When these features are perpetually reproduced, a sudden and radical discontinuity with the past is implied which confuses us in our attempts to fashion realistic responses to the current actualities and dilemmas.

Post-War Lift Off: Teds Under the Beds

It goes without saying that there have been a number of moral panics concerning young people since the Second World War. Indeed, Stanley Cohen's seminal work *Folk Devils and Moral Panics* (1972) was formulated in response to one such set of incidents — the mod/rocker disturbances at southern English seaside towns in the early 1960s. Since then there have been numerous episodes of alarm — about football hooligans, skinheads, muggers, punks, chavs and hoodies — leading into the current concerns with street gangs, stabbings and shootings. However, it was the 1950s that gave the post-war years lift-off in the context of youth panic. Summarising the concerns of the previous decade, in 1960 the British Medical Association (BMA) decided to inaugurate a discussion on a 'Special Topic' and predictably chose 'The Adolescent'. Young people were said to be growing up in an atmosphere of 'bewildering change':

> ... the whole face of society has changed in the last 20 years ... unaccustomed riches ... materialism without effort ... in his worst light the adolescent can take on an alarming aspect: he has learned no moral standards from his parents, is contemptuous of the law, easily bored ... vulnerable to the influence of TV programmes of a deplorably low standard...
>
> *BMA, 1961: 5-6*

It goes without saying that for the BMA, the 'adolescent' is a boy, not a girl, and nor were they writing about other doctors' children. Rather, it was the 'Teddy Boy' they were concerned with, described by Paul Rock and Stanley Cohen (1970: 289) as 'the first and greatest' of the post-war emblems of shocking modernity. Dressed in their finery of long drape jackets with velvet collars — originally tailored for City toffs who wanted to sport a bit of retro Edwardian chic — the 'Teds' were instantly recognised as symptomatic of affluence. Although as one of the informants in T R Fyvel's *The Insecure Offenders* (1963: 40) described them, 'they were market porters, roadworkers, a lot of van boys, all in jobs that didn't offer a lot—labourers would cover the lot'.

One notable feature of the Teds was their attachment to the new rock-and-roll music from the USA. In Richard Hoggart's portrait of the 'juke-box boys' in *The Uses of Literacy* (1958: 248) they were 'boys between 15 and 20, with drape-suits, picture ties and an American slouch'. This effortless, 'American-ised' appearance where 'Americanisation' figures in the English imagination as a signifier of modernity and a portent for the dreadful future, was central to the structure of feeling arranged around 'unaccustomed riches', 'materialism without effort' and 'sex in shiny packets' as Hoggart described it. This trope was put to even more outlandish use elsewhere, as when the *Daily Mail* ran front-pages editorials on 'Rock 'n Roll Babies' in response to cinema riots greeting Bill Haley's 'Rock Around the Clock'. These described the music as 'a communicable disease' and 'the music of delinquents'. 'Rock, roll and riot' is sexy music. It can make the blood race. It has something of the African tomtom and voodoo dance'. And then, the awful unblemished truth about the musical force that was rocking the nation:

> It is deplorable. It is tribal. And it is from America. It follows rag-time, blues, dixie, jazz, hot cha-cha and the boogie-woogie, which surely originated in the jungle. We sometimes wonder whether this is the negro's revenge.

> *Daily Mail, 4-5 September 1956*

Since the War: Which War was That?

The Teds were tailor-made for the post-war lament that from politicians, the police, the media and other social commentators began to organize itself around the youth question, describing how everything was going to the dogs 'since the war'. The complaint had been perhaps first fully rehearsed in the post-war years by the Conservative Party publication, *Crime Knows No Boundaries,* in the mid-1960s which declared:

> We live in times of unprecedented change—change which often produces stress and social breakdown. Indeed the growth in the crime rate may be attributed in part to the breakdown of certain spontaneous agencies that worked in the past. These controls operated through the family, the Church, through personal and local loyalties, and through a stable life in a stable society.

> *Conservative Party, 1966: 11*

One must ask oneself: was this 'stable life in a stable society' meant to refer to the Great Depression of the 1930s, the ingrained worklessness and poverty, the unemployed riots of 1931, the General Strike of 1926, and the bitter aftermath of the First World War? No matter, the British people know this post-war lament off by heart; it runs in our veins, it is part of our DNA. It is part of the daily gossip in pubs, launderettes and bus queues, TV chat shows and popular journalism. Here it is again:

> That's the way we're going nowadays. Everything slick and streamlined, everything made out of something else. Celluloid, rubber, chromium-steel everywhere ... radios all playing the same tune, no vegetation left, everything cemented over ... There's something that's gone out of us in these 20 years since the war.

And again:

> The passing of parental authority, defiance of pre-war conventions, the absence of restraint, the wildness of extremes, the confusion of unrelated liberties, the whole-sale drift away from churches, are but a few characteristics of after-war conditions.

And yet the immediate problem is that each of these last two complaints about what has gone 'wrong since the war' were both written *before* the war. The first is from George Orwell's pre-war novel *Coming Up for Air* as the main character, grumpy old George Bowling hunts around for traces of his lost boyhood (Orwell, 1939: 26, 168). The second is from James Butterworth's *Clubland* (1932: 22) where a Christian youth worker reflects on his experiences in the Boys' Club movement in the Elephant and Castle area of working-class London.

This 'post-war blues' was widespread in the inter-war years. 'Post-War people, compared with Pre-War people, have lost confidence in things human and divine', wrote F W Hirst in 1934 in his summary of *The Consequences of the War to Great Britain*. Continuing, Hirst (1934: 74) stated 'The post-war generation suffers from a sort of inward instability ... There seems nowadays to be no desire to provide for the future or look beyond tomorrow'. Writing in *The Law-Breaker* in 1933, Roy and Theodora Calvert (1933: 60-1) believed that 'this rejection of conventional standards' and 'the greater freedom from constraint which is characteristic of our age' meant that 'we are passing through a crisis in morals'. In the cultural sphere, one active focus of discontent was the 'Scrutiny' group gathered around F R Leavis at Cambridge that repeatedly thundered against 'this vast and terrifying disintegration' of social life. 'Change has been so catastrophic', Leavis wrote in 1930, that 'the generations find it hard to adjust themselves to each other, and parents are helpless to deal with their children'. 'It is a breach of continuity that threatens', Leavis warned, 'It is a commonplace that we are being Americanised' (Leavis and Thompson, 1933: 87; Leavis, 1930: 6-7).

Fears of 'Americanisation' often figured centrally in these troubled discourses on 'post-war' social change—just as they do now. In the 1930s, this fear was most forcibly registered in the response to the demoralising effects of the Hollywood movies, and from their very beginnings the silent movies that had been condemned for 'the distorted, unreal, Americanised way of life it presented' (Russell, 1917: 6).

The silent movies, and then later the 'talkies', also invited the more specific charge that they encouraged imitative crime among the young—a complaint that we usually think of as belonging only to the age of television and video nasties. So, Hugh Redwood in his book *God in the Slums* (1932: 43) described how boys 'are children in their love of pictures and music' and that 'Hollywood's worst in the movie line has recruited hundreds of them for the gangs of race-course roughs, motor-bandits and smash-and-grab thieves'. A correspondent in *The Times* (12th April 1913) had earlier alleged that many children 'actually begin their downward course of crime by reason of the burglary and pickpocket scenes they have witnessed'. In his book *Children in the Cinema* (1939) Richard Ford collected a number of such accusations. So in 1938 one psychiatrist had confidently asserted that 'seventy per cent of all the crimes were first conceived in the cinema'. In the same year, the Central Women's Advisory Committee of the Conservative Party described their own view of the problem: 'We all know that there is a very great increase in juvenile crime… It is the considered opinion of those who know that this is very largely due to the effect of unsuitable films upon children and the youth of today'. Even among those who clearly did not know, such as a 70-year-old magistrate who proudly boasted that 'I have never been to the pictures in my life', the view still held: 'These lads go to the pictures and see dare-devil things, and they are imitating them' (Ford, 1939: 71-2).

The theory connecting cinema to copy-cat crime had become so well established that even as early as 1913, it had become a matter to joke about. In that year the prosecuting counsel in a London Sessions case involving a boy burglar observed that, 'it was perhaps an example of retributive justice that one of the houses broken into belonged to a cinematograph owner'. The judge, on the other hand, was in no mood to laugh. He was quoted thus: 'Cinematograph shows were responsible for the downfall of many young people,' he thought, and 'a grave danger to the community' (*The Times*, 25 October 1913).

So the accusations have rolled out over the years against faltering discipline, crime and immorality. A couple of decades later, the Children and Young Persons Act 1933 became a target of hostility for undermining the authority of the courts by embracing a welfare model of justice rather than one based on firm punishment:

> There has been a tendency of late to paint a rather alarming picture of the depravity of the youth of the nation ... Headlines scream the menace 'of boy gangsters'. Elderly magistrates deplore the abandonment of their panacea, the birch ... by gloomy forebodings in the Press of the inevitably disastrous results of the leniency and weakness of the present day.
>
> *The Times, 4 January 1937*

As the war clouds gathered in 1939, A E Morgan in his King George's Jubilee Trust report on *The Needs of Youth* summed up the general mood:

> Relaxation of parental control, decay of religious influence, and the transplantation of masses of young persons to housing estates where there is little scope of recreation and plenty for mischief ... a growing contempt by the young person for the procedure of juvenile courts ... The problem is a serious challenge, the difficulty of which is intensified by the extension of freedom which, for better or worse, has been given to youth in the last generation.
>
> *Morgan, 1939: 166, 191*

Street Fights and Music Halls: Queen Victoria's Hooligans

In many ways these inter-war complaints seem like carbon-copies of our own contemporary grievances, and those voicing them were often found to be looking back to happier times 'before the war'. Indeed, the late Victorian and Edwardian years hold a special place in the national memory as a time of unrivalled domestic harmony and moral worth: the cosy fug of the music hall; the rattle of clogs on cobbled streets; and the unhurried pace of a horse-drawn civilisation. Before the motor-car, before the cinema, before all the other disorienting effects of modernity, here lies the true home of moral certainty and 'Old England'. This, however, was not how it was described at the time.

There were already gloomy rumblings in the editorial pages of *The Times* (6 February 1899; 16 August 1899; 17 August 1898) about 'the break-up or weakening of family life', no less than 'the break-up or impairment of the old ideas of discipline or order' in the cities where there was 'something like organized terrorism in the streets'. Nor would we find much comfort from Robert Baden-Powell as he boomed off in the first edition of *Scouting for Boys* against football as a 'vicious game when it draws crowds of lads away from playing themselves to be mere onlookers at a few paid performers'. Oh the good old days:

> Thousands of boys and young men, pale, narrow-chested, hunched-up, miserable specimens, smoking endless cigarettes, numbers of them betting, all of them learning to be hysterical as they groan or cheer in panic unison with their neighbours — the worst sound of all being the hysterical scream of laughter that greets any little trip or fall of a player. One wonders whether this can be the same nation which had gained for itself the reputation of a stolid, pipe-sucking manhood, unmoved by panic or excitement, and reliable in the tightest of places.
>
> *Baden-Powell, 1908: 338*

Once again, this was perceived as a generational shift. 'The tendencies of modern life', wrote Mr. C G Heathcote, the stipendiary magistrate for Brighton, 'incline more and more to ignore or disparate social distinctions, which formerly did much to encourage respect for others and habits of obedience and discipline ... the manners of children are deteriorating ... the child of today is coarser, more vulgar, less refined than his parents were' (Howard Association, 1898: 22). Mrs Helen Bosanquet agreed: 'A somewhat unpleasant characteristic of the present day', she thought, was that 'there is among the children a prevailing and increasing want of respect towards their elders, more especially, perhaps, towards their parents' (Bosanquet, 1906: 310). A chorus of voices agreed on his point.

A few years later, Mary Barnett (1913: 6) wrote that, 'One of the most marked characteristics of the age is a growing spirit of independence in the children and a corresponding slackening of control in the parents'. 'The class of lads and young men who spring up in every city', wrote Sir John Gorst in *The Youth of the Nation* (1901: 11), 'have emancipated themselves form all home influence and restraints'. That young people 'have tasted too much freedom' or had 'no idea of discipline or subordination' was a tireless accusation (Government Papers, 1904: qu. 2107; Braithwaite, 1904: 189). They lived 'a bandit life away from their homes', said a Government Report of 1910, 'free of all control' (Government Papers, 1910: xxviii). 'Speaking generally', according to Reginald Bray (1911: 102), 'the city-bred youth is growing up in a state of unrestrained liberty'. Writing under the cloak of anonymity in 1912, one author suggested that, 'rejoicing in their newly found freedom from school discipline, and with more surplus cash than they will ever again possess', youths were 'tempted to spend as little time at home as possible ... the street, rather than the sleeping place, is the home of the average youth' (Anon, 1912: 263).

Perhaps the most authoritative account of this widespread feeling of a generational discontinuity was given by the young Liberal Charles Masterman in *The Heart of the Empire* where he thundered out his warning of inevitable decline as a result of 'a perpetual lowering in the vitality of the Imperial Race in the great cities of the Kingdom through over-crowding in room and in area'

Clearly, it was the 'new breed' of inner-city youth:

> Turbulent rioting over military successes, Hooliganism, and a certain temper of fickle excitability has revealed to observers during the past few months that a new race, hitherto unreckoned and of incalculable action, is entering the sphere

of practical importance — the 'City type' of the coming years; the 'street-bred' people of the twentieth century; the 'new generation knocking at our doors'… The result is the production of a characteristic physical type of town dweller; stunted, narrow-chested, easily wearied; yet voluble, excitable, with little ballast, stamina or endurance.

Masterman, 1902: 7-8

What was this 'Hooliganism' that Masterman mentions? The word 'hooligan' made an abrupt entrance into the English language in the aftermath of an extremely hot and rowdy Bank Holiday celebration in working-class London which resulted in hundreds of people being brought before the police courts on charges of drunkenness, disorderly conduct, assault and assaults on police officers.

One aspect of this turbulent street life that was highlighted by the Bank Holiday disturbances was the fierce hostility to the police in many working class neighbourhoods. The *Pall Mall Gazette* (19 February 1901) offered the opinion that, 'the constable in certain districts is apparently looked upon as the common enemy whom it is right to kick and beat'. Under the headline, 'Boot "em" at Waterloo', the *South London Chronicle* (15th October 1898) described how a hostile mob raised the cry of 'Boot them against the police' when they attempted to make an arrest in the open street. From the same source, on the very same day, when they attempted to arrest two youths the police were faced with such hostility that 'they had to draw their truncheons and fight their way out of the crowd'. Some indication of how badly used the police were can be gleaned from the 1899 Report of the Metropolitan Police Commissioner and the Royal Commission on the Metropolitan Police of 1908 which indicated that one-in-four of London's police officers were assaulted each year in the course of their duties, and consequently one in ten of them would be in the sick list for a fortnight or more (Government Papers, 1900 and 1908: qu. 79). Taking one consideration from another, a policeman's lot was not a happy one.

At the height of the Bank Holiday outrage, a number of newspapers picked up on what one described as a 'MIDNIGHT RIOT' in the vicinity of Euston Road and Drummond Street in London when five policemen attempted to deal with a disorderly woman who 'began to shriek, and … screamed that she was being choked'. Surrounded by a hostile crowd that 'began to hiss and hoot', one officer swept a semi-circle with his truncheon to make space while another blew his whistle for assistance. 'Unfortunately for the constable', we were told, 'this only had the effect of bringing reinforcements to the mob. A roar went up of "Rescue! Rescue!" and among those alerted to the commotion were the notorious "Somers Town Boys"' (*Evening News*, 13 August 1898; *News of the World*, 14 August 1898; *Daily Mail*, 15 August, 1898).

During the following weeks and months there were any number of reports in the press of Hooligan gangs—the 'Somers Town Boys' who were said to be the pests of Gower Street and Euston Square; the 'Lion Boys' from the Lion and Lamb in Clerkenwell; the 'Drury Lane Boys'; the 'Fulham Boys' from Land's End; the 'Chelsea Boys'; the 'Pinus Gang' from Leather Lane in Clerkenwell; the 'Girdle Gang' from South London which took its name from Thomas alias 'Tuxy' Girdle; the so-called 'Clerkenwell Pistol Gang'; the 'Velvet Cap Gang' from Battersea; the 'Waterloo Road Gang'; the 'Pickell Gang'; 'McNab's'; the 'Rest Gang'; the 'Plaid-Cap Gang' from Poplar; and a band of youngsters who had adopted the dare-devil title of the 'Dick Turpin Gang'. Whereas in Hammersmith *The Sun* (6 August 1898) described how 'the King Street larrikins do just as they like', while gangs who romped about Great Church Street were said to be 'NOT "HOOLIGANS" BUT WORSE'.

The word 'larrikin' was an old Australian term to describe rowdy gangs of youths and was often used inter-changeably when the Hooligans first appeared as in an article in *The Spectator* (27 August 1898) on 'The London Larrikins'. The Larrikins, who can be traced back to 1870 in Australia, were also organized into local gangs or 'pushes' (Ajax, 1884; Pratt, 1901). The 'Scuttler' gangs of Manchester and Salford can also be traced back to the 1870s, and in Andrew Davies's detailed study of Scuttlers, *The Gangs of Manchester* (2008) he identifies more than 500 individual gang members mixed up in the fierce rivalries between gangs such as the 'Bengal Tiger' of Ancoats, the 'Meadow Lads' from Angel Meadow, 'Lime Street' from Miles Platting, the 'Little Forty' from Ardwick, 'The Adelphi', 'Hope Street', the 'Bungall Boys', the 'Grey Mare Boys' from Bradford, and 'Buffalo Bill's Gang' from Salford. These gangs fought pitched battles amongst themselves, over many years, and in some cases female Scuttlers were as fearsome as the boys.

What soon became clear, as the press coverage continued, was that London hooligans had adopted a uniform dress code (Pearson, 1983: 50, 92-101). The main features were bell-bottom narrow-go-wide trousers, cut tight at the knee and flared at the bottom, often pictured with a tasty buttoned wide-vent in the leg; a peaked and a neck scarf; together with heavy leather belts, often worked with ornamental designs using metal studs; and heavy boots, which according to *The Sun* (7 August 1898) in one part of south London were said to be 'toe-plated in iron and calculated to kill easily'. Gang members also had identical hair-styles, the hair clipped close to the scalp, except for tuft on the crown that was pulled forward to form a 'donkey fringe'. Manchester Scuttlers had an almost identical dress sense, pointed clogs substituted for boots, and they also sometimes wore 'billycock' hats as well as peaked caps. Alex Devine, a police court missioner from Salford in 1890, was particularly struck by the ornamental patterns on the Scuttlers' belts which they made with metal pins and studs:

> These designs include figures of serpents, a heart pierced with an arrow (this appears to be a favourite design), Prince of Wales' feathers, clogs, animals, stars, etc., and often either the name of the wearer of the belt or that of some woman.

He also listed weapons that had been confiscated from Scuttlers when their street fights had been broken up:

> Old cutlasses, pokers, pieces of strap having iron bolts affixed to the end, the tops of stone 'pop' bottles fastened at the end of a piece of string and used for whirling round the head, specially made pieces of iron, knives and loaded sticks. But the favourite weapons are stones and belts ... the most dangerous part of the belt is the buckle.
>
> *Devine, 1890: 2*

The fights or 'Scuttles' that took place between the gangs might involve unannounced raids by one gang on the territory of another (including raids on local pubs) or could be pre-arranged confrontations such as one reported in November 1890 from Holland Street in Miles Platting, said to be a 'pitched battle' involving between 500 and 600 people (Home Office papers, 1890).

Violent engagements between local gangs were probably more likely to be more modest affairs. In one such incident that was widely publicised, a gang of about twenty youths known as the 'Chelsea Boys' and 'armed with sticks and stones were fighting a contingent of similar young ruffians from Battersea' at the fashionable neighbourhood of Cheyne Walk by the river Thames, opposite Albert Bridge (*The Daily Graphic*, 18th August 1898). A few months earlier, around the corner in Oakley Street, 19-year-old John D'Arcy, described by the *News of the World* (30thOctober 1898) as 'a youth of the Hooligan type', had stabbed another youth to death and was sentenced to hang. In the aftermath to this affair, a women who had given crucial evidence against D'Arcy was ill-treated by her neighbours and eventually turned out of her Oakley Street home amidst 'a terrible scene' (*South London Chronicle*, 5th November 1898).

More commonly in the weeks and months following the Bank Holiday disturbances Hooligans were depicted in the press cluttering up the streets in noisy gatherings, swearing at passers-by, spitting on them, and sometimes assaulting and robbing them. *The Daily Graphic* (15 August 1898), for example, described 'Some dozen boys, all armed with sticks and belts, wearing velvet caps, and known as the "Velvet Cap Gang", walking along… pushing people off the pavement, knocking at shop doors, and using filthy language'. And then, a few days later, a similar story from another part of London: 'A gang of roughs, who were parading the roadway, shouting obscene language, playing mouth organs, and pushing respectable people down. The young ruffians were all armed with thick leather belts, on which there were heavy brass buckles' (*The Daily Graphic*, 25th August 1898). The following year *The Morning Advertiser* (16 October 1900) could be found describing 'HOOLIGANS AT HACKNEY', 30 or so people 'shouting disgusting language and knocking at the shutters of the shops with sticks… Quite a riot ensued, and sticks, stones, and beer cans were thrown in all directions', but particularly at the police. Elsewhere under the headline 'HOOLIGAN BOYS' the *South London Chronicle* (22 October 1898) told of three boys, aged 17 and 18 years, went into Emma Bennett's coffee house, ate tea and eggs, then laughed at her and refused to pay.

The frequent reports of people being hustled, or pushed off the pavement, might have derived from the practice among working-class youths known as 'holding the end'. This violent ritual of territorial supremacy was described by Walter Besant in his book *East London* (1901: 177): 'The boys gather together and hold the street; if anyone ventures to pass through it they rush upon him, knock him down, and kick him savagely about the head; they rob him as well … the boys regard holding the street with pride'. Besant provided other details of these violent street gangs, describing how the boys of Cable Street would 'constitute themselves, without asking the permission of the War Office, into a small regiment'. A formidable force, they:

> arm themselves with clubs, with iron bars, with leather belts to which buckles belong, with knotted handkerchiefs containing stones — a lethal weapon — with slings and stones, with knives even, with revolver of the 'toy' kind, and they go forth to fight the lads of Brook Street. It is a real fight (*Ibid*: 176-7).

The extent to which the London 'Hooligans' — who were sometimes known as the 'Belt and Pistol' gangs — resorted to the use of firearms is particularly difficult to unravel (Pearson, 1983: 101-106). Cases of pistol shootings were certainly not unknown. Reporting one case under the headline 'PISTOL GANGS IN LONDON. A SCHOOLBOY COMMITTED', *The Daily Graphic* (15 February 1989) had recounted the case of a 13-year-old boy, John Bird from Camden, who had appeared before Marylebone magistrates' court. The magistrate described it as 'an extraordinary tale of life in London', saying that 'these pistol cases are getting much too frequent'. The youngster had shot at an 18-year-old greengrocer's son, shouting 'You won't touch me when I have this. I'll put daylight into you'. In a case reported by the *Illustrated Police News* (5th November 1898) another 13-year-old boy, without provocation, had shot an 18-year-old in the leg on a canal tow-path; whereas a month earlier the *News of the World* (16th October 1898) had carried the story of a 14-year-old boy, Henry Green from Westminster, charged with shooting his two year-old brother Edwin with a 'toy pistol' and a box of cartridges. The magistrate commented on the ease with which these 'dangerous toys' could be bought.

A few months before the 'Hooligan' was officially christened by the news media, the *London Echo* (7 February 1898) had already remarked that 'no one can have read the London, Liverpool, Birmingham, Manchester and Leeds papers and not know that the young street ruffian and prowler, with his heavy belt, treacherous knife and dangerous pistol, is amongst us'. In a discussion of 'Those Pistol Cases' as its chosen 'Topic of the Day', *The Daily Graphic* (15 February 1898) had agreed that they 'are getting much too frequent' and that 'the latest pistol cases have almost all been of boys, hardly in their teens, deliberately using pistols as weapons of aggression ... those 'gangs' of young ruffians ... seem to think little more of discharging them than they would of throwing stones. It is a practice that will have to be suppressed; and if birching and short sentences will not stop it, then more birching and longer sentences will have to be tried'. A couple of years later, with anxiety about the use of pistols still active, the *Graphic* (16th November 1900) would even assert that 'the pistol is the ideal weapon of the Hooligan ... his love for it can be traced directly to the influence of the "penny dreadfuls"'.

With this accusation against popular comic literature, 'Hooliganism' is re-connected to that long, weary catalogue of complaint that blames youth crime and disorder on demoralising popular amusements — whether the cinema, television violence, video-nasties, gangsta rap, or the music halls. Asking 'how far a Music Hall programme may be held to encourage lawlessness', a correspondent in *The Times* (26th September 1898) writing on 'Hooliganism and the Halls' thought that the great majority of Music Hall songs 'could never have been written if the loafer, the liar, the drunkard, the thief, and the sensualist had been regarded as subjects unfit to be glorified in song'. 'This kind of garbage is part and parcel of the repertoire of nearly every Music Hall in the Kingdom' asserted another critic writing in the *Contemporary Review* (1900: 138) who thought that 'spicy' jokes and suggestive songs so much in favour in the Halls 'put decency and clean-living at a discount, and glorify immorality all round. Early in the new century, in his collection *Manchester Boys*, Charles Russell (1905: 94) recounted how 'horrible murders and terrific tragedies were enacted before the footlights', leading to 'so many instances of violence on the part of young men in the backstreets of the city'.

It was a judgement that had echoed down through the nineteenth century, from the time of the furore about 'juvenile depravity' in the mid-century where young people attending cheap theatres, penny gaffs and two-penny hop dancing saloons had been held up as incitements to crime and immorality. 'The corruption of youth from spectacles, songs, etc., of an indecent nature' had excited C. F. Cornwallis in his thesis *On the Treatment of the Dangerous and Perishing Classes of Society* (1853: 41) no less than others who described how the daring enactments of the outrages of Jack Sheppard, Dick Turpin and Claude Duval 'inculcate the same lesson, exhibit to admiration noted examples of successful crime' (Worsley, 1849: 94) and thereby 'attract the attention and the ambition of these boys and each one endeavours to emulate the conduct of his favourite hero' (Beggs, 1849: 97).

So, in the first decade of Victoria's long reign, there was already considerable disquiet about the nation's youth. Edwin Chadwick in his great *Sanitary Report* of 1842 had passed shuddering judgement on the British people, finding 'a population that is young, inexperienced, ignorant, credulous, irritable, passionate, and dangerous' and concluded that during the riots of Manchester, Bristol and elsewhere, 'the great havoc ... was committed by mere boys' (Chadwick, 1965: 267-8). The following year, Lord Ashkey, the Earl of Shaftesbury, rose before Parliament to urge the need for a system of elementary education for the children of the 'dangerous classes'. 'The vicious habits of the parents,' were condemned, 'many of whom are utterly indifferent to the moral and physical welfare of their offspring', so that 'a vast number of children of the tenderest years ... are suffered to roam at large through the streets of the town, contracting the most idle and profligate habits'. He portrayed lads, 'with dogs at their heels and other evidence of dissolute habits', girls who 'drive coal carts, ride astride upon horses, drink, swear, fight, smoke, whistle and care for nobody', together with the great acquaintance if young people with the exploits of Dick Turpin and Jack Sheppard, 'not to mention the preposterous epidemic of a hybrid negro song'. And so her arrived at a tumultuous conclusion: 'The morals of the children are tenfold worse than formerly' and cited one authority that the rising generation were 'more and more debased ... than any previous generation for the last 300 years' (*Hansard*, 28th February 1843).

The profound historical amnesia surrounding the youth question can be measured against a remarkable sermon on the coming of *The Last Days* at the dawn of the Industrial Revolution, rolling out the carpet about parental neglect in the 'last thirty years', and rising juvenile crime:

From this relaxation of parental discipline … doth it come to pass that children who have been brought up within these thirty years, have nothing like the same reverence and submission to their parents … This is the cause of juvenile depredation: this is a chief cause of the increase of crime, especially amongst children … the domestication of man's wild spirit is gone … Oh, oh! what a burden hath the Lord laid upon his ministers, to stand amidst the wreck of a dissolving society, and, like Canute, to preach unto the surging waves!

Irving, 1829: 79, 84, 86–7

Dead-End Discourse

The summer riots of 2011 brought this dead-end discourse fitfully back to life. Amidst the clamour about the feral children of a 'feral underclass', dysfunctional families and communities, a 'moral landslide' and a-moral materialistic nihilism, 'Bagehot' the political correspondent of *The Economist* (16 August 2011) identified some of the worst offenders among these social commentators from Left and Right. First, Bagehot cited the *Daily Mail's* Melanie Phillips 'giving it both barrels: 'The violent anarchy that has taken hold of British cities is the all-too-predictable outcome of a three-decade liberal experiment which tore up virtually every basic social value. The married two-parent family, educational meritocracy, punishment of criminals, national identity, enforcement of the drug laws, and many more fundamental conventions were all smashed by a liberal intelligentsia hell-bent on a revolutionary transformation of society'. Next, he points the finger at the *Daily Mirror's* Paul Routledge for 'attacking foreign music and British materialism': 'I blame the pernicious culture of hatred around rap music, which glorifies violence and loathing of authority (especially the police but including parents), exalts trashy materialism and raves about drugs. The important things in life are the latest smart phone, fashionable trainers and jeans and idiot computer games'. Then, Bagehot picks up on the historian David Starkey's remarks on the BBC that young white working class people had 'become black': 'The whites have become black. A particular sort of violent, destructive, nihilistic gangster culture has become the fashion … This language, which is wholly false, which is this Jamaican patois that has intruded England. This is why so many of us have this sense of literally a foreign country'.

The judgement of foreignness is very much part of the dead-end discourse against troublesome youth: whether we think of the 'Americanisation' of the Teds in the 1950s or the Hollywood inspired delinquents of the inter-war years, the 'street Arabs' and 'English Hottentots' of the 1840s, or late Victorian England's brilliant inspiration of giving its 'Hooligans' an Irish name. What is most remarkable is that each time these social anxieties crystallise around the youth question, they are accompanied by the same vocabulary of historically-illiterate complaints that are repeatedly re-cycled as is they were new — invoking family discipline, increasing irresponsibility, increasing disrespect, and demoralising popular amusements. It should be said in this respect that the significance of implicating Facebook as the viral accelerator of the riots is less a question of whether this was true, than that Facebook joins the history of the contaminating and corrosive influences such as the music halls, movies, video nasties, etc. that are accused of encouraging 'copy-cat' crime.

It is not that nothing changes. Of course things change. But this long, connected vocabulary of complaint seems itself immune to change. The dead-end discourse surrounding the youth question is a kind of moral dodo-ism that seems incapable of keeping pace with a world in motion. Everything changes, nothing moves.

References

Anon (1912) 'Religious Influences on the Adolescent', in Whitehouse, J. H. ed., *Problems of Boy Life*. London: King.

Baden-Powell, R. (1908) *Scouting for Boys*. London: Horace Cox.

'Bagehot' (2011) 'Civil Disorder and Looting Visit Britain: We Have Been Here Before', *The Economist*, 16 August 2011.

Barnett, M. G. (1913) *Young Delinquents*. London: Methuen.

Beggs, T. (1849) *An Inquiry into the Extent and Causes of Juvenile Depravity*. London: Gilpin.

Besant, W. (1901) *East London*. London: Chatto and Windus.

Bosanquet, H. (1906) *The Family*. London: Macmillan.

Braithwaite, W. J. (1904) 'Boys' Clubs', in Urwick, E. J. ed., *Studies of Boy Life in our Cities*. London: Dent.

Bray, R. (1911) *Boy Labour and Apprenticeship*. London: Constable.

British Medical Association (1961) *The Adolescent*. London: British Medical Association.

Butterworth, J. (1932) *Clubland*. London: Epworth.

Calvert, R. and Calvert, T, (1933) *The Law Breaker*, London: Routlege.

Chadwick, E. (1965) *Report on the Sanitary Condition of the Labouring Population of Great Britain*. Edited by M. W. Flinn. Edinburgh: Edinburgh University Press.

Cohen, S. (1972) *Folk Devils and Moral Panics*. London: MacGibbon and Kee.

Conservative Party (1966) *Crime Knows No Boundaries*. London: Conservative Political Centre.

Cornwallis, C. F. (1853) *On the Treatment of the Dangerous and Perishing Classes of Society*. London: Smith, Elder and Co.

Davies, A. (2008) *The Gangs of Manchester. The Story of the Scuttlers Britain's First Youth Cult*. Preston: Milo Books.

Devine, A. (1890) *Scuttlers and Scuttling*. Manchester: Guardian Printing Works.

Ford, R. (1939) *Children in the Cinema*. London: Allen and Unwin.

Gorst, J. (1901) *The Youth of the Nation*. London: Methuen.

Government Papers (1900) *Report of the Commissioner of the Police of the Metropolis 1899*. Cd. 399. London: HMSO.

Government Papers (1904) *Report of the Inter-Departmental Committee on Physical Deterioration*, Vol. 2 (Minutes of Evidence). Cd. 2210. London: HMSO.

Government Papers (1908) *Royal Commission on the Duties of the Metropolitan Police* Vol. 2. Cd. 4260. London: HMSO.

Government Papers (1910) *Report of the Departmental Committee on the Employment of Children Act*, 1903. Cd. 5229. London: HMSO.

Hirst, F. W. (1934) *The Consequences of the War to Great Britain*. Oxford: Oxford University Press.

Hoggart, R. (1958) *The Uses of Literacy*. Harmondsworth: Penguin.

Howard Association (1898) *Juvenile Offenders*. London: Howard Association.

Irving, E. (1829) *The Last Days: A Discourse on the Evil Character of These Our Times*. London: Seeley & Burnside.

Leavis, F. R. (1930) *Mass Civilisation and Minority Culture*. Cambridge: Minority Press.

Leavis, F. R. and Thompson, D. (1933) *Culture and Environment*. London: Chatto and Windus.

Masterman, C. F. G. (1902) *The Heart of the Empire*. London: Fisher Unwin.

Morgan, A. E. (1939) *The Needs of Youth*. Oxford: Oxford University Press.

National Council of Public Morals (1917) *The Cinema*. London: Williams and Norgate.

Orwell, G. (1939) *Coming Up For Air*. 1962 edn. Harmondsworth: Penguin.

Pearson, G. (1983) *Hooligan: A History of Respectable Fears*. London: Macmillan.

Redwood, H. (1932) *God in the Slums*. London: Hodder and Stoughton.

Rock, P. and Cohen, S. (1970) 'The Teddy Boy', in V. Bogdanor and R. Skidelsky eds., *The Age of Affluence*. London: Macmillan, pp.288-320.

Russell, C. E. B. (1905) *Manchester Boys*. Manchester: Manchester University Press.

Russell, C. E. B. (1917) *The Problem of Juvenile Crime*. Oxford: Oxford University Press.

Wilson, A. (1900) 'Music Halls', *Contemporary Review*, Vol. 78, July.

Worsley, H. (1849) *Juvenile Depravity*. London: Gilpin.

Steven Hirschler is a doctoral student within the Department of Politics and Centre for Applied Human Rights at the University of York. His research centres around asylum policy in the UK and the privatisation of housing and support services for asylum-seekers in cities throughout Britain. Steven Hirschler studied International Relations at the University of California Los Angeles (UCLA) before going to York to pursue an MA and PhD.

4

RIOTS IN RETROSPECTIVE:
IMMIGRATION AND THE CRISIS OF THE 'OTHER'

Steven Hirschler

Introduction

Emotive declarations of Britain's 'moral collapse' following the August 2011 riots warned of a rising 'feral underclass' of vicious youths suffering from over-exposure to popular media culture. However, accusations were also levelled against intruding foreign cultures that had threatened to transform 'the British way of life'. For example, Melanie Phillips (2011) believed it was multiculturalism which had led to the wholesale reverse discrimination of white people, leaving the 'bad behaviour' of minorities to go unpunished. David Starkey declared that 'whites have become black' and that Enoch Powell's prophecy of a burning Britain had come true on the streets of Tottenham and Clapham Junction (Quinn, 2011). Shortly after, David Cameron and Theresa May expressed their aims to tighten immigration controls and to abandon Britain's agreement to Article 8 of the European Convention on Human Rights in order to limit the number of foreign families entering the country.

The recent modern-day condemnation of Britain's culturally diverse society is reminiscent of the warnings of Cyril Osborne, Stephen Maydon and Enoch Powell, who disapproved of a mixed society and sought to tighten immigration control following the riots in Notting Hill and Nottingham in 1958. In the early 1960s, an incorrect diagnosis of the nation's social ills led to increasingly restrictive immigration policies over the course of the decade and set a standard for legislation in subsequent years. By identifying previous instances of urban discord throughout the last century, this chapter challenges the belief that the August 2011 riots were 'unprecedented'. With reference to specific discussions within the House of Commons, the House of Lords and the Cabinet, I demonstrate that immigration controls were viewed as a possible solution to urban unrest and that suggestions of stricter immigration legislation resulted from the perceived racial nature of the riots in 1958 and 1981. In questioning whether heightened immigration controls can resolve problems relating to poverty and social exclusion, I suggest that any commitment to such legislation will only exacerbate tensions and that considerations should extend beyond identifying individual rioters' motivations to understanding the state's role in fostering the conditions from which riots develop.

Whatever Happened to the British 'Golden Age'?

Declarations of 'Broken Britain' saturated media discourses following the August 2011 riots. For some commentators and politicians, the riots were symptomatic of the degradation of a reserved and deferential British culture. Contemporary violence, the savagery of the nation's youth and a culture of permissiveness were situated against an imaginary past in which British citizens maintained respect for the authorities. However, British history is replete with instances of urban unrest. The disruption of the 1981 Brixton riots was viewed as unprecedented for its time, but that disorder succeeded similar violence in the 1958 riots in Notting Hill and Nottingham. 'Gangs' of 'destructive youths' menaced store owners in the 1920s and, at the turn of the nineteenth century, the press noted the rise in 'hooliganism' as a disruptive force during the Bank Holiday violence in August 1898 (Pearson, 1983). Recent assertions that the 2011 riots were distinctly modern and indicative of new attitudinal shifts amongst the nation's youth therefore prove problematic when urban discord is considered in its broader historical context.

During a speech in Witney, Oxfordshire a week after the riots, Prime Minister David Cameron declared that the 'past few generations' suffered from 'slow-motion moral collapse' due to absent fathers, disorderly schools thereby permitting criminality; the idiom 'live and let live' had transformed into 'do what you please' (Cameron, 2011b). The once moral British society was in decline. Iain Duncan Smith, the Secretary of State for Work and Pensions, stated that the disintegration of 'stable families' and a greater dependency on the welfare state contributed to street violence (Mulholland, 2011). Writing for the *Daily Mail*, Melanie Phillips did not want to be equated with 'right-wing nutters who wanted to turn the clock back to some mythical golden age'. However, her concluding remarks reaffirmed her entrenched belief in an idealised past. She was mournful of 'Broken Britain', a once 'ordered society that was the envy of the whole world—the most civilised, the most gentle and law-abiding'. The 'sickness' amongst 'pockets of society' was due to 'the breakdown of the family'. Phillips called for the return of a 'Biblical morality' that would help the British state reclaim its role as global civiliser (Phillips, 2011). Indeed, for Max Hastings (2011), the unruliness of British youths increased as teachers and parents were no longer allowed to punish them for their misdeeds. He found their disrespectfulness appalling: 'A century ago, no child would have dared to use obscene language in class. Today, some use little else'. Hastings also levelled judgement against a culture of permissiveness within the police force, writing that the 'police, in recent years, have developed a reputation for ignoring yobbery and bullying'.

These statements point to a society currently affected by a social phenomena specific to a new amoral age which therefore views the riots, and the attitudes of those participating in them, as unprecedented and symptomatic of the insolence and cynicism of our time. However, these reflections are neither novel themselves, nor do they convey new sentiments. One need only recount previous responses to urban unrest to demonstrate the expression of similar viewpoints. After the 1981 riots in Brixton, John Stokes, the MP for Halesowen and Stourbridge declared: 'Riots on this scale have not happened for 200 years. Are not these riots something new and sinister in our long national history?' (quoted in Benyon, 1984a: 4). In his official report to Parliament addressing the causes and consequences of the 1981 riots, Lord Scarman observed:

> [T]he British people watched with horror and incredulity an instant audio-visual presentation on their television sets of scenes of violence and disorder in their capital city, the like of which had not previously been seen in this century in Britain.
>
> *Scarman, 1981: 1.2*

Accounts of this nature, which focus heavily on the contemporary abandonment of a culture of lawfulness and restraint in Britain, are founded
upon a wholly apocryphal reality. They are, as Geoffrey Pearson suggests,
symptoms of 'cosy nostalgia' afflicting sufferers of 'historical amnesia' (Pearson, 1983: 22,38). Pearson's *Hooligan: A History of Respectable Fears*, published
two years after the 1981 Brixton riots, serves as a reminder that the perceived
'deterioration' of the present is not a new phenomenon, but rather the most
recent development in a long history of disorderly conduct in Britain. Pearson attempts to bury presumptions that a 'permissive' culture has given rise
to delinquency amongst the British youth; he questions whether an idealised
past in which order and respect for authority were the mainstays of British society can truly be identified. Following the 2001 riots, the *Economist*'s
Bagehot columnist realised the salience of Pearson's work as a response to
the 'sweeping historical claims' of those like Paul Routledge, Melanie Phillips and David Starkey, and reminded readers that 'we have been here before'
(Bagehot, 2011).

In his book, Pearson contradicts views that street violence is a new occurrence by highlighting periods throughout the 20th century during which
civil unrest was prominent in Britain's urban areas. He explains that groups
of 'Teddy Boys' in Edwardian-style clothing instigated 'gang fights, vandalism' and 'street robberies' during the 1950s (Pearson, 1983: 18). Metropolitan
police files released in August 2002 confirm Pearson's account, revealing that
Teddy Boys were largely responsible for the harmful physical attacks against
West Indian residents during the riots in Notting Hill in 1958 (Travis, 2002).
Pearson further explains that 'the disruptive behaviour of the youth' was not
limited to the post-war era, but also featured in the 1920s as an increase in
store theft and vandalism gave rise to criticisms of family breakdown and
the destructive influence of the cinema (*Criminal Statistics for England and
Wales, 1928* in Pearson, 1983: 34-35). During a House of Lords debate following the 1958 riots, Earl Winterton reflected on previous periods of unrest in
'the old days' when riots erupted in Liverpool and in Glasgow. He praised
the 'baton charge' of the police in response to public disorder at that time,
stating: 'Even if a few people did get broken heads, it was better than that
others should be seriously injured or the public peace endangered' *(Hansard, 1958d: C10)*.

The belief that riots were symptomatic of a violent youth culture that had arisen out of a lack of parenting and ineffective disciplinary methods is also not limited to the current era. A *Juvenile Offenders* report from 1898 cites deficiencies in parenting, a lack of discipline in schools and the entry of women into the workforce as contributing to the misconduct of the nation's youth (Howard Association, 1898 in Pearson, 1983: 55). Pearson points to even earlier diagnoses of societal decline in Britain, which identified the Industrial Revolution as the era of family breakdown as mothers went to work in an 'unnatural arrangement' that led to their abandonment of 'domestic duties' (Hill, 1953 quoted in Pearson, 1983: 165).

Pearson suggests, an 'altered moral terrain' has led to a reassessment of the severity of certain types of crime, which has generally resulted in stricter sentences over time. He implies that authorities did not always deem crimes like vandalism and petty theft to be as destructive as 'real crime' and thus treated these forms of deviancy more leniently (*Hansard*, 30 June 1933 in Pearson, 1983: 36). With this observation, Pearson is perhaps in danger of developing an idealised past of his own, as appropriate methods of punishment were just as contested prior to the Second World War as they are now. For instance, in June 1933, Viscountess Astor discussed increases in juvenile crime during a House of Commons debate and encouraged a greater use of the probation system as an alternative to sending more young people to jail. She suggested that juvenile crime could be expected to increase along with rising unemployment (*Hansard*, 30 June 1933: c1833). Douglas Hacking, the MP for Chorley, disagreed with Astor; he doubted the effectiveness of 'alternatives to imprisonment' and suggested that fines and probation were no longer appropriate responses to youth criminality (*Ibid*: c1853). Disputes of this kind reveal that youth crime was as much a policy consideration for politicians in the 1930s as it is for their contemporaries today. The mythical British 'Golden Age' loses its lustre when one considers the possibility that criminality has always existed and that it is society's response to it that changes over time. Bailey (1988: 42) writes:

> It would be false … to portray the pre-Second World War period as a 'golden age', when working-class communities reared children with a sense of respect for other people's property. Such nostalgia for the 'British way of life' is understandable in

light of present fears about a seemingly irreversible crime wave, but it squares with neither the social reality nor the social perceptions of crime in the earlier years.

These historical accounts help raise the veil of nostalgia that distorts our understanding of the past. The reality is then made clear: British society was hardly 'gentle' in bygone days, but was in fact marked by intense episodes of street violence. The same fatalistic diagnosis of a broken society due to familial breakdown and the influence of new technologies was as much the rhetoric then as it is now. The 'Golden Age' thus revealed is in fact an age of pyrite. As the haze of romanticism clears, once obscured commonalities between periods of urban discord become more apparent, and the singling out of the 'Other' as a source of violence can be identified as a recurring response to episodes of unrest throughout history.

The 'Alien' Offender and Reinforcing Britishness

In the aftermath of the 2011 riots, news agencies scrambled to secure interviews with hastily anointed 'experts' and opened the door for right-wing commentators to make swift judgements about the deteriorating social health of Britain. Theories advanced addressing possible sources of unrest rested upon the belief that an invasive 'black' culture was in the process of assimilating an otherwise wholesome (white) British society. Paul Routledge, writing for the *Mirror*, blamed the 'pernicious culture of hatred around rap music' for generating an anti-establishment fervour amongst Britain's youth (Routledge, 2011; Bagehot, 2011). Melanie Phillips (2011) faulted multiculturalism for creating a 'victim' culture in which foreigners with dubious hardship claims were coddled while white Britons suffered the deterioration of their heritage. Most contentiously, these points were epitomised by David Starkey's proclamation on 'Newsnight' that 'whites have become black' (Quinn, 2011).

English Defence League marches in South East London in September 2011, a month after the riots, revealed that possible accusations of a failed multicultural state went beyond the grandiloquent columns of *Daily Mail* commentators (BBC News, 2011a; Townsend, 2011). Similar feelings were also evident through surveys. Dr Matthew Goodwin and fellow researchers at Nottingham University used data gathered in two YouGov polls, one conducted in July and the second in mid-August 2011, to investigate British attitudes toward foreigners in the aftermath of the riots. The analysis of survey responses from a total of 3,000 participants across Britain revealed a five per cent increase in feelings of cultural threat and a ten per cent rise in feelings of insecurity (Taylor, 2011). While these results do not demonstrate a causal relationship between the riots and heightened fears of outsiders, they at least point to increased anxiety about perceived cultural tensions.

Paul Routledge and David Starkey found it difficult to grasp that British citizens were capable of violent action of their own accord. Disorder and 'savagery' were not 'British traits', but those of the foreigner; they were the qualities of 'blacks'. Early attempts to blame the riots on black youth lost traction as it became apparent that whites were prominent in the unrest throughout English cities, such as Nottingham, Birmingham and Manchester (Lewis and Harkin, 2011). Unable to point to individual 'aliens', Starkey and Routledge were left to indict the culture of the outsider. For Routledge, that culture was rap music, and for Starkey it was 'a particular sort of violent, destructive, nihilistic gangster culture' (Routledge, 2011; Quinn, 2011). The Prime Minister distinguished the rioters from 'real' British citizens, stating: 'Those thugs we saw last week do not represent us, nor do they represent our young people — and they will not drag us down' (Cameron, 2011b). Iain Duncan Smith referred to rioters' otherness by likening them to 'child soldiers of the third world' whose only role models included 'the violent and the criminal' and whose knowledge was only that of 'anger and violence' (Mulholland, 2011). The imagery of a 'dark' foreign interloper was unmistakable. To re-establish a sense of order, it became necessary to differentiate the familiar from the unfamiliar, the white from the black. Disruptive behaviour became foreign — *un*British — as it had been in the aftermath of previous instances of disorder during the last century.

The belief that innate cultural incompatibilities was particularly pronounced following the 1958 riots in Nottingham and Notting Hill, as the fear of future disorder corresponded with steep rises in immigration rates in the early 1960s. As skirmishes erupted in August 1958, news media were quick to label the disturbances as 'race riots' (Small and Solomos, 2006: 242). A *Daily Mirror* article released on the 3rd September 1958 titled, 'Black v White', featured an image of two faces spliced together — one side black, the other white—bearing a caption that read: 'The Problem … in one picture'. The article declared that the violence was a direct result of racial antagonisms and that Commonwealth citizens should be denied entry into the UK unless they had a job to come to (*Daily Mirror,* 1958b). In Parliament, Cyril Osborne, the MP for Louth and a notorious opponent of immigration, proclaimed that 'the unfortunate riots in Nottingham and Notting Hill' were evidence of extreme racial tensions in the country. 'Like real dynamite that accumulates in greater quantities', he declared, '[immigration] could become increasingly dangerous'. Osborne suggested immediate restrictions on immigration (*Hansard,* 1958b: cc1552-1554; *Hansard,* 1958a: c195). In the House of Lords, Lord Elton warned of 'the problems arising from West Indian immigration into the United Kingdom' and he reminded his audience of 'race riots' in Liverpool and Cardiff prior to the First World War and riots in Tyneside, London and Glasgow in the first half of the century (*Hansard,* 1958c: c655).

Others within government cautioned against reducing the 1958 riots to racial factors alone. The MP for Durham, Charles Grey, condemned Cyril Osborne, referring to him as 'often misguided and sometimes not entirely accurate'. Grey insinuated that MPs like Osborne had inaccurately described the riots as racially motivated and had negatively influenced the attitudes of those living in Notting Hill and Nottingham (*Hansard,* 1958b: cc1564-1566). He then described his efforts to reverse public perceptions about the nature of the riots:

> [Residents] have got the whole position out of perspective, and no one could tell them anything else, so that it was our job—and I believe we did our job effectively—to convince the people out there that race riots as such did not occur in this country. I would have been much happier if the Press had done more to tell these people the truth, but the truth, as they saw it out there, was that these were race riots, because the Press was more or less magnifying the position out of all perspective. (*Ibid.,* c.1566)

Martin Lindsay, MP for Solihull, also disputed Osborne, stating that the riots were more a display of 'hooliganism' than of racial discord. He went further to say: 'I do not take the view that those deplorable racial—if that is the correct adjective—riots which we have had are strictly the result of racial pressures'. However, Lindsay still used the opportunity to call for the deportation of those that 'come [to Britain] because they prefer to live on National Assistance here rather than in poverty in their own country' (*Ibid.*, cc1561-1563).

There was little consensus in the immediate aftermath of the 1958 riots that racial tensions were significant factors in the disturbances. Even the *Daily Mirror*, the same paper that called for the immediate deportation of 'coloured … no-goods' (1958b), acknowledged that the violence in Nottingham on 30 August 1958 involved 'no coloured people' (1958a). Indeed, when 4,000 people descended onto the streets of Nottingham, few blacks were present; whites began fighting amongst themselves and dozens of people were arrested (Pressly, 2007). However, the realities of the riots did not necessarily correspond to people's perceptions, and as time passed, the collective memory of the riots began to shift towards issues of race. In 1961, Stephen Maydon, the MP for Wells reminisced: 'It was not so long ago, we remember with shame, that we had the Notting Hill riots. What else were those but a manifestation of racial discrimination?' (*Hansard*, 22 March 1961, v637: c512). During a House of Commons debate in July 1963, Benjamin Parkin was reminded of the 'racial riots of Notting Hill when night after night there was nothing less than civil war in that area' (*Hansard*, 08 July 1963, v680: c927). Peter Griffiths remarked that he believed the 1958 riots arose out of the British population's 'resentment against immigrants' (Griffiths, 1966: 154). When Griffiths emerged victorious in Smethwick, West Midlands after running an explicit anti-immigrant campaign, it became clear that exploiting citizens' fear of the 'Other' was the ground on which one could win an election.

For some, the mixing of cultures was deemed a source of current and future conflict. The letters Enoch Powell received following his infamous 'Rivers of Blood' speech in April 1968 reveal that many of his supporters believed that a society consisting of distinct cultures was doomed to fail. A woman writing from Ealing on 22 April 1968 stated: 'Asians … simply seem not to want to know anything of us or our way of life. This frightens me' (POLL, 8/1/8). A resident of Birmingham wrote that Powell's words were those of 'every domesticated, family-loving Englishman', thus implying that the opposite qualities were true of the immigrant. The author continued: 'These coloured people do not want to adapt to our standard of living or our ways. They would bring their children up in there [sic] own ignorant way' (Birmingham, 21 April 1968, *ibid*). Another respondent from North Kensington said: 'I for one do not hate every coloured person, but the ones that live around me are like animals' (London, undated, *ibid*). Powell's speech resonated with a concerned retired headmistress who exclaimed: 'Obviously, then, immigration if continued is likely to create an explosive situation, and you [Powell] were correct in describing us as mad to allow the seeds of such conflict to be planted here' (Surrey, 22 April 1968, *ibid*). A teacher from Bedford emphatically proclaimed: '[A]s a Catholic, I do object to the foreign influence which is present in excess in this country today' (Bedford, 19 November 1968, *ibid*). These examples, while limited in their overall representativeness of British society, underscore the anxiety felt by those opposed to continued immigration. Disorder and unrest were viewed as natural features of a state marked by cultural difference. In failing to adopt the qualities of white British citizens, foreigners presented a threat to national identity.

These feelings were also prevalent in later instances of disorder in 1981 and 2001. The *Daily Mail* described the 1981 Brixton riots as a 'Black War on Police' (*Daily* Mail, 7 July 1981 in Benyon, 1985: p.409). In a retrospective article describing the events of 1981, the *Daily Mail* again emphasised the supposed racial tensions prevalent during the unrest, claiming that 'thousands of black youths were fighting pitched battles with some 3,000 policemen' (Sandbrook, 2011). Another article attributed violence to 'thousands of West Indian youths' (Reid, 2011). Enoch Powell weighed in on the disorder, believing it to be largely a result of racial frictions within the affected areas (Benyon 1984a: 6). In contrast to these claims, a Home Office *Statistical Bulletin* released in 1982 revealed that 67 per cent of those arrested following disorder in London, Liverpool, Manchester and other locations around Britain in July 1981 were white (Benyon, 1985: 410). Sarah Neal's study of the media responses to the Scarman Report found that the media were generally willing to accept Lord Scarman's depiction of Britain as a nation divided into 'three or four societies' (Neal, 2003: 61). This passive resignation that Britain was 'naturally' divided due to innate differences between cultural groups perpetuated the presumption that 'racial tensions' were the primary cause of disorder. Few lessons were learned in the aftermath of the Brixton riots;

when disturbances erupted in Bradford 20 years later, commentators offered many of the same underdeveloped insights into potential sources of unrest.

According to Paul Bagguley and Yasmin Hussain, the media responses following the disruptions in Bradford, Oldham and Burnley in 2001 were concerned with South Asians' lack of Britishness. Instead of explaining the riots, they wrote, 'official reports ... focused ... on the broader issues of segregation, social cohesion and proposals to instil a liberal conception of citizenship into the minds of South Asians' (Bagguley and Hussain, 2003; Cantle, 2001; Denham, 2002; Kalra, 2002 in Hussain and Bagguley, 2005: 407). Media reports describing the 'race riots' focused on an 'apparently stark ethnic/racial divide' and 'the notion of difference became a recurrent theme through these debates' (Alexander, 2004: 527-529).

In identifying the 'Other' as a harbinger of civil discord and associating 'real' Britishness with peacefulness and lawfulness, violence is rationalised as something external to British culture. During periods of unrest, an indictment of British identity is unnecessary, as the 'qualities' of disorder and criminality can be attributed to the 'Other'. Multiculturalism is perceived as a threat, because it allows foreign cultures to maintain their distinctiveness within Britain's borders; it sanctions the autonomous existence of the criminal-outsider. Multiculturalism is therefore viewed as the mechanism that allows 'alien criminals' to 'take their place alongside subversive enemies within' (Gilroy, 1982: 48). Writing in response to the 2001 Bradford riots, Claire Alexander states that 'riots are constructed as being about recalcitrant foreign cultures and failed integration as much as about social exclusion and discrimination. Multiculturalism is thus placed as part of the problem' (Kundnani, 2002 in Alexander, 2004: 530).

Multiculturalism is therefore interpreted as a threat to state authority, because it undermines the state's efforts to homogenise communities within its borders. It impedes the pursuit of a single national identity, which is believed necessary to hold together a population that might otherwise be torn asunder due to geographic, linguistic, religious or socio-economic divisions (Koopmans and Statham, 1999; Pattie *et al*, 2004: 21). However, the uniformity needed to ensure the strength of this identity is exclusionary by nature. Hussain and Bagguley argue that national identity expressed through citizenship is 'racialised', with an elitist community serving 'as a model for the nation as a whole'. They suggest that, in Britain, a distinction is made 'between Whites and "others" by maintaining dichotomies in which Englishness continues to reproduce Blackness as its "other"' (2005: 409,413-414). Stam and Spence (1983: 4) elucidate this point:

> It is hardly accidental that the most obvious victims of racism of are those whose identity was forged within the colonial process: blacks in the United States, Asians and West Indians in Great Britain, Arab workers in France, all of whom share an oppressive situation and the status of second class citizens.

The 'alien', as a manifestation of the 'unfamiliar' and the 'strange', is the preferred target for those attempting to identify sources of disorder. The inculcation of the nationalist ideal into the collective mind requires an acceptance of the immutableness of culture and a belief that sameness is tantamount to order. During riotous periods, when *dis*order seemingly reigns, it is the unknown, the bizarre — the alien — that is emphasised. Where assimilation is not possible, the expulsion of the 'Other' is deemed necessary. Just as 'native' criminals can be separated from the rest of society through the process of incarceration, aliens can be imprisoned in detention centres and eventually deported. However, these processes only address the perceived symptoms of disorder rather than its source.

The Wrong Prescription

When David Cameron declared the failure of multiculturalism and damned the 'corrosive influence' human rights laws have on people's 'behaviour and morality' (BBC News, 2011b; Falloon, 2011; Shipman and Walker, 2011), he was not simply announcing that the state project of social inclusion had been unsuccessful; he was suggesting that the very introduction of foreignness into British society had undermined British identity. If we accept that homogeneity leads to a stronger sense of identity and this identity in turn strengthens the state, then a heterogeneous society is one that is fundamentally anaemic. In this way, multiculturalism can be viewed as a major stumbling block in the development of national identity. Pattie, Seyd and Whiteley (2004: 3) explain:

When nearly all the citizens of a given country share the same ethnic, historical and cultural backgrounds, that makes the task of building the social contract relatively straightforward, though this does not of course eliminate political conflicts. In contrast, when citizens of a country have very heterogeneous identities deriving from different ethnic, cultural and religious backgrounds, particularly if these identities involve fundamental disagreements about values, then the task of building a social contract is much harder.

For those looking to emphasise a loss of imagined community, the 2011 riots became symbolic of the divisiveness inherent in multicultural society. Viewed in this way, the real source of discord during the riots was not simply the existence of the 'Other', but the lax policies that allowed the 'Other' to arrive in the first place. As with a trail of ants disrupting an otherwise peaceful picnic, the initial response was to eliminate those in plain view and the secondary reaction was to attack them at their source. This attitude gave rise to the kinds of anti-immigrant rhetoric that surfaced following the riots. It also encouraged the government to vocalise its plans to introduce more restrictive immigration controls and limit the protections guaranteed through European human rights agreements. It was a method employed by legislators following the 1958 riots in Nottingham and Notting Hill, and perhaps to a more limited extent, by lawmakers responding to the disorder in Brixton in 1981. It may be coincidental that major pieces of immigration legislation followed in the wake of two previous instances of urban unrest, but there is evidence to suggest that revised immigration policies were viewed as a salve for a wound made deeper by the intrusion of foreign nationals.

Discussions of expanded immigration legislation were static during much of the 1950s. When suggestions of stricter controls did arise, they were often abandoned in favour of employing a 'wait-and-see' tactic. When the Cabinet met in March 1954 to discuss Commonwealth immigration, it concluded that restrictions would threaten business interests and 'the unity of the Commonwealth' (Spencer, 1997: 63). There was also some hesitation to introduce controls on Commonwealth citizens specifically, as it would seem that the UK Government was discriminating on racial grounds. Lord Swinton supported legislation, but believed it should not be drafted in 'discriminatory terms' as the government 'cannot conceal the obvious fact that the object is to keep out coloured people' (Swinton to Salisbury, 15 March 1954, CAB 124/1191 in Spencer, 1997: 64).

Following the 1958 riots, politicians' attitudes shifted with public perceptions and real consideration was given to the portentous exhortations of those like Cyril Osborne who had been calling for immigration controls for years. Spencer writes that the riots led to a 'second intensive phase [of debate] which this time was to culminate in the decision to legislate' (*Ibid*: 87). The government's preoccupation with the riots and its belief that immigration was a major source of unrest were revealed in its consideration to put forward a Deportation Bill during a Cabinet meeting held on 20 January 1959. The Lord Chancellor's memorandum states:

> It would be better for the Government to take the initiative and introduce legislation as a result of mature consideration of the problem, rather than to wait until more race riots compelled its hurried introduction, possibly in a more drastic form, to meet an urgent public demand.

CAB 129/96, 20th January 1959, para. 7(v).

Within two years, the pursuit of immigration controls began in earnest. The Secretary of State for the Home Department expressed the possible need for 'some measure of statutory control' as immigration into the UK increased rapidly at the start of the 1960s (CAB 129/103, 15 November 1960, para. 1-3). R. A. Butler warned of the dangers of immigration and stated that 'social tensions ... were a potential source of serious disturbance'. He continued:

> Although it would represent a breach with tradition, it might become necessary to introduce legislation to control immigration from the Commonwealth and to empower the Secretary of State to deport Commonwealth citizens.

CAB 128/34, 25 November 1960, s.8 para. 3

The Commonwealth Immigration Act 1962, which developed out of proceedings such as these, placed significant restrictions on those British subjects once considered equal citizens, particularly by limiting the entry of Commonwealth workers to only those possessing employment vouchers. Further legislation in 1968 subjected all foreign nationals to immigration control if they did not have a parent or grandparent who was born in the UK (Bloch, 2000: 31-32). Iain Macleod later reflected on the 1962 legislation, citing it as a preventative measure that had averted further unrest. In a *Spectator* article written in 1965, he stated that since the legislation had been passed in 1962, there had been 'no repetition of the sorry scenes at Nottingham and Notting Hill' (*Spectator,* 12 Feb 1965 quoted in Shepherd, 1994: 491). While Spencer cautions that the riots should not be viewed as a primary cause for the passage of the Commonwealth Immigrants Act 1962, they raised public awareness of issues surrounding immigration, which had previously 'been of only occasional public and media concern' (Spencer, 1997:101). From the early 1960s onwards, limiting immigration became a priority for both major parties. It was under Harold Wilson's Labour Government that the 1965 and 1968 Acts were introduced. The Immigration Act 1971, which came into force while Edward Heath was Prime Minister, retained some of the features Enoch Powell had suggested throughout the 1960s, such as a government-funded repatriation scheme to rid the country of foreigners (Powell, Eastbourne, 16 November 1968 in Shepherd, 1996: 377; Immigration Act 1971, s29(1)).

After the Brixton riots in 1981, the MP for Basildon, Harvey Proctor, warned about the possibility of further disturbances and described immigration as a source of public discord. Those who supported 'multiracialism', Proctor declared, were 'engaged in a sustained attack on authority, law and order and on our way of life in the United Kingdom as we know it and as we want it to remain'. He concluded:

> Immigration has unsettled our institutions and traditions that have been nurtured over the centuries and abruptly changed the complexion and texture of our national life. Immigration makes us assume grave burdens and incur grave risks that would otherwise not arise ... I believe that it would be fairer to black and white alike in our country if we were firmer [on immigration].

> *Hansard, 28 June 1982, v26, c662*

The British Nationality Act 1981, which came into force on 1st January 1983, redefined the boundaries of British citizenship. Principally, the legislation stripped those born in the UK of guaranteed citizenship unless they were descendants of a British citizen (Bloch, 2000). Birthright citizenship was all but abandoned, though an exception was made for deserted newborns whose parents could not be identified (British Nationality Act 1981, s1(2)(a)). The division of citizenship categories into three distinct groupings with varying degrees of rights resulted in full British citizenship becoming a much more exclusive classification following the 1981 Act. As restrictive legislation continued to develop through the 1990s, culminating in the Immigration and Asylum Act 1999, it became increasingly clear that Britain was home to 'real' citizens as well as various categories of imposters.

The current Coalition Government has no intention of bringing to an end the legacy of exclusionary immigration practices of its predecessors. New limits on student visas and the introduction of new language requirements for those hoping to enter through the employment route significantly restrict outsiders' access to the UK (Home Office, 2011a; Home Office, 2011b). The August 2011 riots gave rise to calls for the deportation of foreign nationals involved in the unrest. Damian Green, the Minister of State for Education, exclaimed that the government would pursue an uncompromising effort to deporting any foreign nationals involved in the unrest (Holehouse, 2011). Following the riots, David Cameron expressed a desire to re-examine the 'right to family life' currently guaranteed by the European Convention on Human Rights and he has suggested that 'operational changes' may be necessary to end the enabling practice of 'twisting and misrepresenting ... human rights' (Cameron, 2011a). The government has also used its power to remind its population what it means to be a 'good' citizen. It has attempted to manufacture respect for law and order by dispensing severe punishments for those both participating and threatening to participate in protest movements (Jones and Bowcott, 2011; Bowcott and Carter, 2011), and Iain Duncan Smith has supported a family tax break to incentivise marriage, which he views as 'the best antidote to the celebrity self-obsessed culture we live in' (Wintour, 2011).

In the state's capacity as population manager and its use of 'laws as tactics' (Foucault, 2007: 99), it has gone to great lengths to ensure the territory of the outsider is limited to areas beyond Britain's borders. For Enoch Powell, the objective was clear: 'the alien element', including immigrants and their descendants, needed to be reduced through legislation and repatriation. Integration was not a solution for Powell, but neither was a culturally diverse society. In sum, immigrants and their UK-born offspring were a threat to the British way of life. Human rights legislation would only allow them to 'consolidate their members, to agitate and campaign against their fellow citizens, and to overawe and dominate the rest with legal weapons'. Powell's 'Roman', the white British citizen, was threatened with ejection from his own homeland and faced the ominous signs of conflict manifest in 'the River Tiber, foaming with much blood' (Powell, 2007). If, as Powell suggested, immigration and its attendant social ills are real sources of discord, it stands to reason that public action should have waned as immigration legislation became more restrictive. However, as the 2011 riots in Tottenham, Bethnal Green, Manchester, Nottingham and Birmingham demonstrate, discontentment regarding police brutality, disappointment over a lack of opportunity and feelings of marginalisation are not limited to 'racial dimensions' alone.

Discussion

Reports comparing the August 2011 riots with those of previous eras appeared even before disruptions had ceased in many of the affected areas around the country. These stories pointed to similarities between events themselves, such as the stabbing of Michael Bailey in 1981 and the shooting of Mark Duggan in 2011, and also possible parallels to the sources of unrest, such as economic uncertainty, high levels of unemployment, racial tensions, and police distrust (see Bagehot, 2011; Carey, 2011; Lewis *et al*, 2011; Newburn *et al*, 2011; Taylor and Lewis, 2011; Thomas, 2011; Wheatle, 2011). It is useful to address these similarities to understand how a riot can evolve when social conditions are such that citizens feel that it is the only form of expression left to them. The works of Kundnani (2002), Lea (2003), Hussain and Bagguley (2005) take this analysis further by considering underlying notions of identity and the social and economic effects of cultural segregation. Kundnani (2002: 68-70) remains critical of multiculturalism, believing it to be a form of 'institutional racism' and an 'ideology of conservatism, of preserving the status quo intact, in the face of a real desire to move forward'.

He describes the classification of culture as a 'cage', which serves to limit the opposition of minority communities. While categorisation as a means of control must certainly be challenged, it is also necessary to consider the potential alternatives, such as the complete assimilation of identity through a nationalisation project that would homogenise all under a single set of cultural or phenotypic traits.

As history shows, immigration legislation following periods of unrest has increasingly limited the type of people allowed to identify themselves as British citizens. It has, in no uncertain terms, made British identity the privilege of whites. Describing the work-voucher system introduced in the Commonwealth Immigrants Act 1962, the Secretary of State for the Home Department, R. A. Butler declared: '[A]lthough the scheme purports... to be non-discriminatory, its aim is primarily social and its restrictive effect is intended to ... operate on coloured people almost exclusively' (CAB 129/107, 6th October 1961, para. 4). Public policy designed around these aims only serves to intensify social division, whether real or imagined, between communities within Britain as marginalised groups are ever reminded of their place on the outskirts of society. A border is therefore drawn between the 'real' citizen and the imposter, and the door is opened for future commentaries of the failure of the multicultural state.

References

Alexander, C. 2004 'Imagining the Asian Gang: Ethnicity, Masculinity and Youth After "the Riots"'. *Critical Social Policy.* 24(4), pp.526-549.

Bagehot. 2011. *Civil Disorder and Looting Hits Britain: We've Been Here Before.* http://www.economist.com/blogs/bagehot/2011/08/civil-disorder-and-looting-hits-britain-0 (Accessed 17 September 2011).

Bailey, V. 1988. 'Crime in the Twentieth Century'. *History Today.* 38(5), pp.42-48.

BBC News. 2011a. 'EDL protest in east London sees 60 arrested'. http://www.bbc.co.uk/news/uk-england-london-14778429 (Accessed 18 September 2011).

BBC News. 2011b. 'State multiculturalism has failed, says David Cameron'. http://www.bbc.co.uk/news/uk-politics-12371994 (Accessed 22 September 2011).

Benyon, J. 1984a. 'The Riots, Lord Scarman and the Political Agenda. In John Benyon, (ed). *Scarman and After: Essays Reflecting on Lord Scarman's Report, the Riots and their Aftermath*, Oxford: Pergamon Press, pp.3-19.

Benyon, J. 1985. 'Going Through the Motions: the Political Agenda, the 1981 Riots and the Scarman Inquiry. *Parliamentary Affairs.* 38(4), pp.409-422.

Bloch, A. 2000. 'A New Era or More of the Same? Asylum Policy in the UK'. *Journal of Refugee Studies.* 13(1), pp.29-42.

Bowcott, O. and Carter, H. 2011. 'Facebook Riot Calls Earn Men Four-year Jail Terms Amid Sentencing Outcry'. http://www.guardian.co.uk/uk/2011/aug/16/facebook-riot-calls-men-jailed (Accessed 2012 February 2012)

British Nationality Act 1981. (c61), London: HMSO.

CAB 128/34. 25 November 1960. *Conclusions of a Meeting of the Cabinet.* National Archives.

CAB 129/103. 15 November 1960. *Coloured Immigration from the Commonwealth.* National Archives.

CAB 129/107. 6 October 1961. *Commonwealth Migrants.* National Archives.

CAB 129/96. 20 January 1959. *Commonwealth Immigrants.* National Archives.

Cameron, D. 2011a. '*David Cameron: Human Rights in my Sights.* http://www.express.co.uk/posts/view/266219/David-Cameron-Human-rights-in-my-sights (Accessed 20 September 2011).

Cameron, D. 2011b. *Full transcript—David Cameron—Speech on the fight-back after the riots*. http://www.newstatesman.com/politics/2011/08/society-fight-work-rights (Accessed 10 February 2012).

Carey, S. 2011. Riots and randomness: the search for an explanation. http://www.newstatesman.com/blogs/the-staggers/2011/08/randomness-explanation-riots (Accessed 07 February 2012).

Daily Mirror 1958a. '400 clash in 'colour' riot'. *Daily Mirror*, 1 September.

Daily Mirror 1958b. 'Black v White: what we must do'. *Daily Mirror*, 3 September.

Falloon, M. 2011. *Multiculturalism Has failed in Britain—Cameron*. http://uk.reuters.com/article/2011/02/05/uk-britain-radicalisation-idUK-TRE71401G20110205 (Accessed 10 February 2012).

Foucault, M. 2007. *Security, Territory, Population: Lectures at the Collège de France, 1977-78*. Basingstoke: Palgrave Macmillan.

Gilroy, P. 1982. 'The Myth of Black Criminality'. *Socialist Register*. 19, pp.47-56.

Griffiths, P. 1966. *A Question of Colour?* London: Leslie Frewin.

Hansard. 1933. *HC Debates, Police, England and Wales & Prisons, England and Wales*. 30 June. Volume 279, cc1811-1876.

Hansard. 1958a. *HC Debates, Debate on the Address [Second Day]*. 29 October. Vo 594, cc146-288.

Hansard. 1958b. *HC Debates, Immigration (Control)*.5 December. Vol. 596, cc1552-1597.

Hansard. 1958c. *HL Debates, Colour Prejudice and Violence*. 19 November. Vol. 212, cc632-724.

Hansard. 1958d. *HL Debates, Provincial Police Forces*. 8 December. Vol. 213, cc4-55.

Hansard. 1961. *HC Debates, Union of South Africa (Withdrawal from Common-wealth)*. 22 March. Vol. 637, cc441-532.

Hansard. 1963. *HC Debates, Housing and Urban Land Prices*. 8 July. Vol. 680, cc871-940.

Hansard. 1982. *HC Debates, Immigration Regulations*. 28 June. Vol. 26, cc633-704.

Hasting, M. 2011. *Years of Liberal Dogma Have Spawned a Generation of Amoral, Uneducated, Welfare Dependent, Brutalised Youngsters*. http://www.dailymail.co.uk/debate/article-2024284/UK-riots-2011-Liberal-dogma-spawned-generation-brutalised-youths.html (Accessed 11 February 2012).

Holehouse, M. 2011. *England Riots: Foreign Rioters Will be Deported*. http://www.telegraph.co.uk/news/uknews/crime/8711623/England-riots-foreign-rioters-will-be-deported.html (Accessed 25 February 2012).

Home Office. 2011a. Government Outlines Overhaul of Student Visas. http://ukba.homeoffice.gov.uk/sitecontent/newsarticles/2011/march/54-student-visas(Accessed 13 February 2012).

Home Office. 2011b. Reforming Family Migration to Promote Better Integration. http://www.ukba.homeoffice.gov.uk/sitecontent/newsarticles/2011/september/40-migration (Accessed 13 February 2012).

Hussain, Y., and Bagguley, P. 2005. 'Citizenship, Ethnicity and Identity: British Pakistanis After the 2001 'Riots'. *Sociology*. 39, pp.407-425.

Immigration Act 1971. (c77)., London: HMSO.

Jones, S. and Bowcott, O. 2011. *England Riots: Anti-poverty Groups Question Evictions and Benefit Cuts*. http://www.guardian.co.uk/uk/2011/aug/15/england-riots-poverty-evictions-benefits (Accessed 25 February 2012).

Koopmans, R. and Statham, P. 1999. 'Challenging the Liberal Nation-State? Postnationalism, Multiculturalism, and the Collective Claims Making of Migrants and Ethnic Minorities in Britain and Germany'. *American Journal of Sociology*. 105(3), pp.652-696.

Kundnani, A. 2002. 'The Death of Multiculturalism'. *Race & Class*. 43(4), pp.67-72.

Lea, J. 2003. *From Brixton to Bradford: Ideology and Discourse on Race and Urban Violence in the United Kingdom*. http://www.bunker8.pwp.blueyonder.co.uk/misc/riots.htm (Accessed 20 February 2012).

Lewis, P. and Harkin, J. 2011. *Who Are the rioters? Young Men from Poor Areas. But That's Not the Full Story*. http://www.guardian.co.uk/uk/2011/aug/09/london-riots-who-took-part (Accessed 12 February 2012).

Lewis, P. and Newburn, T., Taylor, M. and Ball, J. 2011. *Rioters Say Anger with Police Fuelled Summer Unrest*. http://www.guardian.co.uk/uk/2011/dec/05/anger-police-fuelled-riots-study (Accessed 11 February 2012).

Mulholland, H. 2011. *Duncan Smith Blames Riots on Family Breakdown and Benefits System*.http://www.guardian.co.uk/politics/2011/oct/03/duncan-smith-riots-benefits-system (Accessed 10 February 2012).

Neal, S. 2003. 'The Scarman Report, the Macpherson Report and the Media: How Newspapers Respond to Race-centred Social Policy Interventions'. *Journal of Social Policy*. 32(1), pp.55-74.

Newburn, T., Lewis, P. and Metcalf, J. 2011. '*A New Kind of Riot? From Brixton 1981 to Tottenham 2011*. http://www.guardian.co.uk/uk/2011/dec/09/riots-1981-2011-differences (Accessed 22 February 2012).

Pattie, C., Patrick, S. and Whiteley, P. 2004. *Citizenship in Britain*. Cambridge: Cambridge University Press.

Pearson, G. 1983. *Hooligan: A History of Respectable Fears*. London: The Macmillan Press Ltd.

Phillips, M. 2011. *Britain's Liberal Intelligentsia Has Smashed Virtually Every Social Value*. http://www.dailymail.co.uk/debate/article-2024690/UK-riots-2011-Britains-liberal-intelligentsia-smashed-virtually-social-value.html (Accessed 18 September 2011).

POLL 8/1/8. 1968. *The Papers of Enoch Powell*. Cambridge: Churchill Archives Centre.

Powell, E. 1972. *Still to Decide*. London: B.T. Batsford Ltd.

Powell, E. 2007. Enoch Powell's 'River of Blood' Speech. http://www.telegraph.co.uk/comment/3643823/Enoch-Powells-Rivers-of-Blood-speech.html (Accessed 8 August 2011).

Pressly, L. 2007. *The 'Forgotten' Race Riot*. http://news.bbc.co.uk/1/hi/uk/6675793.stm (Accessed 19 September 2011).

Quinn, B. 2011. *David Starkey Claims 'The Whites Have Become Black'*. http://www.guardian.co.uk/uk/2011/aug/13/david-starkey-claims-whites-black (Accessed 18 September 2011).

Reid, S. 2011. *Heroes or Anarchists? The 1981 Brixton Riots are Now Being Hailed by the Left as a Heroic Uprising. The Truth is Rather Different*. http://www.dailymail.co.uk/news/article-1377495/Heroes-anarchists-The-1981-Brixton-riots-hailed-Left-heroic-uprising-The-truth-different.html (Accessed 10 February 2012.

Routledge, P. 2011. *London Riots: Is Rap Music to Blame for Encouraging this Culture of Violence?* http://www.mirror.co.uk/news/uk-news/london-riots-is-rap-music-to-blame-146671 (Accessed 10 February 2012).

Sandbrook, D. 2011. *Why 1981 Was the Year That Forged Modern Britain*. http://www.dailymail.co.uk/news/article-1381370/Why-1981-year-forged-modern-Britain.html (Accessed 11 February 2012).

Scarman, L. 1981. *The Brixton Disorders, 10-12 April 1981: Report of an Inquiry by the Rt. Hon. the Lord Scarman, OBE*. London: HMSO.

Shepherd, R. 1994. *Iain Macleod*. London: Pimlico.

Shepherd, R. 1996. *Enoch Powell*. London: Pimlico.

Shipman, T. and Walker, K. 2011. *Cameron's War on Feckless Families: PM Attacks the Human Rights Laws and Backs National Service*. http://www.dailymail.co.uk/news/article-2026163/David-Cameron-UK-riots-speech-PM-attacks-human-rights-laws-backs-national-service.html (Accessed 10 February 2012).

Small, S., and Solomos, J. 2006. 'Race, Immigration and Politics in Britain : Changing Policy Agendas and Conceptual Paradigms 1940s–2000s'. *International Journal of Comparative Sociology*. 47(3-4), pp.235-257.

Spencer, I. 1997. *British Immigration Policy Since 1939: The Making of Multi-racial Britain*. London: Routledge.

Stam, R., and Spence, L. 1983. 'Colonialism, Racism and Representation'. *Screen*. 24(2), pp.2-20.

Taylor, M. 2011. *British Public 'Are More Prejudiced Against Minorities after Riots'*. http://www.guardian.co.uk/uk/2011/sep/05/british-public-prejudiced-minorities-riots?cat=uk&type=article (Accessed 18 September 2011).

Taylor, M. and Lewis, P. 2011. *Opportunism and Dissatisfaction with Police Drove Rioters, Study Finds*. http://www.guardian.co.uk/uk/2011/nov/03/opportunism-dissatisfaction-police-rioters-study (Accessed 12 February 2012).

Thomas, S. 2011. *We Must Nurture a Forgotten Underclass*. http://www.independent.co.uk/opinion/commentators/sheldon-thomas-we-must-nurture-a-forgotten-underclass-2337224.html (Accessed 8 February 2012).

Townsend, M. 2011. *EDL London March HaltedBy Police*. http://www.guardian.co.uk/uk/2011/sep/03/edl-march-halted-by-police (Accessed 18 September 2011).

Travis, A. *After 44 Years Secret Papers Reveal Truth About Five Nights of Violence in Notting Hill*. http://www.guardian.co.uk/uk/2002/aug/24/artsandhumanities.nottinghillcarnival2002 (Accessed 19 September 2011).

Wheatle, A. 2011. *Tottenham 2011 and Brixton 1981—Different Ideals, Similar Lessons*. http://www.guardian.co.uk/commentisfree/2011/aug/09/tottenham-2011-brixton-1981 (Accessed 22 February 2012).

Wintour, P. 2011. *Marriage Ruined by Hello! Idea of weddings—Iain Duncan Smith*. http://www.guardian.co.uk/lifeandstyle/2011/feb/09/marriage-wedding-iain-duncan-smith (Accessed 25 February 2012).

Dr Tim Bateman is Reader in Youth Justice at the University of Bedfordshire. He has a background in youth justice social work as a practitioner and prior to joining that university in 2010, he was employed as a senior policy development officer in Nacro's Youth Crime Section. His research focuses primarily on youth justice and youth crime and he has a particular interest in the experiences of children who break the law. Tim is co-editor of the *Safer Communities* journal, news editor of *Youth Justice* journal and is a member of the editorial board of *Child and Family Law Quarterly*. He is a trustee of the National Association for Youth Justice and Secretary of the London Association for Youth Justice.

5

WITH THE BENEFIT OF HINDSIGHT:
THE DISTURBANCES OF AUGUST 2011 IN HISTORICAL CONTEXT

Tim Bateman

All that we got, it seems we have lost;
We must have really paid a cost.
(That's why we gonna be)
Burnin' and a-lootin' tonight;
Burnin' and a-lootin' tonight.

Bob Marley, 1973

Introduction

Rioting is exceptional in the sense that it is a relatively infrequent occurrence. For this reason, it is often presented as unpredictable; rooted in hedonism and a breakdown in morality, or instigated by 'outsiders'. While immediate political accounts generally encompass such explanations, socio-structural analyses of disturbances tend to develop only as the events recede in time. This chapter proposes that, as a consequence of such tendencies, it may be helpful to consider the events of August 2011 through the lens of previous experience, identifying earlier episodes of social unrest which have parallels with the recent events in order to inform current analysis with the benefit of hindsight.

The intention is not to present a comprehensive analysis of the disturbances of August 2011 but rather to identify previous occurrences of rioting that might help inform such an analysis. It is argued that the Brixton riots of 1981 can provide a template with which the disturbances of August 2011 might be usefully compared. By drawing out some of the similarities and differences between the two episodes of rioting, separated by 30 years, a provisional outline is offered of how an understanding of the former might illuminate our assessment of the latter. In particular, such a comparison can help to provide an answer to the question of whether August 2011 might be best conceived as a manifestation of the 'mob' (violent outbursts with no underlying political meaning) or of the crowd (a political expression of dissent). The chapter begins by examining the nature of rioting.

The Exceptional Nature of Riot

Almost by definition, riots are exceptional occurrences in a number of respects. First, they involve simultaneous activity by a large collection of people who, at other times, operate as individuals or as part of a relatively small group. In addition, they tend to be short lived, as participants become tired and revert to routine, the forces of law and order disperse those engaged in disorder, and pent up anger is exhausted, if only temporarily. In this respect, while rioting might be regarded as a form of protest, other, more durable and organized forms of resistance are required if momentum is to be maintained. For instance, the disturbances that followed the student demonstrations of November and December 2010 in London took place against a background of college occupations and other ongoing expressions of dissent.

However, these features lend themselves to the presentation of riots—at least in the immediate aftermath of any disturbance—as exceptional in a rather different sense; as events which are unlinked, unpredictable, out of national character, attributable to feral denizens of the affected areas or to outside troublemakers. A consensus as to the importance of structural, socio-economic, considerations—which, as Bob Marley's lyrics remind us, is frequently an essential element of any adequate understanding of the phenomenon—tends to develop as the rioting recedes from the immediate headlines, with the benefit of hindsight.

Media coverage of, and political comment in relation to, the events of 6th to 9th August 2011 might easily lead one to believe that such outbreaks of disorder were near unprecedented. Thus David Cameron (2011a) described them as 'sickening acts on our streets' that generated 'moral outrage ... because this is Britain'. His words were redolent of Minister of State for Policing, Nick Herbert's (2010) assertion in relation to the student protest of November 2010 that 'there is no place for such behaviour in *Britain's* democracy' (emphasis added) as if such forms of disorder might be acceptable in other (lesser?) democracies. But the fact that senior politicians have had to resort to a 'lack of Britishness' twice within the space of nine months to explain significant disorder, undermines the explanatory power of a breakdown in national character and might alert us to the possibility that the riot is not as rare as such professions of indignation would imply. Indeed, rioting in the cities of the United Kingdom has a lengthy history.

George Rudé, for instance, who provided the seminal history of what he referred to as 'the crowd' (Rudé, 1964), suggests that, during the early part of the 18th century, 'popular rioting ... [was] endemic' (Rudé, 1962:13). While the latter part of the 20th century may have witnessed less frequent outbursts of disorder, John Pitts (2011) is nonetheless able to identify 38 acts of riot between 1958 and 2010; approximately three every four years. This level of prevalence suggests that, contra Cameron and Herbert, rioting is something of a British custom. Further, it provides previous experience of various types of disorder on which to draw to illuminate our understanding of the recent conflicts through the more objective lens provided by temporal distance.

Not all Riots are the Same

All riots have elements in common. So, while the number of participants required by legal definition has changed over time, rioting involves group—as opposed to individual—activity which takes place in public space (Navickas, 2011). Violence, or at very least aggression and damage to property, is integral to disorder of a magnitude that warrants the term. Confrontation between rioters and the forces of law and order is, as a consequence, an invariable feature of the phenomenon. As recent events confirm, there is a tendency too for authorities to condemn roundly both the behaviour involved and the motivation of those who participated: as Flett (2011) notes, the promise of tough retribution is routine.

But precisely because riots are not simply acts of wanton criminality, the form they take varies considerably. As Bohstedt (1994: 257) has argued, riots are complex manifestations of:

93

social/political behaviour set in historical contexts comprising distinctive social networks, conflicts, and ideologies that create and equip the opposing collective actors and thus shape both the incidence and dynamic of riots.

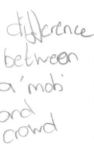

difference between a 'mob' and crowd

Rudé (1959) draws a distinction between the actions of the 'mob' and activities associated with the 'crowd', implying that while the former are generally reactionary or without political meaning, the latter are a mechanism — frequently unconscious — by which dissent was expressed in a (largely) progressive direction. But this helpful distinction is inadequate to delineate the full range of disorders. For instance, the behaviour of English football fans following the defeat of their team by France in the opening group match of Euro 2004 in Portugal might be thought to represent a clear example of 'mob' action on Rudé's account. By contrast, the occupation of Millbank Tower on 10th November 2010, following a demonstration in London objecting to the government's policy in relation to tuition fees and the two subsequent days of protest on 24th and 30th November over the same issue, correspond more closely to the actions of the 'crowd'. But it is not so obvious where to locate the events of August 2011. Most commentators, *pace* Cameron and Herbert, would accede that social and economic factors played a part in the disturbances in a manner that ought to distinguish them from violence occasioned by the national team losing a game of football. On the other hand, there was no direct association between the disturbances during August 2011 and political campaigning as there was in the case of the protests over tuition fees.

The large majority of those caught up in the 'student' riots of November 2010 had attended the demonstrations which preceded them and most of the participants would have been able to give an explicit political rationale for their presence. The targets of the disturbances were similarly chosen for their political symbolism — as well as their location, within close proximity to the route of the various marches. In this respect, the November events were more similar to the occupation of Fortnum and Masons that followed the Trade Union Congress March for the Alternative on 26 March 2011 (BBC News, 2011) than to those that took place across England in the early part of August of the same year. Participants in the latter incidents were significantly less likely to be actively associated with a political campaign or cause, and one might accordingly anticipate that they would be less able to give a political articulation of the reasons for their involvement. Similarly, the disorder itself tended to occur in, or close to, the communities of those who took part rather than in locations proximate to the venue of a planned protest. It is not true, however, that all of the August disorder took place near to where those involved lived. As Smith (2011) notes:

> [A] contrasting picture emerged in Birmingham and Manchester where people appear to have travelled into the city centre from quite distant neighbourhoods to join in the looting and disturbances.

If one were to look for prior parallels, one might conclude that the riots of August 2011 had more in common with disturbances in Brixton some 30 years before, rather than, say, the 'poll tax' riot of 1990. Adequate time has elapsed since those earlier events to allow more objective explanatory accounts to emerge. Considering the similarities or differences between Brixton and the 2011 disorders accordingly provides an historically-informed mechanism for assessing whether the latter ought properly be ascribed to the actions of the crowd or to those of the mob.

Brixton 1981 and August 2011: The Immediate Response of the Authorities

During the weekend of the 10th to 12th April 1981, the streets of Brixton, London, witnessed scenes of violence and disorder 'the likes of which had not previously been seen in [the 20th] century in Britain' (Scarman, 1982: 13). On the Saturday night alone, 279 police officers were injured alongside an unknown number of members of the public. Twenty eight buildings were damaged and destroyed by fire. Petrol bombs were used for the first time on the British mainland (Scarman, 1982). While perhaps most imprinted on the nation's collective conscience, the Brixton events were not isolated: they were preceded in the previous year (1980) by rioting in the St Pauls area of Bristol (Harman, 1981); within a period of months after Brixton, major urban disturbances occurred in Southall (an area of West London with a sizeable Asian community), Toxteth in Liverpool, and Moss Side in Manchester (Rex, 1982). These were interspersed by a rash of less serious outbreaks of violence in areas that included Finsbury Park, Wanstead, Ealing, Hackney, Walthamstow and Wood Green (all in London), Hull, Southampton, Birmingham, Luton, Bedford, Leeds, Bolton and Reading among others (Harman, 1981).

The immediate response of the authorities was predictable. Margaret Thatcher, then prime minister, condemned the rioters in terms that provided a template for David Cameron's assessment three decades later:

> No one should condone violence. No one should condone the events … They were criminal, criminal.
>
> *Pilkington, 2011*

As John Lea and Jock Young (1982: 6) argued at the time, from a conservative perspective, rioting was a symptom of a lack of social discipline and a breakdown of the work ethic:

> [I]t is the entry of the police into … criminal areas in an attempt to stamp out crime which precipitates rioting. Riots are thus seen as no more or less than the attempt by the criminally minded to resist the imposition of law and order upon them. What is therefore necessary first and foremost is firm policing. If the stable discipline of working life is absent and of family discipline regrettably lacking, then the state authorities must provide the necessary element of coercion.

Responding to suggestions that unemployment might be at the root of the disturbances, Norman Tebbit, Employment Secretary, famously bragged that during the 1930s, his unemployed father had not rioted but had 'got on his bike and looked for work, and kept looking until he found it'.

The parallel with Justice Minister Kenneth Clarke's description of those involved in the more recent riots as belonging to a 'feral underclass, cut off from the mainstream in everything but it's materialism' (Lewis *et al*, 2011) is patent. It chimes too with David Cameron's (2011a) image of a 'broken society', and the Coalition Government's broader reliance for its social policy on notions of welfare dependency. Such analysis supports the notion of the August events as a manifestation of the mob.

But the Conservative Government of 1981 soon recognised that the gravity of the disturbances warranted further investigation. William Whitelaw,

Home Secretary in the Thatcher administration, tasked Lord Scarman with investigating the Brixton riots. While his conclusions have been criticised as representing 'liberal concern' (Lea and Young, 1982: 19) and for displaying latent racist assumptions in respect of culture and tradition (Barker and Beezer, 1983), they nonetheless fatally undermined the government's account. In the preface to the report, Scarman (1982: xiii) notes that 'public disorder usually arises out of a sense of injustice'. In conclusion, he cites US President Johnson's 1968 address to the nation proposing that the solution to problems, such as he had been asked to review, lay in mounting an attack upon:

> The conditions that breed despair and violence. All of us know what those conditions are: ignorance, discrimination, slums, poverty, disease, not enough jobs.

> *Johnson, 1968, cited in Scarman, 1982:210*

Such a perspective speaks to an understanding of riots as the actions of the crowd rather than of the mob. Since the publication of the Scarman report, few serious commentators have relied upon the authorities' initial response as an adequate explanation of the Brixton disturbances. If there are more resemblances between August 2011 and the 1980s than distinctions, one might be justified in extending that analysis to the more recent events.

But such parallels have been denied. David Cameron for instance, in the immediate aftermath of August 2011 rebuffed any suggestion that there was any need for an inquiry as there had been following events 30 years previously:

> This was not political protest or a riot about politics. It was common or garden thieving, robbing and looting. And we don't need an inquiry to tell us that.

> *Cited in Newburn, Lewis and Metcalf, 2011*[1]

Similarly, David Lammy, opposition MP for Tottenham, was at pains to distance the 2011 riots from those that erupted on the Broadwater Farm estate in the same borough in 1985, claiming that:

---

1. In the event, refusing to hold a review was not a position that the Prime Minister was able to maintain.

> The vast majority of people in Tottenham reject what happened here. This is
> nothing like the sorts of scenes we saw in Tottenham 25 years ago....This is an
> attack on ordinary people, shopkeepers, women, children...

Gilligan, 2011

If the attribution of the August events to the mob is implicit in the
reactions of the political elite, it becomes explicit in the analysis of radical
philosopher Slavoj Žižek (2011) who argues that the rioters, in contrast to student demonstrators of November 2010, had 'no message to deliver' and might
appropriately be seen as fitting 'the Hegelian notion of the 'rabble' (Žižek,
2011). In this context, the question of how closely the 2011 disturbances did
in fact resemble those in Brixton 1981 becomes important for determining
how best to characterise participation in the more recent episodes.

'Othering' the Rioters

The response of the authorities to the two sets of events, separated by 30
years, provides another point of commonality. In both cases, there was an
attempt to 'other' (Said, 1978) those involved in the disturbances, to suggest that somehow they were not part of the 'real' local community. In the
1980s, blame was attributed to outsiders in the form of political agitators,
particularly anarchists and adherents of far left organizations (Rex, 1982).
Certainly, *Socialist Worker*, the mouthpiece of the Trotskyist Socialist Workers Party, welcomed the Brixton riot as an 'insurrection' and a 'festival of the
oppressed' (Ward, 2011). But there is no credible evidence that such agitators
played anything other than a fringe role. Indeed, Rex argues that far from
being infiltrated by revolutionary provocateurs, the 'whole local community
had been radicalised' (Rex, 1982: 103).

Scarman, although patently sympathetic to the idea that outside organization was to blame, was able to find little that might substantiate such a
charge. The sum total of corroboration, which he acknowledged was 'too
slight to amount to proof in a court of law' (Scarman, 1982: 75), included
reports of a woman participant with an American accent, 'the presence of
the white and black man apparently directing operations in Railton Road'
(p.74), and the testimony of a police constable to the effect that he did not

recognise many of the 'black people opposing him and his colleagues … as Brixton people' (p.75). In the face of such slim evidence, the report is forced to conclude that, while once the rioting had started, some outsiders were inevitably attracted to the area by the publicity, the disorders 'originated spontaneously. There was no premeditation or plan' (Scarman, 1981: 77).

In 2011, the nature of 'outsiders' had changed. The decline of the radical left in the intervening period would have made the charge of external political agitation even less credible than it had been in 1981 (Muddle and March, 2005). One might note too a corresponding waning of the influence of radical black political organization (Palmer and Pitts, 2006). David Lammy's condemnation of the Tottenham rioters in 2011, for example, stands in stark contrast to, the then councillor, Bernie Grant's suggestion, following Broadwater Farm in 1985, that the police had been given a 'bloody good hiding' (Rose, 1992: 79). But a similar dynamic of attempting to characterise involvement in the riots as 'other' was nonetheless evident. Within days of the disturbances, David Cameron (2011a) explicitly linked the events to gangs and gang culture, arguing that the 'thugs' who participated in the disturbances 'did not spring out of nowhere last week'. Similarly, Theresa May, the Home Secretary, in the foreword to the government's gang strategy published in November 2011, maintained that the riots had brought home 'to the whole country, just how serious gang and youth violence has now become' (HM Government, 2011:3). Unfortunately, for such accounts, the Home Office's (2011) own data, already in the public domain prior to the Home Secretary's intervention, had confirmed that just 13 per cent of those arrested for involvement in the riots were suspected gang members. Perhaps more significantly, research conducted by the London School of Economics found that, where gang members did take part, they did not do so as affiliates of the gang but were, on the contrary, behaving atypically (*Chapter 2*; Newburn *et al*, 2011).

More recently, Cameron has tried another tack. In a speech delivered in December 2012, to coincide with the 400th anniversary of the publication of the King James Bible, the prime minister suggested that the development of multiculturalism, and an associated tolerance of alternative value systems, was at the root of:

the riots last summer, the financial crash and the expenses scandal, or the ongoing terrorist threat from Islamist extremists around the world.

Cited in Butt, 2011

The implication that the riots were somehow alien to the British character/ Christian ethos has already received some attention. The unstated assumption that disturbances occurred in areas largely populated by minority ethnic communities is considered in the next section.

Race and Riots

The flashpoints that triggered Brixton 1981 and Tottenham 2011 were both incidents involving confrontation between members of the black community and the police. One might cite similar triggers in relation to St Pauls in 1980, Toxteth 1981, Brixton 1985, and Broadwater Farm 1985 (Rex, 1982; Harman, 1981; Angel, 2012; *Chapter 6*). This is not just a feature of UK disturbances. As Angel (2012: 25-26) points out, all the major riots in the United States, from Watts in 1965 onwards, were sparked by 'perceived police brutality and racism'. No doubt, antagonistic relations between minority ethnic communities and the constabulary contributed to an underlying mood of resentment that made it more likely that police intervention would lead to a broader disturbance. The Scarman (1982) report acknowledged that there had been a wholesale loss of confidence in the police by the local community, caused in part by 'hard' policing methods, discriminatory stop and search, and, in some cases, police harassment.

But it would be a mistake to see either the episodes of 1981 or those of August 2011 as riots that revolved primarily around such antagonisms. Unlike the American experience, participation in the disturbances was not confined to members of the minority community. In Brixton 1981, those involved represented a 'fair cross section' (Harman, 1981:14) of the local community, while in Moss Side the same year, the large majority of those arrested for public order offences (78 of 106) were white (Harman, 1981). As Rex (1982:106) put it:

One conclusion to be drawn from [the] spreading of riots to other cities and to white youth was that what was happening was not specifically, or only, a revolt against racial oppression and mistreatment … even though racial conflict had been at the heart of the first events.

> The contingent nature of the link between race and riots is further underlined by Power and Tunstall's analysis of 13 incidents of violent disturbances recorded between 1991-1992 showing that 'the vast majority of rioters were white and British born' (Power and Tunstall, 1997: 1).

Research into the 2011 events paints a similar picture. Respondents reported that a widespread anger with the police fuelled the unrest. Many indicated that they believed that they were participating in 'explicitly anti-police riots' but did not consider them to be necessarily about race (Lewis, Newburn *et al*, 2011). Ministry of Justice (2011) data confirm that the majority of those arrested in Greater Manchester and Merseyside were white (see *Chapter 13*); while the reverse was true in London and Nottingham, white defendants still constituted a third. In interpreting the figures, the high concentration of minority communities within the affected localities should be borne in mind. Moreover, as Lea and Young (1982:15) noted in relation to the riots of 30 years ago 'black youth are the worst sufferers from a situation facing youth in general in the inner cities' and in that context may have less to lose by taking to the streets. It is now time to turn to the situation faced by inner-city youth.

Recession and Revolt

Ponticelli and Voth (2011) have demonstrated a strong empirical link between economic factors, specifically in the form of government cutbacks, and social disorder across Europe over the past century. They argue that instability, including general strikes, demonstrations, assassinations and riots, is linked to fiscal retrenchment rather than simply economic downturn. The relevance of this analysis for understanding Brixton 1981 and August 2011 is unmistakable.

In relation to the former, unemployment had been rising since the onset of the recession associated with the oil crisis of 1973. Between 1971 and 1976, for instance, manufacturing jobs fell by 20 per cent in Manchester/Salford, 21 per cent per centin Liverpool, 23 per cent in Birmingham and by 30 per cent per cent in inner London. Each of these areas was to become a scene of unrest in 1981 (Harman, 1981). Young people were hit particularly hard with the average rate of unemployment for those aged 16 to 24 years standing at twice the average for the broader population. But this worsening financial climate did not generate widespread instability in the immediate term.

The widespread strike action of the 1978/9 'Winter of Discontent' provided the first signs of civil dissent; a reaction to the Labour Government's policy of holding down public sector wages increases below five per cent (Wolfe, 1991). But it was the election called in the wake of that series of industrial disputes that marked the turning point. The new administration, headed by Margaret Thatcher, came to power with a neoliberal agenda that was intent on reducing the power of the trade union movement and cutting public spending as a proportion of gross national product (German, 1990). The latter proved more difficult than anticipated since social security payments inevitably continued to expand in line with unemployment which grew much faster than in the years before the election, peaking at three million in 1986 (Hicks and Allen, 1999). In early 1981, official statistics showed that 13 per cent of the population of Brixton were unemployed. More than one in four of those registered as jobless were from a minority ethnic group (Scarman, 1982). Nevertheless, cuts were imposed where the administration was able to do so. Spending on social housing fell by 60 per cent under the Thatcher Government: average council tenant rent quadrupled during the 1980s (Jones O, 2011). Funding for education also suffered significant reductions (Hills, 1998). Those towards the lower end of the economic scale were hit particularly hard when the formula, that had ensured that benefits and pensions would rise in line with the cost of living, was abandoned (Hill, 1998).

At the same time, despite a fall in the rate of income tax, the Thatcher administration presided over an overall increase in tax receipts, largely as a consequence of a rise in value added tax (Hill, 1998). Those on lower incomes were inevitably disadvantaged by the regressive realignment of the tax burden. The riots thus appear to be associated with the election of a government ideologically committed to measures of austerity which would impact upon the poor in particular.

The parallels with the Coalition Government's assumption of power are apparent. The recession of 2008 did lead to a rise in unemployment but there was a qualitative leap once the Coalition Government's austerity measures started to bite. The rate of joblessness rose from 7.8 per cent per cent in September/ November 2009 to 8.4 per cent per cent in the same period of 2011. For those in the 16 to 24 age range, the equivalent rise was from 17.6 per cent per cent to 20.1 per cent (Office for National Statistics, 2012). Minority groups were disproportionately affected. In the final quarter of 2010, the unemployment rate for black/black British males stood at 17.7 per cent (Office for National Statistics, 2011). Underlying the government's rampant neoliberal plans to fix the 'broken society' is an ideological commitment that the reduction of the budget deficit should take priority over other considerations, and economic and social policy has been subjected to this imperative. The tripling of higher education fees, the abolition of the education maintenance allowance, the cuts to local authority budgets, the breaking of the linkage between housing benefit and rents, the freeze on public sector pay, the attack on public sector pensions and the rise in value added tax to 20 per cent per cent, all contributed to a five year plan for public spending anticipated to be the tightest since at least the Second World War. As Brewer *et al* (2011) have noted:

> Out of 29 leading industrial countries, only Ireland and Iceland are forecast by the IMF to deliver sharper falls in spending.

Projections from the Institute for Fiscal Studies suggest that the proportion of children living in absolute poverty will rise between 2010 and 2013 from 19.9 per cent to 23.2 per cent (Joyce, 2011). Tellingly, one commentator has noted that many of the areas experiencing riotous activity had made substantial cuts in their youth services and Connexions provision in the previous year (Higgs, 2011). Inevitably, there is some lag before the impact of such austerity measures filters through to those most adversely affected. Significantly, the time delay between the introduction of cutbacks and civic unrest is similar in both of the cases under discussion. The first riots in the 1980s, at St Pauls in Bristol, occurred 14 months after Thatcher's election. The August 2011 events took place 15 months into Cameron's tenure.

As noted above, Lord Scarman had no doubt about the impact of austerity in Brixton. The young black population inevitably harboured a sense of 'frustration and deprivation' exacerbated by daily contact with the police whom they saw as

> Visible symbols of the authority of a society which has failed to bring them its benefits or do them justice.
>
> *Scarman, 1982:29*

Research into the more recent events has revealed a similar pervasive sense of injustice:

> For some this was economic: the lack of money, jobs or opportunity. For others it was more broadly social: how they felt they were treated compared with others. Many mentioned the increase in student tuition fees and the scrapping of the education maintenance allowance.
>
> *Lewis and Newburn et al, 2011*

August 2011: Crowd or Mob?

In attempting to provide a context for understanding the riots of August 2011, this chapter began by posing the question of whether those events were manifestations of the mob or the activities of the crowd. Benefit of hindsight allows us to view the 1981 Brixton riots as fitting closely Rudé's account of the crowd. It has been suggested that the two sets of disturbances, though separated by three decades, have substantial elements in common and are more alike than has frequently been assumed.

In particular, drawing a distinction between 1981 and 2011 on the basis that the latter events were not political, as Žižek (2011) and others have attempted to do, is misplaced. Zoe Williams (2011) denies a political agenda to the more recent rioters because of the extent of looting. But this is to forget the widespread occurrence of the same phenomenon noted by Scarman. Harman (1981:2) cites a contemporary report in *The Guardian* describing 'an assumption that anyone who was not police would help themselves'. Indeed, as Bob Marley (1973) implies looting is a frequent concomitant of rioting irrespective of the nature of the injustice to which they are a response (see also Jones, J, 2011).

It might be contended that political sentiments were not so explicitly articulated by participants in the events of August 2011. As we have seen, this is not entirely accurate (Lewis, Newburn *et al*, 2011). But to the extent that there is merit in the argument, it is largely a manifestation of the decline of an organized left and the erosion of a politically aware black solidarity movement (Palmer and Pitts, 2006), able to give effective political expression to underlying grievances which are, nonetheless, of a political nature. It does not point to a qualitative difference in the motivations of those involved in rioting in 1981 and those who took to the streets in 2011. Both were manifestations of the crowd and not the mob.

There is one further differentiation between the two sets of events that warrants mention. The disturbances of August 2011 were over within four days. Brixton, by contrast, was one of a large number of episodes that commenced in May 1980 in Bristol and continued throughout much of 1981. Indeed, some commentators would see subsequent riots in Brixton and Broadwater Farm, four years later, as part of the same chain of events. From this perspective, the riots of 2011 were a compressed, truncated affair. It might be suggested that this is, in part, a consequence of things developing more rapidly — perhaps a consequence of the impact of social media on the speed with which events unfolded (see for instance, Baker, 2012). An alternative assessment, might propose that in fact we are simply looking down the wrong end of the telescope. From a broader perspective, the series of episodes that started on 6th August 2011 may not yet have run its full course.

References

Angel, H (2012) 'Viewpoint: Were the Riots Political?' in *Safer Communities* 11(1): 4-32.

Baker, A (2012) 'From the Criminal Crowd to the "Mediated Crowd": The Impact of Social Media on the 2011 English Riots' in *Safer Communities* 11(1):40-48.

Barker, M and Beezer, A (1983) 'The Language of Racism—An Examination of Lord Scarman's Report on the Brixton Riots' in *International Socialism* 18:108-125.

BBC News (2011) 'Anti-cuts demo unrest sees 149 charged', *BBC News*, 28 March 2011, at www.bbc.co.uk/news/uk-12876705.

Bohstedt, J (1994) 'The Dynamics of Riots: Escalation and Diffusion/Contagion' in Potegal, M and Knutson, J (eds.) *The Dynamics of Aggression: Biological and Social Processes in Dyads and Groups.* Hove: Psychology Press.

Brewer, M, Emmerson, C, Johnson, P and Miller, M (2011) 'Tax rises and spending cuts will hurt, but little room for Budget easing'. Press release February 2011. London: Institute for Fiscal Studies.

Butt, R (2011) 'Cameron calls for return to Christian values as King James Bible turns 400' in *The Guardian* 16 December 2011: www.guardian.co.uk/world/2011/dec/16/cameron-king-james-bible-anniversary?newsfeed=true.

Cameron, D (2011a) 'We are all in this together'. Speech in Oxfordshire, 15 August 2011.

Cameron, D (2011) Speech outside number 10 Downing Street, on 9 August 2011.

Flett, K (2011) 'I Love the Sound of Breaking Glass: The London Crowd 1760-2010' in *International Socialism* 130:155-171.

German, L (1990) 'The Last Days of Thatcher?' in *International Socialism* 48:3-52.

Gilligan, A (2011) 'Tottenham and Broadwater Farm: A Tale of Two Riots' in the *Daily Telegraph,* 7 August 2011: www.telegraph.co.uk/news/uknews/crime/8687879/Tottenham-and-Broadwater-Farm-A-tale-of-two-riots.html.

Harman C (1981) 'The Summer of 1981: A Post-riot Analysis' in *International Socialism* 14:1-43.

Herbert, N (2010) 'Public Disorder' (NUS Rally). Statement to the House of Commons, 11 November 2010.

Hicks, J and Allen, G (1999) 'A Century of Change: Trends in UK Statistics Since 1990'. Research Paper 99/11. London: House of Commons Library.

Higgs, L (2011) 'Youth Services are Slashed in Riot Hit Areas' in *Children and Young People Now* 18 August 2011: www.cypnow.co.uk/Youth_Work/ article/1085555/youth-services-substantially-cut-riot-hit-areas/

Hills, J (1998) 'Thatcherism, New Labour and the Welfare State'. Case paper 13. London: Centre for the Analysis of Social Exclusion.

HM Government (2011) *Ending Gang and Youth Violence: A Cross Government Report including Further Evidence and Good Practice Case Studies.* London: The Stationery Office.

Home Office (2011) *An Overview of Recorded Crimes and Arrests Resulting from Disorder Events in August 2011.* London: Home Office.

Jones, J (2011) 'August 2011: A Riot of Our Own' in *International Socialism* 132:35-58.

Jones, O (2011) *Chavs: The Demonization of the Working Class.* London: Verso.

Joyce, R (2011*) Poverty Projections Between 2010 - 11 and 2013 - 14: A Post-Budget 2011 Update.* London: Institute for Fiscal Studies.

Lea, J and Young, J (1982) 'The Riots in Britain 1981: Urban Violence and Political Marginalisation' in Cowell, D, Jones, T and Young, J (eds.) *Policing the Riots.* London: Junction Books: 5 - 20.

Lewis, P, Newburn, T, Taylor, M and Ball, J (2011) 'Rioters say anger with police fuelled summer unrest' in *The Guardian*, 5 December 2011: www.guardian. co.uk/uk/2011/dec/05/anger-police-fuelled-riots-study (Accessed 31 January 2012).

Lewis, P, Taylor, M and Ball, J (2011) 'Kenneth Clarke blames English riots on a "broken penal system"' in *The Guardian*, 5 September 2011: www.guard- ian.co.uk/uk/2011/sep/05/kenneth-clarke-riots-penal-system.

Marley, B (1973) 'Burning and Lootin''on *Burnin'* by Bob Marley and The Wailers.

Ministry of Justice (2011) *Statistical Bulletin on the Public Disorder of 6*[th] *to 9*[th] *August 2011*— October update. London: Ministry of Justice.

Muddle, C and March, L (2005) 'What's Left of the Radical Left? The European Radical Left Since 1989: Decline and Mutation' in *Comparative European Politics* 3(1):23-49.

Navickas, K (2011) 'Fire and Fear: Rioting in Georgian London and Contemporary Britain' in *History and Policy Newsletter,* Summer 2011.

Newburn, T, Lewis, P and Metcalf, J (2011) 'A new kind of riot? From Brixton 1981 to Tottenham 2011' in *The Guardian* 9 December 2011: www.guardian.co.uk/uk/2011/dec/09/riots-1981-2011-differences.

Newburn, T, Topping, A, Ferguson, B and Taylor, M (2011) 'The four day truce: gangs suspended hostility during English riots' in *The Guardian* 6 December 2011: www.guardian.co.uk/uk/2011/dec/06/gang-truce-english-riots.

Office for National Statistics (2011) *Labour Market Status by Ethnic Group.* Updated February 2011. London: ONS.

Office for National Statistics (2012) *Summary of Labour Market Statistics.* Updated January 2012. London: ONS.

Palmer, S and Pitts, J (2006) '"Othering" the Brothers: Black Youth, Racial Solidarity and Gun Crime' *Youth and Policy* 91:5-22.

Pilkington, H (2011) 'What's pure and simple about what's happening on Britain's street?': http://sociologyatwarwick.wordpress.com/tag/explaining-riots/

Pitts, J (2011) 'Riotous Assemblies' in *Youth and Policy* 107:82-98.

Ponticelli, J and Voth, HJ (2011) 'Austerity and Anarchy: Budget Cuts and Social Unrest in Europe 1919 - 2009'. Discussion paper number 8513. London: Centre for Economic Policy Research.

Power, A and Tunstall, R (1997) *Riots and Violent disturbances in Thirteen Areas of Britain.* Social Policy Research Findings 116. York: Joseph Rowntree Foundation.

Rex, J (1982) 'The 1981 Urban Rots in Britain' in *International Journal of Urban and Regional Research* 6(1):101 - 113.

Rose, D (1992) *Climate of Fear: The Murder of PC Blakelock and the Case of the Tottenham Three.* London: Bloomsbury Publishing.

Rudé, G (1959) 'The London Mob of the 18th Century' in *Historical Journal,* 2(1):1-18.

Rudé, G (1962) *Wilkes and Liberty.* Oxford: Oxford University Press.

Rudé, G (2005) *The Crowd in History: A Study of Popular Disturbances in France and England 1730-1848.* London: Serif.

Said, E (1978) *Orientalism.* London: Vintage Books.

Scarman, Lord (1982) *The Scarman Report: The Brixton Disorders 10-12 April 1981.* Harmondsworth: Pelican.

Smith, K M (2011) *Young People and the 2011 'Riots' in England—Experiences, Explanations and Implications for Youth Work.* Infed: www.infed.org/ archives/jeffs_and_smith/young_people_youth_work_and_the_2011_ riots_in_england.html

Ward, P (2011) 'Brixton 1981: The Great Insurrection' in *Socialist Worker Online.* 9 April 2011: www.socialistworker.co.uk/art.php?id=24408.

Williams, Z (2011) 'The UK riots: the psychology of looting' in *The Guardian*, 9 August 2011: www.guardian.co.uk/commentisfree/2011/aug/09/ uk-riots-psychology-of-looting.

Wolfe, J (1991) 'State Power and Ideology in Britain: Mrs Thatcher's Privatization Programme' in *Political Studies* 39(2):237-252.

Žižek, S (2011) 'Shoplifters of the World Unite' in *London Review of Books Online.* 19 August 2011: www.lrb.co.uk/2011/08/19/slavoj-zizek/ shoplifters-of-the-world-unite.

Sheldon Thomas is an ex-gang member from Brixton whose life took a dramatic twist when someone standing next to him in a dance hall was shot in the head and the blood splattered on his face whilst watching the man fall to the ground right at his feet. This was not the first time he had seen someone murdered but having someone killed in front of him changed his life. This was the beginning of his journey of redemption in 1986, which was realised with the assistance of his mentor Bernie Grant. Along with his wife and eldest daughter, Sheldon runs a successful gangs mentoring business that re-shapes the mind-set of high-profile gang members whilst developing their potential and transferring their street skills knowledge into corporate business sense.

6

REVISITING BRIXTON:
THE WAR ON BABYLON 1981

Sheldon Thomas

Introduction

What we saw across London in August 2011 gave us some clue that particular problems endemic to urban communities across the country still remain unresolved; in particular the tensions between minority ethnic communities and the police. To me, it seems little has changed over the last 30 years—despite recommendations made from Lord Scarman's report on the 1981 Brixton riots and the McPherson Report written as a response to the death of the black teenager, Stephen Lawrence. The violence and disorder which gripped the country in 2011, although different to Brixton 1981 in many ways, had some similarities, and reminded me of my experiences as a young black man and why I took part in uprisings in the 1980s. This chapter is a reflexive account of what took place in Brixton, London in 1981. In the first part of the chapter, I set the scene for my experiences and participation in the 1981 disturbances by discussing the black community, the social climate at the time and its relations with Britain as well as place our experiences and treatment in a historical context. I then move on to talk about how these experiences went from simmering to boiling point in April 1981, resulting in what we called the Brixton uprisings. Some of you may be surprised to learn about the level of anger and frustration people like me had at the time but the fundamental aim of this chapter is to show you how these feelings layered over time; the important point to note is that, as we saw it, our violence was not senseless, but of our *violation*.

Setting the scene: How We Were (or Are?) Depicted

I have grown up in a British society, which at first did not except me for who I was and, if I dare say it, may even at times struggle now with who I am (a black man). It was not until much later in life as an adult that I began to understand why I felt so much frustration and anger. So when I was mentored by Bernie Grant and Jessie Jackson as a young man (whilst on a trip to America with Bernie as part on the newly formed National Black Caucus), they both imparted some very wise words, they said, 'Don't state the obvious' (the white man hates me), 'look beyond what's being said' (hate, get's you to hate, so you spend your life hating). To me this seemed true; if you begin to dissect what people tell you, and that includes what you tell yourself, you begin to realise; hate only stops you from living. That's to say to address injustice, its best to look at things without hate in your heart. But as I grew up, I started to feel various forms of hate, dislike, and difference towards me manifested in various forms of racism in British society.

I know some of you may be thinking, that 'this could not have happened, not in Britain'. Maybe some of you will ask me 'where did you get your research from' or if I have a PhD, where is my 'data' but here's the thing, I grew up a black man whose experience cannot be taught, put into research for social scientists to analyse. Many of my experiences are equal to data which could be collected for most PhDs or someone making some documentary on urban life (even the word 'urban', seems to have been offered as some way of politically correctly referring to 'black culture'). Sometimes I feel that unless you lived it, survived and came through that journey of redemption, pain and sacrifice, then it is difficult for research or documentaries to capture. To me, when I read some research reports on 'gangs', it feels like the interviewers were very far from the real world of the people they are supposed to be researching; that is, 'man's on road', the 'Gullyside', the 'hood', (basically referred to as 'deprived communities' in some social science reports). But this is historical. It also felt quite patronising that they asked Lord Scarman, who was far distanced from the tense police/community interactions in Brixton, to tell the black community living there why the 1981 riots happened.

Even to this day, it's very difficult for people like me to receive social scientists when they come into our communities feeling they already know how they can help us. They are given very large amounts of money by government (regardless of whichever party is in power) to write papers on gangs, 'deprived communities', black boys, bad parenting, riots, the list goes on. Yet, despite these investigations and the recommendations which follow, our problems remain. Similar things happen with the way in which we are depicted in the media, by film directors, producers, and all the TV channels; they all follow a similar pattern. Someone disconnected from the real scenery of street life writes some film/documentary/drama about some issue around black people. Adding insult to injury, they try and tell us our story about our lives and sell it back to us. These accounts fail in a number of ways to reflect our pain and can do more damage than good. Take 'Bullet Boy' or 'Top Boy',[1] where the violent exchanges and oppressive interactions are given precedence over examining the root causes of young black peoples' hostility.

Here in 2012, I sometimes feel that these mediums still think they can tell our story and know what the solutions are to our problems. Maybe news media and government officials don't want the issues in our community to change, and often what happens in the black community, because I see these depictions as poisonous, bringing more damage and dividing our community. But it is unfortunately a divide which has long existed; as far back as I can remember when I was growing up the 1970s.

Our World in the 1970s

So where does my story start? Believe it or not, back home in the West Indies; not because my friends and I were there, but because we saw what was happening to our Jamaican homeland. When America invaded Grenada and the CIA supplied guns to Edward Seaga's supporters in the 1980 Jamaican elections, which went down as one of the bloodiest elections in Jamaican history, Britain stopped buying bauxite (aluminium) from Jamaica. The American company Chiquita forced the World Trade Organization to stop Britain

---

1. Dramas about growing up in gang life in London; however, they did nothing other than glamourise gang life.

from buying its 9 per cent share of Banana's from the Caribbean and this is when the political climate changed. We believed that Britain had done the right thing by giving us independence but now it all seemed under threat, because Jamaica had to borrow back from the IMF before getting punished by structural adjustment. Many people were made unemployed and struggled to get by on a day-to-day basis. Jamaica became politically and socially unstable, violence increased and this was the first layer of our anger.

I am the son of Jamaican parents and was born and grew up in the UK. However, living in Britain was no different just on a smaller scale; we still had to struggle for basic things. I felt at the time, the politics were about 'put the blacks in the worst housing', 'offer them low-paid jobs', 'tell them in school that they cannot become solicitors, doctors, teachers or run their own business' but of course tell them they 'can work in Ford motors, play football, do athletics and work for others'. So the second layer of our anger was something a little more obvious, a little more close to home. Our opportunities were denied, downplayed because of our perceived inferiority.

In London during the 1970s, we were persistently violated by police officers, make no mistake about that. Although some of our black leaders back then were strong, as the 1970s drew to a close, our leaders began jostling for positions to become councillors and the like. As they moved into these positions, we lost our representation and these few key community figures began to present less of a challenge to the systemic social problems. This meant we were further exposed to racist abuse from the police. So when sus laws[2] came about, our community leaders, who now had more prestigious positions, had no idea about our anger, hate, and worst of all, the violence that was to come. It felt like it was a step away from assimilation into British culture.

When the Conservative party came to power in 1979, it felt like they wanted to crush our spirits and what better way than to make it legal for the police to stop and search us. I remember feeling that now it was legal to shout racist abuse at us and violently abuse their power. For many of us, this was why we formed 'posses' (the word used today is 'gangs'), because we needed to defend ourselves. Many of us decided we would seek retribution because we wanted to get our own back on what many of us believed

---

2.   From the term 'suspected person', the law permitting the search of a suspect.

at the time was 'white people looking to keep the black man down'. We had seen how our parents, who had come over from countries like Jamaica, were subservient, passive, and meek; they didn't want to upset anyone, let alone have an uprising in a country they looked up to. My parents' generation felt that Britain had 'saved them'. When I had my first argument with my father, he told me to respect Britain because the country had given him a job but I knew that the British politics had structurally undermined Jamaica — it had created the political instability in the first place so we couldn't succeed in our own country! Had my generation in the late 1970s been in the same position, maybe we would have had the same reservations: a strange country, grey skies, freezing cold weather, treated as second class citizens, spoken to as if we didn't understand English, given the worst housing, and to top it all, given the lowest jobs and made to feel we owed them (England) in social terms.

But for the second generation Caribbean offspring, the seed was already sown decades earlier: we were not going to be like our parents, we were not going to allow a system to repress us. Even though many of us did not have the understanding to look beyond what the State was trying to do to our spirits, hate had already begun to engulf and cement itself in our hearts. Many of us now wanted nothing more than to take revenge, getting into fights with police officers and bus drivers when we received racist abuse. It was a similar experience when we were victimised by the National Front which is why some of us were tempted to join forces with the IRA. This may come as a surprise but, to some degree, we had the same struggles as our Irish comrades; well at least I know a few of my posses did.

The Rage

In this late-1970s period, three life-changing things happened to me but which also affected the Brixton black community. For the community, it was the TV broadcast of the series 'Roots' — a programme on the history of slavery[3] and then the very public trauma of the far right National Front announcing marches through a black area, Lewisham in south London. For

---

3. This was the first series showing the history of slavery. Alex Haley traced his roots in slavery and wanted to find out how he got from West Africa to America. During this process, he realised the brutality of the colonial West.

me, it was when my brother was beaten by a group of skinheads to within an inch of his life. Collectively, this set me, as well as most of the Brixton black community on a collision course that would ultimately take decades for many in my generation to recover from and begin to self-reflect, dissect and give therapy to ourselves.

The TV broadcast of 'Roots', well, this broke to camel's back. Having come home from school and as usual in a Caribbean household, it was homework, look after your little brother and sister, wash the dishes and make sure the house was clean. Even though we were dirt poor, my dad and mum had great pride in keeping the house clean; my mum would say 'Becah wi brok nu mean seh'[4] (Because we're broke it doesn't mean people should know) but she had pride despite our poverty. We then sat down to watch TV, which in those days had three channels. Then 'Roots' came on. I was completely stunned and for the first time I think I swore in my head (in most Caribbean houses you couldn't swear at all). You see up until then we had not been told by our parents that our ancestors were taken as slaves. To make matters worse we were stolen from Africa and our lands taken over and every mineral and natural resource was used to prop up the industrial revolution in the UK and build up other European cities in Spain and France. I think for the first time my house was silent. Tears began to run down my face because I was seeing black men and women being beaten, raped (I didn't know it was rape at the time, I was 12), thrown off ships, tied up in chains, and crammed together like sardines and being sold like cattle. I was never the same, and this was what made me react so passionately against the National Front when it marched in Lewisham that same year.

The next day at school, it was obvious everyone had seen 'Roots'. For the first time, the school was divided; all the blacks refused to associate or even talk to anyone who looked remotely white, black kids that were normally well behaved started to change their attitude, and there seemed to be a sinister feeling in classes. It was at this point I stepped up to lead the revolt in school, because I felt so violated, so hurt, so in pain, so angry, that even as a second year student (which would now be a schoolchild in year eight), I made sure all the black kids felt the same way as I did and if they didn't I

---

4. This is Jamaican patois.

beat them up (even though I was not the best fighter in the school, I was only 12, but had a big posse) and that included my older brother whom I threatened to kill if he didn't stop seeing his white girlfriend.

I remembered most of my brethren[5] at the time wanted to know why our parents didn't tell us about slavery and we wanted to know why the school hid it from us. We felt we were lied to by our parents, it was then that some of us,I believe, began to lose some respect for them and even though we would never say this to their faces, most of my generation rebelled and for many of us, that rebellion nearly destroyed a whole generation of black boys. We were consumed with hate. I began to dig deep into history, reading as many books as possible on slavery. As a 12-year-old I began to think, 'Does everyone hate black people,' what is it about 'us' that would make people treat us like that. During these dark days, most people in the black community went to church; it was like a prerequisite to being black. The church was the backbone of our community, and I even remember, asking God, 'Why does everyone hate blacks?' I'm not sure if I got an answer, but I remember listening in church one day as the preacher read scripture from the old testament, 'an eye for an eye', so to me I felt this was God saying 'Sheldon, the white man steps to you, bury him'. I have no doubt now, that this voice was not God, but the hate in me, driving me to seek retribution. This was my decline.

These feelings were exacerbated when my brother was nearly killed by 15 skinheads in Clapham Common Park because he was 'black'. I wanted to hunt them down but my father had this old view of 'going to the police'. But my father hadn't experienced the racist treatment of the police that I had and I lost more respect for him when he said that. So when the National Front marched through Lewisham was the moment my friends, my posse, were waiting for: to batter some racists even though there were only 12 of us. It was all out war, and we didn't even live in Lewisham, but we saw our brothers and sisters in the area needed us. We ambushed the National Front from the side streets, throwing bottles as they marched, and this gave us the training—even though we did not know at the time—we would use these same tactics in Brixton in 1981.

---

5.   Meaning 'friend' or in modern-day terms 'man dem'.

The Hate

However, during this period, more Jamaicans (Yardies[6]) started to arrive in the UK, especially in areas like Brixton, St Pauls in Bristol, Handsworth in Birmingham, Toxteth in Liverpool and Chapletown in Leeds. At first they came with reggae music, the Jamaican sound system, even though Sir Coxone, Small Axe, and Serpano B (which became Stereograph, the best sound system to come out of the UK) were already in full flow, the Jamaicans came with MCing, which flipped the script on the reggae music scene. But their arrival also brought a new breed of gangster criminal, the nine millimetre gun. In those days, guns were controlled by the white gangsters or 'the firm' as they were then known (later adopted white crime families, e.g. the Richardson's, Noonan's, the Brindles and of course the Adams). Therefore only the top black men got hold of guns, even though all the guns came via the white crime families. So when the Yardies came over with an 'I don't-give-a-damn' attitude, sticking two fingers up to these crime families, and some of us looked up to them; for us it was again showing the establishment, albeit white criminals, we were running things.

By the time 1980 had come around, I had been arrested so many times, I had lost count. In those days, the Caribbean household believed this brought 'shame on the family', but you see I didn't care anymore, didn't respect my parents; I saw them as weak and because they hid our history from us only made me feel contempt towards them. Most of us in my posse of young black youths decided we were no longer going to associate ourselves as 'British'; we were now 'African/Caribbeans' and ones, like me, who had real hate in their hearts. Although I was British born and bred, I didn't even recognise I was born in Balham, I was now a Yardie; collectively, we felt that as far as we were concerned, Britain was dead to us.

The Brixton Uprisings

This is what the police said about why the Brixton riots occurred:

---

6. 'Yardies' were already involved in crime in Jamaica but in the 1980s fled to countries like the US and UK. They used sound system to make links and act as cover for or deter attention from some of illegal activities in Britain. However, they soon realised that there was little money to make from fighting the police and National Front, and moved into selling drugs and robbing people.

A serious increase in street robbery in Lambeth caused the District Commander to institute a plain clothes operation known as Operation Swamp 81, which resulted in a significant number of black youths being stopped and searched. This intensified the resentment of a group who already frequently protested against and obstructed police actions on the street.

Metropolitan Police, 2011

What this statement misses is that the 1981 Brixton uprisings had already been written decades earlier and the time bomb that had been slowly ticking finally ran out of time on that April Friday evening, when a young black boy was stabbed and the police refused to take him to hospital. So the uprisings were going to happen; it was just 'when' and that 'when' was now. There was no turning back the clock, slavery had happened, colonialism had happened, Jamaica's structural adjustment, 'Roots', racist police officers, the National Front, Maggie Thatcher and the Conservative squeeze, our parents hiding the truth, the church losing support in the community, the Yardie's, they all happened and worst of all, hate happened and had consumed us all. We were all charged. What started with bricks on a Friday night, turned into all-out attack on the police and all the businesses in Brixton, as none were owned by any blacks apart from a few record shops? We had nothing to lose. This was it, it was payback.

The Next Day

I arrived at my friend's garage, which was on the notorious Angel Park Estate in Brixton (well before 'gangs' like 28s, Hangman, Invincible, Tottenham Man Dem (TMD), Poverty Driven Children (PDC), O-Tre, Gas from Brixton, were even born). We were fortunate to have an up-and-coming sound system, and, in a way, we kind of made history because we were the first youth man sound to challenge the dominance of Sir Coxone and other big man sound and yes, before Saxon, Love Injection, Java, Jamdown Rockers, Nasty Love and all other youth man sound that sprang up years later. We were testing the equipment for big sound clash in Angel Park in Brixton, and had totally forgotten about the night before, because it was normal for us to fight the police, until a bus on diversion came down our road and busses never came down our road. We knew it was on, we knew of the impending violence.

We ran out to Brixton High Street, and what we saw reminded us of TV footage of Soweto in 1976, where there were thousands of black people on one side of the road and the police on the other; the former were demonstrating when the police opened fire on them. It was the first time that we were standing side by side with the most violent youth black group in Brixton, Small Axe. So when Keytie from Small Axe, the most notorious sound system/posse in Brixton, arrived we wasted no time in organizing the line of attack. Keytie was a lot older than us, he was in his late-20s or maybe even early-30, and, by 1981, we were 16 and did not care. When the first of our bricks hit the meat wagon (the police van), that was it, and some of us lost our minds and full-scale violence erupted like never before. We were not going stop until Brixton was brought to the ground.

This was going to be our night, this was payback for years of systematic bullying and exploitation, a night where for just that one moment in time, and we were going to control our own destiny. We were going to live out our dreams and, although we were hurting, for some of us this was therapy, this was our release. Years of pent up anger, and hate (especially the younger black boys at the time): hate that was now driving us, hate that brought such rage and bitterness. So when Keytie led the first charge towards the police line, we were glowing with excitement, turning over cars, setting buildings on fire and throwing anything and everything towards the police; we could see and smell the fear in their eyes and that gave us great strength.

The War on Babylon[7] Continues: 2011

Almost three decades later whilst sitting in my Tenerife hotel room, again the uprisings seem to have taken London by surprise. Can you imagine: my family and I are watching the TV in Tenerife thinking, 'It's happened again.' This time, however, there was something far more serious and sinister behind these uprisings because between this 30-year period, we have seen more young men die at the hands of other young men, especially young black boys in the

---

7. We referred to the biblical 'Babylon' as the movement which King Nebuchadnezzar used to systematically repress the Jews. We felt the modern-day repression was through Maggie Thatcher.

name of 'gangs'. The August riots could have seen even more killings take place, but instead we saw gangs rivalries disappear as they joined forces to again fight Babylon. The country was very much blind to this, and did not see it coming, and our community leaders could only watch as shops and cars were burnt or looted.

What did society miss (again)? Well when you ignore gang violence, ignore the 40 murders from 2008 which have taken place in London alone at the hands of youth violence, and where most of the victims and perpetrators were black, I am not surprised that the tensions were missed. To me, local authorities always seem to talk big about how crime, shooting and stabbings have come down, but the most important statistic which cannot be measured is that of tension. None of the London boroughs even acknowledge the word 'tension', instead we have self-indulgent heads of youth offending teams (YOTs), community safety services and youth services, whose sole purpose is to number crunch. They don't seem to know the issues at all. Some of these public-sector bodies only tend to use the community when it suits them and only invite the third-sector organizations (who are closer to the 'problem'), but it's all too last minute, and to me it's hardly surprising that tensions in the black community never get mentioned and even when it does, it's completely ignored.

Just like 1981, unemployment today is a significant issue. Back then, aside from manual labour apprenticeships, we were also called into action because the avenues supposedly available to us were pretty much closed. Despite this, the same groups always seem to be left outside 'opportunity' these days. Take the Olympics for example. When we won the bid to host the Olympics, Lord Coe said, 'This will bring employment to the local area and regenerate most of Newham and parts of East London', but between him and Ken Livingston (who was the mayor at the time), it was one big con and minority ethnic young people in Hackney and Newham never really benefitted. In fact, they made it so difficult for these groups to sign up through the website because of the exhaustive application process. For the last year, I have been working in Hackney and Newham where these promises of Olympic opportunity have supposedly been made. I can't see any improvement in the schools in East London. Hackney Borough in 2008 was only offered six apprenticeships, and at first I thought they must have missed the other six off (66), but no, six was what the Olympics offered, in one London borough. It's difficult to see how tokenistic efforts like this help the youth of today, hardly surprising, in my view, that young people took to the streets during August 2011.

Discussion

Why did I write this chapter? It's quite simple. There were some real fundamental core reasons why the 2011 uprising took place which were very similar to those in 1981 and 1982 in Brixton, Handsworth/Birmingham, Toxteth/Liverpool and Chapletown/Leeds. Firstly, both 1981 and 2011 seemed to be triggered by tensions between the police and the black community, predominantly because of stop and search. Secondly, unemployment, which was also at the centre of the uprisings in 1981, has been increasing in recent years; half of black youth across the country are currently unemployed (ONS, 2012). Another striking comparison with 1981 is that the death of a young black youth again lies at the centre of it. What happened in 1981 made us feel very angry and it did Mark Duggan's family and friends in 2011. Let us remember the uprisings took place because the underlying social issues in both 1981 and 2011 had been completely ignored and to add insult to injury, most of our black MPs and councillors are too scared to even address these systemic problems. Perhaps Diane Abbott has tried but in the Houses of Parliament, the rest seem to spend their time pleasing the cabinet, and don't seem to have any respect from the people who matter on the streets.

I have also tried to chart the reasons for participation in the Brixton riots 1981 in this reflexive passage. I hope you don't misinterpret my words because they are true to my experience and that you can empathise with what it was like for some people like me in the early 1980s. My rage was not connected to any defunct psychological problem, but a general frustration about my social position, which I had come to learn, was historical, structural, social and, consequently, subjective. I was very bitter that few others could see what I saw which is why I started to take revenge. Even though I have come a long way since the days of 1981, I still can feel the emotion of the evening of the Brixton riots. It is extremely close to my heart.

These days, I run a gangs programme to help young people who are likely to face similar situations to those I did earlier in my life — disoriented with the education system, facing unemployment, caught up with gang life, and with criminal convictions. Like some black youth today, I had persuaded myself to believe that the world was against me. Do we need to 'deal with gangs' just because there are riots? Why is property damage and loss of business more important than young people dying at the hands of gang violence?

To me there is a dark irony: the posses of 1981 are the gangs of today and, on a daily basis, I still see the same problems between the black community and the police. However, I believe we need to at least acknowledge how our black communities lived through the scourge of racist treatment from police officers, the National Front, gang violence, the Conservative hell. Only then, can we begin to bring the real expertise and knowledge of what is needed to stimulate actual change in our communities. For me, community leaders are a thing of the past; they are political puppets only interested in making sure they sit at the Home Secretary's round table discussions along with some organizations that spend their time creating flash booklets, stating how their programmes are so successful with gangs. Perhaps they help in some way but I have been at some meetings and asked some of these organizations to name one gang with which they have worked: suddenly there is a very uncomfortable silence and an awkward shuffling in seats. Now I see new parallels with what my mentors, Bernie Grant and Jessie Jackson used to tell me because today, although I 'state the obvious' about the current situation, with 'gangs' and 'youth crime', I've passed 'looking beyond what's being said', because I am now more concerned with what's not being said.

References

ONS (2012) 'Ethnicity by Employment: Latest ONS Data Release'. March 2012, London: ONS.

Metropolitan Police (2011). *History of the Metropolitan Police: Brixton Riots 1981*, cited on March 14th 2012 online at http://www.met.police.uk/history/ brixton_riots.htm

Dr Axel Klein is a social anthropologist with an interest in the convergence of conflict, culture and policy. He is particularly interested in official and unofficial techniques of conflict management, and how policies designed to protect society generate their own harmful consequences. He regards the role of social analysis as being to identify policy perversities and the counterproductive impact of well-intended interventions. The riots in London and other parts of England are part of a wider engagement with questions of state-society relations (see Klein, Axel, 2012, 'Policing as a Causal Factor—A Fresh View on Riots and Social Unrest', *Safer Communities*, Vol.11, No.1: pp.17-23). He has also written widely on drugs and drug policies (including *Drugs and the World* (2008), London: Reaktion) as well as on civil war, conflict in the work place and the treatment of immigrants.

7

MORE POLICE, LESS SAFETY?
POLICING AS A CAUSAL FACTOR IN THE OUTBREAK OF RIOTS AND PUBLIC DISTURBANCES

Axel Klein

Introduction

Unrest is an opportunity for reviewing the relationship between the state and wider society. In the UK, this review is currently taking place in the context of 'austerity': the inability of the state to maintain funding levels for key public services. Yet maintenance of public safety is perhaps the primary aim of the state, hence, there is an argument of preserving the police and other criminal justice agencies from the cutbacks on public-sector spending. However, the stakes are high in any contest over resource distribution, even more so at a time of economic contraction. It is therefore important to establish a clear understanding of the dynamic and two-way relationship between policing, and the maintenance of law and order. What we can learn from the 2011 riots is that tactical errors by police officers on the ground become amplified against structural policing deficits, and can be a fuse for social unrest, even revolution. While post-riot analyses will identify a need for closer scrutiny, accountability and dialogue between the police and all sections of the communities they serve, the definitive problem is political and reverts to a general question about the functions the police. Indeed, one of the reasons why trust relations have eroded between police and sections of the population is that the functions of the police force now extend well beyond the maintenance of law and order in the pursuit of public safety.

Much of police activity is therefore directed towards maintaining public morality, public health and social services, which should arguably be left to the 'Big Society' or other arms of the state. Young people are caught in-between the failure of government managing of economy and welfare, and as targets for an overzealous law enforcement machinery. Much police time is spent controlling the young, at precisely the point where economic contraction excludes them from the labour market.

This chapter discusses these areas in greater depth, drawing on examples from other countries where public disorder has surfaced as a result of policing. It looks at the political economic context of public unrest, and draws parallels between the political response to protest in different countries. It then argues that protest takes place within a moral economy, with a vaguely articulated but strongly perceived sense of right and wrong. While media attention has focused on criticising the police response to the outbreak of violence, this chapter looks at the responsibility of the police in causing the violence in the first place. It takes a critical look at stop and search tactics, and the relationship between the police and sections of the community. It then argues that the important policy lesson is to review the role and purpose of the police at a time of budgetary constraint.

[handwritten margin note: *Public disorder as a response to Police / Policing*]

Political Protest

Public unrest was a defining political theme in 2011, with a range of protests in countries in North Africa and the Middle East escalating into revolutions that overthrew governments and changed the political landscape. To some observers the events were so defining that *Time Magazine* named 'The Protester' as person of the year (*Time Magazine*, 26 December 2011). Known as the 'Arab Spring' — a term redolent with memories of democratisation movements in southern Europe — they generated immense support in Western countries where the sympathies lay largely with the demonstrators in Tunisia, Egypt, Syria, Yemen and Qatar. Peaceful but determined in the face of heavy intimidation, they won much admiration in their demand for what were widely seen as basic, political rights. Unbeknown to the tax-paying electorate in Europe, their political leadership had for years been complicit with autocratic Arab regimes, providing economic aid in exchange for stability, pro-Israeli policy, and a locale for the forceful interrogation of terror suspects. Relations between the political elites were so close that Michele Alliot-Marie, the French Foreign Minister, spent his Christmas vacation in a Tunisian resort owned by that country's ruler Zine el-Abidine Ben Ali and even offered to lend the expertise of the French police to contain the unrest. But sensing the mood both in North Africa and at home, European policy-makers were quick to change tack. They abandoned their regional allies and threw their weight behind the protestors. According to David Cameron, the UK Prime Minister, the general approach to North Africa had been flawed. 'The EU needs to look hard at its role in the region', said Cameron in national parliament on the 7th February 2011. He continued: 'It is time for Europe to take a more hard-headed approach where the conditions on which we give money are real and insisted upon' (Vogel, 2011). Stability was no longer enough. A few months later, Cameron and the French President, Nicolas Sarkozy were able to go even further, by throwing military weight behind the demands of protestors in Libya. A short but hard-hitting aerial campaign allowed both leaders to burnish their credentials as 'liberators', position their countries advantageously for lucrative oil contracts and to settle an old score with Colonel Gaddafi. If this was one example of regime change where foreign military intervention had been decisive, it seemed no less deserving of public sympathy.

The explanatory framework for such Western support re-opens the last chapter of a seminal text by the historian Francis Fukuyama (1989). In his view, the establishment of democratic governments is the logical end point of historical progress that will eventually produce a universal and homogenous state. Applied for the first time to the North African/Middle Eastern region, the model rejects explanations of cultural or religious particularism, and instead claims that all people are capable of democratic government. Fuku-yama would therefore see popular support for the Arab revolts in the West as a continuation of the claims and ambitions of the Enlightenment—the idea of universal values, of inalienable rights, and a social contract between government and the governed. As the latest inheritors of the 'rights of man' the agitators of the Arab Spring were taking up the torch from the protesters on the streets of Berlin, Warsaw, Prague and Moscow in 1989, in the long march towards global democracy.

Economic Protest

Inspired by and contemporaneous with the Arab Spring were the demonstrations in cities along the northern shore of the Mediterranean. Protestors were also attracted to civic landmarks in the cityscape to vent their frustrations at the mismanagement of public finance and the social costs of economic contraction. While the very act of public assembly and the call for change in the Arab countries had been surrounded by tension and was seen as a challenge to the regime, protestors in Europe were moving well within their democratic rights. Though there was excessive use of violence by protestors and police forces in Greece, most of the protests were peaceful, well managed and often carnivalesque rather than revolutionary. Commentators in northern Europe, once again, were largely goodwilled in view of the deep economic crises faced by southern Europe and massive unemployment experienced by young people in the spring of 2011. The high levels of youth unemployment in Spain, for example, were part of a two-tier labour market that privileged unionised job-holders over job-seekers. Governments, political parties and trade unions had constructed a system of social protection that made it hard for workers to get fired but just as difficult for school or university leavers to get hired (*Economist*, 2011a). While the actual demands of the *indignados* gathering at the Plaza de Sol in Madrid were vague and general, it was agreed by liberals and conservatives that economies across Southern Europe were held back by restrictive practices, closed shops and cronyism (*Economist*, 2011b).

The economic problems in southern European countries such as Spain, Italy and Greece stimulated calls for political change; yet here the issue was not for wider participation in the political process or freedom of expression. Protesters were in the streets to defend their living standards and to fight for the right to work. Northern European observers and financial backers were encouraging of economic reform in Greece, Spain, Italy and Portugal including the expansion of the economy to competition, the downsizing of the state, and a restructuring of expenditure. What was unclear was whether their political systems would be able to rise to the challenge.

Interestingly, the protests in Europe were not too dissimilar to what, throughout the 1990s, became a common phenomenon in large parts of the developing world. Government after government was structurally adjusted by teams of economic advisers from the World Bank and International Monetary Fund (IMF). Both the painful reforms and the futile public protests were part of the long march towards market economies: the economic reverse of democratic government. Though the political processes around the Mediterranean remain unresolved at the point of writing, most observers placed fault with politicians, for either 'cooking the books' to meet the criteria for joining the single currency, or living beyond national means. The protestors, in turn, were largely seen as morally justified, and the moment of crises thereby providing an opportunity for economic restructuring and a redefinition of the state.

Protest as Crime

When protests broke out on the streets of England at the height of the summer of 2011, the response by the political leadership and the media commentariat was remarkably different. The Prime Minister, a fervent backer of stone-throwers in Benghazi and Cairo, was quick to give his verdict on protesters at home: 'This is criminality, pure and simple' (Sparrow, 9 August 2011), he said at a meeting with top security officers. The criminal justice system responded with a swift screening of CCTV footage, leading to 1,715 arrests, 24 courts and tough sentences (*The Guardian*, 24 November 2011). Most notorious, perhaps, were the four year custodial sentences meted out to young people for using social media for 'incitement'. These punishments are far in excess of what is normally handed out to people who commit violent or sexual crimes.

The dissonance between HM Government's robust resort to repressive measures at home and the fulsome praise for protesters abroad was not lost on foreign observers. The Iranian Government issued a travel warning to Iranians planning to visit the UK and asked the UN Security Council to intervene. With a gesture of generosity, it even offered to provide humanitarian observers to monitor the street protests to ensure that the human rights of protesters were not violated and an objective account could be given to the world (Dehghan, 10 August 2011). Newspapers close to the government in both Saudi Arabia and China (*People's Daily*, 18 August 2011) were delighted with David Cameron's warning about the pernicious effect of social media, and his consideration of censorship, in situations where 'it would be right to stop people communicating via these websites and services when we know they are plotting violence, disorder and criminality' (BBC, 11 August 2011).

Individuals caught up in the wheel of justice became symbolic scapegoats, with long sentences passed for their deterrent effect. However, the arrestees in England served another function—they provided concrete evidence of how the riots started. Here another parallel opens up from government reactions to the outbreak of public violence; the official position is that the riots are the product of conspiracy involving distinct groups, preferably with links to the outside. This allows for the discussion to be moved away from the original causes and underlying conditions and focus on the identity of the perpetrators. In North Africa, governments characterised protesters as Islamists and foreign agents, in London the culprits were described as 'gangs'. Indeed, the Home Secretary Theresa May, said 'gang' culture was a critical contributory factor for the unrest (May, 2011; see *Chapter 10*).

The fearful breakdown of public order across large parts of England's inner cities was seized on to provide a rationale for greater police funding and powers. Arguments for additional resources for maintaining public order in times of crises entered into spending reviews in times of budgetary cutbacks. The mayor of London, Boris Johnson, was arguing persuasively that in times of crises 'This is not a time to think about making substantial cuts in police numbers'. The riots had shown how quickly control could slip away from the security forces, and the widespread damage this could cause. With the UK economy stagnating, the government was set on course to cut police budgets by 20 per cent by 2014/15, and there were fears that public safety could no longer be guaranteed.

But while there is widespread intuitive support for Boris Johnson's argument that austerity is not the time for trimming police budgets, the understated assumptions behind this reasoning are worth exploring. First, far from constituting a 'freak event' the riots could be seen as part of wider and more general protests against cuts, including demonstrations against increases in university tuition fees and public sector strikes. Second, the riots did not represent British exceptionalism but were part of popular revolt sweeping across large parts of Europe (Taylor-Gooby, 2011). The correlation between economic recession and public unrest has been established across the world (Ponticelli and Voth, 2011). What this suggests then, is that the riots are the product of economic decline and accompanying social tensions that cannot be dismissed as what David Cameron described as 'criminality, pure and simple'.[1]

The Moral Economy of Rioting

If we examine historical precedents and comparative material from around the globe we find that need often generates turbulence with unanticipated consequences. The turbulence in North Africa and the Middle East in 2011, for instance, was causally intertwined with the rise in food prices (Mason, 2012). The European revolution of 1848, was triggered by poor harvests and sharp increases in bread prices, while what is arguably the 'mother of revolutions', in Paris in 1789, was to a large extent caused by the collapse of public finance under a massive mountain of debt. Senior police officers must certainly be scenario planning for an increase in public disturbances, even while force strength is shrinking

Yet while establishing the correlation between deprivation and unrest is helpful, even if only by demonstrating the validity of an intuitively grasped relationship, it does not provide an explanation for any particular event. In this respect, there is a risk of making the mass action appear mechanical, the automatic outcome of certain preconditions which diverts from the human reality. In a detailed study of unrest in the 18th century the historian E. P. Thompson cited contemporary explanations for regular disturbances at times of rising food prices as spasmodic. They were quite different from instances of mob violence directed at particular targets and often manipulated by the authorities. The attacks on the homes, churches and places of association (including the Lunar Society) of dissenters in Birmingham during the 1791 'Priestley riots' for instance were thought to have been planned by local officials. The authorities, in any case proved slow to respond and reluctant in the prosecution of ringleaders (Jay, 2000).

---

1. Analyst Louise Taggart at security consultancy AKE said that in time urban unrest worries could make it harder to cut other programmes as well, including sorely needed education and community services. It went well beyond Britain. 'Across Europe, we've already seen some incidence of civil unrest', she said, saying it would almost inevitably impact on policy. 'There's definitely a likelihood that similar scenes might erupt when austerity cuts really start to be felt'.

The crowd in the bread riot, by contrast, has no such rationale, and no agency. It is like a gigantic beast reacting instinctively to external stimuli. Thompson notes the psychological empowerment of people congregating in numbers for market days, the sense of common purpose, and the exceptional reversal of power relations vis-á-vis the authorities. But he goes further to restore a rational causality to the action of the crowd and a moral compass. In the 18th century, this was tied to economic activity, with a strong, deeply entrenched sense of rights and obligations. Much of the violence shaking English cities at the time was occasioned by conflict over antagonistic notions of the economy. Most of the rural poor subscribed to the idea that regionally produced food should be used to feed local populations as part of a moral economy. Many landowners, on the other hand, were trading these long-established communitarian values for the profit motive of a political economy in which demand was attracting supply. It was therefore differences in underlying value systems that explained the conflict.

For violence to erupt, however, there had to be an incident in which the established rights of the poor were breached. This was usually by way of established, customary rights, such as the sale of wheat to the cities, but could also include incidents of fraudulent practice. The discovery of false measurements by a retailer, for instance, could incite the crowd to fury and unleash a attack by the crowd on the shop. The crowd, then, does not only operate within a moral framework, it also has to have a sense of justice. Action is triggered by an affront. The violence of the mob then, far from constituting a breach of the law, is a corrective action, and in the view of the rioters at least, to assert a higher justice. Not that this may hold for long, because once it has kicked off, the events quickly slip beyond their control of the instigators and spill over into targets that are quite unrelated to the original offence.

The crowds in London, just as in southern parts of Europe, North Africa and the Middle East were also operating within a moral framework and not simply 'criminal'. There is little doubt that much of the crowd's initial action was opportunistic and gratuitous because it was a sense of outrage that motivated protestors, not greed.

The Critical Role of the Police in the Outbreak of Violence in Tottenham

In Tottenham, as in other parts of London, relations between the police and the community, particularly the black community, are tense. There is historic mistrust of the police among young black men, with widespread allegations of deliberate and persistent harassment. A disproportionately high number of people dying in police custody are Afro-Caribbean, and some police stations have gained notoriety for the use of violence on these groups. On the evening of the August 4th Mark Duggan was killed by armed police officers. The story was not widely reported by the national media, preoccupied with events in Libya at the time, but pictures of Duggan's dead body surrounded by police officers went viral on social media within a short time after his death. For many local people seeing a picture of a dead black man surrounded by police the picture conjured notions of injustice (Briggs, 2012).

The police meanwhile provided newspapers with the following account: the deceased was a known criminal and had for some time been subject of an investigation (*Daily Telegraph*, 4 August 2011; *London Evening Standard*, 5 August 2011). As Duggan was driving his silver Toyota Estima in Ferry Lane, close to Tottenham Hale tube station on Thursday night, a police patrol tried to pull his car over. Duggan pulled out a weapon and opened fire on the police officers who then shot him dead. To the family of the deceased, it was indicated that the killing had been an act of self-defence, and this was the final provocation. On Saturday, a crowd of family and friends marched to the police station in Tottenham to demand an explanation and an apology. Faced with a volatile situation, police officers did not try to negotiate their way out but instead shut down the station. When stonewalling[2] did not work, they tried to disperse the crowd with force. It was at this point that the anger exploded into violence. It was only on Tuesday 9th August that the Independent Police Complaints Commission (IPCC) released the ballistics report that Mark Duggan had not been shooting at the police after all. It was another incident of an innocent man getting killed by armed police officers. It later transpired that a team consisting of officers from the Metropolitan

---

2. A behavioural communication technique of non-cooperation by refusing to provide information.

Police Operation Trident unit, the Special Crime Directorate 11 and armed officers from CO19 had planned to arrest him that night.

It is evident that the misjudgment by police officers at that particular moment was the main event that unleashed the outbreak of violence. However, it is debatable that the damage could have been contained and widespread rioting been avoided if the situations had been managed thereafter. Instead, the police compounded an already difficult situation with a number of errors which helped blow a local story and personal tragedy into a national crisis by:

1. Concealing the way in which Duggan was killed (that he fired the first shots) which was met by disbelief among family and friends;

2. Refusing to meet protesting family members outside the station to negotiate;

3. Denying responsibility for the shooting; and

4. Failing to disperse protestors, including the grieving family members who came to protest outside the police station in Tottenham.

When considered in this light, the outbreak of disturbances does not come as a surprise. A family that has suffered a loss and is then first insulted and then assaulted by the perpetrators could be understood to be reactive. From a public order perspective, the quality of law enforcement agencies is marked by their skill in defusing tension and neutralising conflict. However, community relations was not really on the list of priorities of police commanders, indicated by the failure of senior officers to attend the town hall meetings in Tottenham, which were held to rebuild community relations. Local MP David Lammy commented at the time:

> We are here very much today as a community. So it is with tremendous dismay and disbelief and huge disappointment that I express my sadness on behalf of the people of Tottenham that senior police officers have not come today.

It can even be understood that the anger of the mourners and sympathisers spilt over into a more general violence. What took everybody by surprise, however, was how this local outbreak sparked off disturbances all over London and other cities. Social media made the rapid communication possible but the messages transmitted via cyber circuits (as well as more conventional means of communication) could incite a population that was already motivated by shared experience and common grievance. One interesting observation made early on in the riots was the 'truce' established among neighbourhood gangs. Rivalries were set aside in the struggle against a common enemy. Briggs cites on informant as saying 'this is not about postcode war, it is "us" against "them" and "forget our beef with each other and lets get the police"'. Gangs from Hackney, the borough next to Tottenham, were not mourning the loss of a family member or friend. Violence kicked off not because of a particular incident relating to an individual (Briggs, 2012). It was not an expression of solidarity or an action run in order to lend support. What happened across many cities in England over those few days was an uprising by mostly young people against a clearly perceived enemy. It was not that the killing of Mark Duggan provided a cover of legitimacy for anything other than the initial protest, and indeed, the family of the deceased very quickly distanced itself from the violence. But the first series of clashes created an opportunity to rise and wreak violence against the authorities.

In the UK, criticism of the police centred on their ineffective response to the violence. According to the *Daily Mail*, for example, the disorder spread because 'by not getting a grip on the violence, officers allowed the impression to take hold that the streets have been surrendered to thousands of yobs' (*Mail Online*, 28 November 2011). It was argued that if the police had been more proactive early on in the riots, disorder would not have spread as it did, and far less damage would have been caused. This is a disingenuous line of reasoning, that purports to be critical of the police when effectively the criticism is not that there was too much, or the wrong kind, but simply to little policing. In any event, arguing over the merit of different tactical operations in order to contain violence has diverted attention from the core problem—the role of law enforcement in triggering public unrest.

Comparative Material from Riots Around the World

Comparisons with the unrest in the Arab country is illustrative for the critical role of law enforcement as a cause of public unrest. In Tunisia, the unrest that overthrew a government and rung in political change across North Africa was triggered by the suicide of an unlicensed vegetable trader. Mohamed Bouazizi had taken the drastic cause of action after being harassed, again, by law enforcement agents ostensibly checking licences but widely believed to be looking for bribes. A few weeks later, protestors began marching in Egypt mobilised again by the death of a young man in police custody. In other parts of the world too, the trigger to public outrage is often police action. So called 'race riots' erupted in Detroit in 1967 after police officers broke up an after-hour drinking club used by Afro-American Vietnam vets. A racially motivated killing of a black motorist by four white police officers, and their subsequent acquittal by a white jury set off violence across the Los Angeles district of Watts and neighbouring areas. In Clichy-sous-Bois, Paris riots broke out in 2005 after police officers chased a group of youths into a tangle of power cables, where they died.

Senior police officers will concede instances of misconduct and lament the few 'bad apples' that are found inevitably in every force but the suggestion of exceptionalism does not explain the massive scale of the action. For violence to spread from a flash point across a city and even a country there have to two elements: (1) identification with the victim and (2) a shared perception of the perpetrator as enemy. Rioters in London, Cairo, Tunis, Los Angeles, Detroit and Paris identified with the victim in categorical terms, in that the protagonists of the unrest felt equally disadvantaged by class, race or age group. But without personal ties and in the absence of an over developed sense of social solidarity, this would not suffice to motivate people into action. What was critical was that shared experience of victimisation at the hands of the police.

The Demonisation of Youth

There have been no suggestions so far that the English summer riots of 2011 were racially motivated, even though the relationship between the police and the black community is far from ideal. Anger towards the police extended well beyond the black community and was reported by 85 per cent of 270 informants interviewed (*Guardian* and LSE, 2011). Individuals stated strong feelings even 'hatred' towards the police, and saw the riots as an opportunity to get back at them. While there has been a distinct decline in public trust of the police since the 1950s the outright hostility is mainly reported by a younger age group. Even given that young males have always been vulnerable to being drawn into offending behaviour, and one of the critical categories of the dangerous classes, there has possibly been a qualitative shift in relations between youth and law enforcement in recent years. The preoccupation of law enforcement with young people is on its current scale and extent a recent phenomenon, reflective of changes in both society, and the workload and function of the criminal justice system.

In the US, the demonisation of young people has been tracked by the work of Michael Males. He has studied media and popular representations of young people as 'super predators' or 'drug and alcohol bingers'. But it appears that both consumption patterns and offending behaviour is far more prevalent in older age cohorts. Whereas serious youth crime has remained steady for the last 25 years, felony arrests for the 30-50 year age cohort have more than doubled. Alcohol and drug use patterns are also higher, particularly for problematic patterns of use, among the ageing 'babyboomers' than among young people (Males, 2010).

All over the western world, the emergence of the teenager as a separate category between childhood and adulthood was one of the big sociological changes of the 1950s and 1960s. It was linked to sharp rises in prosperity, to transformations in the workplace, family structure, and in a wider, yet under explored sense, the relationship between society and state. While the expansion of the market economy, with its emphasis on consumption, provided a sense of individualism and with that, of liberty, it was also accompanied by a steady increase in the functions of the state. From the 1980s onwards the model of state intervention shifted in the US. The welfare state was progressively dismantled and replaced by a security state. As budgets for education and welfare were driven down, spending on law enforcement and the prison service increased. This was accompanied by a direct reallocation of resources, away from childcare, social housing, and food stamps, and into policing and incarceration. It is possibly best exemplified by schools in many US cities which have cut back spending on teachers and classrooms to use the funds to hire retired police officers as security agencies and metal detectors at the entrance.

These trends have been echoed in the UK under the New Labour Government which introduced a string of targeted pieces of legislation in the guise of the anti-social behaviour agenda. It has been argued that these have eroded established criminal justice principles by a 'hyper active state' intent on demonstrating its activism (Crawford, 2009). While policy-makers introduce new powers and penalties and award funding, the decisions on how they will be implemented are always made at street level. It is the criminal justice agencies, but particularly the police who decide when and how to bring the new powers to fruition. Legal powers furnished to enhance public safety mesh with the priorities and practical convenience of individual officers on the ground. This can lead to the unfair targeting of certain youths who are deemed to be less respectable and undeserving of leniency. This, in turn, relates to the resources available to the young and disadvantages those without access to safe recreational facilities who then come into adversarial contact with the police as the 'usual suspects' (Crawford, 2009b; McCara 2005).

The blanket use of these extensive powers was underlined by *The Guardian* and LSE study, which found over two thirds of respondents, reported having been stopped and searched in the past year. In the worst cases these experiences can produce a labeling process where agencies define certain categories of young people as deviant, who then, upon encountering the systematic suspicion and mistrust of the authorities, internalise the behaviour. Though policing powers have been issued for ostensibly preventative purposes, the results seem to be more ambiguous. In some cases the attentions of the authorities seem 'to recycle certain categories of children into the youth justice system, whereas other serious offenders escape the tutelage of the formal system altogether. The deeper a child penetrates the formal system, the less likely he or she is to desist from offending' (McAra and McVie, 2007: 328). As with adult offenders, where exposure to the criminal justice system, and particularly to prison, is a predictor to future offending, the extension of formal interventions can be counter-productive.

Discussion: Reviewing the Purpose of Policing and the Political Representation of the Young

It therefore appears that the cumulative effect of extending police powers, of lowering the threshold for criminal justice interventions and the age of criminal responsibility, and the heavy investment in policing over the past decade has not led to a dramatic increase in public safety, but to the contrary. Instead, the expansion of police powers and resources has placed a strain on relations between the police and the urban young. We can now identify the consequence of excessive policing as a major contributing factor to the outbreak of violence at the onset of the 2011 riots, leading in due course to multiple deaths and injuries, the arrest of over 4,000 people and massive damage to public and private property. While there are several contextual factors involving wider notions of legitimacy and the role of the state, one of the main learning points should be to re-examine the precise role and function of the police force.

Since the first introduction of an organized, uniformed police, there has been a steady increase in their size and capacity but also in their responsibilities. A corollary of this expansion has been the withdrawal of civil society, leading to a reduction of the public sphere and a moral nihilism in civic affairs. There is therefore a push-pull situation, where the very existence of a police service, as opposed to a police force, allows a general abandonment of responsibility. It is now widely accepted by both police officers and the public that the police is the 'service of last resort'. This has taken the agency a long way from the erstwhile objective of maintaining law and order to uphold public safety.

Returning to the international parallels we find that in each case the errors made in the course of policing practice that trigger violence are made possible by structural factors of governance. In the riots in Detroit, Los Angeles and Paris, policing was an extension and a reflection of systemic racism. In North Africa, corrupt regimes used the police and an array of other official and secret agencies to repress protests and opposition. In return these agencies were given licence to abuse their position to extract benefits and favours from the populace. In the absence of a Rule of Law there was nowhere where they could take their grievance short of direct action.

This is a further lesson to learn from the riots in England. While young people have crystalised as a discrete social entity they do not have political voice. This seems incongruous given the dominance of the young in international image markets. But there is a hiatus between aesthetic hegemony and political representation. At a time then when the demographic change with an ageing population shifts an increasing economic burden onto the young, their defining experience of the state is negative, while their means to redress these by participating in policy discourse is diminished. None of these reflections should be misread as a licence for looting, but in order to preclude the recurrence of events the analysis of the riots should stretch beyond incrimination of the perpetrators.

References

Allen, C. (2007), *Crime, Drugs and Social Theory: A Phenomenological Approach*, Ashgate, London.

BBC (2011), 'England riots: Cameron says police admit to wrong tactics', BBC, 11 August 2011, www.bbc.co.uk/news/uk-14485592 (Accessed 3 October 2011).

Bradford, Ben (2011) 'Convergence, Not Divergence?: Trends and Trajectories in Public Contact and Confidence in the Police'. *British Journal of Criminology* January 1, 2011 51: 179-200.

Briggs, D. (2012) 'What We Did When It Happened: A Timeline Analysis of the Social Disorder in London' in *Safer Communities Special Edition on the Riots*, Vol 11 (1):6-16.

Browcott, O. (2011), 'UK riots: court of appeal upholds lengthy sentences', *The Guardian* (Accessed 18 August 2011).

Centre for Crime and Justice Studies (2006), 'Breakdown Britain', Centre of Justice Studies, London.

Crawford, A. 2009a. 'Governing Through Anti-social Behaviour: Regulatory Challenges to Criminal Justice' *British Journal of Criminology* November 1, 49:810-831.

Crawford, A. 2009b 'Criminalizing Sociability through Anti-social Behaviour Legislation: Dispersal Powers, Young People and the Police' *Youth Justice* April 1, 9: 5-26.

Daily Mail (2011) cited online at http://www.dailymail.co.uk/news/article-2067178/How-police-abandoned-streets-riot-mobs-Officers-gave-impression-surrender.html#ixzz1ltNc5HXw

de Botton, A. (2004), *Status Anxiety*, Hamish Hamilton, London.

Daily Telegraph, 4th August 2011. 'Man killed in shooting incident involving police officer. A policeman's life was saved by his radio last night after gunman Mark Duggan opened fire on him and the bullet hit the device'.

Dehghan, S. K. (2011), 'UK riots: Iran calls on UN to intervene over "violent suppression"', *The Guardian*: www.guardian.co.uk/uk/2011/aug/10/uk-riots-iran-un-mahmoud-ahmadinejad (Accessed 6 October 2011).

The Economist, 2011a. 'Austerity in southern Europe Spain's cry of pain: How to get the protesters out of the plazas and into jobs'. May 26th 2011.

The Economist, 2011b. 'Spain's indignants Europe's most earnest protesters. They may not know what they want, but they are starting to get it'. Jul 14th 2011.

Fukuyama, F. (1989) *The End of History and the Last Man*, London: Penguin.

The Guardian, 7 February 2012 'David Lammy condemns police for failing to show up at riots meeting': http://www.guardian.co.uk/uk/2012/feb/07/david-lammy-tottenham-police-riots

The Guardian 24 November 2011 'Riots broken down: who was in court and what's happened to them?': http://www.guardian.co.uk/news/datablog/2011/sep/15/riot-defendants-court-sentencing.

Her Majesty's Inspectorate of Constabulary (2011), 'Adapting to Austerity', Her Majesty's Inspectorate of Constabulary, London.

Jay, M. (2009) *The Atmosphere of Heaven: The Unnatural Experiments of Dr Beddoes and His Sons of Genius.* Yale: Yale University Press.

London Evening Standard, 5th August 2011. 'Father dies and policeman hurt in "terrifying" shoot-out'.

London School of Economics and *The Guardian*, 2011. 'Reading the Riots: Investigating England's Summer of Disorder—Full Report': http://www.guardian.co.uk/uk/interactive/2011/dec/14/reading-the-riots-investigating-england-s-summer-of-disorder-full-report (Accessed 14th January 2012).

McCara, L. 2005 'The Usual Suspects? Street-life, Young People and the Police' *Criminology and Criminal Justice*, Vol. 5 No. 1: 5-36.

McCara, L. and McVie, S. 2007. 'Youth Justice? The Impact of System Contact on Patterns of Desistance from Offending'. *Journal of Criminology* July 2007 Vol. 4 No. 3:315-345.

Males, M. 2010. *Teenage Sex and Pregnancy: Modern Myths, Unsexy Realities.* St. Barbara, California: Praeger.

Mason, Paul, 2011 *Why It's Kicking Off Everywhere.* London: Verso

May, T. (2011), Speech on Riots, Made to the House of Commons, London, 11th August: www.homeoffice.gov.uk/media-centre/speeches/riots-speech (Accessed September 2011).

Nozick, R. (1975), *Anarchy, State and Utopia*, Basic Books, New York.

Ponticelli, J. and Voth, H. J. (2011), *Austerity and Anarchy: Budget Cuts and Social Unrest in Europe, 1919-2009*, Centre for Economic Policy Research, London.

Sparrow, A. (2011), 'David Cameron announces recall of parliament over riots', *The Guardian*, 9th August 2011: www.guardian.co.uk/uk/2011/aug/09/david-cameron-announces-recall-parliament (Accessed 3 October 2011).

Taylor-Gooby, Peter, 2011 'Riots, Demonstrations, Strikes and the Coalition Programme' Occasional Paper, University of Kent.

Thompson, E. P. (1971), 'The Moral Economy of the English Crowd in the 18th Century', *Past and Present*, Vol. 50, pp.76-136.

Tilly, C. (1985), 'War Making and State Making as Organized Crime' in Evans, P., Rueschemeyer, D. and Skocpol, T. (eds.), *Bringing the State Back In*, Cambridge: Cambridge University Press.

Tyler, T. and Fagan, J. (2008), 'Legitimacy and Cooperation: Why Do People Help the Police Fight Crime in their Communities?', *Ohio State Journal of Criminal Law*, Vol.6, pp.31-75.

Vogel, T. (2011) 'EU under pressure to reassess aid to Egypt' *The European Voice*: http://home.earthlink.net/~mmales/uscrime.txt (Accessed 10th February 2012).

Part II

WHO, HOW AND WHY?

Professor Steve Hall is Chair of Criminology at Teesside University. After dropping out of university in 1974 he became a nomadic musician, general labourer and avid reader of anything political or philosophical. In the 1980s he worked with young offenders in the de-industrialising North-East of England, and he was active politically during the steelworks and mine closures in County Durham. In 1988, he returned to university, and, after graduating in 1991 began teaching, researching and publishing. Essentially a sociologist, he has also published in the fields of history and radical philosophy. He is the co-author of *Violent Night* (Berg, 2006). His co-authored book *Criminal Identities and Consumer Culture* (Willan/Routledge, 2008) has been described as 'an important landmark in criminology'. He is also the author of *Theorizing Crime and Deviance: A New Perspective* (Sage, 2012).

Simon Winlow is Professor of Criminology at Teesside University. He is the author of *Badfellas* (Berg, 2001), co-author of *Bouncers* (Oxford University Press, 2003), *Violent Night* (Berg, 2006) and *Criminal Identities and Consumer Culture* (Willan, 2008). He is also the co-editor of *New Directions in Criminological Theory* and *New Directions in Crime and Deviance* (both Routledge 2012).

8

GONE SHOPPING:
INARTICULATE POLITICS IN THE ENGLISH RIOTS OF 2011

Simon Winlow and Steve Hall

Introduction

In this chapter, we suggest that the riots of August 2011 contained within them an amalgamation of apparently contradictory narratives. In particular, we will argue that the riots were both political and apolitical; destructive, but also strangely conformist. It is clear that dissatisfaction with life chances and urban social conditions played a role in framing the riots, but the nihilism of the looting suggests a context of political and historical inertia and the depressing triumph of liberal capitalist ideology. Our goal here is to suggest a few intellectual paths forward that might allow us to contextualise and historicise the development of contemporary advanced marginality and the occasional outbursts of collective rage that appear intimately wedded to this process.

Large scale urban unrest of the kind we saw across England in the summer of 2011 is not a new phenomenon (see Lea, 2011). Indeed, urban disorder appears to be closely tied to the regular and destructive economic convulsions that are a structural feature of capitalism (see Harvey, 2010; Hall, 2012). Riots appear to the multitude as entirely random occurrences; the apparent result of a unique assortment of urban, political and cultural contingencies that can neither be predicted nor planned. In fact, rising inequalities and systemic injustices appear to collude with a general erosion of popular hope for the future, and a sense of social wellbeing and collective sentiment. Mediated by everyday social experience and engagement, these background dynamics frame the immediate foreground issues that catalyse disorder (Winlow and Hall, 2012). As such, we should not be particularly surprised that England was beset by such widespread social disorder in the summer of 2011. The trigger event — the shooting of Mark Duggan, and the resulting micro-political and non-violent protest that followed his death — produced a slight rupture in the thin layer of normative civic order, allowing a wellspring of durable social antagonisms and dissatisfactions to burst forth in a spectacular manner.

Tim Newburn (2011), the academic lead of the *The Guardian's* rapid investigative study into the riots, has called for a concerted empirical investigation into the riots. We support him in this endeavour, but we would also point out that without a concerted theoretical investigation we will fail to develop an adequate understanding of the riots and the people who were involved in them. Empirical accounts of the situational factors that led individuals to become involved in the disorder must be placed alongside a critical investigation of what it means to live in poor communities and in the shadow of such extravagant and ostentatious wealth. Specifically, we must seek to understand the nature and causes of the antagonisms and dissatisfactions that are such a key feature of the 2011 riots. In this chapter we will try to offer a few very basic observations about the nature of the deep-seated social frustration that is such a demonstrable aspect of the cultural life of areas of advanced marginality and permanent recession (Hall *et al*, 2008). We will also attempt to link these frustrations to the widespread looting that tends to differentiate these riots from others that have occurred in Britain in recent history.

The Academic Response

Many academics were quick to highlight what appeared to be the uncanny similarities between the 2011 riots and those of the 1980s and 1990s. While this is not an entirely unreasonable claim, it is worth noting that there is an enduring tendency among sociologists and criminologists to play things down, to attack the idea that riots of this sort are unusual in some way, and then to return to the comfort of finding patterns and applying established formulas. Of course there is much that is unique about the 2011 riots, and this uniqueness reflects the specific historical context in which they took place and our individual and collective experience of the rising inequality and social antagonisms that are such a disturbing feature of contemporary liberal capitalism (Hall, 2012). Too many criminologists in their response to the riots immediately reached for the most obvious intellectual framework, that enduring and established conceptual tool, first created in the 1960s, that magically still appears to possess the lustre of critical theoretical engagement: the 'moral panic' (Cohen, 1973).

Those interested in the 2011 riots should prepare themselves for yet more interminable chatter among the left liberal intelligentsia about a disproportionate criminal justice response as the state once again engages in the politics of distraction and identifies a new generation of internal enemies upon which Middle England can focus its righteous indignation. It is not that this framework is entirely mistaken in identifying the power of the conservative establishment to wilfully discard the democratic ideals of justice and fairness and aggressively denunciate marginalised social groups. Its critique of the myopic moral codes of the mainstream media appears entirely justified. It is true that right-wing media were quick to demonise those involved in the riots, and post-riot sentencing was clearly disproportionate. However, the application of the moral panic thesis fails to yield the new ideas that are vital if critical criminology is to regenerate itself and advance social understanding of the brutal realities of life in Britain's most marginalised neighbourhoods. After 40 years of left liberal criminological orthodoxy, didn't we expect the media to respond in this way? Didn't we know ahead of time that the state's response would be punitive? Why should we be surprised that the media vilifies rioters and their families and the criminal justice system abandons its stated commitment to equality before the law? If it is true that state and media responses to social disorder are, and have been for some time, entirely predictable, what good does it do us to endlessly return to the 'moral panics' framework and act as if we are seeing these trends for the first time? The 'moral panics' framework takes us only to places we have already been. Might it not be more fruitful for critical criminologists to return to our intellectual roots and reaffirm our commitment to actually explaining the root causes of our recent summer of disorder?

If criminology is a discipline that seeks to explain the social, cultural, economic or psychological 'root causes' of crime, then one could be forgiven for thinking that the 'moral panic' thesis represents a kind of liberal anti-criminology; an attempt to subvert the foundations of the discipline. Moral panic theory neatly sidesteps the complexity of causal mechanisms that propel the individual towards crime in order to make an ideological point about oppressive statestate power. It reduces crime to a one-sided power game dominated by those who have the authority to define what crime is and the ability to manipulate how people feel about it. One could be forgiven for thinking that moral panic theorists are encouraging us to believe that the very real crime problems that beset working-class neighbourhoods throughout the country are nothing more than media creations that function to induce fear in the multitude. For moral panic theorists, these condemnatory media creations ultimately produce the 'crime' that they are so keen to condemn: the righteous indignation of those aggressively labelled by established power structures in the media and politics prompts the marginalised to kick back at the system that oppresses them. For Cohen (1973), crime itself is a response to the very attempt to control it. Moral panic theory then encourages us to look away from the painful reality of our decaying neighbourhoods and towards the obscene power of a media apparatus to manipulate public sentiments in the hope of shoring-up the status quo.

If we are to truly advance our understanding of the riots of 2011, we must move away from the seductive siren call of established ideas and begin to think about the social and economic realities that frame the lives of the rioters. We cannot content ourselves with yet another analysis of media and governmental reactions to the riots. If we do so, criminological theory will once again find itself reiterating ideas from its dim and distant past; as if 1960s liberal radicalism is still radical in the second decade of the 21st century and as if the world economy and the entire structure of British society have not changed beneath our feet. Criminological theory must endeavour to construct a critical account of the riots that is unsentimental and rooted in the harsh social realities of the post-industrial revanchist city at a time when the global neoliberal economic project stumbles onwards despite its recent destructive failure. Only by constructing new ideas can we re-energise criminology. The half-hearted reiteration of ideas that are already in circulation simply confirms the intellectual stasis of our discipline (see Hall and Winlow, 2012). Rather than focusing upon predictable media and governmental responses, and thus on what happened *after*—rather than before and during—the riots, we avoid the ultimate truth of these historic and destructive events.

But, as Tony Jefferson (2011) has asked, if the riots and the reaction to them cannot be explained by the moral panics thesis, then how are we to explain them? What can we say about these disturbances that moves the argument forward and provides us with new ways of interpreting the complexities of social order and disorder during a time a profound economic turmoil? Below we will attempt to respond to Jefferson's request by offering a few very brief and rather basic theoretical observations about the riots of August 2011.

Cynical Realism

Perhaps the most notable change that has occurred between the riots of the 1980s and the riots of 2011 is that, for those involved in the disturbances, attacking the police no longer appears to be the paramount concern (see Topping and Dawdon, 2011; Prasad, 2011). A considerable number of the disturbances that took place across the country were clearly geared towards looting (*Ibid*), and this new focus offers us some insight into the complex causes of the riots and the motivations of many of those involved. The dark spectacle of the riots of 2011 had a strangely conformist aspect, and the focus upon the looting of consumer goods indicates the huge power of consumer imagery and the ideological uniformity of the contemporary neoliberal period. Those who rioted were not politicised groups fighting for a more just and equitable world. They made no demands to those in power, and they were not possessed of an ideological vision of a new and progressive historical path. Consciously, they wanted to change nothing. They were subsumed by the experiential adventure of the riot and, with regard to the looting, they wanted to grab what they could while they could (Prasad, 2011; Carter, 2011). Subconsciously, they wanted to change everything relating to their own being-in-the-world.

On the surface of things the riots were profoundly apolitical. Public reaction tended to support the view, offered by David Cameron and others, that the rioters were simply selfish and avaricious barbarians basking in the fleeting pleasures of mob rule. No obviously political targets were identified and no manifesto for change was forthcoming. Any attempt to position the riots as a genuinely political event was immediately dismissed as the unworldly ideological myth-making of the radical left. However, it was just possible to identify beneath the surface a dark resignation and a gloomy nihilism exhibited by the rioters at the very moment of what appeared to be their carnivalesque triumph. The looters appeared to be gripped by a strange joy-less joyfulness, a depoliticised depressive hedonia (Fisher, 2010) that is the necessary endpoint of the new cultural injunction to enjoy (*Žižek,* 2002). The central claim we hope to advance in the coming pages is that those involved in the riots appeared to be acting out an objectless and unconscious rage that, in the absence of alternative political narratives of the present, cannot be adequately symbolised.

A Dark Cloud of Cynicism Envelops the World

The responses of politicians and mainstream commentators have been entirely predictable. The right were quick to denounce the disorder as nothing more than criminality; mindless violence carried out by feckless, anti-social savages (see Squires, 2011). The progressives of the liberal-left have also swung into action, blaming the concentration of joblessness, the failure of welfare and rising inequality. Others have reasonably identified the anti-social behaviour of feral elites and suggested that corrupt politicians and venal bankers exacerbate a culture of base instrumentalism that erodes modernist ideals of inclusivity, citizenship and progress. It is difficult to deny the liberal-left's account of the harms of advanced marginality and the huge problems created by highly unstable labour markets. It is certainly true that it has become almost impossible for the unskilled working-classes to find anything approaching a reasonably stable and satisfying job that grants the individual access to the privileges of inclusion (Standing, 2011). However, there is also the sense that the political debate between left and right on these issues has become entirely non-dialectical, especially in the social sciences. Instead, we see the left and the right return to the same issues and offer the same arguments, unable to truly advance our understanding of the apparently insurmountable problems and fears that structure the lives of the marginal-ised in contemporary post-industrial cities. Might there not be issues relating specifically to the problem of post-modern subjectivity that can help us to understand the profound *sense of lack* that is exhibited by so many young people these days? In a political and economic system that encourages us to think that we are free to make active decisions about our lives, there seems to be a durable, nagging sense that something unidentifiable is missing; that we are not quite whole, and that we must search for something to fill in the absent centre of our being (Hall *et al*, 2008). Of course, this is an economically functional sense of absence.

Our consumer and media culture offers us a panoply of experiences, goods and services that purport to transform the subject into a secure being, finally happy with their reflection in the social mirror. But consumerism is now an established cultural system, despite its commitment to neologism and its ability to regularly shed its skin. We know very well that another shopping expedition will only provide us with a very brief frisson of excitement, yet still we make the journey. We become locked in an orbit that takes us from desire, to experiences that appear to represent fulfilment, and back again (Bauman, 2007), a process that appears to make us rather wane and disinterested but incapable of imagining a radically different path. What we are experiencing is a new super-ego injunction to enjoy (Hall *et al*, 2008): an incessant order to seek out enjoyment and personal pleasure upon the field of contemporary consumer culture. Of course, being ordered to enjoy makes enjoyment itself impossible in any real sense. Isn't this what we see in the lives of bored teenagers, surrounded by gadgets and gizmos and reality TV? Their consumer lifestyles do not appear to yield any durable sense of satisfaction. Rather, they provide a mild, reassuring comfort that these young people appear unable to live without. Are they not, in reality, searching for a *genuine experience* free from the obscene spectacle of contemporary consumer indulgence?

We believe that this enduring *sense of lack* lies at the very heart of these riots. The young people involved in the riots seem as engaged as they are disengaged. For them the riot is a distraction from the humdrum reality of everyday life, momentarily absorbing, but in the absence of real politics, incapable of yielding the progressive change that the subject subconsciously desires. As we explain below, the rioters were attempting to address their own unconscious unease and dissatisfaction with the world, their own nagging sense that something isn't quite right. This dissatisfaction provides the raw energy that gathers in areas of social and economic marginality and can burst forth when some aspect of their immediate social experience provides the catalyst.

The riot's profoundly apolitical foreground of destructive nihilism and conformist consumerism concealed an incoherent and inarticulate political desire to change the entire socio-economic field upon which everyday social experience is built. The riots reflected a dissatisfaction with the harsh realities of life in these places of advanced marginality, but this deep dissatisfaction remained unclear and incommunicable for both those involved and those watching at home. The riots were clearly a reaction against something, but the precise character and coordinates of this drive to resist remain unclear. We suggest that, in the riots of August 2011, the political remained hidden and subconscious. Politics appeared to be a hazy background dynamic informing the nature of the unrest, but it could not be brought to the fore to offer a genuine political account of the social reality of those involved in the disturbances, an objectification of their dissatisfaction or a structured demand for change. In the absence of genuine politics, the riots took the form of a blind, impotent and aggressive outburst, in which the tension of social experience rises to such a level that it cannot be contained within the usual structures of everyday life. Similarly, the rioters were rebelling against something which had eaten away at their ability to live relatively dignified lives, but the actual form of the riot, and especially the looting, perversely reiterated the primacy of neo-capitalist ideology, an ideology that has taken on the appearance of common sense in the absence of realistic alternatives.

While a broad range of liberal academics have thoughtlessly and prematurely announced the death of ideology, ideology continues to shape our social experience. It is now 'common sense' to adopt an instrumental and individualised attitude to social life, and to believe that what gets called 'society' is merely the sum of a broad collection of atomised and individualised subjectivities existing in mutual competition for status and recognition (see Hall *et al*, 2008). We are almost willing to risk the contentious claim that, for many of those involved in the disturbances, the regressive logic of self-interest structures their approach to civic life to the extent that the unique opportunity presented by the riots to do some free shopping was stripped of much of the usual moral and ethical considerations one might associate with such activity. In a society in which everyone is out for themselves, why not take this opportunity to grab what you can? This is a complicated claim that requires some contextual discussion.

Post-Political Riots

It is now clear that we are living through a post-political age (*Žižek*, 2008). At election time politicians line-up to tell us that they do not see themselves as 'ideological'. Instead they see themselves as dedicated pragmatists who will make judicious adjustments to all the instruments of government to pursue a programme concerned with the maintenance of basic human rights, rising standards of living, and the defence of a legal apparatus geared towards ensuring that 'the other' does not intrude on the sanctity of the subject and his or her individualistic lifestyle concerns. This is what democratic politics has become in the West: a high-stakes competition between media-savvy game-show hosts, all trying to convince you that you'll be a little bit better off with them rather than the other guy. In relation to this dominant field of political pragmatism, all utopianism seems anachronistic, a throw-back to an earlier, less sophisticated age when it seemed reasonable to publicly declare one's fidelity to an ideological truth. The political debate is now waged on TV screens, and policy is constructed in relation to the feedback from focus groups rather than in accordance with fundamental ideological visions of a better world.

The differences between our political parties these days are of course negligible, and the message that emanates from this mediated and hyper-real world is that the formula for the best possible society is already at hand. Liberal democracy coupled with free market capitalism is unequivocally the best of all political and economic systems. All alternatives to this system appear barbarous in comparison. So wedded are we to the infinite expansion of consumerism and material wealth that to abandon liberal capitalism for an economic system geared towards sustainability or social justice seems absurd. Even a return to the welfarist social democratic capitalism seems like an impossible dream.

Similarly, we cannot imagine a political system based upon anything other than parliamentary democracy. We cling to the image of liberal democracy as 'the fairest', despite the growing public recognition that our electoral system has failed to animate the electorate. Our politicians look the same, sound the same, believe in the same things, and often attended the same schools. There is no vigorous political debate about our economy, our environment or our collective future together. We even persevere with this image of democracy despite knowing that are there is widespread corruption and cheating and that the entire process is polluted by the interests of elites. This is how ideology operates today: we all know about the profound injustices of capitalism, and we all know about the huge problems of liberal democracy. But this knowledge of the reality of our world no longer contains any emancipatory potential (Badiou, 2002). Contemporary capitalism continues onwards by opening up a gap between social knowledge and social behaviour. That is to say that we know of all the huge historic problems that beset the current system, but this knowledge merely encourages us to develop a cynical distance between ourselves and the world we occupy (Briggs, 2012). We believe we see the truth of capitalism, and that our knowledge of this truth somehow separates us from the logic of our economy and its complex ideological system. Capitalism now stages its own critique in the media and throughout our culture, sure in the knowledge that recognising the injustices of its markets will immobilise the subject, rather than encourage the subject to embark upon a political attempt to change it. Laughing at the stupidity of capitalism and knowing of its grotesquely exploitative and environmentally destructive growth fetish allows the subject to continue onwards safe in the knowledge that capital cannot pull the wool over its eyes, and that it sees the truth of the world as it is (see *Žižek,* 2008). The climate of contemporary post-modern cynicism encourages us all to believe that any alternative politics is corrupt from the outset and that all ideological idealism or working-class collectivism eventually leads to dictatorship and the erosion of the personal freedoms and consumer lifestyles we have come to hold so dear. Our embedded post-political cynicism and fear of change means that what we have remains, even though we know that what we have is deeply flawed and profoundly unjust.

So the couplet of liberal democracy and liberal capitalism enforces a horizon upon acceptable forms of political governance and economic management. These days, all acceptable politics must now take place on this field. All mainstream politicians know that proposing anything that moves beyond this system ensures that they will be mercilessly lampooned and shunted to the political margins to suffer the ignominious political death of 'not being taken seriously' (Winlow, 2012).

Liberal democracy has traditionally held out the promise of inclusivity. Every election offers the electorate the opportunity to change things. If the last Labour administration doesn't measure up, then the voter has the chance to give the other guys a try. The problem here is that contemporary liberal democracy devolves to a perverse politics of rejection, in which voters are perennially disappointed with forms of political representation and float between parties that are incapable of delivering real change. Of course, the difference between the Conservatives and Labour is so small that voters must focus on surface issues in order to come to a judgement on who deserves their vote. Labour, Conservative, Liberal Democrat: the ultimate end-point is the same. The voters can do no other than endorse a political party dedicated to the politics of the possible, a depressing realm of fake practicality, opposed to all idealistic strategies that might alter the shape of contemporary politics and economy. The elected government of the day is tasked only with managing our political institutions and acting as custodian for the free market economy. The hidden truth of this situation suggests that a post-modern reversal has taken place that has transformed practicality into idealism, and idealism into practicality. Given the huge historic problems we face, isn't it in fact ridiculously utopian to believe that liberal capitalism can continue on indefinitely? Isn't it absurd to think that we can fix the problems of contemporary global capitalism by pumping more money into the system and tinkering with interest rates? In comparison, isn't the 'practical' thing to do to begin in earnest the search for an alternative? Shouldn't we be working towards a sustainable and just economy? Shouldn't we be thinking in radical new ways about the production of new energy sources? In times like these, contemporary politics, in delivering 'more of the same', simply gives us more of what we don't need. What we do need is the courage to address the harsh realities of our position and to strike out in a different direction so that we might avoid the destructive historic events that lie a little further down the path we are now on.

The pallid appearance of post-politics is seen most clearly at election time. No matter who you vote for, what you get is liberal democracy and a free market economy. Upset at the current Labour administration and widening inequalities, political and economic corruption, or the fact that the poorest are now shouldering the burden created by the profligate and irresponsible economic activities of the super-rich? Then vote Conservative or Liberal Democrat, and get, well … more of the same.

Gradually, and incrementally, liberal democracy descends into a perverse 'making do', a system of weak pragmatism that ensures free and open elections become a mere representation of change rather than change itself (*Žižek,* 2002). On the fluid and shimmering surface of liberal democracy we see rigorous electoral processes that guarantee that every vote is equal—the faceless multitude joining together to collectively determine a political route forwards. However, underneath the surface, the social, economic and political bedrock of our world remains unmoved. Our right to vote is reduced to a mere indication of the legitimacy of a system that seeks to endlessly perpetuate itself. The obvious ideological corollary is that contemporary pantomime politics closes off the possibility of a genuine transformative politics pushing beyond these narrow parameters and opening up the field for genuine political contestation and arguments about justice, fairness, equality and collective life (Winlow, 2012).

There is a deep perversity at work in our post-political system that reverses the standard positions of pragmatism and idealism. Our pragmatic and post-political politicians tell us that the only practical and reasonable approach to dealing with the global economic crisis is to continue onwards with the neoliberal project, perhaps making a few slight adjustments along the way. Similarly, they tell us that the global ecological crisis can be addressed by already-in-place structures of governance and the fluidity of global markets. For them, any attempt to change this system represents stupid idealism, the mere utopian thinking of educated elites who have lost all connection to the real world. But the true reality of the situation is, rather, the reverse. It is their belief that we can continue to live this way that signals unworldly utopianism, their belief that markets will prevent ecological degradation, their belief that neoliberalism can continue indefinitely. Their utopianism wears the clothes of pragmatism, but the truly pragmatic response to the problems we face begins with the stark realisation that real change is needed if we are to prevent the gradual but continued degradation of our current mode of life (*Ibid*).

But what has this depressingly bland political vista to do with the urban riots that erupted across England in 2011? Quite a lot, actually. This post-modern process of depoliticisation is also exhibited in the social body. The people are no longer animated by the political process or moved by fundamental, deep-seated political values. All genuinely progressive politics develops from a shared sense of common interests and shared destiny. For some decades now, all forms of collective identity have been transformed from a source of security and a site of individual identity building into a fetter that restricts egoistic self-expression. We are increasingly compelled to see ourselves as the agents of our own destiny, and our identities as something that we thoughtfully construct for ourselves by making free and informed choices relative to our own individualised tastes and dispositions. A significant proportion of the critical social theory from the last 20 years or so finds some agreement on this issue: we are now a society of confirmed individualists keen to secure our material and symbolic interests.

For the post-modern subject, the old idea that the interests of the self are best secured by improving the collective wellbeing of one's community seems dangerously anachronistic. It is worth reminding ourselves that traditional working-class communities once gave rise to a labour movement that became capable of intervening in political decision-making to ensure that the drive for profit did not ride roughshod over the drive for just rates of pay and safe working conditions. During modernity's 'Golden Age', many young people were exposed to political ideas that reinforced a sense of collective destiny and the ethic of anti-utilitarianism (Winlow and Hall, 2006; Rose, 2001). These important political sentiments are now very difficult to find in contemporary 'working-class communities', if it is still possible to use such a phrase. The triumph of individualism and instrumentality seems almost complete. For the contemporary working-classes, the problem of creating a reasonable standard of living and a publicly valued social identity cannot be folded into a class narrative in which 'people like us' suffer the same indignities and humiliations for the same structural reasons. Instead each member of the working classes must understand and deal with these things subjectively, and the absence of a popular, alternative political account of the various tribulations of the contemporary working-classes exacerbates this problem significantly.

This absence of progressive politics was laid bare in the recent riots. While it is clear that the disorder resulted from the declining chances of our inner city and marginalised youth creating a reasonably satisfying and legitimate life for themselves from the low-paid and precarious work opportunities available to them, it is also apparent that the riots were not a direct reaction to the gross inequities of contemporary capitalism. In fact, in reacting against humiliation and the suffocation of hope, the riots and the looting indirectly indicated the total ubiquity of consumer capitalism's ruling ideology. In the absence of genuine political alternatives, the unconscious dissatisfaction the rioters felt about their place in the world could only be expressed by further engagement with the meaning system of late capitalism. The rioters were not disgusted at the symbols of social distinction that are routinely applied by consumer items, or the culture of envy that has been so assiduously cultivated by consumerism (Hall *et al*, 2008). Instead, they wanted those symbols for themselves. One might imagine the embodiment of contemporary consumer capitalism looking on contentedly as even the poorest and most marginalised exhibit a subjective enchantment at the seductive promises of its consumer symbolism.

The looting reflected the me-first, grab-what-you-can, everyone-is-out-for-themselves logic of contemporary consumer society, but this does not mean that the looters were simply dedicated consumerists rabid at the prospect of grabbing a quick bargain as law and order collapsed around them. Instead, we would suggest that consumerism acted as a perverse default position that achieves its primacy only in the absence of more appealing or progressive alternatives. So when the usual restrictions placed upon social comportment were momentarily suspended, how does one fully take advantage of this unique opportunity? The depressing conclusion seems to be that nicking a new pair of trainers and a few other bits and pieces represented the limits placed upon their desire. There was no attempt to change those social processes and systemic abuses that contribute to the subjective experience of rage. The rioters' genuine frustration and dissatisfaction could find no articulate form of expression. For many of those involved desire extended no further than grabbing a few trinkets. One might imagine that, once the heady tumult of the riot subsided, the objects stolen seemed a bit of a let-down. In this way, in its very destructiveness and acquisitiveness, the looting represented the dull normality of consumer capitalism, a system that sets out to destroy all alternative sources of value. Here, even an inarticulate opposition to the reality of capitalism perversely reasserts the dominance of capitalism itself.

Inarticulate Rage

One might reasonably argue that rage has always been the driving force behind the development of western society (Sloterdijk, 2010). The development of the civilising process (Elias, 2000) ensured that this rage was sublimated and was no longer allowed to suddenly burst forth in response to frustration or provocation. Sloterdijk (2010) claims that the power of leftist politics resides in its capacity to absorb the subjective frustrations and dissatisfactions of ordinary people. Leftist politics promises a future in which those responsible for injustices will be called to account and an egalitarian society will be constructed that is free from the forms of humiliation and discrimination that afflict the present. These days, however, it is no longer possible to fold individual humiliation into a progressive political project. Instead, the individual is compelled to stew these problems subjectively. As a direct consequence, the left fails to accumulate enough 'rage capital' (Sloterdijk, *ibid*) to drive a progressive political intervention. The post-modern subject no longer seems capable of properly symbolising her own rage, and is therefore compelled to sublimate that rage, feeling forever dissatisfied and aggrieved but in many cases incapable of fully articulating what it is that produces this profound and durable sense of unease. Rather than driving a progressive politics, this sublimated rage instead tends to pollute the lives of individuals who cannot account for their own suffering and dissatisfaction. They become pissed off about something they cannot objectify or give form to. Their dissatisfaction is a background force that shades the immediacy of everyday social encounters, but it cannot be consciously accessed, accounted for or made real.

So, we might reasonably claim that the post-modern subject is full of rage yet incapable of becoming fully conscious of the fact. The only way to overcome this deadlock appears to lie in the creation of an alternative politics that is capable of popularising an account of the structural and external causes of this rage and can promise a future call to account. The West's barren post-political landscape does not yet seem capable of supporting the growth of such a political movement but, as we see with the Arab Spring, genuine truth events appear to rise from nowhere and can completely transform the coordinates of acceptable knowledge. A genuine truth event suggests something that, once we have lived through it, ensures that our lives can never truly be the same again. We have become aware of a social reality that we were completely blind to before the arrival of the event. A truth event of this magnitude might encourage us to look back at our world under the orthodoxy of free market capitalism and ask: how could we ever have been so stupid? How could we have become so obsessed with consumerism and consumer lifestyles that we were willing to risk destroying the planet so that they might continue? How could we countenance the rise of such grotesque social inequalities? How could we let so many people languish at the bottom of society, incapable of building reasonably rewarding and fulfilling lives for themselves? Our great hope is that we do not have to wait for a destructive ecological catastrophe before we are willing to create a more just, equal and sustainable life together.

Discussion

We have tried as much as possible to avoid the well-trodden areas of post-riot analysis. In our view it is vital that we move the debate forward and situate the riots of 2011 firmly in the post-political present. Analysing these disturbances necessitates a thoughtful investigation of the specific historical conjuncture in which they occurred. We need to think clearly and incisively about economic and social marginality, but we must also be willing to address the complexity of subjectivity and the emotional consequences of living a life in the shadow of ostentatious wealth and indulgent hedonism. What we have tried to do in this chapter is to attempt to explain why it is that those involved in the disturbances were unable to form an articulate political response to the pressures they face. This is not the 1970s, and the entire field of politics and social class has changed. There is no political opposition to contemporary liberal capitalism, and so the subjective torments of the individuals involved cannot be invested in and carried forward by an articulate political opposition that promises a more just and equitable social and economic system.

Just as it is totally witless to suggest that the riots were 'criminality, pure and simple', it is not enough for the liberal left to ignore the difficulties of emotion and subjectivity and rush to lambast the right-wing establishment for their heavy-handed response to the riots, and the media's ability to distort 'reality' by whipping up aggressive sentiments towards our most marginalised groups. The challenge for contemporary sociology and criminology is to display the nerve necessary to move away from the broadly accepted intellectual frameworks of the past and actually say something new about the present.

References

Badiou, A. (2002) *Ethics*, London: Verso.

Bauman, Z. (2007) *Consuming Life*, Cambridge: Polity.

Briggs, D. (2012) *Crack Cocaine Users: High Society and Low Life in South London*, London: Routledge.

Carter, H. (2011). 'Rioter Profile: "Looting was nothing personal. Just business"', *The Guardian*, 5-12-11.

Cohen, S. (1973) *Folk Devils and Moral Panics,* London: HarperCollins.

Elias, N. (2000) *The Civilising Process.* London: Wiley-Blackwell.

Fisher, M. (2009) *Capitalist Realism*, London: Zero Books.

Jefferson, T., (2011) 'English Riots of 2011: Moral Panic... or What?' Urban Unrest Conference, University of York, 22-23 September 2011.

Hall, S. (2012) 'Consumer Culture and the Meaning of the Urban Riots in England' in S. Hall and S. Winlow (eds) *New Directions in Criminological Theory*, London: Routledge.

Hall, S. and Winlow, S. (eds) (2012) *New Directions in Criminological Theory,* London: Routledge.

Hall, S., Winlow, S. and Ancrum, C. (2008) *Criminal Identities and Consumer Culture: Crime, Exclusion and the New Culture of Narcissism,* Cullompton: Willan.

Harvey, D. (2010) *The Enigma of Capital,* London: Profile Books.

Lea, J. (2011) 'Riots and the Crisis of Neoliberalism', cited online on 1st March 2012: http://www.bunker8.pwp.blueyonder.co.uk/misc/riots2011.html

Prasad, R. (2011), 'Rioter Profile: "I saw an opportunity to take stuff"', *The Guardian,* 5 December 2011.

Rose, J. (2001) *The Intellectual Life of the British Working Classes,* London: Yale University Press.

Sloterdijk, P. (2010) *Rage and Time,* New York: Columbia University Press.

Standing, G. (2011) *The Pracariat*, London: Bloomsbury Academic.

Squires, P. (2011) 'There's nothing simple about "simple criminality"', UCU online, cited online on 1st March 2012: http://uc.web.ucu.org.uk/files/2011/10/UC2Online.pdf

Topping, A. and Bawdon, F. (2011), 'It was like Christmas: a consumerist feast among the Summer riots', *The Guardian* 5 December 2011.

Winlow, S. (2012) 'Is it OK to Talk About Capitalism Again?' in S. Winlow and R. Atkinson (eds) *New Directions in Crime and Deviance*, London: Routledge.

Winlow, S. and Hall, S. (2006) *Violent Night: Urban Leisure and Contemporary Culture,* Oxford: Berg.

Winlow, S. and Hall, S. (2012) 'A Strangely Obedient Riot: Post-politics, Consumer Culture and the English Riots of 2011', *Cultural Politics.*

Žižek, S. (2002) *Welcome to the Desert of the Real,* London: Verso.

Žižek,, S. (2008) *Violence,* London: Profile Books.

Dr Stephanie Alice Baker holds concurrent positions as a Lecturer at the University of Greenwich, London, and a Research Assistant at the Institute for Culture and Society, University of Western Sydney, Australia. Her research interests include the sociology of emotions, cultural sociology, aesthetics, media culture, crowd theory, and historical sociology, with particular emphasis on ancient Greece and Rome. She is in the final stages of completing a book for Palgrave's Cultural Sociology series on the emotional and cultural dimensions of 'social tragedy'.

9

POLICING THE RIOTS:
NEW SOCIAL MEDIA AS RECRUITMENT, RESISTANCE, AND SURVEILLANCE

Stephanie Alice Baker

Introduction

Much has been speculated about the role of new social media in orchestrating the 2011 English riots. In the early aftermath of the riots, a moral panic emerged about the role these technologies played in stimulating the violence, with commentators reverting to a form of 'technological determinism' at the expense of understanding the emotional and cultural dimensions of the unrest. While these instant, mobile forms of communication inexorably contributed to the speed and scale of the riots, precisely how new social media was used to counteract the violence has been largely overlooked. In this chapter, I compensate for this neglect by exploring how those who chose not to riot employed new social media, interrogating the extent to which these communication mediums altered their perception and response to the events. In-depth interviews with those affected by the riots are cross-referenced with social media platforms, police and press reports, to account for the dynamic role of new social media in preventing, resisting and policing the crisis. It is argued that debates focusing only on the negative implications of new social media to orchestrate the riots are limited and that understanding the impact of these emergent technologies requires examining the complex interplay between social structures and agency, old and new media, as well as online and offline forms of communication. Finally, it is suggested that acquiring a more nuanced understanding of the diverse ways that new social media were employed during the 2011 riots undermines the current moral panic while providing insight into the capacity for these novel communication technologies to operate as modes of recruitment, resistance and surveillance in the media age.

New Social Media: A New Moral Panic?

In *Policing the Crisis* (1978), Stuart Hall *et al* analysed the moral panic created around mugging in 1970s Britain. Hall *et al*'s thesis drew on Stanley Cohen's (1972) notion of 'moral panics': the 'fundamentally inappropriate' reaction by much of society (e.g. the mainstream media, politicians, law enforcement agencies, and the public) to relatively minor events. In such circumstances, Cohen argued that the seriousness of a condition was distorted as posing an exaggerated threat to society. In this chapter, I argue that speculation surrounding the role of new social media[1] in igniting the 2011 English riots represents a new form of moral panic. This is not to undermine the severity of the recent riots, nor their impact on victims and communities, but rather the 'fundamentally inappropriate' response by certain commentators who framed new social media as the catalyst of the disorder.

After four days of rioting and looting that spread rapidly across parts of Britain, new social media became a familiar target used to explain the unrest. While the country experienced recurrent incidents of rioting throughout the 20th-century, the speed and scale with which the 2011 riots evolved distinguished the events from previous incidents of civil disorder. This 'new form' of rioting explains, in part, why new social media was blamed for the 'contagion' (Baker, 2011). Speaking in the House of Commons, Britain's Prime Minister, David Cameron, declared, 'Everyone watching these horrific actions will be struck by how they were organized via social media'. The main finding of the Metropolitan Police Interim Report (2011) on the August disorder echoed these views suggesting that 'the speed, geographical distribution and scale of this escalation set these events apart from anything experienced before'. As the country tried to make sense of the riots, the impression emerged of a technology-obsessed, deviant, youth culture,

---

1. I distinguish between 'new' and 'social media' when referring to a particular technology, and employ the concept 'new social media' when referring to both mediums in general.

so-called 'Twitter rioters' (France and Flynn, 2011), responsible for what was referred to as the 'Facebook riot' (Bowcott, *et al*, 2011) and the 'BlackBerry Riots' (*Economist*, 2011). As Blond (2011) put it:

> The August riots were new in that gangs of predominately young unemployed men were able, using new media, to launch a series of semi-organized disturbances for the purpose not of protest, but of criminal gain.

Despite insufficient evidence to verify a causal connection between new social media and the riots (Ball and Lewis, 2011), this did not prevent local authorities, MPs and police from drawing premature conclusions and discussing a possible intervention to switch off social media platforms during the height of the disorder. Addressing an emergency session of parliament convened after four consecutive nights of rioting and looting, David Cameron declared:

> We are working with the police, the intelligence services and industry to look at whether it would be right to stop people communicating via these websites and services when we know they are plotting violence, disorder and criminality.

David Lammy, the MP for Tottenham, reiterated these views, appealing for RIM (Research In Motion), the company responsible for the BlackBerry product line, to shut down the service after claims it played a key role in orchestrating the unrest. This view was echoed by the UK Home Secretary, Theresa May, who arguably contributed to the moral panic by scheduling meetings with the police and social media industry (Facebook, Twitter, RIM) to discuss their responsibility in 'policing the crisis' (although a spokeswoman for the Home Secretary denied that switching off such services was on the agenda). While it is not surprising, given the speed and scale of the events, that these new communication technologies emerged on the political agenda, suggestions that authorities intended to censor social networking services by removing certain hash tags, temporarily shutting down services, and banning individual users thought to be responsible for inciting the riots appeared to undermine the moral tenets of Britain's liberal democracy. Talk of such a move drew parallels to contemporary methods of censorship used by authoritarian regimes during the Arab Spring, and was consequently publicly criticised.

Beyond the legal issues associated with infringing upon people's civil liberties, it is problematic to infer that censoring social media services would have prevented the riots. Not only has Britain had an established history of rioting prior to these technologies, the moral panic surrounding new social media misrepresents the emotional and cultural dynamics of collective action (Baker, 2011). Such arguments point to a broader debate between those who overemphasise the impact of new social media on the riots and those who neglect the effect of these technologies altogether. Focusing on the medium of the riots rather than their message, the former risks reverting to a form of technological determinism by insinuating social media has human agency instead of viewing it as a tool through which people communicate. Yet, it is equally problematic to deny that new social media played a part in the recent riots, or to view the disorder simply as part of a continuum of British rioting. As I have argued elsewhere (Baker, 2011, 2012), the recent riots were emblematic of a nascent 'mediated crowd' phenomenon whose many manifestations in 2011 traversed beyond the geographical boundaries of contemporary Britain. In such instances, it is crucial to recognise the substantive effect of new social media by analysing the complex interplay between these emergent communication technologies and embodied social actors in physical space.

The moral panic surrounding new social media appears, in part, to be a corollary of contemporary studies on the riots. To date, very little empirical research has been conducted into exploring whether new social media was used to prevent people from participating in the riots, or precisely how these communication technologies were employed by those whom refrained from engaging in the unrest. To understand the impact of new social media on the riots requires a consideration of those who participated in the disorder as well as those who chose not to participate (where the decision not to participate was itself a form of action). This study analysed 30 in-depth interviews[2] with participants from riot-affected London boroughs in con-

---

2. This project was granted ethics approval by the University of Greenwich Ethics Committee. Pseudonyms were used to maintain the anonymity of all participants. While participants' names have been altered for ethical purposes, their gender and borough were not disguised as these factors were considered important means of contextualising their responses.

junction with social media platforms (Facebook, Twitter), police and press reports to acquire a more nuanced understanding of the impact of these technologies on the events. Here, I contend that to comprehend the role of new social media in the riots requires more than a survey-like analysis of 'what mediums were the preferred method of communication during the unrest'. Crucially, this inquiry necessitates understanding the effect these technologies had on users, that is, the capacity for interaction via these mediums to alter people's perception, experience and response to the riots.

There are invariably limitations with this approach. Even when using qualitative interview techniques to allow those affected by the riots to articulate their decisions and actions, responses may be rationalised as participants attempt to explain their behaviour in hindsight. There are also a range of unconscious, pre-reflective thoughts and feelings that may have influenced their actions, and of which respondents are not necessarily aware. These potential limitations do not, however, undermine the importance of such data in revealing latent and manifest emotional responses to the use of new social media, namely, how respondents consciously perceived and experienced the riots through such mediums.

Recruitment: The Emergence of the 'Mediated Crowd'

A common criticism regarding the way in which the riots were depicted in the mainstream media was the propensity for commentators to blame social media for its role in recruiting rioters and looters. Such beliefs are problematic as they endow what is ostensibly a communication device with human agency and, in so doing, overlook the underlying reasons that 'people' were motivated to riot. For example, when those interviewed were asked if they were solicited to riot through social networks, respondents were quick to suggest that, despite empathising with the motivations of protesters, they were not the 'sort of people' inclined 'to get involved'; as if to suggest that the 'rioters' were 'different' to them:

> No, because I'm not the sort of people [sic] to get involved. I think the view was that everybody in Tottenham was involved when that wasn't the case.
>
> *Daphne, Tottenham*

A view echoed by Levy from Greenwich:

> No they didn't, but even so, they would not have had to because it wouldn't have been my style to participate in them [the riots] anyway.

While one would not want to reify rioters as possessing a certain type of character, these responses indicate the complex interplay between emotions, thought and action where the decision not to act was itself a form of action. More specifically, in revealing an embodied agent behind the medium, such insights overcome the propensity for research on social media to revert to technological determinism.

A further criticism regarding media coverage of the riots is that the impact of new and social media was confounded: new media referring to emergent forms of digitalised technology (e.g. smart phones, mobile handsets), social media denoting social networking platforms (e.g. YouTube, Tumblr, Facebook, Twitter), characterised by user driven content and dialogue rather than the one-way communication conventionally associated with 'old' media (e.g. television, radio). Initial findings suggest it was BlackBerry's Messenger (BBM) service, not social media, that was the main medium used to recruit rioters and looters (*The Guardian*, 2011). The use of BBM as the preferred method of recruitment has been explained by pointing to key differences between new and social media: the latter, characterised by open access social networks, in contrast to BlackBerry's closed messenger service, which enables encrypted, private messages to be disseminated instantly, en masse (Eddo-Lodge, 2011). Others suggest that this efficient, secure recruitment procedure was merely the 'unintended consequence' of the ubiquitous ownership of BlackBerrys by 'thousands of young people prone to riot', given that this new media service was affordable and accessible to young rioters and looters from 'economically deprived communities across England' (Ball and Brown, 2011). Despite the fact that these new technologies were employed as the primary method of recruitment during the riots, interviews indicate that rioters made use of existing connections and social networks rather than recruiting random members of the general public; with those interviewed commonly suggesting that 'it [the riots] would have happened regardless of social media' (Daphne, Tottenham).

While initial studies suggest that BBM was the preferred method of recruitment for many rioters (Ball, 2011),[3] it would be spurious to infer that social media played no part in the unrest. To date, research on the use of social media during the riots has been largely based on content analysis of social networking sites, such as Facebook and Twitter (*Guardian* and LSE, 2011). The capacity for authorities to edit online content, however, highlights the limitations of relying on current posts as an indicator of the type of communication that took place during the events. For example, content on social networking sites perceived to be 'egregious during sensitive times like the UK riots' is subject to the discretion of reviewers and removed when necessary to 'disincentivise bad actors on the site', as representatives from Facebook pointed out.[4] Moreover, respondents interviewed for this study—that is, those who chose not to riot—provided important insights into the role and effect of social media on the unrest. When asked to recollect their emotional responses to the representation of the riots through social media, the instant, visual form of these mediums (particularly symbolic images posted on Facebook of burning police cars in Tottenham, and protesters calling on members of the community to avenge Mark Duggan's death) were repeatedly referenced:

> It was really quick and the way that things moved about [through] pictures. I was really surprised how social media was so efficient and very effective. I was thinking that social media was really powerful in posting pictures ... To a certain degree it [pictures displayed via social media] would have made people want to join in.

A notable effect of new social media was that these mediums engendered a sense of social cohesion by connecting actors from disparate geographies into a common symbolic space. While new social media did not initiate the unrest, by representing one man's death as a vivid symbol of widespread

---

3. Ball (2011) suggests, for example, that 'the role of Facebook and Twitter in fuelling August's riots was marginal at best: analysis of more than 2.5m tweets obtained by *The Guardian* found only a tiny fraction of users attempting to incite trouble—and even these were generally shouted down'.

4. On this point, a recent study documenting 'tweets' made during the 2011 Egyptian Revolution highlighted that 'a year after the Egyptian Revolution, 10 per cent of its social media documentation is already gone' (Garber, 2012).

social injustice, what I refer to as a 'social tragedy' (Baker, 2010; 2013), these emergent mediums played a key role in facilitating the events. In fact, a common feature of the 2011 protest movements was that these forms of 'mediated crowd' membership largely emerged in response to a perceived 'social tragedy', wherein the interactive online relationships enabled by social media connected aggrieved users into intense relationships that transpired offline. This communicative effect is not unique to new social media, of course, with moral panics generated around old media (e.g. television) in the aftermath of the 1992 Los Angeles riots and 2005 French riots. What is new is the ubiquitous ownership of 3G wireless technologies (e.g. mobile phones, handsets), which make instant messenger services, and 24-hour online social networking sites powerful tools to mobilise and sustain collective action through rapid, multimedia messages that can be communicated en masse.

I think it's just a communication effect. Just a news tweet, or even an update with people talking, it just got so many people talking, as opposed just to knocking on someone's door. It's just really quick and very efficient in that when something kicks off everyone starts talking about it.

Hence, while closed networks, such as BBM, provided rioters with more security than open social networks accessible to police (e.g. community pages posted on Facebook or Twitter), this is not to deny that social media contributed to the disorder by facilitating feelings of solidarity and empowering collective action. One is reminded here of Marshall McLuhan's (1964) notion of technological mediums as 'any extension of ourselves', a view resonating with George Herbert Mead's (1907) research on the effect of the human hand on perception and experience:

> The vast importance of the human hand for perception becomes evident when we recognise how it answers to the eye, especially among the distance senses. The development of space perception follow in normal individuals upon the interaction … mediated through the manipulating hand.

When considered to be an 'extension of ourselves', the introduction of new social media in the early 21st century has made substantial contributions to social interaction by broadening, and indeed transforming, the spatial and temporal configuration of contemporary public life. When applied to the recent riots, these mediums undeniably altered the dynamics of collective action with the instant, mobile interactions afforded by these technologies engendering a 'double-reflexive crowd' experience in which the user can simultaneously 'occupy' online and offline public space (Baker, 2012). Whereas traditional crowd theory focused on crowd formation in spatial and temporal proximity, these emergent technologies have contributed to a new form of 'mediated crowd' membership—an interactive community that traverses and intersects geographic and virtual arenas (Baker, 2011). In such circumstances, the crowd is mediated both in the sense that members communicate through media technologies, as well as mediating social networks both online and off. Here, the riots are understood as emblematic of an emergent 'mediated crowd' phenomenon, not to be confused with subsequent notions of the 'virtual crowd'[5] (Cookson and Ilbury, 2011), in which the 'virtual' is demarcated from the 'real'.

To reduce the recent riots, or other forms of 'mediated' protest, to online 'virtual geographies' is limited. The 2011 English riots were mobilised by embodied participants in lived urban environments, which notions of the 'virtual crowd' appear to obscure. Moreover, interviews conducted for this study reveal that the riots combined both online and offline modes of communication. Even when social media was used to inform people about the riots, these forms of online communication often occurred simultaneously with face-to-face, interactions in offline geographies (common examples included public transport, users' places of residence or employment). Recalling how she first heard about the riots in Tottenham, Daphne exemplified that contemporary interactions typically traverse both physical and digital modalities:

> It wasn't through the news. My brother told me about the protest at Tottenham and showed me pictures. These were mostly through BlackBerry notifications from

---

5. With regard to the wave of protest movements in 2011, Cookson and Ilbury (2011) have suggested that 'Research now shows that similar behaviour can occur in both real and virtual crowds where they share a sense of collectivity, driven by common goals and interests. Whereas individuals in a physical crowd may take their cue from the visible behaviour of others, fund managers and online gamers take theirs from changes on a screen'. Studies such as these are problematic in that they revert to a form of 'digital dualism' by endorsing the view that technology creates an alternate, virtual universe supposedly separate from 'real' social life.

> my brother … and speaking to the community activists [face-to-face] helped me
> to get a perspective as to why it happened.

Such responses indicate that, even if one did not use social media directly, these online social networks inexorably impact their offline lives. In fact, the proliferation of social networking services, together with the ubiquity of new mobile technologies, mean that we are increasingly susceptible to being influenced indirectly by these mediums in our physical interactions with users, whom restructure our experience without consensus or online participation. The result is that online and offline forms of communication, old and new media become increasingly merged with some arguing, 'There is no "Cyberspace"'[6] (Rey, 2012) and others declaring that 'There is only Cyberspace' (see Antley, 2012).

It is also important to note that despite the proliferation of these new technologies that 'new' media did not displace 'old' forms of communication during the riots. Many of those interviewed for this study perceived a disjuncture between the personalised messages they received from friends and family via new social media (images sent via Facebook and BBM, for example), compared to the representations put forward by authorities and journalists on 'old' (mainstream) media. As Daphne, from Tottenham, explained:

> I think it [new social media] was more realistic. And speaking to the community
> activists [face-to-face] helped me to get a perspective as to why it happened, as
> opposed to the news.

Or, as said by Mina from Peckham:

> On TV and radio it was more a question of politics and with the new media
> representation it was from a more personal representation since it was the people
> living it, which were reporting it.

And Levy from Greenwich:

---

6.   On this point, it has been argued that the notion of 'Cyberspace', first introduced in 1982 by William Gibson as a 'consensual hallucination' in his short science fiction story 'Burning Chrome', is deeply problematic in describing the contemporary social web because the web is neither consensual, nor a hallucination (Rey, 2012).

Something else that I noticed was the difference in the ways that the same form of 'old' media reported the riots. Some (e.g. the *Daily Mail*, and *Mirror* as to be expected) were more sensationalist than others, and tended to continually 'hone in' on specific groups, including kids from working-class and minority backgrounds although people from all walks of life were involved. Channels such as Sky news also did a similar thing and in one case seemed to show the same reportage of some looters being interviewed in Greenwich over and over again. I am certainly not condoning their behaviour because having seen firsthand the damage caused to people and property by the looters in places like Lewisham, Croydon and Camberwell and then Birmingham, I was really quite annoyed. However, at the same time, repeated negative focus on certain groups is the sort of thing that can reinforce negative labels against all members of those groups even though the vast majority had no intentions of doing anything like this.

In fact, some respondents indicated that the perceived disconnect between the representation of the riots on old and new media itself contributed to the unrest:

Basically the way it was portrayed [in the mainstream media] was that it was our [Tottenham residents] stupidity. So I wasn't really happy with the way it was portrayed. So, it was a bit patronising ... there was so much speculation and rumours going on. But basically they made it out that it was Mark Duggan. We had that situation in 1985. Again that was with the riots that took place in Broadwater Farm. The news sparked it off because they were trying to make the police like [sic] the victim, when really it was the lady [Cynthia Jarrett] who was the victim. The same tensions again. So why did we have that situation again?

Daphne, Tottenham

Others, however, particularly those less sympathetic towards rioters and looters, emphasised their reliance on old media to provide accurate news on the events: 'Since I was on Sky News and BBC news live (television) I had very clear up-to-date info' (Carmen, Lambeth). In this instance, new social media was perceived as a less reliable medium, prone to unsubstantiated claims and bias. 'New' is a relative term, of course, and any attempt to distinguish old and new media, requires situating these mediums in their cultural context. Even traditional forms of communication, such as, the letter, the novel, pamphlets, television, radio and cinema — what we now perceive to be 'old' — were once considered 'new', arousing moral panics in their day. Moreover, while new social media is typically associated with two-way social networking, as opposed to the one-way communication thought to comprise old media technologies, such beliefs fail to recognise that new social media is not immune from its own power structures and hierarchies (whether this take the form of the Twitter accounts of mainstream media, influential users, celebrities, or political authorities). Claims such as these also overlook the fact that old media is regularly informed by emergent technologies and can, in certain circumstances, be highly interactive as exemplified by talk-back radio, a conventional telephone call, and more abstract forms of communication between an actor and a book, for example. It was significant, however, that those interviewed for this study consistently suggested 'the medium is the message', thereby, echoing Marshall McLuhan's (1964) paradoxical aphorism. Interviews indicate that, while the content displayed on these mediums was consequential and significant, users had preconceived ideas about their legitimacy and, in the case of new social media, perceived these mediums to signify a challenge to centralised forms of authority.

Resistance

The use of social media as a means of resistance — that is, to oppose a force by action — was evident not only by those who rioted, but also those that chose not to riot, many of whom remained active participants in resisting the riots (whether their involvement took the form of disseminating information, ensuring public safety, preventing others from rioting, fundraising, or in the clean-up operations that followed). In the aftermath of the riots, popular belief and academic theories overwhelmingly limited their analysis of resistance to understanding the motivations of rioters (*Guardian* and LSE, 2011). From this perspective, it was the rioters who were held to have used social media to resist police during the unrest (although social media services have recently been introduced to resolve tensions between youths and police[7]). Such studies have the potential to provide valuable insight into the underlying causes of the riots, and may mitigate the chance that such events recur in the future. Resistance, however, takes many forms and need not be reduced to dichotomies regarding those rioting, on the one hand, and policing the riots, on the other.

New social media played a key role in ensuring the safety of those members of the public affected by the riots. Respondents interviewed for this study consistently suggested that the visibility and accessibility of new social media made these mediums reliable, convenient ways of communicating during the unrest. This was particularly the case in riot-affected areas, such as, Tottenham and Clapham Junction. Tottenham resident, Daphne's comment that 'friends from Tottenham used social media to see if I was ok and safe', was indicative of the use of new social media more generally by those interviewed for this study. The founder of Riot Cleanup (2011), a popular Twitter account dedicated to resisting the riots, also used social media for this purpose:

I was on a bus on Kingsland Road in London when the rioting spread beyond Tottenham. I spent a couple of hours in the pub watching it all go down on television. A good friend of mine was stuck in Clapham and I was using the #londonriots tag along with many others to spread information. I continued to follow the tag throughout the night to see activity.

In such instances social media operated as a valuable source of public information during the riots, the utility of which exceeded their use by rioters and looters. While initial findings suggest that BlackBerry's instant messenger service operated as rioters' preferred method of recruitment, social media platforms were regularly employed by the general public to provide instant reports during the disorder,[8] and to aggregate information on the crisis[9] (in addition to disseminating unsubstantiated rumours — see Ball and Lewis, 2011).

---

7. A 'Stop and Search' App developed by Aaron Sonson, Satwant Singh, and Gregory Paczkowski in 2011 has been endorsed by the Independent Police Complaints Commission (IPCC) for attempting to aid police relations with youths. The App enables young people to collate 'stop and search' patterns, to obtain information about their rights, and to rate their experience of being stopped and searched by the police.
8. Popular URLs established to provide up-to-date information regarding the riots included: @londonriot; @manchesterriots; @tottenhamchoir.
9. Common hashtags used to aggregate information during the riots included: #londonriots;

It is therefore important to acknowledge that social media was also used to mobilise public support and coordinate the cleanup efforts that followed the unrest. The most popular of these, Riot Cleanup (2011), was established within days of the unrest, 'dedicated to coordinating the clean-up after the recent UK riots'. Recalling the aim of the Twitter account, the founder explained:

> I saw tweets … in regards to helping to clear up some of the mess. I could see that many others were willing but the times and locations were varying. As a result I thought it best to try and organize a central feed so the information of meeting points was accurate and that we had strength in numbers (Riot Cleanup, 2011).

Here, Twitter operated as an extension of the public sphere by broadening users' social networks in a way not possible had communication been limited to standard face-to-face interactions. Tens of thousands of people supported the cleanup operation with Riot Cleanup's Twitter page accumulating more than 57,000 followers in ten hours, and maintaining close to 60,000 followers six months after the riots. While this form of resistance commenced on Twitter, it was not limited to online communication, but traversed offline into collective action in the urban geographies most affected by the disorder (e.g. Bow, Hackney and Clapham Junction). Together with Facebook pages[10] dedicated to various riot-related clean-up operations and fundraising projects,[11] the Twitter feed aggregated all the information spread through the group's hashtag:

> Riotcleanup was the sum on [sic] many parts, thousands of whom are anon [sic].

Riot Cleanup, 2011

---

10. #riots; #englandriots; #prayforlondon.
11. For example, Post riot clean-up: Let's help London.
11. Social media was used for a range of fundraising purposes with Twitter (e.g. @riotremedy; @riot_rebuild; @riotrescue; @tottenhamgig) and Facebook community pages (e.g. One London, Riot Rebuild Project, the Riot Raffle), employed as platforms to raise funds for those communities and local residents whose businesses were destroyed by rioters and looters. Hashtags, such as, #keepaaroncutting and #helpsiva, operated as memes to aggregate information and acquire donations to help Aaron Biber, an 89 year old barber, and Siva Kandiah, a local shopkeeper, restore their barbershop and local convenience store respectively after they had been ransacked by rioters and looters.

What is crucial here is that by extending the public sphere, these online social networks connected users from disparate offline geographies as fused members of civil society, whose mediated interactions (both online and off), although coordinated by key individuals, were irreducible to any single user.

In this sense, Riot Cleanup operated as a collective act of resistance against rioters with online social networks transpiring into an offline social movement. Here, resistance was not framed as opposition through violent force or protest, but resistance to the notion of a country in decline; members of Riot Cleanup fused through feelings of social solidarity as encapsulated by the movement's mottos: 'unite against rioters',[12] and, 'clean up the streets, community and unity', displayed on their respective Facebook and Twitter pages. Illuminating this broader understanding of resistance, as a movement formed around unity and a reconstitution of the social order, the founder explained:

> The action has changed things. People have said they woke up this morning feeling fear, but they now feel optimistic. There's talk of reclaiming the streets from violence just by being there and talking. The broom, raised aloft, and cups of tea carried on riot shields have become today's iconic images. How British. How beautifully British. And how very, very London … It's a movement.
>
> *Thompson, 2011*

This form of 'mediated crowd' membership was both spontaneous and coordinated with resistance taking the form of regular updates, recruitment, donation drop offs, and, of course, sweeping. Indeed, 'the broom' may be remembered as the sacred symbol of civic resistance, literally cleansing the community and symbolically set apart from the profane, however, the various online forums dedicated to the cleanup operations indicate that social media was a powerful means of engendering *civitas* and collective action. What is

---

12. While respondents generally expressed feelings of resentment towards looters, there were mixed reactions to those whom rioted. On this point, respondents highlighted the need to distinguish between rioters and looters: 'What the news need to differentiate is that there is a difference between rioters, who were there to support Mark Duggan, and looters, who were there to loot. The news gave the image that the rioters were looters when this wasn't the case' (Daphne, Tottenham).

evident here is a complex process of social inter-action with social media services used as online platforms to disclose, exchange and coordinate ideas that transpire into public, offline relationships, thereby, illuminating the salience of place. From this perspective, it was precisely by broadening the scope of the public sphere to fuse online contacts from disparate locales that social media was employed to reconstitute the social order as a mode of resistance.

Surveillance

One of the most common criticisms to emerge in the aftermath of the riots was that the police were ill-equipped to deal with the technological tactics of this new 'mediated crowd' phenomenon. While rioters employed a range of on and offline modes of communication, the impression emerged of an intelligence failure centred on outdated policing methods, unable to integrate emergent forms of communication and, therefore, unable to respond in time. Critics have subsequently suggested that better use of new social media could have made the police much more effective in anticipating and policing to the riots. On this point, Jon Silverman (2011) highlighted the need for the Metropolitan Police to convert its information on media networks into surveillance strategies, with Twitter providing crucial information when 'tweets' are verified by distinguishing facts from rumours.

Police responded to these claims by emphasising the need for greater surveillance of new social media as an emergent tactic in policing the riots. In fact, the decision to integrate social media services into policing strategies was one of the main findings of the Metropolitan Police Interim Report (2011) following the August disorder: 'Professionalising the police use of social media both as an engagement and an intelligence tool'. Within days of the unrest, the Greater Manchester Police used their official Twitter account to caution that social media could be used as a police tactic:

> If you have been using social networking sites to incite disorder, expect us to come knocking on your door very soon.
>
> *@GMPolice, 10 August 2011*

Essex Police's acting assistant chief, constable, Maurice Mason, reiterated this warning:

We are watching social networking sites closely, and if there are any criminal offences being committed we will track down the people responsible and deal with them.

Phillips, 2011.

In light of the perceived intelligence failures, attempts by some individuals to use social media to encourage rioting and looting resulted in severe punishments. Several men were sentenced with four-year jail terms within days of the riots for inciting disorder through Facebook, despite these attempts never manifesting action (Taylor, 2011). Consequently, while police were initially criticised for their inability to integrate these emergent technologies in their surveillance strategies, social media has subsequently played an important role in policing the riots.

One of the most striking responses to the 2011 riots was the way in which members of the public used social media services as a mechanism of surveillance. Resonating with Foucault's (1977) model of power, in which power is exercised through decentralised social relations, social networking sites operated as public surveillance platforms to locate those responsible for the unrest. The blogging platform Tumblr, for example, hosted an account called, 'Catch A Looter', which encouraged users to disseminate photos of looters and, thereby, expose their identities to police (although the site has subsequently been pulled down presumably for legal purposes). The founder of the account, an anonymous citizen, considered 'Catch a Looter' to be part of a wider social movement to police the riots:

You can't just stand idly by letting people do what they want ... I am just someone who wanted to try, in some way, to fight back against thugs and criminals ... I was irritated by some people blaming social media ... in my opinion it's just thieving.

Harrison, 2011

What these social networking sites demonstrate is a collective desire for justice actualised by novel 'mediated' interactions rather than conventional policing methods. From a Foucauldian perspective, these communication mediums also operated as efficient, decentralised forms of surveillance to support the body politic in policing the riots. Again this resistance movement points to the varied role of social media during the riots. These examples highlight that to understand the effect of these mediums is not merely a matter of whether Facebook, Twitter or BBM were used during the riots, but how these mediums helped to create a common identity and mobilise collective action.

Discussion

While the riots raised legitimate questions about the state of British society, new social media has emerged as a new moral panic for supposedly inciting the unrest. I have argued that this moral panic is problematic for two reasons: first, such beliefs reveal a tendency towards technological determinism, and second, existing research tends to limit the use of these technologies to nefarious practices, consequently obscuring the variety of ways in which new social media was employed during the riots. Conducting in-depth interviews with those who chose not to riot, I emphasise that although new media appeared to be rioters' preferred mode of recruitment, this does not render social media irrelevant with these emergent technologies operating as a valuable means of resisting and policing the riots.

New social media have made substantive contributions to nascent forms of 'mediated crowd' membership, not least of which was revealed by the speed and scale of the recent riots. This study has demonstrated that these instant, visual forms of communication are significant in so far as these mediums have the capacity to evoke strong emotional responses and engender social solidarity by connecting users from disparate offline geographies as fused participants. By broadening and transforming the public sphere, new social media can mobilise groups more effectively than traditional forms of old media. Although the argument put forward here has been critical of the propensity to blame emergent technologies during times of crisis, I suggest that there are key differences between old and new media, emphasising the need to recognise how these mediums configure contemporary communication practices. In fact, a notable insight acquired from this study was that respondents regularly attributed the perceived disjuncture between the representation of the riots on old and new media with preconceived ideas about the legitimacy of these mediums (politically and symbolically). Despite respondents attributing the medium with the message, it would be erroneous to suggest that media operate in such a dualistic way. I have pointed out that although social media is defined, in part, by its capacity to generate online social interaction, these mediums can also operate in a more unilateral manner, and uphold traditional power structures by publicising the voices of extant authorities (similarly, old media is regularly informed by emergent technologies and can, in fact, be highly interactive). On this point I highlight that, while new social media empowers users in their capacity to disseminate knowledge, these ubiquitous mobile technologies and decentralised social networks have not overcome extant power structures altogether. I demonstrated, moreover, that one form of communication does not simply displace the other entailing that just as old media continues to be used in conjunction with new technologies, online social networks commonly configure embodied social interactions in offline geographies indirectly without knowledge or consensus.

Here, I propose that any study investigating the impact of new social media on the recent riots must recognise that the disorder was the result of complex, interactive relationships between the actor and their social environment, both on and offline. New social media itself contributes to these interactive relationships by broadening the public space for communication and self-constitution with the medium perceived to be an 'extension of ourselves'. The question shifts then from 'did social media catalyse the recent riots' to 'what role did these technologies play in "mediating" the events.' I have argued that while new social media was not the cause of the unrest, these emergent technologies certainly altered how the riots were perceived and experienced. Invoking Hall's renowned study,[13] I contend that the current moral panic must be re-evaluated in light of these considerations to avoid deflecting blame onto a supposed technologically obsessed, deviant youth culture and obscuring the profound structural inequalities and emotional grievances that motivated people to riot.

---

13. While this study resonates with Hall *et al.'s* research on moral panics, the approach, political and economic orientations between the studies remain remarkably different.

References

Antley, J., 2012. 'Between Reality and Cyberspace'. *The Society Pages*, 8 February: http://thesocietypages.org/cyborgology/2012/02/08/between-reality-cyber-space/ (Accessed 10 February 2012).

Baker, S. A., 2010. *Zidane in Tartarus: A Neo-Aristotelian Inquiry into the Emotional Dimension of Kathartic Recognition.* Ph.D. University of Western Sydney: http://arrow.uws.edu.au:8080/vital/access/manager/Repository/uws:8257

Baker, S. A., 2011. 'The "Mediated Crowd": New Social Media and New Forms of Rioting'. *Sociological Research Online*, 16(4), 21.

Baker, S. A., 2012. 'From the Criminal Crowd to the "Mediated Crowd": The Impact of Social Media on the 2011 English Riots'. *Safer Communities*, 11(1), pp.40-49.

Baker, S. A., 2013. *Social Tragedy: Evoking the Nation Through Symbol, Ritual and Emotion in the Media Age* (Cultural Sociology Series). New York: Palgrave, forthcoming.

Ball, J., 2011. 'Social media has its own class divide'. *The Guardian*, 8 December: www.guardian.co.uk/commentisfree/2011/dec/08/social-media-blackberry-messenger (Accessed 13 December 2011).

Ball, J. and Brown, S., 2011. 'Why BlackBerry Messenger was rioters' communication method of choice'. *The Guardian*, 7 December: www.guardian.co.uk/uk/2011/dec/07/bbm-rioters-communication-method-choice (Accessed 13 December 2011).

Ball, J. and Lewis, P., 2011. 'Riots database of 2.5m tweets reveals complex picture of interaction'. *The Guardian,* 24 August: www.guardian.co.uk/uk/2011/aug/24/riots-database-twitter-interaction (Accessed 13 December 2011).

Blond, P., 2011. 'England's Riotous Values'. *The New York Times*, 24 August: www.nytimes.com/2011/08/25/opinion/25iht-edblond25.html (Accessed 25 November 2011).

Bowcott, O., Carter, H. and Clifton, H., 2011. 'Facebook riot calls earn men four-year jail terms amid sentencing outcry'. *The Guardian*, 16 August: www.guardian.co.uk/uk/2011/aug/16/facebook-riot-calls-men-jailed (Accessed 15 January 2012).

Cohen, S., 1972. *Folk Devils and Moral Panics*. London: MacGibbon and Kee.

Cookson, C. and Ilbury, D., 2011. 'Crowd Behaviour: United they stand'. *Financial Times*, 27 December: www.ft.com/cms/s/0/9eec57ac-2c8e-11e1-8cca-00144feabdco.html#axzz1kCM2wQyA (Accessed 14 January 2012).

Economist (Anonymous), 2011. 'Technology and Disorder: The BlackBerry Riots'. 13-19 August, p.22.

Eddo-Lodge, R., 2011. 'Twitter didn't fuel the Tottenham Riot'. *The Guardian*, 8 August: www.guardian.co.uk/commentisfree/2011/aug/08/tottenham-riot-twitter (Accessed 10 September 2011).

Foucault, M., 1977. *Discipline and Punish: The Birth of the Prison*. New York: Pantheon Books.

France, A. and Flynn, B., 2011. 'Nail the Twitter rioters'. *The Sun*, 9 August: www.thesun.co.uk/sol/homepage/news/3741129/Cops-vow-to-nail-the-Twitter-rioters.html (Accessed 12 January 2012).

Garber. M., 2012. 'A Year After the Egyptian Revolution, 10 per cent of It's Social Media Documentation Is Already Gone'. *The Atlantic*, 16 February: www.theatlantic.com/technology/archive/2012/02/a-year-after-the-egyptian-revolution-10-of-its-social-media-documentation-is-already-gone/253163/ (Accessed 17 February 2012).

The Guardian (Anonymous), 2011. 'Live webchat: social media and the riots'. Reading the Riots: Investigating England's Summer of Disorder (series), 8 December: www.guardian.co.uk/uk/reading-the-riots-blog/2011/dec/08/social-media-riots-live-web-chat (Accessed 10 December 2011).

The Guardian and LSE, 2011. Reading the Riots: Investigating England's Summer of Disorder (series). *The Guardian*: www.guardian.co.uk/uk/series/reading-the-riots (Accessed 12 December 2011).

Hall, S., Critcher, C., Jefferson, T., Clarke, J. N. and Roberts, B., 1978. *Policing the Crisis: Mugging, the State and Law and Order*. New York: Palgrave Macmillan.

Halliday, J., 2011. 'Gang recruitment' videos: MPs back call for police to have blocking power'. *The Guardian*, 8 November: www.guardian.co.uk/media/2011/nov/08/social-media-block-videos-gangs (Accessed 12 January 2012).

Harrison, T., 2011. 'DIY JUSTICE: Catch a Looter'. *The Huffington Post*, 9 August: www.huffingtonpost.co.uk/tara-harrison/diy-justice-catch-a-loote_b_922088.html (Accessed 31 January 2012).

Ingram, M., 2011. 'Network Effects: Social Media's Role in the London Riots'. *Bloomberg Businessweek*, 8 August: www.businessweek.com/technology/network-effects-social-medias-role-in-the-london-riots-08082011.html (Accessed 12 August 2011).

McLuhan, M., 1964. *Understanding Media: The Extensions of Man.* New York: McGraw Hill.

Mead, G. H., 1907. 'Concerning Animal Perception'. *Psychological Review*, 14, pp.383-390.

Metropolitan Police Interim Report (Anonymous), 2011. August Disorder, 30 November: http://content.met.police.uk/News/August-Disorder—Police-Interim-Report/1400005002176/1257246745756 (Accessed 02 February 2012).

Phillips, T., 2011. 'UK riots: Arrests over Facebook' incitement' to more violence'. *The Metro*, 10 August: www.metro.co.uk/tech/871945-uk-riots-arrests-over-facebook-incitement-to-more-violence (Accessed 16 August 2011).

Rey, P. J., 2012. 'There is no "Cyberspace"'. *Cyborgology*, 1 February: http://thesocietypages.org/cyborgology/2012/02/01/there-is-no-cyberspace/ (Accessed 4 February 2012).

'Riot Clean-up' (Anonymous), 2011. Interview on Twitter. Interviewed by Kate Bussmann [Twitter], 7 December 2011: http://atwitteryear.tumblr.com/ (Accessed 3 January 2012).

Silverman, J., 2011. 'The State of Britain Today. 19 October The riots of summer 2011: Causes, Calamities and Consequences': www.socialsciencespace.com/2011/10/the-riots-of-summer-2011-how-did-we-come-to-this/ (Accessed 12 January 2012).

Taylor, J., 2011. 'Four years in jail for failed attempts to incite looting on Facebook'. *The Independent*, 17 August: www.independent.co.uk/news/uk/crime/four-years-in-jail-for-failed-attempts-to-incite-looting-on-facebook-2338860.html (Accessed 13 September 2011).

Thompson, D., 2011. 'Get up, clean up, sweep away the riots'. *The Guardian*, 9 August: www.guardian.co.uk/commentisfree/2011/aug/09/clean-up-riots (Accessed 13 January 2012).

Dr Simon Harding has 25 years experience working in crime reduction and community safety in central and local government. He joined the teaching staff at Middlesex University in 2011 where he lectures in Criminology, Community Safety and Policing. Simon Harding has just completed a three year study into violent urban street gangs in south London as part of a doctorate in Youth Justice. He also completed a three year study into the phenomenon of status dogs and weapon dogs in the UK and this was published by Policy Press in 2012 in his book *Unleashed*.

10

STREET GOVERNMENT:
THE ROLE OF THE URBAN STREET GANG IN THE LONDON RIOTS

Simon Harding

Introduction

In this chapter, I contend that the riots in London, which occurred after
the initial Saturday night rioting in Tottenham, all had their genesis in the
urban street gang. Over the last decade, urban street gangs have emerged
as an identifiable feature of many of the deprived neighbourhoods in London. Their presence is increasingly visible in these excluded neighbourhoods
where their own forms of social control and authority operate within their
own social field—which I argue represents a form of 'street government'.
While this street government came together to fight the authorities during
the riots it also provided an opportunity for the sudden temporal expansion
of this social field. The so-called 'gang truce', which captured this expansion, also generated a gravitational pull for others, familiar with this social
field, to participate in rioting and looting. The riots in London therefore not
only revealed significant aspects of UK gang organization but also interesting features of an urban street culture which I feel are important starting
points to understanding these disturbances. Let us first look at how gangs
were linked to the riots.

The Claims Against 'Gangs' During the Riots

The involvement of gangs in the disturbances in London during August
2011 remains contested. Initial statements just after the conclusion of the

disorder suggested: 'Gangs were at the heart of the protests and have been behind the coordinated attacks', David Cameron, 11th August 2011. This view was echoed by the Ministry of Justice (MOJ), Metropolitan Police (Met) and MPs in several London boroughs, the Centre for Social Justice and by several youth workers working directly with neighbourhood gangs (de Castella, 2011). The immediate government response was to 'crack down' on UK gangs by establishing a Gangs Task Force and seeking the advice of former US police chief, Bill Bratton.[1] Furthermore, despite their pilot status, gang injunctions (so-called gangbos) were to be implemented nationally.

However, three weeks later, in early September 2011, there was by a political retraction by the Home Secretary who stated that the role of gangs was 'not as high as people first thought'. Whilst acknowledging 'some gang activity taking place in terms of encouraging people to take part in these events' (BBC News 2011), she reported to the Home Affairs Committee that 'the majority of people involved were not individuals who've been involved in gangs', (BBC News 2011). This new position followed a downward revision by the Met that the number of people arrested with known gang-affiliations was not 33 per cent but 19 per cent.

The report by the Ministry of Justice (2011), published shortly afterwards, informed us that nationally only 13 per cent of those arrested in the riots were identified as gang-affiliated. This was supported by a Home Office (2011: 19) statement that 'in terms of the role gangs played in the disorder, most forces perceived that where gang members were involved, they generally did not play a pivotal role'. This suggests the Home Office had made sweeping assumptions based on data analysis of those presenting in courts. This statement obfuscated variations in the profile of rioters across the different city locations affected by the rioting. The report also indicates that the profile of participants differs depending upon gender, age, ethnicity, socio-economic indicators, educational history, previous criminal history and city location.

This initial targeting of gangs as the locus for the riots, followed by this swift retraction, has led to considerable confusion with regard to the role of gangs. The report, 'Reading the Riots' (*Guardian* and LSE, 2011: 4) adds

---

1.   Bill Bratton was previously the police commissioner for NYC and Boston and police chief for Los Angeles. His policing style is influenced heavily by broken windows theory and he is associated with developing a zero-tolerance approach towards crime.

further confusion noting that 'gangs behaved in an entirely atypical manner for the duration of the riots', before continuing, 'on the whole the role of gangs in the riots has been significantly overstated'. These statements are at once contradictory and curious; the former statement is accurate whilst the later misreads the evidence. On 25th October 2011, *The Guardian* reported that 'gangs did not play central role in riots, inquiry finds' and worryingly, many academics accepted this headline unquestioningly. When reframed, this statement could offer a different perspective which should be considered in closer detail: that in London, one in five involved in the disturbances had gang-affiliations. As this figure relates only to those appearing before the courts and is not representative of those participating in events (see *Guardian* and LSE, 2011; Briggs, 2012), it is likely that gangs may have played much more of a significant role than first assumed. The role of the gang has therefore been downplayed twice, firstly by the Home Office and secondly by academic commentators. Whilst it is inescapable that in London gangs played a significant role, their role in the rioting occurring in the provincial cities is unclear. It is entirely possible that government rhetoric has been based on assumptions relating to the gang issues presenting in London. If this is the case then government responses regarding a national 'crack down on gangs' may be pre-emptory. If it is not, then the evidence is yet to be fully presented.

One obvious difficulty is gaining agreement on what the government mean by the 'gang role' (Lewis, 2011) in the disturbances. This question precipitates further confusion over meaning, rhetoric and definitions which further complicate data-analysis. Many commentators interpret questions about gang involvement as implying that participants were 'solely' or 'overwhelmingly' gang members; that they were responsible for the riots, or that the events were visibly orchestrated as a gang activity or gang outing, without the involvement or participation of other groups. But these accusations were false. Firstly, because such post-scriptum analysis implies that gangs are instantly identifiable, homogenous groups when research has indicated that 'gang-affiliation is far more complex and relational' (Pitts, 2008) or fluid (Hallsworth and Young, 2008) Secondly, because such misunderstandings are evident in interview transcripts with gang-affiliates e.g. 'the social disorder was "not a gang ting"'(Briggs, 2012: 13) and 'the government needed someone to blame and [put] everything together under "gangs"' (*Guardian* and LSE, 2011: 22). Furthermore, post-hoc analysis contains few gang member testimonies about their involvement. So the narrative of 'gangs' as some locus to the disturbances is lost while narratives highlighting politics, grievances with bankers, globalisation, lack of jobs and poverty are foregrounded. This led some media commentators and academics to generalise about broad social disorder rather than localised events, (NatCen 2011).

The Social Field of the Gang

To understand the role of gangs in the riots in London, we must first consider how gangs function and operate within their own domain. In this respect, the concept of 'social field' by Pierre Bourdieu (1985) provides a useful lens for analysis. The social field exists as a social world/domain where actors are in perpetual conflict and struggle to achieve mutually-validated goals, notoriety or elevated social status, (which Bourdieu calls 'distinction') (Bourdieu, 1984). The value of these goals is historically validated and perpetually revalidated by field participants. Furthermore, all actions undertaken by them are determined and coordinated by the habitus (Bourdieu 1985). For Bourdieu, the habitus represents internalised dispositions arising from local traditions, local and personal histories and habits. These actions are generated by the constraints of the social field or by the available life opportunities and how they are mediated by field participants (Bourdieu, 1985).

So the social field in the context of gangs would exist predominantly in areas of poverty borne out of deprivation, lack of amenities, residualised housing, decimated youth services, and a lack of opportunities. It is under these conditions that gangs often evolve in the forgotten areas, where marginalised communities and new immigrant arrivals struggle to stay above the poverty line. Coupled with this downward trajectory is the gradual retreat of state-support mechanisms and political disenfranchisement. Collectively, this environment forms the physical, psychological, socio-structural and emotional landscape which is the social field of the urban street gang in the UK.

The social field of the gang does not exhibit physical boundaries but relational boundaries. In this way, the social field therefore relates to other urban young people who are not gang-affiliated but are familiar with that lifestyle. Many aspects of the social field will be instantly familiar and recognisable by these young people; for example they will be aware of gang tensions at school or be aware of restrictions on free movement across 'gang' neighbourhoods. It may not necessarily impact upon older members of the local community which is why it is possible to live in a gang-afflicted estate and have no interaction with a gang at all. For these reasons gangs are difficult to identify in some communities. This had led some sociologists to contest their very existence (Hallsworth and Duffy, 2010), claiming they are mythical, and that practitioners, academics and statutory authorities who recognise their existence are guilty of making mythology manifest simply by talking about it (Hallsworth and Young, 2008).

Within the social field of the gang, participants are engaged in 'an arena of struggle' (Bourdieu and Wacquant, 1992). As participants struggle for distinction, they aim to generate economic capital. However, in all areas of multi-layered deprivation, and specifically within the social field of the gang, such economic capital is scarce. To compensate for this, participants engage their 'street capital' (Harding, 2012) which is used as an amalgam for cultural, symbolic and social capital, alongside habitus and personal history, thereby acting as the prime capital within the field. The difficulty is that street capital venture, status and reputation relies on aggression, intimidation and violence as a measure by which participants in this field strive for success. Indeed, these young people therefore strive to build street capital to achieve localised distinction and this is done by building and maintaining a reputation at any cost. Respect is gained by the acquisition of brand names, through violence and undertaking carnival acts which are filmed and broadcast on social networking sites. Broadcasting generates instant respect from peers while group disorder reinforces gang cohesion and branding. Involvement in a fracas or riot confers bragging rights upon individuals providing an opportunity to enter gang mythology by dominating oral history and moulding biographical accounts which lionise their actions.

As with any, the social field (Bourdieu 1984; 1985) of the gang operates with a clear hierarchy (Pitts 2008); this operates with new entrants and recruits entering at the bottom of the hierarchy as Youngers, later rising to become Olders and then Elders. Youngers engage in largely expressive crime, in order to build self-reputations. They may undertake street robbery against other Youngers, however as Olders are involved in more instrumental crimes, often drugs and street robbery. As Olders, street robbery now tends to be against other drug dealers (Briggs, 2008) Information networks operate through which drugs and stolen goods are exchanged for economic capital or are quickly dispersed to ready markets. The social field of the gang hosts multiple local gangs and thus the struggle for success is both intra-gang and inter-gang. Gang rivalries or 'beefs' are commonplace resulting in young people restricting their movements to avoid victimisation. Known locally as 'Postcode Beefs', its rules demand that gang members may not enter the designated territory of rivals unless invited. Such 'violations' are considered disrespectful and can be met with violent group reprisals.

The social field of the gang, as with all social fields, is structured vertically. Gangs are positioned upon the vertical axis within the field. For Bourdieu (1984, 1985) all social fields exhibit similar patterns of vertical differentiation. Those just starting out are located at the bottom of the rung, whilst those that are the longest established, most notorious or most violent are located at the top of the hierarchy. This means there are 'winners' and 'losers'. Perhaps unsurprisingly, the social field is one of perpetual flux as gangs constantly shift and alter position on the vertical axis, which gives the impression of fluidity. Each gang struggles to dominate the field and achieve distinction, and violence occurs between gangs as this struggle for supremacy is played out on social housing estates and local streets. The challenge therefore is to situate the police within this social world.

The Police as 'Gang'

As noted by one respondent in 'Reading the Riots', 'to me the worst gang is the police though' (*The Guardian* 2012). Similar refrains have also been made by street-oriented youth and gang-affiliated youth are that the police operate as 'the biggest gang on road'. This perception not only relates to police tactics and use of aggression against them but also to a belief that the police are heavily involved in the social field of the gang. Street-oriented youth and gang-affiliated youth claim that the police are also 'Playas', e.g. who understand and manipulate the Street Codes[2] to their advantage. In this

---

2. Recognised behaviours and norms which dictate street life, e.g. knowledge of the rule of not grassing, rules of respect, how and when the Code of Silence operates etc. Famously espoused by Elijah Anderson (1999) in his work *Code of the Streets*.

way the police function within the field in much the same way as other rival gangs; their key purpose being to thwart gang activity by employing tactical manoeuvres to frustrate and arrest suspected gang-affiliates. Rather than a form of disruption, gang affiliates, view this as disrespect. Police presence on an estate is considered a violation in much the same way as it would be if undertaken by a rival gang: 'They violate us!' Police stimulate this disrespect through the deployment of their prime tactical weapon — stop and search. This provides an opportunity for ritualised humiliation of young gang-affiliates: an activity which compounds hatred for the police, not because it interrupts their social time, but because it diminishes the accumulated respect held by a gang-affiliate.

As the prime authority in the public domain, the police can enter the social field of the gang at will. They too seek to achieve symbolic and street capital within the field by intervening to disrupt gang activity with low-level harassment tactics, interfering with free movement and, if possible, 'decapitation' of the gang elite: goals which vary little from those of rival gangs. In this way, the police operate within the social field of the gang, but they are not situated on the same vertical axis as the gangs. Their struggle within the field occurs instead along the vertical axis (vertical differentiation), i.e. gangs seek distinction by dominating their rivals. However, it is not possible to dominate the police in this way. The presence of the police within the social field presents a constant challenge. They cannot be overcome or dominated as with other gangs; they must therefore be accepted or accommodated as an occupational hazard within the field. In this way they therefore represent a horizontal differentiation within the field.

The ability of the police to enforce legislation also suggests an asymmetrical differentiation within the social field of the gang. This imbalance indicates a bias of power to the police. However, police resources are spread thinly meaning interactions with gangs may be limited, temporal and targeted. Police are thus intermittent players, operating at half strength, with limited resources in a constantly changing social field. Therefore the advantage sits with the gang because they can make effective use of the intimate personal knowledge of the environment, social networks, the residents, the deals, the favours, and the gossip Consequently, the habitus recalibrates this symmetry, allowing the gang to sit on the same horizontal axis as the police, effectively diminishing the police's asymmetrical advantage. In this way, urban street gangs view the police as a permanent presence, a 'rival gang' which cannot be overcome and so rather, must be avoided. If the police are seen as a 'rival gang', then the logic of the social field declares that attacks are permissible with no remorse. As with other gang rivals, retribution and revenge become motivations for confrontation and, in the context of the English riots, these are mediated as anti-police narratives.

How the Riots Developed

Briggs (2012) and the *The Guardian* and LSE (2011) provide detailed accounts of how the riots unfolded in London and across England during August 2011. However, a key fact remains obscured: whilst at first glance events followed broadly similar sequential patterns, there were in fact distinct differences in many rioting locations as to how these events unfolded. This suggests a different local signature based on local dynamics. Researchers have yet to fully examine these differences; for example, the Tottenham riot appeared to arise from grievous anger following the death of Mark Duggan, subsequent protests and disrespect of a black family; described by Angel (2012: 25) as the 'trigger event'. Later events in Birmingham and Manchester, however, appeared to have followed a different template, i.e. one which was heavily influenced by mediated accounts of events in London (described by some as copy-cat events). However in London, the majority of episodes of social disorder (in over 31 neighbourhoods) occurred in areas acknowledged by the Met police as 'gang-affected' (e.g. Hackney, Lewisham, Croydon, Ealing). It is useful to consider, post-Tottenham, a number of other unique developments which are now relevant and may change the way we consider what happened in the context of gangs:

Many London youth viewed the Tottenham riot as the first major confrontation of this type with the Met police since 1985 at Broadwater Farm. Therefore, for many, it was the first such event in their lifetime (as opposed to politically-motivated disturbances, e.g. poll tax riots of 1991, student demonstrations of 2010). The events in Tottenham are an important signifier for what was to develop in other cities.

From the late-1990s, London has witnessed the emergence of neighbourhood street gangs, (Pitts, 2008; 2010). Operating in areas of severe deprivation, these gangs provided a locus for young people to group together for protection, to make money and generate street capital.

Unlike 1985, BlackBerry, SMS and social networking sites were alive with messages bringing a social imperative to get involved in the 2011 riots; giving locations, filming opportunities and the thrill of real-time developments. A single text was able to potentially attract scores of peers to participate in the carnival of crime.

In the week prior to the riots, Hackney police mounted an invasive policing operation on the Pembury Estate, (home to the Pembury Boys—one of the most recognised gangs in London) seizing firearms, drugs, cash, mobile phones and making 23 arrests, (Angel, 2012: 26). Thus a revenge narrative is constructed by local gangs and the Met police failed to recognise tensions were running high.

The events unfolding in Tottenham on the evening of 6th August 2011 were for many, unfamiliar. However, for gangs in London, this was viewed as an opportunity to quickly establish and verify local police presence, police activity and tactical responses: a learning opportunity. And they learned quickly.

The Governance Vacuum

Over the past two decades, state authorities, notably the council and the police, have increasingly retreated from 'difficult to manage' urban areas of multiple deprivation. This fact is already familiar to those in the social field of the gang. Their daily lives are lived in discredited estates where the authority of the state and its agents has long since dissipated. Governance of these dangerous and discredited neighbourhoods is now frequently undertaken by force as a result of this declining legitimacy. This often leads to increasingly militaristic policing tactics. As Manuel Castells (2000: 303) notes, 'the state still relies on violence and surveillance, but it does not hold their monopoly any longer'. As the state retreats, alternative agents and actors 'now exercise authority and control outcomes that previously were the domain of the state' (Susan Strange, cited in Castells, 1998: 185, n39). State retrenchment and retreat compounds a loss of faith in the state apparatus leading to the appearance of localised non-state groups with greater local legitimacy. As the riots evolved, gang networks quickly established that police were absent from the streets or, at best, sparsely deployed. Gang-affiliates assumed that police would flood into Tottenham leaving other town centres 'thinly policed' and actively monitored police activity on an hourly basis, thus enabling them to take quick advantage of an emerging governance vacuum.

Street Government

As the police (the primary authority in the public domain) diminish in their neighbourhood presence, their authority weakens. When this occurs, secondary authority in the community may rise to take control and fill the governance vacuum. This may vary considerably depending upon time and place, but may include local authority staff, street wardens, housing department housing officers and caretaking staff. It may also include vigilantes, criminal families, or street gangs. In London, localities where gang affiliation is high—which is often on these disadvantaged estates—this secondary authority is often the gang. For some urban young people, gangs are the only relevant authority in their environment, operating their own rules of social control and discipline, acting as a form of 'street government' (Hagedorn, 2008). The gang is also often the community operative with the most intimate knowledge of, and connectivity to, the street environment. Gangs can mobilise swiftly, through the use of BlackBerry Messenger (BBM) and social network sites, thereby generating large numbers, establishing a broader presence through threats of violence. The momentum then brings recognition of the shift in governance to 'the street'. The absence of primary authority—the police—also designates a 'permission to act'. For gang-affiliated youth and street youth, (those who are not gang-affiliated but are street-oriented), this instils a growing sense of control, empowerment and invincibility. Gang Olders and Elders were now fully alert to these developments during the riots and youngers were instructed to 'test the waters'; to find out if the police were present on the streets, and if so, their movements along with the speed and nature of their responses to disorder or criminal activity. Sporadic pilfering escalated to targeted attacks on pre-identified key locations, e.g. electrical stores such as Currys in Lewisham when the primary authority failed to materialise or assemble itself in a form which may bring more social control. Street activity therefore becomes increasingly visible and audacious as more gang networks learn of the opportunities.

These key developments altered the horizontal differentiation within the social field, shifting the asymmetrical advantage further in favour of the gang. The gang then moves quickly to capitalise on this advantage, knowing from shared oral history and experience this will be a short-lived opportunity. This asymmetrical tilting in favour of the social field of the gang allowed three things to happen in quick succession during the riots in London:

1. Expansion of the social field of the gang

The pervading social field of the community with its established cultural authority of the police and the state embodies a 'moral alignment' between citizens (Klein, 2012: 19). As the cultural authority shifts, so too does the social field. Therefore, community social norms quickly altered as the social field of the gang expanded. At this point, the normative actions of the social field of the gang—violence, revenge and retribution—became permissible and favoured. Local residents, and those living in areas unaffected by gangs, articulate shock and outrage at this sudden explosion of violence which, to some of them, is so alien to their social norms and values. This view contrasts sharply with those already operating within the social field of the gang and those within its wider social field of deprived estates who recognise these new norms and values as familiar.

As the social field of the gang expanded, other young people adopt the values and norms of the social field. The public domain became 'the street' domain: the values became street values operating to the 'Code of the Streets' (Anderson, 1999). This term is used by Anderson in relation to the identifiable culture of the streets which often leads to violence. Anderson (1999: 34) views these street codes as a 'cultural adaptation to a profound lack of faith in the police and judicial system'. This transformation is noticeable by initial onlookers and bystanders who reported 'a change in the feel of the place', and 'a dark mood taking over'. It quickly became apparent that new rules were operating on the street. Ordinary members of the public removed themselves hurriedly; whilst those who understand these new rules and can operate or function within them, gravitated towards the action. Participants who can operate under these newly emergent rules are adept at spotting those who are suddenly and unexpectedly unfamiliar in this new social field. Often unable to read the signs or feel the change in mood, they may be unaware of their vulnerability. Bystanders and those traversing the area were now targeted (e.g. the Malaysian student who was assaulted and then robbed by those allegedly offering assistance). Therefore those navigating this new social landscape within the new rules do so with impunity. It therefore became an imperative to move with the pack, look like the pack and respond to police tactics as a pack. To do otherwise implies individual isolation — acting outside your social field — and this increases the risk of personal attack.

For those immersed in the new rules of this altered social space, the only true danger was the only other gang likely to be operating within the field … the police. In general, confrontation with the police was avoided, however, some sought direct confrontation. Those familiar with avoiding 'the Law' did so adroitly. Those new to this social field, or recent adherents, are required to take their social cues from more experienced participants around them. By following their cues to move, recent adherents will reduce the risks of being singled out or targeted. As a result, individuals will group and swarm in animation. The gang social field now pervades as the significant cultural authority — a street government; that is, it is street values and norms which are ascendant and in control. Those 'on road' or active in 'street life' now exercise authority over the local area.

2. The gang truce

Gang Olders and Elders were heavily involved in exchanging information. Through discussions, agreements to temporarily suspend hostilities were brokered. This so-called 'gang truce' was one of the most notable, but remains one of the least researched, features of London riots. The truce refers to spatially diverse gangs temporarily suspending violent rivalry to act in unison. *The Guardian* report, 'Reading the Riots', (2011: 22) addresses this point thus:

> What most of the reports on the riots thus far have missed is that the four nights of rioting saw a truce as otherwise hostile gangs suspended ordinary hostilities to focus on other targets.

> Daniel Weston, a Brixton youth worker reported the temporal abandonment of territorial divisions with gangs issued with *"hood passes"* — a slang term meaning

that youths were allowed to travel into another neighbourhood without reper-cussions thereby permitting both gang-affiliated and non gang-affiliated young people freedom of movement not normally permitted in gang-affected areas. He further comments that 'the gangs came together and forgot their rivalries', although he continues, 'the informal truce didn't last long however' (de Castella, 2011). Such observations matched my own conversations with those working with gang-affiliated youth. The town centre loci of these congregations also fitted the concept of the establishment of neutral territories and spaces for gangs. The truce was facilitated through the use of BBM and worked at intra-gang and inter-gang level. The phone conversations and BBM between gangs served to confirm new rules and permissive actions, ratifying any expansion in the social field of the gang.

3. Creation of a safe space — Non-gang participants

Clearly not everyone involved in the riots was gang-affiliated and it would be quite incorrect to claim so. The gangs merely created the opportunity for the social field to be temporarily rebalanced and then tipped in their favour which allowed others to adhere to this social field. As numerous reports tes-tify (*Guardian* and LSE, 2011; NatCen, 2011) a wide spectrum of people were involved, generally described as local youth, students, adults, those with a grievance against the government anarchists, agitators, etc. Those participat-ing in the riots who were not gang-affiliated, (the majority of the crowd), largely share the same habitus as participants who were gang-affiliated, i.e. they may share the same environment, social housing, local community, college, social housing estate, outlooks in life or aspirations and thus may believe they share the same 'social fate'[3] (Bourdieu 1985). Others may oper-ate on the fringes of criminality or move within the social field of the gang, opting for only tangential or minor involvement. This shared habitus then both determines and coordinates what is possible within this social field. The new, temporal adherents to the social field quickly moulded their behav-ioural norms to this social field, enjoying the new found freedom provided by the change in the social field and the new 'street government', perhaps also excited that the speed of the events evoked a sense of revolution.

3. Considered by Bourdieu to mean their acceptance of their life trajectory and, by and large, their inability to break away from this trajectory.

Adhesion to this new social field therefore took these forms:

- It was temporal. Some participants engaged for only one night before returning home to later regret their actions. Others, e.g. adrenaline junkies (Ferrell *et al*, 2008) may enjoy two or three nights of fun before returning to 'real life'.

- It was relational. Those in close proximity to the social field of the gang, through the gang network, school, extended family or because they share the same habitus or social field, are the most likely adherents.

- It was emotional. Some participants used this moment to activate their Second Life persona (Presdee 2000), bringing to life a hidden personality. Such participants expressed a variety of narratives, e.g., those angry at their lack of social or commercial power or social exclusion or political impotence. Other adherents include those more inclined to the carnivalesque elements of the crowd (Presdee 2000); those embracing the edgework margins (Ferrell *et al*, 2008) and voyeurs.

- It was novel. For some young people, entering this new social field is novel, and thrilling, generating a new excitement which they find difficult to leave once events are underway.

Numerous media interviews have identified these different experiences. To the average citizen they read as a jumble of different reasons for participation. This creates general confusion regarding motivations permitting space for speculation and politicking.

'Whose Streets, Our Streets!'

The truce created a safe space whereby others — those normally reluctant to enter or move around the social field — come out and participate in the full knowledge that they will not be targeted by rival gangs. Many people then entered the streets; some young people felt suddenly empowered as the bridles governing their daily movements, (gangs and the police) were both suddenly removed, absent or powerless. This generated narratives of exuberance, freedom and 'getting high' from their experience of 'being in control of the streets' (Kelly and Gill, 2012: 69). The expanded social field during the truce created a new safe space for participants, facilitating a number of permissible actions all viable within the social field. As the disturbances unfolded reputations were generated in different ways. Younger people, empowered by these events, often felt drawn to direct confrontation with the absent authority through street violence and fighting. As Klein (2012: 19) notes, the 'authority of the state is dissipated ... its manifestations become targets.'

Both gang-affiliated and non-gang-affiliated sought a more instrumental outcome, through the acquisition of goods by looting. Media reports and interviews are replete with accounts of goods being removed in wholesale fashion from electronic retailers, such as Currys, being loaded onto white vans and lorries. This was certainly the situation in the small retail park near my home in Lewisham. My own research and numerous mediated accounts confirm that gang Olders and Elders were instructing gang Youngers to take advantage of the liberated moment (*Guardian* and LSE, 2011: 4). One youth worker said to me 'the older generation were the puppet masters pulling the strings. They weren't the ones doing the looting but they were getting the stuff' (de Castella, 2011).

The street confrontations and the looting then became a Reputational Extravaganza (Presdee, 2000; Harding, 2012) whereby the acquisition of stolen goods is quite secondary to the acquisition of street reputation and respect from peers. That's to say, it is not the goods themselves they seek—but the reputation from having looted it because the reputation will last longer than £50 received for selling, for example, a 50' inch plasma TV. Two additional developments occurred during the rioting in London, arson and home invasions (Briggs, 2012); both of which incurred high-levels of street capital for those who engaged in these activities. Arson levels were noticeably high during the riots as such events acted as opportunities for participants to increase their street capital by filming these events. Others led small groups on home invasions, terrorising families by rampaging through their homes: again such events are reputation-making activities. All these activities, from street violence to looting to fencing stolen goods, permit generation of copious amounts of street capital (Harding, 2012).

Explaining the Data

What then of the comments by the Home Secretary regarding the role of gangs? The Home Secretary's comments based on the arrest statistics mis-interpret the data, suggesting that as only 19 per cent of arrestees were gang affiliated, this indicates low-levels of gang involvement (Ministry of Justice 2011). Are academics looking for a higher percentage threshold as positive proof that gangs were involved? If so, this suggests a fundamental misun-derstanding of how gangs work and how they became involved in these disturbances. This 19 per cent statistic invites several critiques:

Firstly, I would have expected a lower number of gang-affiliated youth to feature in the arrest statistics because they are advanced in their social field, and are familiar with the law and how they will be dealt. Urban street gangs operate effectively every day in their social field, it is thus a domain they understand well, i.e. they utilise face coverings; stolen goods are quickly dispersed; alibis are easily constructed; participants will not grass. In short, they are more proficient than 'temporal adherents'. Either they were easily identifiable and thus arrested or the overall proportion of gang-affiliated youth on the street was high. Either way a figure of one in five you being gang-affiliated indicates a high level of involvement.

The first cohort of arrestees were known gang members and prominent nominals.[4] This led to inflated reports of gang-affiliated young people. As the arrests increased, non-gang-affiliated youth and adults were taken into custody — thus, the initial figure was always going to be revised downward. The police also made considerable efforts when they formally started to respond to get who they knew first — those who had previous convictions or were known (Briggs, 2012); those likely to be gang affiliates.

Later arrests relied heavily upon CCTV analysis. Here non-gang affiliated youths and 'temporal adherents to the social field' appear with uncovered faces. This behaviour differs significantly from gang-affiliated youth who are familiar with CCTV locations; police surveillance tactics and risk manage their street behaviour by having their face covered. Only naive participants engage in street activity without face coverings.

---

4. Those identified by the police as persistent offenders.

Relatedly, gang members are highly proficient at the dispersal of stolen goods, having into highly organised networks/markets for effective distribution while naive adherents to the social field have no such networks. Whereas gang-affiliated youth transferred and dispersed stolen items quickly, non-gang-affiliated youth experienced some difficulty in shifting multiple items.

The sudden influx of newly looted goods acquired by 'novice' looters and 'temporary adherents' led to saturation for stolen goods in the local neighbourhood market. This, in turn, led to market newcomers seeking to quickly off-load their 'hot' property by making heavy discounts. This has the effect of undercutting markets already successfully operated by local gangs. To ensure their position as market leaders, established gangs used police hotlines to report non gang-affiliated youth and remove them from the marketplace.

It wasn't long before gang relations returned to their customary position because when the 'gang truce' ended, rival gangs raided flats to rob rivals of recently acquired earnings from the sale of stolen goods.[5]

Discussion

Firstly, to be clear, gang involvement in rioting was not apparent in all the cities affected by the disorder in England. However, urban street gangs and those who associated themselves within this social field, in my view, had central involvement in the rioting in London. As gangs are not easily identifiable or visible, this view is easily obscured, not least by the jumbled narratives emerging from post-hoc analysis, by long-standing disagreement over gang definitions and by confused government rhetoric regarding the gang 'role'. Collectively, 'Reading the Riots' (*Guardian* and LSE, 2011) which downplayed the significance of 19 per cent of arrestees having gang-affiliation, and central government rhetoric, both failed to provide an adequate exposition of gang involvement. Academic and media research has further masked the involvement of gangs in London by offering up a panapoly of highly individualistic narratives regarding motivations for participation. Public consciousness was further influenced by one-sided media depictions and the misinterpretation of arrest data (*Guardian* and LSE, 2011) which has now calcified views that gangs were not or only very slightly involved in the riots.

---

5.   Information provided by respondents interviewed by author.

Angel (2012: 30) suggests that when analysing the disturbances academics need to 'distinguish between political intent and political significance'. Similarly if we are to have a more nuanced perspective of the role of gangs we must consider both intent and significance. This is, in my view, best achieved by examining the social field of the gang and its influence upon events. The intent of the urban street gang in London was to capitalise quickly on unfolding events. Following the riot in Tottenham, a depleted police presence created a vacuum of authority in many areas: an issue quickly identified by gangs. Through established networks, gangs seized the initiative by instigating a gang truce in many neighbourhoods. This temporarily shifted the horizontal differentiation of the social field in favour of the gang. The social field was only later rebalanced when police flooded the streets of London. By acting in this way, street gangs expanded their own social field thereby ensuring their normative values became the dominant street values. The truce provided a temporary 'confederation' of gang activity allowing gang-affiliates to confront the only 'gang' rival still visibly providing opposition in the social field—that of the police.

However, the gang truce did more than simply cease mutual hostilities. It created a 'safe space' where those peripheral to gangs could actively participate knowing they would not be targeted by rivals. This permitted free movement and association in ways normally heavily restricted for young people in gang-affiliated neighbourhoods. These new field participants quickly adhered to the social norms of the gang and their values. The actions of gang-affiliated youth and most street-oriented youth was coordinated by a shared habitus and determined by the logic of the social field of the gang. This logic would indicate that the social field operates as an 'arena of struggle' (Bourdieu and Wacquant, 1992) where young people strive for status and distinction through the acquisition of street capital. Acts of looting, arson and physical violence were therefore undertaken to generate street capital. Thus the opportunity provided by the riots was primarily one of 'reputational extravaganza' for earning street capital and only secondarily about obtaining goods. In this short lived process, all actors benefit as participants in events which generate oral history and street capital for years to come: benefits that will surely outlast any new trainers acquired from Footlocker.

Whilst I believe the significance of gang involvement in the riots in London (post-Tottenham) should not be obscured, overlooked or underplayed, my analysis does signal some interesting questions: Does this spectacular flourishing of gang activity across the capital mark a further evolutionary step of gangs in London? Might we now see increased gang confederation? Will the events act as a recruitment drive for gangs? Will it happen again? One last noteworthy point gives rise for optimism: curiously, the ability of gangs to suspend mutual hostilities perhaps suggests that the violence, so endemic in the social field of the gang, is either preventable or stoppable.

References

Anderson, E. (1999) *Code of the Streets*. New York: W. W. Norton.

Angel, H. (2012) Viewpoint: 'Were the Riots Political?' *Safer Communities*, Vol 11, No. 1 pp.24-32 Emerald Group Publishing.

Baker, S. A., (2012) 'From the Criminal Crowd to the "Mediated" Crowd: the Impact of Social Media on the 2011 English Riots', *Safer Communities*, Vol. 11 No.1 pp.40-49 Emerald Group Publishing.

BBC News (2011) 'Theresa May says most rioters were not in gangs', 8 September 2011: www.bbc.co.uk/news/uk-politics- 14834827 (Accessed on 14 September 2011.

Bourdieu, P. (1984) *Distinction: A Social Critique of the Judgement of Taste,* translated by Richard Nice, Cambridge, Mass: Harvard University Press.

Bourdieu, P. (1985) 'The Genesis of the Concepts of Habitus and Field', *Sociocriticism* 2:11-24.

Bourdieu, P. and Wacquant, L. (1992) *An Invitation to Reflexive Sociology* Chicago: University of Chicago Press.

Briggs, D (2008) 'Robbery Careers and Desistance Attempts' in *Safer Communities* Vol. 7(3): 27-34.

Briggs, D. (2012) 'What We Did When it Happened: A Timeline Analysis of the Social Disorder in London', *Safer Communities*, Vol.11 No.1 pp6-16 Emerald Group Publishing.

Castells, M. (2000) 'The Rise of the Network Society', Vol. 1 *The Information Age: Economy, Society and Culture*, Malden, Mass: Blackwell.

Castells, M. (1998) *End of Millennium Malden,* Mass: Blackwell.

De Castella, T. (2011) 'England Riots: What's the evidence gangs were behind the riots?' BBC News Magazine: www.bbc.co.uk/news/magazine-14540796 (Accessed on 14 September 2011).

Ferrell, J. Hayward, K. and Young, J. (2008) *Cultural Criminology*, London Sage Publications'.

The Guardian (2011) 'Reading the Riots: Investigating England's Summer of Disorder' (Guardian Shorts) Manchester: Guardian Books.

Hagedorn, J. (2008) *A World of Gangs,* Minneapolis: University of Minnesota Press.

Hallsworth, S. and Duffy, K. (2010) 'Confronting London's Violent Street World: The Gang and Beyond, A Report for London Councils. London': CESR, London Metropolitan University.

Hallsworth, S. and Young, T. (2008) 'Gang Talk and Gang Talkers: A Critique'. *Crime, Media and Culture* 4(2): 175-195.

Harding, S. (2012) 'A Reputational Extravaganza? The Role of the Urban Street Gang in the Riots in London', *Criminal Justice Matters*, March 2012.

Home Office (2011), *An Overview of Recorded Crimes and Arrests Resulting from Disorder Events in August 2011*, Home Office: London.

Kelly, L. and Gill, A. (2012) 'Rotis not Riots: A Feminist Dialogue on the Riots and Their Aftermath', *Safer Communities*, Vol.11 No. 1pp.62-72. Emerald Group Publishing.

Klein, A. 'Policing as a Causal Factor –A Fresh View on Riots and Social Unrest', *Safer Communities*, Vol.11 No. 1 pp.17-23 Emerald Group Publishing.

Lewis, P. (2011) 'England riots: top advisor warns against overplaying role of gang', *The Guardian*, 11th November 2011.

Martin, J. L. (2003) 'What is Field Theory?' *American Journal of Sociology* 109 No 1:1-49.

May, T. (2011), 'Speech on riots' made to the House of Commons, London, 11 August: www.homeoffice.gov.uk/media-centre/speeches/riots-speech (Accessed September 2011).

Ministry of Justice (2011) *Statistical Bulletin on the Public Disorder of 6th—9th August 2011*: ww.justice.gov.uk/publications.

NatCen (2011) *The August Riots in England: Understanding the Involvement of Young People*. London: National Centre for Social Research www.natcen.ac.uk.

Pitts, J. (2008) *Reluctant Gangsters*, Cullompton: Willan Publishing.

Pitts, J. (2010) 'Mercenary Territory: Are Youth Gangs Really a Problem?' In Goldson, B. (ed.) (2011) *Youth in Crisis? Gang's, Territoriality and Violence*, London: Routledge.

Presdee, M. (2000) *Cultural Criminology and the Carnival of Crime*, London: Routledge.

Strange, S. (1996) *The Retreat of the State: The Diffusion of Power in the World Economy*, New York: Cambridge University Press.

Dr Aisha K Gill (B.A., M.A. [Di], PhD (University of Essex)) PGCHE, is a Reader in Criminology at University of Roehampton. Her main areas of interest and research are health and criminal justice responses to violence against black, minority ethnic and refugee (BMER) women in the UK, Iraqi Kurdistan and India. She has been involved in addressing the problem of violence against women (VAW) at the grassroots level for the past 14 years. Her current research interests include rights, law and forced marriage; gendered crimes related to patriarchy; 'honour' killings and 'honour'-based violence in the South Asian/Kurdish Diaspora and femicide in Iraqi Kurdistan and India; missing women; acid violence; post-separation violence and child contact; trafficking; and sexual violence; gender and the England riots.

Professor Liz Kelly is a feminist researcher and activist, who has worked in the field of violence against women and children for over 30 years. She is the author of *Surviving Sexual Violence*, and many book chapters, journal articles and research reports. She is director of the Child and Woman Abuse Studies Unit (CWASU), London Metropolitan University, which is recognised as one of the world leading research centres on violence against women. The Unit has completed over 100 research projects (see www.cwasu.org for a complete list) and are known for their work on making connections — between forms of gender-based violence, and between violence against women and abuse of children. CWASU also run the only MA on Woman and Child Abuse in Europe, with students from the UK, Europe, Africa, Asia and Latin America. The MA has been designed to provide 'thinking time' for practitioners, to deepen their understanding and reflect on practice from the global North and South. Liz Kelly has been Professor of Sexualised Violence since 2000 and in 2006 she was appointed Roddick Chair of Violence Against Women.

11

READING THE RIOTS THROUGH GENDER:
A FEMINIST REFLECTION ON ENGLAND'S 2011 RIOTS

Liz Kelly and Aisha K. Gill

Introduction

From August 2011 to February 2012, the members of 'Rotis Not Riots', a Facebook-based discussion forum, devoted considerable time and effort to developing a more nuanced, gendered perspective on the riots, the media coverage, and political and policy responses (Kelly and Gill, 2012). The group was set up during the riots with the specific aim of providing a space for feminists to discuss ways to make sense of these events, and has since become a key location for uploading and discussing research on, and commentaries about, the disorder and its implications. Whilst this chapter does not examine these discussions in detail (see Kelly and Gill, 2012), the informal debates on the forum sparked our interest in discovering whether the same key themes were reflected in recent scholarly publications. This chapter therefore explores the extent to which gender was addressed in research and academic commentaries on the 2011 riots in England.

To illuminate this issue, we read two key pieces of research — the interim report of the 'Reading the Riots' study, undertaken by *The Guardian* and London School of Economics (LSE) (2011), and the NatCen project 'The August Riots in London', commissioned by the government (Morrell, *et al*, 2011). We also looked to commentaries on the riots and feminist analyses of previous disorders. Our analysis was structured around three key questions:

1. Is it possible to 'reduce' an analysis of gender to a simple examination of how many men and women were involved?

2. Are women saying similar/different things to male research participants, including both those who took part in the rioting and/or looting and those who did not?

3. To what extent has gender been drawn on to explore the meanings of rioting, looting, protest and community?

The questions reflect our initial observation that, as with work on crime and violence in general, 'gender' is often read as being about women and girls, with little attention paid to men and boys. This contrasts with contemporary gender theory, which explores the construction of both femininity and masculinity. We examine examples of the theoretical frameworks that have emerged from gender theory, demonstrating how they can add an important new dimension to analysis and understanding of the England riots in August 2011. We do not rehearse the events that took place in August 2011 (see *Chapter 2* of this volume for a detailed discussion), focusing instead on the ways in which a more detailed gender analysis can illuminate both alternative narratives about these events and significant gaps in current knowledge.

Theories of Gender and Crime

The Independent Riots, Communities and Victims Panel (IRCVP) interim report made eleven key recommendations, warning that 'while deprivation is not an excuse for criminal behaviour, we must seek to tackle the underlying causes of the riots, or they will happen again' (IRCVP, 2011:14). Concern with the underlying causes of crime, and violent disorder in particular, is a recurrent theme in both academic studies and public policy, but it is one in which gender has occupied a marginal place.

In the mid-1970s, feminist psychologists and criminologists began to explore the links between gender and crime in an effort to explain both why so few women were involved in violent crime and whether violent women were subjected to disproportionate attention and opprobrium. This work challenged explanations that took gender differences for granted and assumed they did not require interrogation (Heidensohn, 1985; Chesney-Lind, 1997). Empirical studies soon followed; these explored girls' aggression in relation to the impact of their family (Viermero, 1996), peers (Messer and Gross, 1994) and school (Artz and Riecken, 1997). These studies highlighted a connection between girls' violence and: (i) their victimisation (physical and sexual) (Chesney-Lind, 1997); (ii) violence in the context of relational disruption (Jack, 1999); and (iii) violence committed for self-protection (Maher and Daly, 1996).

However, many of these studies employed definitions of 'gender' that were similar to those used in previous studies of 'sex': gender was treated as a simple binary, with socialisation the key to explaining behavioural similarities and differences between women and men. Studies focusing on difference tended to posit that violence had distinct emotional roots for men and women, with women's violence being primarily 'expressive' and men's, primarily 'instrumental' (Heidensohn, 1985). Conversely, those who adopted 'similarity' as their point of departure emphasised the impact of shared life experiences and social positioning, especially socio-economic disadvantage (Smart, *et al*, 2001). Each theoretical approach has been revisited and developed, but a common premise in studies of women's violence is that as women achieve greater equality, their rates of criminal offending will increase and start to align with those of their male counterparts (see, e.g., Campbell (1994) on female gangs).

Critically, both positions take men's use of violence and criminality as a norm, to which women's behaviour is compared—what in feminist theory has been termed 'male universalism'. This, in turn, results in a failure to interrogate assumptions about gender in approaches to explaining crime and violence. This lacuna is also evident in how the concept of 'youth', and especially disadvantaged youth, has been employed in research and policy: despite the fact that females and males face similar conditions and limitations in impoverished inner-city neighbourhoods (Herrenkohl *et al*, 2000), the literature has focused almost exclusively on how deleterious neighbourhood conditions influence the behaviour of adolescent males (Ensminger, *et al*, 1996). It is only in the last decade that studies of violence linked to neighbourhood effects and the social environment have incorporated larger female samples (Ingoldsby and Shaw, 2002; Sampson, 2002). Currently, few criminological and social policy studies on 'youth' involve critical gender analysis (Cf. Firmin, 2011). Thus, it remains the case that the ostensibly ungendered categories of 'youth' and 'young people' are implicitly assumed to comprise young men. As a result, attempts to illuminate the relationships between gender, crime and criminality have tended to focus on women, since gender is seldom deemed a significant analytical concept with regard to men.[1] Moreover, most studies continue to draw on conceptions that treat gender as a relatively fixed personality or identity construct within a rigid, dichotomous social system (Cameron and Scanlon, 2010).

In contrast, some contemporary gender theorists argue that gender is always in a reciprocal process of change, and that its social construction continues throughout life: both masculinity and femininity are achieved through 'doing gender' in interactions with others and in relation to normative expectations. There has also been considerable work on variations in gender construction across time, space and socio-economic strata. For example, Connell (2002) suggests that all gender constructs are located within an overarching 'gender order' in which individuals are positioned in relation to a 'hegemonic' masculinity that sets the standard for 'real' (i.e. successful) manhood. This school of thought suggests that, in most western societies, hegemonic masculinity centres on being employed, white and heterosexual. Men who are excluded from these social realms are relegated to 'subordinated' masculinities, while all femininities are subordinated to hegemonic masculinity. Femininities that conform to current norms are termed 'emphasized' femininities, while those that lie outside the norm may be considered 'resistant'. This framework suggests that the study of gender should always be context-specific, encompassing multiple masculinities and femininities as well as their potential overlap. This theoretical framework also presumes that gender is in flux, never being entirely stable: gender orders, gender regimes and gender relations change and adapt, as individuals 'live gender' in complex, intersecting contexts (see also Crenshaw, 1992).

Meanwhile, Eva Lundgren has introduced the concept of 'gender constitution' (1995) to explain how individuals continually become men/women, and how gender influences our everyday lives through both conformity and

---

1. Parallel arguments have been made about race and sexuality regarding the fact that both 'whiteness' and 'heterosexuality' have been implicitly accepted as the 'norm' and, hence, have not been subjected to critical scrutiny.

challenge to current normative frameworks. In her research on intimate partner violence, she argues that in using violence men 'constitute' their masculinity while seeking to enforce a desired femininity in their female victims. Here, violence is not just gendered, but specific masculinities and femininities are (re-)created through its ongoing use, and its impact on and meanings for both victims and perpetrators. Lundgren's interpretation, thus, has wider relevance, including to violence in the public sphere.

Critically, while feminist approaches have directed attention to the relevance of gender analysis in explaining the criminality of women and girls, the question of why law-breaking, and especially violent offending are predominantly masculine activities, remains neglected in both criminology and public policy research.

Reading the Riots

Before reading the two key research studies on the riots through the lens of gender, we present official data on those processed through the criminal justice system for their part in the events of August 2011. Both of the seminal studies we explore sought to distinguish between 'protest', 'rioting', 'looting', 'damage' and 'observing' in terms of what those who participated actually 'did'. However, as the NatCen (Morrell, *et al*, 2011) study points out these activities did not represent mutually exclusive categories. Both studies devote limited attention to gender in their analyses, with the exception of noting that most of the 'rioters' were male, with the women and girls involved depicted primarily as non-violent 'looters'. As Bagguley (2011) argues:

> While the identities of those involved [in riots] may vary, different types of disorder tends [sic] to attract different social groups.... In terms of direct conflict with the police, it is mostly young men, but in terms of looting, it's more mixed [with both] young men and young women involved.[2]

Moreover, the fact that women and girls were involved is far from unprecedented; however, it was considered newsworthy because crime and the use of violence still lie outside most normative constructs of femininity.

---

2. Topping, A (2011) 'Looting "fuelled by social exclusion"': www.guardian.co.uk/uk/2011/aug/08/looting-fuelled-by-social-exclusion (last accessed 19 February 2012).

The Ministry of Justice (MOJ) has since published two statistical bulletins (MOJ, 2011) on the 1,984 people who appeared before the courts on or before 12 October 2011 for offences relating to the August disorder. Just over a quarter of suspects (26) were aged 10-17, while the majority (53 per cent) were young adults under 20 and the remaining fifth (21 per cent) were adults over 20 (MOJ, 2011). Of the young people aged 10-17, the vast majority (88 per cent) were male (MOJ, October 2011: 28). Overall, the percentage of women and girls involved (12 per cent) was not that much higher than in previous disorders, such as the 1991 riots (Campbell, 1994). Where ethnicity was recorded, the data shows that 37 per cent of suspects were white, while a similar proportion (40 per cent) were black and only six per cent were Asian; however, these ratios varied significantly from area to area, reflecting the ethnic makeup of the local population (MOJ, 2011). While useful, these data are limited in two key ways: first, those individuals brought before the courts comprise only a subset of those who took part in the disorder; and, second, it was easier for the police to bring charges against those who did not hide their faces and also those who were involved in looting, which may have boosted the identification of female suspects as women are both less likely to be experienced in law-breaking and more likely to have participated in looting.

The dominant images of the August riots—and the political debates that ensued—focused on groups of angry men. However, 21 per cent (n=56) of the 270 interviews conducted for the 'Reading the Riots' study involved women or girls (Topping, Diski and Clifton, 9 December 2011): in other words, the sampling may be disproportionate, since it represents double the percentage of women and girls who were brought before the courts in relation to the disorder. More than half (n=133) of the 206 young people interviewed in the NatCen study (Morrell, *et al*, 2011) were not directly involved in the disturbances; however, gender statistics are only provided for the sample as a whole. Therefore, while 65 women and girls took part in the study (31 per cent), it is not possible to draw any conclusions about the extent or nature of women and girl's involvement. While we welcome the fact that these studies draw attention to female involvement in the disorder, there is a danger that this 'over-sampling'—interviewing a higher proportion of women and girls than was actually involved in the riots in order to ensure their visibility within the research — may be read as indicating that between a fifth and a third of rioters/looters were female. This seems unlikely given that the documentary and criminal justice evidence tells a different story that is consistent with previous disorders in that few women or girls were involved in direct confrontations with the police or in breaking into commercial properties.

Participants in both studies claimed that enduring grievances — especially poor relationships with the police due to excessive use of stop and search powers and dispersal orders to prevent groups meeting in public spaces — were among their main reasons for rioting. The motivations behind looting, however, were generally more complex. In 'Reading the Riots', nearly half (43 per cent) of the women and girls who were interviewed reported having been stopped and searched (Topping, Diski and Clifton, 9 December, 2011); while this figure is considerably lower than that for the male participants (78 per cent), women and girls also expressed anger at the police's treatment of men in their social networks. Indeed, some female interviewees spoke of feeling more afraid of the police than the rioters, especially when officers began to take more assertive action to quell the disorder.

Unfortunately, the decision to use the ungendered descriptor 'young person', rather than a gender-specific term, renders it impossible to analyse the NatCen data with regard to gender.[3] However, a web-based report on 'Reading the Riots' offers more detail about the range of behaviours young women engaged in during the disorder (Topping, Diski and Clifton, 9 December 2011). Not only were women and girls more likely to be involved in looting, but the things they took were often different from those taken by young men: women and girls tended to steal lower-value items or pick up the spoils others had left behind. In images published by the police and national press, women and girls were shown taking jeans, shoes, crisps, fizzy drinks, nappies, bottles of wine, cigarettes and bags of Tesco value Basmati rice ('London Riots 2011', 3 February 2012; *Daily Mail* Reporter, 9 August 2011). This was poignantly highlighted by one of the NatCen interviewees, who described her actions as 'doing her weekly shopping for free'.

---

3. In conversation, one of the authors explained that the short timescale of the study, and the fact that the central aim was to explore why young people did or did not participate in the disorder, precluded a deeper analysis of gender. However, in some instances the text implies the gender of particular participants.

Almost two thirds of the 150 Members of Parliament who responded to the 2011 ComRes survey believed that greed and opportunism were the key motives behind the disorder; however, this does not reflect the results of the 'Reading the Riots' and NatCen studies. Although many of those who took part in looting referred to the 'buzz' and excitement of being involved, as well as the thrill of obtaining 'free stuff', the banality of many of the items taken by female looters suggests that many did not, in fact, feel that they were entitled to help themselves to high-value consumer items. An interesting theme in the 'Rotis not Riots' discussions revolved around the need for explorations of the links between consumerism and masculinity (Kelly and Gill, 2012): an insight that is confirmed by these findings but is yet to be addressed in any depth.

The importance of recognition from peers and a wider — indeed, global — audience was another recurring theme in interviews with those who had participated in the disorder. However, many media reports centred on accounts of female adolescents gratuitously victimising other members of society. The phrase 'girls gone wild', used by female adolescents to represent their own aggressive behaviour as well as by the authorities — though with vastly different connotations — came to signify the essence of the phenomenon for many. The fact that significant numbers of girls were involved meant that they could not be seen as a tiny minority who had 'lost their way'. Instead, their involvement challenged the stereotype that rioting, looting and violence are anathema to women and girls, feeding into the media's framing of the disturbances as utter chaos brought about by the dissolution of the normal social order. This does not mean that participants showed no remorse. For example, the 16-year-old quoted below expressed regret over her involvement (quoted in Topping, Diski and Clifton, 9 December 2011):

> It's stupid because now everyone's thinking why did we actually do it? Like, you didn't really benefit from it; if anything we're just thinking what did we do to where we live? You're basically breaking your own community.

Both studies reported that women and girls who did not take part in the disturbances were critical of the disorder as a whole, though some distinguished between the initial rioting, seeing this as a legitimate protest, and the looting and destruction that followed. The section on gender from the 'Reading the Riots' study also notes that women and girls were more likely to report having been scared by the events, both as participants and as bystanders (Topping, Diski and Clifton, 9 December 2011). These observations are intriguing, hinting at the possibilities that the violence and destruction created a deeper sense of insecurity for women and girls, and that for some woman and girls the 'buzz' that seemed to animate many participants in the riots was of a complicated sort.

Unfortunately, without an in-depth analysis of the interview material through the lens of gender it is not possible to draw further conclusions. In this regard, it is worth noting that there were no references to gender in the live blog of the 'Reading the Riots' conference, nor does the issue feature even once in more than 200 comments on the blog (Owen, 14 December 2011). Thus, although the 2011 riots followed the general pattern of previous uprisings in Britain, the involvement of women and girls became a focus of populist discourses while remaining at the margins of scholarship.

Desperately Seeking Gender Analysis

As these two key studies offered little analysis of gender beyond comparing the numbers of women and men involved in the disorder, we undertook additional internet research to locate commentaries that addressed gender as a framing concept; this produced thousands of results. The first 70 were examined in detail, but most after this point related to either 'riot girls' (an underground feminist punk movement, which began in the 1990s in America) or 'Gender Riots' (a music track by the German women's band Sister). Only one source offered a critical examination of masculinity, while several academic pieces examined femininity and one blog bemoaned the limited focus on female transgression (Rad Geek, 27 August 2011):

> I'm very interested in how the media has been portraying women in the context
> of the recent UK riots. I've seen some of the usual things, like hysteria centred
> on young women transgressing that doesn't hit young men in the same way, or
> hand-wringing 'Why'?'- type articles about 'good girls gone bad'.... However
> it would be great to get some submissions on specific stories people see in the
> press about women involved in the events (as perpetrators, victims, bystanders,

officers of the law etc.) to start compiling some kind of mosaic of how gender interplays with them.

We concur with this observation, but argue that a further dimension of analysis is needed: one centred on unpicking whether there was a difference in girls' versus adult women's involvement. Currently, the available evidence is extremely limited and only offers ammunition for speculation as to whether girls were more motivated by a sense of injustice and/or excitement, and older women, by the reasons behind the initial protest and a desire to be visible among the community members seeking to quell the disorder in their neighbourhoods.

Although the Economic and Social Research Council's 'Sociology and the Cuts' website stresses the importance of sociologists' contributions to debates on the riots, only one contribution addresses gender in any depth (Allen and Taylor, 2012). This paper focuses on what the authors term 'the (hyper) visibility of women' in media reports and, particularly, their representation as 'troubled' mothers. This trope locates women as parents, specifically working-class or welfare-dependent mothers, who are responsible for the behaviour of their children. The policy announcement by David Cameron (Wintour, 15 December 2011) that 'chaotic families' are to be targeted through new funding measures fits this implicitly gendered framing. As Allen and Taylor (2012) argue, such 'public discourses of "troubled families" and poor parenting are … easily and problematically collapsed into one of "failed mothering"'.

On the other hand, the authors also note that women were prominent in depictions of community members clearing up after the disorder. Both this and the image of troubled mothers locate women in conventional, feminised positions in line with Connell's notion of 'emphasised femininities' (2002). Allen and Taylor (2012) claim that these framing devices also reinforce socio-economic distinctions, a process they term 'class making':

> The gendering of the riots tells us many things, but perhaps most importantly that classed and racialised distinctions and boundaries of failed and ideal femininities are becoming more accentuated under the Coalition Government and its austerity policies.

Despite raising important issues about how government policies and austerity measures are not only disproportionately burdening women and reconfiguring femininity in relation to race and class, the paper only genders the riots with respect to women. The only publication that includes a detailed discussion of masculinity also appears on the web (Bailey, 13 October 2011). Bailey explores young men's accounts of what they 'got' from rioting, identifying five key themes:

1. The desire to be part of, and contribute to, a group, even if that group is a gang or riot mob;

2. The thrill of empowerment and feeling in control;

3. The purposefulness of being part of a focused activity;

4. The value of a clear 'pecking order' in which people know where they stand and what is required to rise to the next level; and

5. The importance of sharing norms with a defined group, even if these norms are not shared by society at large.

Bailey (2011) goes on to argue that, in post-industrial Britain, the disappearance of traditional routes for boys to make the transition to adulthood contributes to the appeal of riots, gangs and other predominantly male peer groups. As this analysis shows, gender has not been a core theme in research or commentaries on the 2011 riots (to date), though it has featured in a few thoughtful reflections published on the internet. However, two key studies of similar riots in the 20th century suggest that this is not because gender has limited relevance to understanding and interpreting recent events.

Gendered Spaces and Social Geographies

The social geography of the August riots (BBC, 2012) solicited paradoxical responses: many discourses constructed the crisis as posing the biggest threat to those who turned out to be least affected. In narratives that spanned the spectrum of popular, academic and political discourses, spatial correlations between crime and poverty were simplistically interpreted as causal links (Lammy, 2011). Socially conservative discourses added to the rhetoric, offering both diagnoses and potential remedies based on the idea that London's urban poor had been cultured into making unwise choices, with the corollary that crime is most effectively curbed through stronger law enforcement responses and deterrent-based sentencing. Recently, the role of parental discipline was introduced to the public debate by the Member of Parliament for Tottenham, David Lammy (2012), who bemoaned the limitations placed on smacking children. The suggestion that violence (of any type) is an effective solution to violent disorder is both logically and morally dubious. Moreover, Lammy's framing of the issue is also implicitly linked to discourses that criticise single mothers: he invokes stereotypes of fathers as dispensers of discipline to illuminate the difficulties that stem from the absence of fathers (or positive father figures) in young men's lives. However, it is not absent fathers who receive the lion's share of the blame as Lammy is keen to hand that to single mothers.

Feminist analyses of previous riots offer a different perspective on which issues we should focus on. For instance, historian Marilynn Johnson (2002) explores three mid-20th century American 'race riots' through the lens of gender, noting that most previous scholarly work had looked only at the participation of women in terms of arrest rates: studies of women's participation showed higher levels of involvement, especially where looting was concerned. More importantly for our purposes, she notes how little attention had previously been paid to the gendered assumptions and ideologies that underpinned individual and group behaviour; few studies had traced the sequence of gendered engagements that preceded the riots and continued throughout them. In her review of previous research, she demonstrates that women rarely featured as riot instigators, though they appeared in many accounts both as looters and as community members seeking to prevent the arrest of family members and neighbours. Critically, Johnson (2002: 255) challenges the view that to be considered active agents women must act like men, arguing instead that their involvement is often structured through conventionally feminine roles as 'consumers, victims, protectors'.

Johnson's insightful analysis draws on gender as a key intersectional category: she explores how the complex interplay of race and gender lit the tinder that ignited the riots then continued to fan the flame behind the disorder. She illuminates how the symbolic importance of both rumours and real cases of gendered and interracial violence against women sparked two of three riots: police brutality and 'man-handling of a pregnant Black woman' were evident in the Watts riot (*Ibid.*, p.271), which was echoed in Detroit in 1967, revealing the significance of white aggression 'towards bodies of symbolically significant black individuals' (*Ibid.*, p.271). Similar real and rumoured incidents were widely reported as the touchstone that transformed the protest over lack of information about the shooting of Mark Duggan into the riot that sparked the wider disorder in England during August 2011. Thus, Johnson suggests that the intersections of race and gender offer a key to understanding how collective violence can be linked to notions of gender and family, which in turn construct notions of race.

Bea Campbell's *Goliath* (1993) examines gender, class and race in relation to the riots that took place in England during the summer of 1991. However, this ground-breaking text has hardly been mentioned in the commentary on the 2011 riots, despite the obvious parallels. For example, recent stories from the 2011 riots echo Campbell's accounts of mothers desperately trying to prevent their sons from taking part in the riots but failing to mute the power of peer groups. The book presents a dense, rich and at times lyrical evocation of the confrontation between 'incendiary young bucks' and the 'Boys in Blue' (*Ibid.*, p.4): two masculinities battling for control over public spaces. At least two of the 1991 riots were sparked by disputes about young men's use and attempted control of specific public spaces. These were sites of struggle 'over young men's criminality and control over their shared streets' (*Ibid.*, p.168). Campbell suggests that while these young men positioned themselves as victims deprived of respect by wider society, many in their communities perceived them as intimidating: the housing estates they lived on had, in the eyes of many inhabitants, become social spaces '*increasingly regulated by organized crime and masculine tyrannies*' (*Ibid.*, p.177).

This crisis of masculinity, Campbell (1993) argues, was linked to the absence of opportunities in the local area for meaningful employment, result-ing in many young men spending a large proportion of their time on the streets in their local neighbourhoods: spaces traditionally associated with notions of community as built and sustained by women. Unaware of, or unconcerned about, normal daily life in these spaces, young men laid claim to them, creating a sense of unease and insecurity on the part of the local women and older people who had previously used them with relative ease.

Campbell (1983) reminds us that a key, though often unheeded, message in the Scarman Report on the 1981 riots revolves around the strength of the extended black family: sustained by women, this strength is often undermined by the dislocation of women's networks and the absence of social support, especially as a result of public spending cuts in times of recession. The book warns against treating mothers as part of the problem rather than part of the solution. Campbell's conclusions offer food for thought in the current context: she argues that 'crime is one of the cultures in which young men achieve the mantle of manhood' (*Ibid.* p.211), pointing to the ways in which the conquest of public space is often an important route to constructing oneself as a man, but simultaneously contributes to the 'erosion of cooperative use of public space' (*Ibid.*, p.320). This analysis of the importance of constructions of what in Connell's framework (2002) would be termed 'subordinated masculinities', based on ownership of public spaces in contexts offering dwindling employment opportunities and no alternative models of masculinity, deserves serious consideration in relation to the events of the summer of 2011.

Discussion

Returning to the questions posed at the start of the chapter, we conclude that there has been very limited engagement with the issue of gender in both research and commentaries on the 2011 riots. Not only is there is little documentation of the involvement of women and girls in the disorder, but it seems that there has been over-sampling in some key research studies. Moreover, failures to refer to the conclusions of research on similar previous riots have created space for the media to invoke a variety of well-established tropes. Critically, conventional models of femininity have been used to suggest that it was strange that so many women and girls were involved, despite the fact that similar ratios of male versus female participants were evident in previous riots, which also saw a higher number of women involved in looting as opposed to rioting. What a more complex gender analysis offers is an alternative to characterising women's involvement as 'acting like men' and, instead, drawing attention to the ways such tropes are linked to particular constructions of femininity, with some aspects reflecting emphasised femininities and others, resistant femininities (Connell, 2009).

The 'Reading the Riots' and NatCen studies offer evidence that women and girls were motivated to protest about enduring grievances common to many inner-city areas, especially complaints over the targeting of 'young people' in the policing of public spaces. The fact that many participants across both studies identified with the collective noun 'young people' suggests that multiple, overlapping peer groups, only some of which are gendered, hold significant currency in the present context. This, in turn, raises the question of whether use of public spaces may be gendered in different ways to those described in *Goliath* (Campbell, 1993). However, at present there is a paucity of research data that addresses both how the wider community in the areas affected understands and interprets the 2011 disorder, and how (and, indeed, whether) the August 2011 disturbances reflect ongoing tensions between genders and generations.

This does not mean, however, that the questions raised by earlier studies are no longer relevant. The limited number of spaces available for young people to meet in may mean that public spaces are now even more important. However, while the frustration that many young people voice about being seen as threatening by adults has been well documented, too little attention has been paid to the fact that some individuals, and groups of young men in particular, experience pleasure and a sense of power through claiming public spaces as 'theirs', intimidating other members of the community who seek to use these spaces.

Uneasy relations between different races and ethnic groups fuel these feelings: the real dangers and social problems that plague many inner-city neighbourhoods then reinforce them. This has deep ramifications for how people live in the areas affected by the riots and how they think about one another. Instead of focusing solely on police responses, we need to consider why 'street'-centred notions of masculinity often result in some community members feeling anxious in, and even excluded from, public spaces, especially since there are indications that a significant number of young women also identify with and participate in 'street'-centred constructions of gender. How can the use of public spaces become more cooperative in diverse communities? In *Goliath*, Campbell (1993) challenged discourses about the 1981 riots that found fault with 'families', using this umbrella term as a politically correct way to point the finger specifically at mothers and especially single mothers. Recognising women's strengths, particularly in terms of their willingness to invest in social networks, offers a different discourse on how to move forwards: one centred on community building, rather than punishment and exclusion, in which gender is both a theoretical and practical resource.

References

Allen, K., Taylor, Y. (2012) 'Failed Femininities and Troubled Mothers: Gender and the Riots', *Sociology and the Cuts* (British Sociological Association), 17 January 2012: http://sociologyandthecuts.wordpress.com/2012/01/17/failed-femininities-and-troubled-mothers-gender-and-the-riots-by-kim-allen-and-yvette-taylor/ (Last accessed 8 February 2012).

Artz, S., Riecken, T. (1997) 'What, So What, Then What? The Gender Gap in School-based Violence and Its Implications for Child and Youth Care Practice', *Child and Youth Care Forum*. 26: 291-303.

Bagguley, P. (2011) 'Who are troublemakers behind UK riots?': http://articles.cnn.com/2011-08-09/world/uk.riots.identity_1_riot-low-income-young-people?_s=PM:WORLD (Last accessed 8 February 2012).

Bailey, A. (2011) 'Rioting… It's a gender thing…' *A Band of Brothers*, 13 October 2011: http://www.abandofbrothers.org.uk/thoughts-from-us/2011/10/13/rioting-its-a-gender-thing.html (Last accessed 8 February 2012).

BBC (2011) 'London Riots: Metropolitan Police Response Report: http://www.bbc.co.uk/news/uk-england-london-15433404 (Last accessed 15 February 2012).

Beckford, M., Gardham, D. (8 August 2011) ''Attack' on teenage girl blamed for start of Tottenham riot', The *Daily Telegraph*: http://www.telegraph.co.uk/news/uknews/crime/8687547/Attack-on-teenage-girl-blamed-for-start-of-Tottenham-riot.html (Last accessed 8 February 2011).

Campbell, A. (1984) *The Girls in the Gang*. Oxford: Basil Blackwell.

Campbell, B. (1993) *Goliath: Britain's Dangerous Places*. London: Methuen.

Cameron, D., Scanlon, J. (2010) 'Talking about Gender', *Trouble and Strife*: http://www.troubleandstrife.org/?page_id=527 (Last accessed 8 February 2012).

Chesney-Lind, M. (1997) *The Female Offender: Girls, Women and Crime*. Thousand Oaks, CA: Sage.

Chesney-Lind, M., Pasko, L. (eds.) (2003) *Girls, Women and Crime*: Selected Readings, New York: Sage.

Connell, R. (2002) *Gender*. Cambridge: Polity Press.

ComRes (2011) 'UK Riots: The Views of MPs': http://www.comres.co.uk/blog-post/12/uk-riots-the-views-of-mps.htm (Last accessed 8 February 2012).

Crenshaw, K. (1992) 'Mapping the Margins: Intersectionality, Identity Politics, and Violence Against Women of Colour'. *Stanford Law Review,* Vol. 43.

Daily Mail Reporter (2011) 'They stole EVERYTHING! Shelves stripped bare and shops ransacked as looters pillage London high streets', *Mail Online,* 9 August 2011: http://www.dailymail.co.uk/news/article-2024012/LONDON-RIOTS-2011-They-stole-EVERYTHING-Enfield-Clapham-shops-stripped-bare.html (Last accessed 8 February 2012).

Ensminger, M., Lamkin, R., and Jacobson, N. (1996) 'School Leaving: A Longitudinal Perspective Including Neighbourhood Effects, *Child Development,* 67, 2400-2416.

Firmin, C. (2011) 'This is It. This is My Life: The Female Voice in Violence Report'. London, ROTA: http://www.rota.org.uk/?q=category/publications/research-publications (Last accessed 25 February, 2012).

Heidensohn, F. (1985) *Women and Crime,* New York, University Press.

Heidensohn, F. (1994) 'Gender and Crime', in M. Maguire, R., R. Morgan and R. Reiner (eds.) *The Oxford Handbook of Criminology.* Oxford: Clarendon Press.

Herrenkohl, T., Mason, W., Kosterman, R., Lengua, L., Hawkins, J., and Abbott, R. (2004). 'Pathways from Physical Childhood Abuse to Partner Violence in Young Adulthood. *Violence Victimology,* 19(2), 123-136.

Home Affairs Select Committee (2011) 'Policing Large Scale Disorder: Lessons From the Disturbances of August 2011', Home Affairs Select Committee: http://www.tvpfed.org/media/documents/policinglargescaledisorder.pdf (Last accessed 8 February 2012).

Ingoldsby, E., Shaw, D. (2002) 'Neighbourhood Contextual Factors and the Onset and Progression of Early-starting Antisocial Pathways, *Clinical Child and Family Psychology Review,* 5, 21-55.

Independent Police Complaints Commission (2011) IPCC Press Release, 'IPCC investigates MPS handling of alleged assault involving firearm' 18 November 2011.

Independent Riots, Communities and Victims Panel, 'Remit', 2011: http://riotspanel.independent.gov.uk/ (Last accessed 17 February 2012).

Johnson, M. (2002) 'Gender, Race and Rumours: Re-examining the 1943 Race Riots'. *Gender and History*, 10:2, 252-277.

Kelly, L., Gill, A. (2012) 'Rotis not Riots: A Feminist Dialogue on the Riots and their Aftermath', *Safer Communities Journal*, 11, 1: 61-72.

Lammy, D. (2011) *David Lammy: Tottenham Past and Present—A Memoir*: http://www.guardian.co.uk/books/2011/nov/18/david-lammy-out-of-ashes (Last accessed 8 February 2012).

London Riots (2011) 'Do you know these looting suspects? Police release just TWELVE pictures (but we've found 30 more to be going on with)', 3 February 2012: http://londonriots.org.uk/2011/pictures-of-london-riots/do-you-know-these-looting-suspects-police-release-just-twelve-pictures-but-weve-found-30-more-to-be-going-on-with/#ixzz1kQB49Jow (Last accessed 11 February 2012).

Lundgren, E. (1995) *Feminist Theory and Violent Empiricism*, Aldershot: Avebury.

Maher, L., Daly, K. (1996) Women in the Street-level Drug Economy: Continuity or Change? *Criminology*, 34, 465-491.

Messer, S., Gross, A. (1994) 'Childhood Depression and Aggression: A Covariance Structure Analysis', *Behaviour, Research, Therapy*, 32: 663-677.

Ministry of Justice (2011) *Statistical Bulletin on the Public Disorder of 6th to 9th August 2011*: http://www.justice.gov.uk/downloads/publications/statistics-and-data/mojstats/august-public-disorder-stats-bulletin.pdf (Last accessed 15 February 2012).

Morrell, G., Scott, S., McNeish, D. and Webster, S. (2011) *The August Riots in England: Understanding the Involvement of Young People*, London: NatCen.

Owen, P. (2011) 'Reading the Riots Conference—Wednesday 14 December 2011 Ed Miliband, Theresa May and Yvette Cooper speak at *The Guardian*/LSE conference on the summer disorder, *The Guardian*, 14 December 2011: http://www.guardian.co.uk/uk/blog/2011/dec/14/reading-the-riots-conference-live-blog (Last accessed 8 February 2012).

Rad Geek People's Daily (2011) 'Rad Geek, "Riots and gender"', 27 August 2011: http://radgeek.com/gt/2011/08/27/riots-and-gender/ (Last accessed 8 February 2012).

Reading the Riots, 'Reading the Riots: Investigating England's Summer of Disorder', *The Guardian* and The London School of Economics and

Political Science, 14 December 2011: http://s3.documentcloud.org/documents/274239/reading-the-riots.pdf (Last accessed 18 February 2012).

Riots, Communities and Victims Panel, 'Five Days in August: An Interim Report on the 2011 English Riots', 28 November 2011: http://www.5daysinaugust.co.uk/PDF/downloads/Interim-Report-UK-Riots.pdf (Last accessed 17 February 2012).

Sampson, R. (2001). 'Crime and Public Safety: Insights From Community-level Perspectives on Social Capital', in Saegert, J. Thompson and Warren, M. (eds.), *Social Capital and Poor Communities* (pp.189-212). New York: Russell Sage Foundation.

Smart, C., Neale, B., and Wade A. (2001) *The Changing Experience of Childhood: Families and Divorce*. Cambridge: Polity Press.

Smith, M. (2011) 'Young People and the 2011 "riots" in England—Experiences, Explanations and Implications for Youth Work': http://www.infed.org/archives/jeffs_and_smith/young_people_youth_work_and_the_2011_riots_in_england.html (Last accessed 8 February 2012).

Topping, A., Diski, R., Clifton, H. (2012) 'The Women Who Rioted: The dominant images of the August riots were of angry men, but our interviews suggest females were a significant presence', *The Guardian*, 9 December 2011: http://www.guardian.co.uk/uk/2011/dec/09/women-who-rioted-english-riots (Last accessed 11 February 2012).

Viemero, V. (1996) 'Factors in Childhood that Predict Later Criminal Behaviour', *Aggressive Behaviour*, 22, 87-97.

Wintour, P. (2011) 'Cameron puts £400m into helping families out of "responsibility deficit"'. *The Guardian*, 15 December: http://www.guardian.co.uk/society/2011/dec/15/cameron-400m-chaotic-families (Last accessed 15 February 2012).

Part III

THE AFTERMATH

Dr Joel Busher is a Research Fellow at the University of Huddersfield. His most recent research is an ethnography of English Defence League activism in Southeast England, based on 15 months of overt first-hand observation at formal and informal EDL events. He has presented on this research to academic and policy audiences, and the respective monograph 'Grassroots Nationalism' is scheduled for publication in 2013.

12

'THERE ARE NONE SICKER THAN THE EDL':
NARRATIVES OF RACIALISATION AND RESENTMENT FROM WHITEHALL AND ELTHAM, LONDON

Joel Busher

Introduction

From the evening of Sunday 7th August 2011 onwards, several groups of local residents had begun to mobilise in different parts of London in order to protect their neighbourhoods against rioting and looting. While the authorities moved to discourage vigilantism, social media such as Twitter and Facebook buzzed with largely celebratory reports of the Sikh community in Southall and of the shopkeepers and residents in Dalston and Harringay, many of whom were Turkish, who were reported to have deterred or chased off looters. On Tuesday afternoon reports also started to emerge that crowds, between 200 and 800 strong, had gathered in Eltham in South London and Enfield in North London. This time, however, the scene was rather different and so too were the politics that would quickly surround these events as it became apparent that the crowds comprised at least in part of a combination of members of local football firms[1] (mainly Millwall in the case of Eltham, Tottenham Hotspur in the case of Enfield) and the English Defence League (EDL). There were even claims that what purported to be a defence of local communities in Eltham was being organized by the EDL; one senior

---

1. People associated with football-related violence.

EDL activist at the time, who identified himself as 'Jack England', said in an interview to the *Daily Telegraph* (10th August, 2011):

> The police are unable to control the streets. Today, these are local people [from Eltham], not EDL, they are patriots that have come out to defend their area. So the EDL has come down, about 50 of us to manage them and control them and to sort of guide them to make sure they don't move out of order.

That Tuesday afternoon and evening, these crowds patrolled Eltham High Street for several hours and footage soon appeared on YouTube of people in Eltham chanting 'E-E-EDL' (see Video A). Some of the crowd were drinking heavily, and after a number of fairly minor public order incidents, the police dispersed the crowd, issuing some people with instructions not to return to the area within 48 hours under section 27 Violent Crime Reduction Act 2006. Despite this, the following night another crowd assembled and there were similar suggestions that the EDL were involved (*The Guardian* Blog, 10th August 2011). As one of the local EDL organizers posted on Facebook:

English Defence League — London Region

> The Barnet meeting has been canceled [sic[2]] tonight as we need people on the street to defend the innocent people & business which may come under attack by criminals. We have drafted in several hundred more EDL enforcement officers from outside London to help out in these times of crisis. Please, show our respect to the police & local communites as we protect and serve ENGLAND.

10 August at 18:50

Accessed from Facebook, 28th December 2011

This time, although the crowd was smaller — estimated to be no more than 200-300 — there was a far larger police presence, with ratios as high as four officers to every crowd member (*The Guardian* Blog, 10th August 2011). The rapport between the crowd and the police was also more hostile than

---

2. All Facebook posts have been left with their original spelling, grammar and punctuation.

the preceding evening and bottles were thrown at the police, who responded with baton charges.

In this chapter I revisit these events. I start the chapter by describing the EDL involvement in the crowds that gathered in Eltham and the response that stories about EDL involvement elicited from the media, police and politicians. I then consider how this short sequence of events was both shaped by and has been situated within: (a) media and mainstream political narratives about the threat of the far right in Britain; and (b) the counter-narratives of EDL activists and supporters and their claims about victimisation at the hands of the state and of mainstream media. In doing so, this chapter provides a further example of how the riots and events surrounding the riots provided a stage on which contemporary social divisions were played out.

In August 2011, I happened to be mid-way through 16 months of ethnographic research about EDL activism in London and the South East. This chapter makes use of a combination of field notes from meetings and informal conversations with EDL activists around the time of the riots; narrative interviews five months after the riots with two EDL activists who were in Eltham on both Tuesday and Wednesday; public interviews given by EDL activists at the time; and Facebook discussions between activists.

EDL Involvement in the Eltham Mobilisation

Since 2009, the EDL has become one of the UK's most controversial social movements. Its leadership, and many of the movement's activists, describe themselves as a peaceful protest group who are opposed only to the spread of 'militant Islam' and have sought to distance themselves from the 'traditional' far right and the racial violence associated with groups such as the National Front (Busher, forthcoming; Copsey, 2010; Jackson, 2011). However, EDL demonstrations have been marked by a number of instances of public disorder and some people who identify as EDL activists have been charged with undertaking religiously-aggravated crimes against Muslims. Certainly counter-EDL groups have rejected the EDL claims that it is a peaceful and legitimate protest movement, while most commentators in the mainstream media have also persisted in using adjectives like 'far right' or 'racist' when referring to the EDL. The police and Home Office also continue to keep a close eye on the movement due mainly to concerns about public disorder.

When the riots started to spread across London, EDL activists expressed opposing views on whether the group should intervene. However, at least initially the position of the local leadership was that this was not a matter in which the EDL ought to be directly involved:

English Defence League—London Region

In light of todays events, we have closed the [Facebook] wall for posting. Please let the Police do their job, and stay away from any trouble areas. This is a public order issue, and not the concern of the EDL. As a Londoner I am horrified and saddened by todays events (as we all are), if you require and further clarification—please contact your division leaders.

8 August at 21:28

Accessed from Facebook, 28th December 2011

This position was not without its critics within the movement. Some activists opined that somebody had to do something, and that perhaps the EDL were as able as anyone to organize groups to protect local neighbourhoods. In the four months prior to the riots, the EDL had undergone a reorganization in London and there were by this time several active borough-level EDL divisions that, it was suggested, could easily gather a group of around 50 people who would be willing to defend shops and other buildings. This was the response to the post cited above:

NAME

im as digusted as u about whats going on. as londoners i feels its our duty to protect our neighbourhoods, towns n cities.

8 August at 21:32

English Defence League—London Region

I understand your anger NAME, but the EDL is not a vigilante group

8 August at 21:42

NAME

It's shocking it's a shame as a group we the EDL can't do anything it saddens me to see what our country is going through so sad

8 August at 21:45

However, for the time being the EDL's position did not change, and broadly speaking the decision not to intervene was supported by activists in and around London. This was partly linked to a number of strategic considerations at the time. As the comments above indicate, there was some debate about the extent to which responding to the riots fitted with the EDL mission, and in recent months there had been growing calls from within the EDL activist community for the movement to retain what was seen to be its original focus: protesting against 'militant Islam'. A number of activists also pointed out that their involvement could further sour relations with the police—something EDL activists were keen to avoid as they had demonstrations planned for the near future. Furthermore, activists were also aware of how easily any response by the EDL to the riots could be framed in such a way as to be used as evidence that the EDL was, after all, a racist movement—an issue of considerable concern to people who had by this point spent more than two years trying to persuade the public and the media that they were neither 'extreme right wing' nor 'racist'.

This situation did begin to change, however, when locals and football casuals came together in Enfield and Eltham on Tuesday. From a strategic point of view, these mobilisations presented what promised to be a good and timely opportunity to network with one of the EDL's main constituencies: football casuals. EDL activists in London were already gearing up to distribute several thousand flyers, many of them to football fans in and around London, in the run up to their planned demonstration in Tower Hamlets at the beginning of September 2011. There were also some activists, like Jack, who saw these mobilisations as an opportunity for a wider public-relations coup, particularly as it seemed by this point that public opinion had swung quite firmly behind the groups that were gathering ostensibly to protect their neighbourhoods.

At this point, it is worth noting however that this shift in position was not mitigated only by such strategic considerations but also by basic psycho-social factors. This seems particularly to have been the case among EDL activists local to Eltham whom I spoke with who argued vehemently that they had gone out on the high street not '*as* EDL' at all (they weren't for example wearing 'colours' — EDL merchandise) but as local residents. For these people, the riots had arrived at their doorstep; they had strong social and cultural ties with the crowd gathering on Eltham High Street; there was something visceral about 'reclaiming the streets' after the chaos and disorder that had gripped London for the last three days and nights; and then there was the sheer buzz and excitement of simply being part of the crowd (see also Sampson, 2011). Whatever the strategic considerations of movement organisers may have been, local activists had no intention of missing out on this:

> I was, I was out working, phone goes. My wife's told me that the boy [his son] and some of his mates had decided that they were going to come up to Eltham and protect Eltham, in fact she said they were already up there, this was in the afternoon. Err, I'd been out since about half past three in the morning, got in about half past six, nobody indoors, wife was out, as she normally is on a Tuesday night. I phoned and she told me to stay indoors because there was about 300 or 400 people up there all protecting the High Street [laughs] which... that was, na I can't stay away from that! I've gone up there and see if I can find the boy and everything else, when I got up here there was 200 people milling about...

> Dave,[3] *EDL activist, 19*[th] *Jan 2012*

---

3. All the respondent names used in this chapter are pseudonyms.

The evidence suggests, however, that in spite of the obvious allure of these crowds, the number of regular EDL activists who went up to Eltham High Street was some way short of the 50 that Jack had claimed. In and around London, there is only a core of approximately 200-300 activists who frequently attend demonstrations and other events, most of whom recognise one another. Of these people, independent estimates from five sources, three of whom were present in Eltham on Tuesday and Wednesday, put the numbers at around eight to ten on Tuesday, and less than this on Wednesday (numbers also in line with comments circulating among members of the Millwall casuals communities). Of these, at least four were from Eltham and one of the others had only travelled the five miles from Bexleyheath.

When pressed about the video footage that showed people chanting 'E-E-EDL', local EDL activists were dismissive, arguing that most of the people that had been chanting 'EDL' had no involvement with the movement and were just joining in with what was going on around them. They even claimed that 'EDL' was not referring to the *English* Defence League but, in a rather tongue-in-cheek way, to the '*Eltham* Defence League' — a claim repeated several times in conversations with EDL activists and some football casuals after the events. One activist said:

> They were just using the EDL as jumping on a band wagon, and it turned out they were using the 'EDL' as the 'Eltham Defence League'.... All the people up there walking down the streets going 'E-E-EDL' and 'England belongs to me' and all that, like doing all the EDL songs, that was Jack [see above] that started that because he was going up to all the reporters saying 'yeah, we're the EDL, we're here and we're here to protect everything'... and then everybody else started singing all the songs and he's marching up and down the road like he's the leader.

Terry, EDL activist, 19th *Jan 2012*

In addition, even though Jack had clearly sought to take a lead in events, local EDL activists were dismissive of the idea that, as a group, they had been involved in organising the crowd[4], or for that matter that anybody could

---

4. A view also supported by the comments of the locals and Millwall casuals who spoke to the media during these events.

243

really have been said to have been *in control* of these events. Instead, they described crowds of people 'running up and down the road like chickens' in response to rumours that swept through the crowd about the approach of 'the Lewisham boys'[5] (Terry, EDL activist, 19th Jan 2012), or people going 'hell for leather' following the latest police car to go 'roaring' by with its sirens blazing (Dave, EDL activist, 19th Jan 2012). One local activist also observed that Jack's claims about the EDL's organising role were giving some other people in the crowd the 'hump' (especially some of the Millwall lads) because they did not want to be associated with the EDL; an account that again tallies with some of the discussion on football casuals forums in the weeks after the riots.

So, as is usually the case with events involving the EDL, there are a number of differing accounts of what happened in Eltham on Tuesday and Wednesday. Based on the available evidence though, it would seem that the scale of EDL involvement in the crowds in Eltham was probably somewhat smaller than was indicated by Jack or reported through news media at the time. There was also some reluctance both from within the EDL community and from some other parts of the crowds which gathered in Eltham for the EDL to take a lead in this mobilisation, and there were certainly differing views among EDL activists about how they should present their role in these crowds. This would appear to be linked to the fact that whilst some EDL activists may have seen this as an opportunity to expand activist networks, others were there for a number of reasons including the simple pleasures of being part of the crowd. However, whatever the 'truths' may be about the EDL's involvement in the crowds in Eltham, whether intentionally or not, reports that EDL activists were descending on Eltham tapped into a number of fears circulating at the time of the riots.

Framing the Events: The Threat of 'Racialisation' and the Far Right

The issue of race hung heavy in the air during public discussions about the riots in London and elsewhere in England. News of the crowds in Enfield and Eltham, and speculation about the involvement of the EDL seemed

---

5.   A reference to the groups of lads from Lewisham that, it was feared, would come up to Eltham.

therefore to resonate with wider political concerns that the riots could yet be racialised, and that this could be exploited by far right groups keen to exacerbate extant community tensions around racial and religious differences. Such concerns were, for example, articulated by Clive Efford, MP for Eltham, in the House of Commons on Thursday 11th August:

> For the last two nights in my constituency I've had a very, very heavy police presence due to right wing extremist groups focusing on Eltham and trying to create unrest and bad-feeling between different racial groups. Whilst we want to support people who are public spirited and coming out to defend their community, like some of my constituents have done, would the Prime Minister join me in saying to those people, 'don't be diverted from your efforts by the extremists seeking to exploit this situation'?

Clive Efford, MP for Eltham, 11th August 2011, Video B

The fact that these mobilisations provoked, or at least provided a focus for, the expression of such concerns is not surprising, particularly in light of the (probably exaggerated) reports which surfaced about the possible extent of the EDL involvement. By Tuesday there were also a number of video clips and anecdotes of skirmishes that hinted at the prospect of racially-aggravated violence in Eltham and Enfield: a video showed a group of white men shouting and throwing objects at a stationary bus containing black youths in Eltham (*Daily Telegraph*, 10th August) and reports appeared of white men chasing after 'blacks' and 'pakis' in Enfield (*The Guardian* Blog, 9th August 2011). The fact that one of these mobilisations was taking place in Eltham lent these events additional symbolic potency of which the media, politicians and, as I discuss later, members of the crowds in the High Street were aware. This is because, much to the chagrin of many Eltham residents, the area has acquired a special place within the politics surrounding racism and anti-racism as the site of the murder of Stephen Lawrence in 1993 (Hewitt, 2005). The timing was particularly unfortunate, with the trial of two of the people accused of the murder of Stephen Lawrence just weeks away.

Then there was also the prevailing view of the EDL and the threat it might pose within an already volatile situation, in which police resources were stretched to the limit, public order seemed unusually fragile, and with community tensions accentuated by fears of further violence and unrest. And at the time of the riots, media and political interest in the EDL was particularly acute. Just two weeks before the riots, Anders Behring Breivik had killed 77 people in Norway, and allegations had since emerged about his links to the EDL. This had generated something of a moral panic about the threat of the 'far right' in the UK. It had left photographers scouring their archives for the money shot of Breivik at an EDL event, journalists and anti-EDL campaigners playing a frantic join-the-dots exercise in the hope of revealing these links, and civil servants and police scrambling to put in place a credible and blame-proof response to the perceived threat of the EDL. To compound matters further, less than three weeks after the riots, the EDL's proposed march through Tower Hamlets was to take it through the home of one of the UK's largest Muslim populations. The march was also to pass Cable Street, one of the most iconic sites in the history of the struggles between the left and the right in Britain, where Mosley's black-shirts were famously denied passage through London's ethnically diverse East End in 1936. The rhetoric from the EDL and from their opponents was therefore already approaching fever pitch.

Given this social and historical context, there was a certain inevitability about the fact that these events would be framed in terms of the risk of their exploitation by the EDL, and the threat of mounting racial tensions. Yet whilst there may have been some kernels of truth within such an interpretation, it risks skating over an interesting and salient point. Rather than encouraging and contributing to the use of racial discourses, there actually appeared to be a concerted effort on the part of members of the crowd gathered in Eltham, and on the part of participating EDL activists who had joined them, to resist the use of such discourses.

The fact that racial discourses were being resisted does not of course mean that racial tensions were absent, nor that EDL involvement could not in some way exacerbate racial tensions. However, whilst some EDL activists may have been seeking to capitalise on this situation in order to expand their activist networks, there was little evidence of overt attempts by the EDL or by other parties on Eltham High Street to 'deliberately create unrest and bad-feeling between different racial groups' as Clive Efford had stated.

Resisting Discourses of Race

As the riots unfolded, it seemed everyone in London was talking about them; there were questions, conversations, arguments and debates about what was causing them, what they represented for society and what should be done to stop them. Individuals and groups from all walks of life were anchoring the dramatic scenes provided by the riots into their pre-existing theories about the world and about the changes underway in contemporary Britain (see Chakroborty, 2011). This was also true of the EDL activist community, even though it quickly became clear that the riots could not easily be incorporated within their main narrative about the threat of 'militant Islam'. So whilst 'left-wingers' interpreted the riots as being at least in part a reflection of what happens when youth services are cut and police use strong-arm tactics, so EDL activists articulated their own set of explanations. For example, some EDL activists (and doubtless many others beyond the boundaries of this particular movement) directed blame towards what they described as years of public life dominated by 'liberalism' and woolly 'lefty do-gooders' (see also Phillips 2011). For example, one activist posted:

NAME

This is the result of years of Liberalism, no discipline in schools, powers taken away from parents and handed over to the kids, soft laws etc ... The thugs rioting on the streets have grown up believing they are invincible. The see the authorities as having no teeth. The police fail to command respect, people don't respect what's seen as 'weakness'!... Well done Liberal, lefty do-gooders ... Turn on your TV and look proudly at the 'MONSTER' you've created ... You do-gooding, misguided fools!

8 August at 23:22

Accessed from Facebook, 28th December 2011

Another theme that was predictably quick to emerge was about the pernicious effects of decades of mass immigration and 'multiculturalism'; the apparent 'failure' of which had been proclaimed recently by both David Cameron (BBC, 5th Feb 2011) and Angela Merkel (BBC, 17th October 2010). As one EDL activist posted:

English Defence League—London Region

We are told by left-wing Politicians that multiculturalism is a success, really? Brixton as a flagship to promote how diversity works ... Walthamstow is promoted as a place where muslims work with the community. How stupid & wrong are you expense stealing twits looking now? We seen 2 nights where muslims, anarchists & their thug friends are attacking London. When you destroy English culture with multiculturalism, instead people being proud and respecting their country they disrespect it (16)

8 August at 14:17

*Accessed from Facebook, 28*th *December 2011*

It was easy to see how race could also surface as another prominent theme in these debates. Indeed, it threatened to do so on a number of occasions. For example, one Facebook comment about race and the riots (which was subsequently deleted by the EDL Facebook administrators) elicited the following response:

NAME A

NAME B, the EDL Are not racist!

9 August at 00:46 · Like

NAME C

Getting UNBELIEVABLY hard not to be, isn't it??? They burn our home-land down and WE have to be very restrained and careful how we voice our opinions about it! Wake up my beloved England!

9 August at 00:51

*Accessed from Facebook, 28*th *December 2011*

Similarly, during video footage from Eltham, there were a number of incidents in which somebody (in most cases not somebody from the EDL) makes a comment about race, only to be 'corrected' by one of their colleagues. Yet what is striking about these incidents is how consistently the encroachment of racial discourse was resisted, even when subjected to the probing of journalists, who seemed intent on asking questions around this theme. As one activist recalled:

Terry: We had the reporters asking us if this was anything to do with race and all that, and we're like 'no it's got nothing to do with race, the rioters are black and white, we're just up here to stop them from coming up here to smash any shops up, because we don't want them up there', and they were trying to twist it to say that we were after the blacks. And we said well no, if any white people come up here and smash the shops up they're going to get done as well... [Then they asked us] 'why are we up here?', 'do you think it's the government's fault?' and 'why are they rioting?' And—well it is the government's fault—but the immigration, that's mainly what they were after for us to say something about immigration and things like that, but we tried not to.

Joel: And... and you say that's what they were after...?

Terry: It was just the type of questions they were asking, you know, 'Do you think, is this about race?' 'Is this about blacks?' 'Is this about whites?' And we're like 'no, it's got nothing to do with race, this is not a black and white thing'. And they was like 'oh okay', and then they'd start asking the question another way round, and you're saying 'mate, no mate you've just asked ...'

Terry, EDL activist, 19th January 2012

There are likely to have been a number of reasons that underpinned this kind of resistance to the use of racial discourse. There was probably a strategic element to it; a concerted effort at 'impression management' (Goffman, 1969), particularly in the case of the EDL activists given their ongoing attempts to refute accusations that the EDL is a racist movement. Some of this resistance might also be attributed to the fact that when people are presented with a journalist's camera or a researcher's dictaphone they tend to say what they think will be received well by their anticipated audience. In addition, there is also a tendency for people to slip back into habitual discourses and well worn phrases when asked to articulate their position, so people who have spent a great deal of time attempting to distance themselves from racism may be likely to repeat their usual repertoire of arguments. These explanations in themselves are interesting as they would, if nothing else, seem to reflect broader shifts in public attitudes towards perceiving overt racism as socially unacceptable.

However, in this chapter I wish to draw attention to a further aspect of this resistance that comes to the fore in Terry's account of his interviews with the journalists. This aspect of resistance is about the construction of moral identity claims. His repeated assertions that the mobilisations in Eltham were 'nothing to do with race', made mandatory by the persistent probing of journalists, can also be read as a refusal to play the role that he and other members of the crowd in Eltham (including EDL activists) felt was being allocated to them by the media in this particular drama: that of the angry, working class whites teetering on the edge of racism.

As Roger Hewitt (2005) describes in great detail, there is, particularly in this part of London, longstanding resentment born of the feeling that certain communities have been portrayed by the media and by some mainstream politicians as being 'racist' or somehow especially prone to racism. As Dave, an Eltham resident and EDL activist complained:

> Because of [the murder of] Stephen Lawrence this area got such a bad name. I mean they virtually called us, we actually complained to Sky about it but they still virtually called us the racist capital of London. It is so, so wrong.

Dave, EDL activist, 19th January 2012

As such, resistance to the encroachment of racial discourses into their accounts of the mobilisations in Eltham was invested with considerable symbolic meaning. It formed part of what Hewitt calls a 'counter-narrative'; an extensive series of stories that anticipates and contests a more powerful and influential narrative that is broadly associated with the social and political elite and in which, EDL activists and others beyond the movement (see Hewitt, 2005) claim, they have been unfairly cast. Ironically, it was through the subsequent contestation of this counter-narrative and of these identity claims by the State that, at least for EDL activists and their supporters, the symbolic value of the events in Eltham was to be greatly amplified.

'Mr. Cameron, We are Not Sick'

The protestations of EDL activists and other members of the crowd that the mobilisation in Eltham was 'nothing to do with race' and was not about inflaming racial tensions appeared to have been given short shrift by those in positions of public authority. First, there was the large and robust policing operation on Wednesday. Then, more importantly, David Cameron's response to Clive Efford's comments (cited earlier in the chapter):

> I think the honourable gentleman speaks not only for his constituents but frankly for the whole house in deprecating the EDL and all they stand for and their attempt to somehow say that they are going to help restore order is: I've described some parts of our society as sick; and there are none sicker than the EDL.

> *David Cameron, 11th August 2011, see Video B*

Not surprisingly, these comments triggered a flurry of outrage from EDL activists, who quickly came to use them as an example both of the unwillingness of the political elite to listen to what they are actually saying, and of the efforts of the authorities and the media to 'discredit' (Dave, EDL activist, 19th Jan 2012) the EDL. For example, one of several statements released by the EDL argued:

> We can't help but think that it was somewhat ironic for the man at the head of a political establishment that is so keen to accuse us of making unfair generalisations about a large group of people, to then utilise exactly the same tactics as we are accused of using against the Muslim community.

> *The English Defence League, 15th August 2011*

Of course, such arguments will have gained little purchase with the majority of people beyond the confines of the EDL and their supporters. However, in the months that followed, Cameron's comments have provided EDL activists and supporters with a particularly effective 'condensing symbol' (Jasper, 2007), a memorable verbal encapsulation of the kind of simmering resentments that the EDL has become adept at using to expand and reinvigorate its support. They have provided the inspiration for countless placards on EDL demonstrations, and were used to generate support for a demonstration on 8th October 2011 when a group of EDL activists marched to Whitehall to tell Cameron that 'we are not sick'. Even at the time of writing this chapter (February 2012), these comments still appear to provide a reliable rhetorical tool for EDL speakers at local and national demonstrations where a comment along the lines of 'some people have called us sick…' invariably elicits a resounding set of boos from the crowd.

Discussion

The involvement of the EDL in the crowd that gathered in Eltham and the response that this elicited from the media, police and politicians provided one of many sub-plots which developed during the course of the riots in London. The precise nature of EDL activists' involvement in Eltham remains somewhat shrouded in conflicting accounts of these events, although the available evidence would suggest that the scale of EDL mobilisation and the role played by EDL activists was considerably smaller than was initially claimed by 'Jack England' and reported by the news media. Yet what these events did, like many others taking place at the time of the riots, was bring into focus some of the social divisions running through contemporary British society. However, and somewhat contrary to the media and political narrative that emerged at the time, the divisions highlighted by this particular sequence of events may be less to do with race *per sé*, than with the politics of racism and anti-racism, and how this intersects with the sense of social and political marginalisation within some parts of white working-class Britain.

The presence of EDL activists in Eltham was quickly and easily framed by political leaders and parts of the media within discourses about the threat of racial violence and the extreme right wing. This was hardly surprising given the reputation of the EDL, the moral panic at the time about the far right and the underlying concerns about the possible racialisation of the riots. Yet while some EDL activists may indeed have sought to exploit these events in order to build public support for the EDL and expand activist networks, there was little evidence to suggest that EDL activists, or other members of the crowds, were trying to stir up racial tensions at the time of the riots. Instead, there was a concerted effort on their part to avoid using racialised frames to describe their actions.

It is of course necessary to acknowledge that there are likely to be multiple explanations for this resistance to the use of racial discourses, and doubtless questions may be asked about the extent to which claims about the mobilisation being 'nothing to do with race' were made in good faith. What I argue in this chapter, however, is that this resistance acquired considerable symbolic significance because of the way that it tapped into longstanding bitterness about what EDL activists, and many others beyond the boundaries of this movement (Hewitt, 2005), perceive as the unfair characterisation of them and their communities as being especially prone to racism. It was this that has made Cameron's hyperbolic rebuttal of their moral claims such an effective condensing symbol for EDL activists, who have since used it to nourish precisely the kind of resentments on which the movement has so far thrived. There are, as Novak observed, 'few quicker ways to stoke smouldering resentment and to awaken an unendurable inner hatred than to look down upon others from some moral height' (Novak p.13, cited in Hewitt 2005 p.130).

Fortunately, the riots in London and the mobilisations in Enfield and Eltham did not result in a proliferation of racially aggravated violence. They did, however, provide another chapter in an ongoing sub-political struggle centred on the contestation of moral identities and grounded in the tense and at times accusatory politics of anti-racism and anti-extremism.

References

BBC (5th Feb 2011). 'State multiculturalism has failed, says David Cameron': www.bbc.co.uk/news/uk-politics-12371994 (Accessed 16th Feb 2012).

BBC (17th Oct 2010). 'Merkel says German multicultural society has failed': www.bbc.co.uk/news/world-europe-11559451 (Accessed 16th Feb 2012).

Busher, J. (Forthcoming). 'Grassroots Activism in the English Defence League: Discourse, Identity and Performance'. In *Extreme Right Wing Political Violence and Terrorism*, edited by Max Taylor, Mark Currie and Donald Holbrook. London: Continuum Press.

Copsey, N. (2010). *The English Defence League: Challenging Our Country and Our Values of Social Inclusion, Fairness and Equality*. London: Faith Matters.

Chakroborty, A. (2011) 'UK riots: political classes see what they want to see'. *The Guardian*, 10th Aug 2011: www.guardian.co.uk/uk/2011/aug/10/uk-riots-political-classes (Accessed 16th Feb 2012).

English Defence League (2011). 'Tommy Robinson: the extremist that makes David Cameron sick': http://englishdefenceleague.org/tommy-robinson-%E2%80%93-the-extremist-that-makes-david-cameron-sick/ (Accessed 28th December 2011).

Goffman, E. (1969). *Strategic Interaction*. Philadelphia, PA: University of Pennsylvania Press.

The Guardian Blog (9th August 2011): www.guardian.co.uk/uk/blog/2011/aug/09/london-riots-day-four-live-blog?INTCMP=SRCH#block-98 (Accessed 28th December 2011).

The Guardian Blog (10th August 2011): www.guardian.co.uk/uk/blog/2011/aug/10/uk-riots-fifth-night-live (Accessed 28th December 2011).

Hewitt, R. (2005). *White Backlash and the Politics of Multiculturalism*. Cambridge: Cambridge University Press.

Jackson, P. (2011). *The EDL: Britain's 'New Far Right' Movement*. Northampton: RNM Publications.

Jasper, J. M. (2007). *The Art of Moral Protest: Culture, Biography and Creativity in Social Movements*. Chicago, IL: University of Chicago Press.

Novak, M., (1972). *The Rise of the Unmeltable Ethnics: politics and culture in the seventies*. New York: Macmillan Publishing Co.

Phillips, M., (2011). 'Britain's liberal intelligentsia has smashed virtually every social value'. *Daily Mail*, 11th Aug 2011: www.dailymail.co.uk/debate/article-2024690/UK-riots-2011-Britains-liberal-intelligentsia-smashed-virtually-social-value.html (Accessed 16th Feb 2012).

Sampson, K., (2011). 'Liverpool riots: I remember the buzz of mob mayhem from 1981'. *The Guardian*, 10th August 2011: www.guardian.co.uk/commentisfree/2011/aug/10/liverpool-riots-mob-mayhem (Accessed 16th Feb 2012).

Telegraph, (10th August 2011): www.telegraph.co.uk/news/uknews/crime/8692872/London-riots-far-right-political-party-protect-Eltham-residents.html (Accessed 28th December 2011).

Video A. www.youtube.com/watch?v=VeX8yoJQNqI&feature=share (Accessed 16th February 2012).

Video B. www.youtube.com/watch?v=CokqrSaTXR8 (Accessed 16th February 2012).

Dr Vicky Heap is a Lecturer in Criminology at the University of Huddersfield. Vicky's interests lie in public perceptions of anti-social behaviour and the implementation of criminal justice policy. She completed her PhD at the Applied Criminology Centre, University of Huddersfield in 2010, supported by an ESRC CASE Studentship with the Home Office.

Dr Hannah Smithson is a Senior Lecturer in Criminology at Manchester Metropolitan University. She has published extensively within the area of youth justice and is currently undertaking research on youth gangs.

13

FROM WORDS OF ACTION TO THE ACTION OF WORDS:
POLITICS, POST-RIOT RHETORIC AND CONTRACTUAL GOVERNANCE

Vicky Heap and Hannah Smithson

Introduction

The riots that took place in a number of English cities over the summer of 2011 caught police and politicians off guard, but was it inevitable? Could the disorder have been precipitated, to some extent, by the range of conduct regulating measures introduced by the Labour Government since 1997? This chapter will critically appraise the criminal justice and social policy frameworks, which serve as the benchmark against which disorderly conduct is measured. We will consider whether modern conceptions of deviance have changed since Labour was elected in 1997. We then critique the policy developments from 1997 to the present day, in an attempt to explain how the spread of contractual governance (behavioural regulation via the negotiation of contracts (see Crawford,2003) and increased legislation around conduct regulation, could have contributed to the societal climate wherein the riots occurred. Finally, we will question the Coalition Government's response to the riots, before examining their current standpoint and whether their populist rhetoric pertaining to heightened regulation can be translated into effective policy and practice for the future. It is important to consider the government's response to the riots to examine whether Coalition criminal justice policies have moved away from the conduct regulating trend of Labour's past, or resorted to it as a default position in light of the riots.

A New Era of Deviance?

New political policies aimed at dealing with 'deviant' and 'disorderly' behaviour emerged when 'New' Labour came to power in 1997. During their years in government, Labour policies shifted away from class politics, becoming more focused on the regulation of conduct (Crawford, 2006). This was achieved by switching the crime agenda to one of low-level disorder (Phillips and Smith, 2003). Arguably the defining criminal justice policy of Labour's time in power, as well as the starting point for increased conduct regulation, was the creation and development of anti-social behaviour (hereafter referred to as ASB) legislation. In the context of this shift, Mooney and Young (2006) suggest that ASB issues were exaggerated in order to demonstrate a tough law and order stance in light of the 'crime drop'.[1] Burney (2005) argues that nuisance behaviours were targeted as a result of perceived inefficiencies in the criminal justice system. Nevertheless, these political developments facilitated significant changes to the types of behaviours and the types of people who were considered deviant and disorderly; the subsequent policies, in the main, tending to further marginalise young people.

Burney (2005:4) states 'once the label "anti-social behaviour' became current, it was very easy to adopt it as a description of any local irritation or the presence of any persons attracting disapproval in the public domain'. Indeed, at the same time, Matthews and Young (2003) suggest that there has been in a decrease in tolerance[2] towards crime and incivilities. This reflects Labour's stance on combating anti-social and nuisance behaviour. It also demonstrates a practical application of Krauthammer's (1993: 20) concept of 'defining deviancy up' which occurs 'as ' part of the vast social project of moral levelling, it is not enough for the deviant to be normalised. The normal must be found to be deviant'. He claims that while the traditional deviancy of criminals is being defined down, ordinary people are simultaneously guilty of new forms of deviancy, such as political correctness. As such, he proposes that while the tolerance and threshold of certain behaviours has increased, others have decreased. Krauthammer's ideas stemmed from reflections made on the modern definition of deviancy; an analysis

---

1. See Hope (2003) and Farrell *et al.* (2010) for further discussions about the 'crime drop'.
2. For further discussions of tolerance see Bannister *et al* (2006); and Bannister and Kearns (2009).

which was initially provided by Moynihan (1993), when he introduced the concept of 'defining deviancy down'. Moynihan suggests that 'we have been redefining deviancy so as to exempt much conduct previously stigmatized, and also quietly raising the "normal" level in categories where behaviour is now abnormal by any earlier standard' (*Ibid.*, 1993:19). He also explains how deviant behaviour has become normalised and almost expected. This suggests that tolerance of disorderly behaviour has increased, although critics such as Krauthammer, believe this is far from accurate.

These theories resonate with the idea of nostalgia discussed by Pearson (1983), who suggests that British society holds a deep nostalgia for the way things used to be and that each generation sees their issues as being disconnected from the past. This implies that defining deviancy up or down is a product of social and moral panics, framed within a current time period. Young (2009: 13) suggests in the modern era, the mass media is 'buttressed by scientific experts and other moral entrepreneurs', reinforcing the legitimacy of the moral panic to a large audience. As such, deviancy can not only be defined up and down, but can also emerge for an indeterminate period of time as the consequence of a moral panic fuelled by the mass media. However, in reality it must be acknowledged that there is no robust way of measuring a decline in behaviour over time, as comparatively, social conditions differ (Burney, 2005). These concepts suggest an ever-changing, dynamic deviancy-determining landscape. Based on this premise, such events as the riots of 2011 contribute to our understanding of deviant conduct and shape our tolerance levels regarding future disorderly behaviour, in both positive and negative ways. Formal sanctions enacted by the government during the period 1997-2010, align to the idea of defining deviancy up, shifting towards an increased focus on conduct regulation and contractual governance. It is important to examine these changes because this was the legislative context which was inherited by the Coalition Government, and it is their policy responses to the riots we will be critiquing.

Criminal Justice and Social Policy Frameworks 1997-2010

The Crime and Disorder Act 1998[3] signalled the beginning of conduct regulating legislation which established various sanctions that regulated a range of behavioural conduct; the most high-profile was the anti-social behaviour order (ASBO). This was followed up by the Anti-Social Behaviour Act 2003, which introduced dispersal orders; allowing the police to disperse groups of two or more people within a designated dispersal order zone, if they were believed to be causing harassment, alarm or distress. These legally enforceable sanctions were supplemented by a number of voluntary agreements, such as acceptable behaviour contracts (ABCs), which could be utilised in settings such as education. The application of contractual governance has increased alongside conduct regulating legislation, with the former now commonly used in situations where the recipient is not an offender or ASB perpetrator. For example, home-school agreements are now regularly used within the education sphere. A final area for consideration in this period is the blurring of boundaries between ASB and gang-related violence, which occurred towards the end of Labour's time in government. The Police and Crime Act 2009 gave provision to grant gang injunctions, so-called 'gangbos', which bear similarities to the ASBO. These civil orders are designed to disrupt gang-related violence by imposing prohibitions relating to association, geography, gang colours, dangerous dogs and the use of the internet/other technologies (Home Office, 2010). Originally restricted to those 18 and over, the Crime and Security Act 2010 proposed its extension to cover those aged 14-17. This reinforced Labour's commitment to conduct regulation through hybrid law (civil orders becoming criminal upon breach) and the necessity to govern the conduct (and potential conduct) of perceived trouble-makers.

Therefore the culmination of Labour's tenure between 1997 and 2010 was to create a society, whose behaviour was heavily regulated through formal means. However, the role of informal social control should also be recognised. Stenson (2005) argues there are competing levels of crime control, including the statutory sovereign agencies such as the police, as well as other informal sites of governance. For instance, 'ethnic, religious and other sites of governance in civil society do more than resist state power. They have their

---

3. Despite examples of ASB being defined in the Housing Act 1996, the Crime and Disorder Act 1998 was the first time the terminology 'anti-social behaviour' had been used in statute.

own agendas of governance, forms of knowledge and expertise deployed to govern and maintain solidarity in and over their own territories and populations' (Stenson, 2005: 267). Furthermore, it is important to simultaneously recognise that communities are not represented by one 'general' public that statutory agencies interact with, hence the systems of formal and informal social control do not exist within a social vacuum (Casey and Flint, 2007).

Additional Societal Factors 1997-2010

It is useful to recognise the broader societal context within which these legislative changes took place. As Mooney and Young (2006) suggest, during Labour's first term in government there were opportunities to focus upon the crime and disorder agenda. This contrasts with the situation they faced from the mid-point of their third term in government, where the country faced recession and a banking crisis, which removed their focus from high-profile criminal justice policies. Instances of conduct regulation were apparent throughout Labour's tenure. Paradoxically, the increased behavioural regulation of the general public was coupled with the simultaneous de-regulation of financial authorities. Consequently, already powerful groups, especially those with financial power benefited greatly. However, by comparison, those in poorer communities (whether offenders or not), who relied upon public services such as social housing found their behaviour under increased scrutiny and regulation. Further societal imbalances were highlighted by political scandals such as the false expenses claims made by MPs, which was exposed at the height of financial instability in 2009 (*Daily Telegraph*, 2009).

We would argue that the societal climate created by Labour is significant in terms of some of the possible explanations for the riots, in relation to both modern conceptions of deviance and financial instability. For example, according to Mervyn King, Governor of the Bank of England, we are experiencing the biggest 'financial crisis the world has ever faced' (*The Guardian*, 2011a). The Conservative-Liberal Democrat Coalition Government face increasing unemployment figures which suggest that youth unemployment will top one million for the first time since the early 1990s (*The Guardian*, 2011b). Absolute child poverty is also predicted to rise by 500,000 to three million by 2015, making it almost inevitable that Britain will miss its legal target of reducing child poverty to ten per cent or less by 2020 (Brewer *et al*, 2011). The Coalition therefore faced some interesting challenges; namely whether it was possible to distance themselves from Labour's reliance upon conduct regulation in the face of an on-going financial crisis.

The Coalition and Conduct Regulation: May 2010–August 2011

The Conservative-Liberal Democrat Coalition appeared keen to distance itself from conduct regulation from the outset. This was signalled very quickly, when Home Secretary Theresa May declared it was "time to move beyond the ASBO" (May, 2010). This was followed by a pledge to empower communities and reduce 'top down' Whitehall-driven national initiatives, with the emphasis firmly placed on local agendas (May, 2010). The commitment to move beyond the ASBO was upheld (partially), with the advent of a Home Office consultation to determine more effective solutions to ASB launched in February 2011. The proposed changes included the streamlining of existing legislation into five new powers, including the replacement of the ASBO with the new crime prevention injunction; although, in reality, this amounts to little more than a terminological change, with added obligations to include positive requirements alongside the prohibitions. The outcome of the consultation was still pending at the time of writing. However, if the consultation goes ahead, the Coalition will have done little to move away from the conduct-regulating traditions of the past.

This is not the only piece of legislation which has been re-branded. crime and disorder reduction partnerships, created by the Crime and Disorder Act 1998 were re-packaged as community safety partnerships (CSPs) in 2010. However, perhaps the most significant change and tangible example of moving away from top-down governance was contained within the Police Reform and Social Responsibility Act 2011. This gave provision for the election of local police and crime commissioners (PCCs), who are to be responsible for holding their local police force to account. This is potentially significant because PCCs will have the power to appoint, as well as dismiss chief constables (Home Office, 2012), which marks a striking shift in power from the Home Office to local communities. The first election of PCCs is due to be held in November 2012.

The final concept to consider here is David Cameron's 'Big Society' agenda, which supports the government's attempts to reduce the amount of conduct regulation within society. How exactly the Big Society will translate into practice remains unclear, however, the guiding principle is to "rebalance the relationship between individuals, society and state, encouraging the sharing of responsibility and placing trust in people' (Mycock and Tonge, 2011: 56). With specific reference to crime prevention, the fundamental elements of this fit within the remit of social methods, with plans to: reduce poverty, increase employability, improve parenting, and to move away from top-down centrally driven policies giving more power to communities and charities (Cameron, 2011a). It also consolidates the de-centralised approach to governance, championing the local agenda once more. This snapshot of criminal justice policies proposed by the Coalition pertains to a renewed emphasis on locally-driven, crime-reduction campaigns but has been further complicated with the advent of the riots.

Policy Responses in the Aftermath of the Riots

After the riots, the government moved swiftly to condemn those involved, while, at the same time, outlining their perspective on the causes and policy responses. On 11th August, Home Secretary Theresa May addressed parliament, stating: 'as long as we wish to call ourselves a civilised society, such disorder has no place in Britain' (May, 2011). Her speech focused upon a number of policy areas which required urgent attention in the wake of the riots including: 'gang' violence, education and social responsibility, and punishment. We now discuss each of these policy areas in detail.

Ending 'gang' and youth violence

One of the first formal political responses on 11th August made apparent that gangs were believed to be responsible for the rioting and disorder that occurred. To quote May (2011) once more, she claimed 'it is clear that many of the perpetrators—but by no means all of them—are known gang members. So we have to do more to tackle gang culture'. The association between gangs and the riots was further reinforced with the announcement that £8 million would be allocated to the cities where rioting had taken place. The government's preoccupation with prioritising gangs as the cause and result of

263

societal breakdown was also illustrated by the Work and Pensions Secretary, Iain Duncan Smith who said: 'I am talking about intervening when the child is conceived, not even when born. The kids we are talking about — half of them [kids] are unable to speak, cannot form sentences, they have no sense of empathy, they cannot share toys at school, they watch their mums get beaten up regularly and sexually abused' (*The Guardian*, 2011c). In addition, legislation contained within the Crime and Security Act 2010, which had started to pilot of gang injunctions for young people, was now to be made immediately available nationwide. This marks a shift back towards the types of conduct regulation associated with Labour, which directly opposes the Coalition initial stance promoting localism.

Despite the early rhetoric suggesting large scale gang involvement in the riots, data released by the Home Office in October 2011 appeared to contradict these claims (also see *The Guardian* and LSE, 2011; Briggs, 2012). Aggregated data produced for all areas that witnessed the disorder found that only 13 per cent of all arrestees had a 'gang' affiliation (Home Office, 2011). Furthermore, the terminology also shifted from gang member to gang 'affiliate', a downgraded associative term which further acknowledges the lack of gang involvement. The report also advises that where gang members were involved in the riots, their involvement was not 'pivotal' (Home Office, 2011) and despite their involvement in a united front against the police, they were not thought to have instigated the violence. This suggests the government's gang-focused response to the riots was disproportionate to their overall involvement. Despite this, it seemed to provide some thin political rationale for the development of new 'gang' policies.

In November 2011, May and Duncan Smith published the post-riot response to gangs in *Ending Gang and Youth Violence: A Cross Government Report Including Further Evidence and Good Pactice Case Studies* (HM Government, 2011). In this report, the Coalition set five key clear aims to prevent gang violence and support those involved in gang culture, namely:

1. Providing support

2. Prevention

3. Pathways out (of violence and gang culture)

4. Punishment and enforcement; and

5. Partnership working.

This will be supported by an investment of £1.2million over a three-year period. The report draws attention to the social problems considered to be at the heart of the riots, particularly the association between gangs and troubled families. The emphasis of the report is centred on identifying and intervening in the lives of 'troubled families', through early intervention, by providing support such as parenting classes. The overall aim is to 'turn around the lives of the 120,000 most troubled families by 2015' (HM Government 2011: 22). According to the Department for Communities and Local Government (2012), a troubled family exhibits at least five of the following characteristics: no one in the family works; living in poor or overcrowded housing; no parent has any qualifications; mothers have mental health problems; at least one parent has a longstanding illness, disability or infirmity; a low income; and the inability to afford a number of food, clothing items.

However, the focus on 'problem' families is not a new phenomenon, having first been mentioned in the Respect Action Plan (2006). Family intervention projects (FIPs) were utilised since the Respect Agenda as a means of providing support, be it in relation to offending, or more generally through the co-ordination of welfare services. Two pieces of evidence published by both the Department for Education (2011b) and Action for Children (2011) show that FIPs have been successful at reducing crime and ASB, as well as reducing health risks and improving educational attainment. This provides a useful indication of successful practice. Therefore, the recent report, which had championed family intervention as a means of reducing gang violence, has been based upon evidence-based good-practice. Potentially one of the biggest challenges facing the Troubled Families Team and the over-arching aim of reducing gang violence is the scale of the problem: it is estimated that 120,000 families require assistance. Figures from the Department for Education (2011b) report show that 5,461 families accepted help from FIPs in the 2010/11 financial year. It is clear that not all 120,000 families would be helped in one year, however some innovative thinking around large scale cost-effectiveness is required, if the target is to be met by the end of this government's term in office.

It was announced in October 2011 that Louise Casey, former 'Respect' tsar and victims' commissioner, was appointed as head of the newly formed Troubled Families Team based in the Department for Communities and Local Government. According to the Department for Communities and Local Government website (2012), £448 million pounds has been allocated to the Troubled Families Team, which requires match-funding from local areas and will be based upon payment by results (exact details of how this will work in practice, including what 'results' are expected, have yet to be announced). It is unlikely that payment by results will contribute towards significant change because the funding is reliant upon families producing results whereby they are no longer in 'trouble'. This is a substantial financial commitment for any agency to undertake in times of austerity, particularly if success is not guaranteed.

Education and social responsibility

Prime Minister David Cameron was also quick to impart his views on the riots in a speech at a youth club in Witney, Oxfordshire on 15 August. He stated: 'In my very first act as leader of this party I signalled my personal priority: to mend our broken society' (Cameron, 2011b). In this speech which echoed his Big Society agenda, he added: 'We must fight back against the attitudes and assumptions that have brought parts of our society to this shocking state' (Cameron, 2011b). He indicated that the areas for improvement were: providing a stronger police presence, reducing police bureaucracy, improved parenting (as seen borne out above), improving educational standards, increased community and social responsibility, and getting people into employment. Here our attention focuses on education and social responsibility, a topic also highlighted by the report from the Riot Communities and Victims Panel (2011).

Education Secretary Michael Gove has been particularly vocal in his opinions about the riots; drawing on the links between 'poor educational attainment' and (towing the party-line mentioned earlier) gang recruitment. He stated: 'We still every year allow thousands more children to join an educational underclass … it is from that underclass that gangs draw their recruits, young offenders institutes find their inmates and prisons replenish their cells' (Gove, 2011). Gove suggested a range of possible interventions to counter poor educational attainment including: reducing bureaucracy for teachers, increasing literacy standards, recruiting more male teachers in primary schools to act as role models, and applying tougher discipline in schools including greater search and restraint powers. How tangible these measures are and the true impact these may have on potential gang members are spurious at best. However, his department has been quick to act upon installing tougher disciplinary measures, with Charlie Taylor appointed as the government's expert adviser on behaviour in schools in autumn 2011. Taylor is a head teacher and behavioural consultant, credited with turning around a failing school in London to achieve an 'outstanding' Ofsted rating. However, Taylor's views on the causes of the riots appear slightly different to that of his departmental head, Gove. Taylor reverts back to the aforementioned focus on families and parenting by suggesting those involved in the riots 'come from broken homes where their mothers and fathers have been unable to perform the most basic of parenting duties' (Taylor, 2012 quoted in the *Daily Mail*, 2012). Perhaps a greater cross-governmental response to the riots is required than at present, if the political rhetoric is going to be meaningfully translated into reality.

While various Conservatives have pledged policy responses, the Liberal Democrats by comparison, have been less active. Their main output has focused on education, with Deputy Prime Minister Nick Clegg announcing plans for summer schools as a means of tackling some of the perceived causes of the riots, such as poor educational attainment. Summer schools are targeted at young people at-risk of 'going off the rails' and involve attending school for a two-week period during the summer holidays, between finishing primary school and starting secondary school. Attendance is aimed at improving their mathematics and English skills and will cost £50 million (Clegg, 2011). Although to achieve the attendance of a student 'going off the rails' during the school holidays, who may not be attending during term time anyway, presents many challenges if success is to be achieved. The summer school proposal marries neatly to a populist policy highlighted by Cameron in his Witney speech about National Citizen Service. He said: 'many people have long thought that the answer to these questions of [promoting] social behaviour is to bring back National Service . . . and that's why we are introducing something similar—National Citizen Service' (Cameron, 2011b).

National Citizen Service (NCS) is an eight week, voluntary programme for 16-year-olds that helps to develop personal skills in preparation for adult life. The programme consists of three weeks of full-time activity, which includes; a ten night residential stay, undertaking structured tasks in outdoor activity centres and community settings. The remaining weeks are dedicated to designing and implementing a 'social-action' task which requires volunteering (to provide sports coaching for example) to improve the local area (Cabinet Office Website, 2012). Thirty-thousand places are available for young people in the pilot scheme of summer 2012 (Department for Education, 2011b). The scheme is supposed to be a contemporary version of National Service, although despite its best intentions there are marked contrasts between the two.

However, the overriding difficulty facing the successful implementation of NCS is the correct recruitment of young people 'at risk' of offending or committing ASB. NCS has adopted a markedly different, but equally concerning approach to summer schools, whereby young people volunteer to join the programme. Subsequently, the young people who need NCS the most may not want to or cannot access the programme. The voluntary nature of scheme enables anyone aged sixteen to apply, with young people being encouraged to apply themselves (Directgov Website, 2011), opposed to being directed to apply through schools or youth services. What incentive is there for at-risk young people to apply? Mycock and Tonge (2011) highlight additional concerns about the long-term positive impact of the NCS for those from disadvantaged backgrounds, where social capital is often lower than in more affluent areas. NCS has been further criticised because it 'does not connect volunteering—essential to civic society—with political citizenship which directly links to civic society and there is little to advance democratic participation as a by-product of community based activities' (Mycock and Tonge, 2011: 63). This demonstrates the wider remit of anticipated benefits from such as scheme that should not be overlooked by focusing too narrowly on criminological concerns.

'Proper' punishment

A further key policy area for attention highlighted by both May and Cameron was punishment. Cameron promised 'proper punishment . . . so no-one should doubt this government's determination to be tough on crime and to mount an effective security fightback' (Cameron, 2011c). He reinforced this message while addressing the House of Commons, by adding: 'anyone charged with violent disorder and other serious offences should expect to be remanded in custody not let back on the streets and anyone convicted should expect to go to jail' (Cameron, 2011c). The proposed imprisonment of those convicted of rioting was also embraced by May, who claimed the disorderly tide was 'turning because the thugs are being arrested and locked up' (May, 2011). Duncan Smith further echoed these sentiments by suggesting that if it was possible to prove someone belonged to a gang, then their prison sentence could be doubled (*The Guardian*, 2011c). These penal-laden statements were made with little tangible policy direction, but strongly hinted at a return to the 'prison works' philosophy from 1986, which was originally associated with former Home Secretary, Michael Howard. Consequently, it would appear that this Conservative faction within the Coalition is attempting to gain public support by returning to their traditional right-wing punishment policies.

Data published by the Ministry of Justice shows that those brought before the magistrates' courts and Crown Courts for participating in the riots, were given more severe sentences in comparison to similar offences committed in previous year. For example, 'the proportion of offenders sentenced who received an immediate custody sentence for offences related to the public disorder at magistrates' courts was 43 per cent. This compares with 12 per cent for offenders sentenced for similar offences in England and Wales 2010' (Ministry of Justice, 2011: 4). Official statistics were supplemented with sensational claims of disproportionate sentencing in the media. For example, a student from London was jailed for six months for stealing water bottles worth £3.50 (*The Guardian*, 2011d).

In the short-term, it appears the notion of 'proper' punishment has been embraced in practice. The Metropolitan Police have named and shamed those convicted of offences connected to the riots. In December 2011, under the auspices of Operation Withern, they posted photographs and personal details of 64 convicted offenders on the website Flickr. The details included the offenders' name, date of birth, street where they live, the sentence they received and the crime they committed. A further two-hundred photographs of those they wish to speak to regarding the riots were also been posted. This demonstrates one way the rhetoric surrounding punishment was translated into reality. However, the government's drive towards 'proper' punishment drew criticism from the Howard League for Penal Reform, who issued a statement suggesting that all sentences 'should be balanced against a key principle of criminal justice, that of proportionality' (Howard League for Penal Reform, 2011).

Implications for the future

Much has been written about the criminalisation of social policy since the early 2000s[4]. Perhaps post-riots, we are moving into an era where welfare policy has an undertone of riot prevention, thereby insinuating an unsubstantiated causal link between welfare dependency and disorderly/criminal behaviour. This would be add further layers of marginalisation to which this group already contend on a daily basis, exacerbating their 'underclass' status (Murray, 1990). It also resonates with the emphasis being placed on harsh punishment, which could impact upon society as whole in relation to; increasing the fear of crime, reducing public confidence in the authorities and the altering contemporary understandings of deviance.

Based on the post-riot policies discussed earlier, it appears there has been a reversion back to top-down governance evident in the national focus on gangs; the recently established, centralised Troubled Families Team; NCS and summer schools; and the renewed emphasis on imprisonment. These Whitehall-driven policies contradict the pledges made by the Coalition early in their term. Furthermore, very little detail has been provided about how the policies will operate in practice. Many aspects of these policies will require local-level delivery but such services have experienced a significant withdrawal of financial support. CSPs will be a crucial vehicle for this implementation, although a reduction in both their financial and physical resources as a result of public spending cuts may curtail their effectiveness.

---

4.   See Gilling (2001); and Squires (2006).

The key issue facing the headline policies on 'gangs', NCS and the Troubled Families Team is the effective targeting of those considered to be 'at-risk' of offending/disorderly behaviour.

Discussion

In summary, the evidence outlined above suggests the Labour Government provided the words of action by introducing a raft of conduct regulating legislation. This has been contrasted by the Coalition, who despite early criticism of Labour's ideology, appear to be reverting back to Labour's legislative actions in light of the riots; providing us with the action of words. The reasons why the current government has reverted back to centrally-driven conduct regulation is unknown. Perhaps the Coalition wanted to assert a greater degree of control over criminal justice policy as a result of the riots. Or, reverting to top-down governance may have simply been considered to be the best (and most populist) decision in light of what was taking place at the time. Equally, it may have been a calculated decision to temper the localism agenda.

It appears that criminal justice legislation is being recycled, with existing legislation being streamlined (ASB powers), only to make way for new conduct regulating legislation to be introduced (gangbos for under 18s). This cycle suggests that the Coalition appears to have resorted to conduct regulation as a default legislating framework when faced with large scale public disorder. Consideration has to be given to whether this cycle of legislation provides tangible conditions for societal change and/or progress, or not. Consequently, if levels of conduct regulation are maintained or even expanded, the societal climate witnessed before the riots (people's lives being subject to conduct regulation without prior offending) may continue and contribute towards future societal unrest and potential disorder. The implementation and effectiveness of the policies outlined above will be pivotal to how wider society is affected. The election of local PCCs has the potential to neutralise some centrally-driven policies if the needs of local communities are perceived to receive attention from the public.

A further consideration is the impact the post-riot policies will have upon contemporary understandings of deviance and methods of informal social control. Only after a period of time will we be able to unravel whether society has 'defined deviancy up' as a result of the riots and the post-riot policies which pertain to that notion. A period of time will also have to pass before we can assess whether informal mechanisms of social control will become more explicit as a result of the riots, as the evidence provided in this book indicates that there was significant community support for both defending local neighbourhoods (*Chapter 12*) and organizing the 'riot clear up' (*Chapter 9*).

Finally, the key issue remains; can and should the post-riot populist rhetoric be translated into reality? Translating criminal justice policy into effective crime reduction practice is not simple. Based on the policies announced to date, further detail is required to fully understand exactly how the rhetoric will become reality.

References

Action for Children (2011) *Intensive Family Support: The Evidence*. Watford: Action for Children.

Audit Commission (2010) 'Place Survey'. Audit Commission: www.audit-commission.gov.uk/localgov/audit/nis/Pages/placesurvey.aspx (Accessed October 2011).

Bannister, J., Fyfe, N. and Kearns, A. (2006) 'Respectable or Respectful?. Incivility and the City'. *Urban Studies* 43 (5): 919-937.

Bannister, J. and Kearns, A. (2009) 'Tolerance, Respect and Civility Amid Changing Cities', in Millie, A. (ed.) *Securing Respect: Behavioural Expectations and Anti-Social Behaviour in the UK*. Bristol: Policy Press.

Brewer, M., Browne, J and Joyce, R (2011) 'Universal Credit Not Enough to Prevent a Decade of Rising Poverty'. Press Release. Institute for Fiscal Studies. London.

Briggs, D. (2012) 'What We Did When it Happened: A Timeline Analysis of the Social Disorder in London' in *Safer Communities Special Edition on the Riots*, Vol 11(1): 6-16.

Burney, E. (2005) *Making People Behave: Anti-Social Behaviour Policy and Politics*. Devon: Willan Publishing.

Cabinet Office (2012) 'National Citizen Service': www.cabinetoffice.gov.uk/news/national-citizen-service-introduced (Accessed January 2012).

Cameron, D. (2011a) Speech on Big Society, made in London, 14 February: www.number10.gov.uk/news/pms-speech-on-big-society/ (Accessed October 2011).

Cameron, D. (2011b) Speech on the Fightback After the Riots, made at a youth centre in Witney, Oxfordshire 15 August: www.number10.gov.uk/news/pms-speech-on-the-fightback-after-the-riots/ (Accessed September 2011).

Cameron, D (2011c) Statement on Violence in England London, 10th August 2011: www.number10.gov.uk/news/pm-statement-on-violence-in-england/ (Accessed October 2011).

Casey, R. and Flint, J. (2007) 'Active Citizenship in the Governance of Anti-Social Behaviour in the UK: Exploring the Non-Reporting of Incidents'. *People, Place and Policy Online* 1(2): 69-79.

Clegg, N. (2011) *Speech to the Liberal Democrat Party Conference*, made at the Liberal Democrat Party Conference, Birmingham 21 September: www.libdems.org.uk/latest_news_detail.aspx?title=Nick_Clegg's_speech_to_Liberal_Democrat_Conference&pPK=00e086ba-d994-4146-bb14-60ce615d05eb (Accessed September 2011).

Crawford, A. (2003) 'Contractual Governance' of Deviant Behaviour. *Journal of Law and Society* 30(4):479-505.

Crawford, A. (2006) 'Fixing Broken Promises? Neighbourhood Wardens and Social Capital'. *Urban Studies* 43(5):957-976.

Department for Communities and Local Government (2012) 'Troubled Families': www.communities.gov.uk/communities/troubledfamilies/ (Accessed January 2012).

Department for Education (2011a) *Statistical Release: Monitoring and Evaluation of Family Intervention Projects and Services to March 2011*. London: Department for Education.

Department for Education (2011b) 'National Citizen Service': www.education.gov.uk/childrenandyoungpeople/youngpeople/nationalcitizenservice/a0075357/national-citizen-service (Accessed September 2011).

Directgov (2011) 'Taking Part in National Citizen Service': www.direct.gov.uk/en/YoungPeople/Workandcareers/Workexperienceandvolunteering/NationalCitizenService/index.htm (Accessed September 2011).

Farrell, G., Tilley, N., Tseloni, A. and Mailley, J. (2010) 'Explaining and Sustaining the Crime Drop: Clarifying the Role of Opportunity Related Theories'. *Crime Prevention and Community Safety* 12:24-41.

Gilling, D. (2001) 'Community Safety and Social Policy'. *European Journal on Criminal Policy and Research* 9(4): 381-400.

Gove, M. (2011) Michael Gove to the Durand Academy Speech, made at the Durand Academy, London 1 September: www.education.gov.uk/inthe-news/speeches/a00197684/michael-gove-to-the-durand-academy (Accessed January, 2012).

HM Government (2011) *Ending Gang and Youth Violence: A Cross Government Report including Further Evidence and Good Practice Case Studies'*. London: Stationary Office.

Home Office (2010) *Statutory Guidance: Injunctions to Prevent Gang-Related Violence*. London: Home Office.

Home Office (2011) *An Overview of Recorded Crimes and Arrests Resulting From Disorder Events in August 2011*. London: Home Office.

Home Office (2012) *Police and Crime Commissioner Powers*: www.homeoffice.gov.uk/police/police-crime-commissioners/questions/pcc-powers/ (Accessed January 2012).

Hope, T. (2003) 'The Crime Drop in Britain?' *Safer Communities* 2(4):14-16.

Howard League for Penal Reform (2011) 'Statement in Reaction to some of the Sentences being Handed Down by the Courts in Relation to the Riots and Disturbances Last Week': www.howardleague.org/sentences/ (Accessed September 2011).

Krauthammer, C. (1993) 'Defining Deviancy Up'. *The New Republic*, 22 November.

Matthews, R. and Young, J. (2003) 'New Labour; Crime Control and Social Exclusion', in Matthews, R. and Young, J. (eds.) *The New Politics of Crime and Punishment*. Devon: Willan.

May, T. (2010) Moving Beyond the ASBO, Speech at the Coin Street Community Centre, London 28 July: www.homeoffice.gov.uk/media-centre/speeches/beyond-the-asbo?version=1 (Accessed September 2011).

May, T. (2011) Speech on Riots, made to the House of Commons, London 11 August: www.homeoffice.gov.uk/media-centre/speeches/riots-speech (Accessed September 2011).

Ministry of Justice (2011) *Statistical Bulletin on the Public Disorder of 6th to 9th August 2011*. London: Ministry of Justice.

Mooney, J. and Young, J. (2006) 'The Decline in Crime and the Rise of Anti-Social Behaviour'. *Probation Journal* 53(4):397-407.

Moynihan, D. P. (1993) 'Defining Deviancy Down'. *American Scholar* 62 (Winter):17-30.

Murray, C. (1990) 'The British Underclass'. *Public Interest* 99:4-29.

Mycock, A. and Tonge, J. (2011) 'A Big Idea for the Big Society? The Advent of National Citizen Service'. *The Political Quarterly* 82(1):56-66.

Pearson, G. (1983) *Hooligan: A History of Respectable Fears*. London: Macmillan.

Riots Communities and Victims Panel (2012) *Five Days in August: An Interim Report on the 2011 English Riots*, London: Riots Communities and Victims Panel.

Squires, P. (2006) 'New Labour and the Politics of Anti-Social Behaviour'. *Critical Social Policy* 26(1):144-168.

Stenson, K. (2005) 'Sovereignty, Biopolitics and the Local Government of Crime in Britain'. *Theoretical Criminology* 9(3):265-287.

Taylor, C. (2012) Speech to Head Teachers, East Sussex 30 January, quoted in *The Daily Mail*: www.dailymail.co.uk/news/article-2094086/Parents-neglected-basic-duties-accused-causing-London-riots.html (Accessed January 2012).

The Daily Telegraph (2009) 'MPs' Expenses: Telegraph Investigation Exposes Allowances'. *The Daily Telegraph* 8 May, 2009: www.telegraph.co.uk/news/politics/5293147/MPs-expenses-Telegraph-investigation-exposes-allowances.html (Accessed September 2011).

The Guardian (2011a) 'Britain in grip of worst ever financial crisis, Bank of England governor fears.' *The Guardian* 6th October: www.guardian.co.uk/business/2011/oct/06/britain-financial-crisis-quantitative-easing (Accessed October 2011).

The Guardian (2011b) 'UK unemployment at 17-year high: Full reaction' *The Guardian* 11th October: www.guardian.co.uk/business/economics-blog/2011/oct/12/uk-unemployment-what-economists-say-full-reaction?INTCMP=SRCH (Accessed October 2011).

The Guardian (2011c) 'Gang culture must be stopped early, says Iain Duncan Smith' *The* Guardian 20th October: www.guardian.co.uk/society/2011/oct/20/gang-culture-stopped-early. (Accessed October 2011).

The Guardian (2011d) 'Riots: Magistrates Advised to "Disregard Normal Sentencing"'. *The Guardian* 15 August: www.guardian.co.uk/uk/2011/aug/15/riots-magistrates-sentencing (Accessed September 2011).

The Guardian and LSE (2011) 'Reading the Riots: Investigating England's Summer of Disorder', London: *Guardian* and LSE.

Young, J. (2009) 'Moral Panics: Its Origins in Resistance, Resentment and the Translation of Fantasy in to Reality'. *British Journal of Criminology* 49(1): 4-16.

Rebecca Clarke is Head of Research and Policy, Greater Manchester Probation Trust (GMPT). She has worked as an applied researcher in Criminal Justice since 1998, initially in prisons prior to joining GMPT in 2001. Rebecca Clarke now heads a unit in GMPT comprising researchers, information analysts and probation practitioners. The unit delivers a range of functions for the trust to support strategic decision-making and practice improvement. It also undertakes research and evaluation for other statutory and third sector agencies, contributing to the wider improvement of criminal justice service delivery in Greater Manchester. She is an associate member of a number of local academic institutions, delivering seminars and lectures to criminology and social policy students.

14

PROFILING THE 'RIOTERS':
FINDINGS FROM MANCHESTER

Rebecca Clarke

Introduction

The disturbances in Greater Manchester began in Salford on the 9th August and quickly spread to other locations including Manchester city centre, with more isolated incidents in the Trafford and Tameside boroughs. The majority of crimes which resulted in conviction and sentence in Greater Manchester were committed on August 9th and 10th. Very quickly, a link was made between the individuals involved and their existing criminal histories. For example, Kenneth Clarke, Secretary of State for Justice, asserted that the rioters were 'existing criminals on the rampage', concluding that the current criminal justice system (CJS) was 'broken'. Perhaps unsurprisingly, the CJS quickly prepared to respond forcefully to those responsible for the disturbances. There was a widely shared view, expressed in the following quote from the Policing and Criminal Justice Minister, Nick Herbert, that in order to deter further disturbances, the CJS needed to act decisively and swiftly, leaving little time to consider either the events or the individuals involved. For example:

> Some severe sentences were rightly handed down in response to mass acts of
> looting and violence, where it is imperative that such behaviour is deterred. Such

sentences were exceptional. But the lesson is that sure justice, where the consequences of offending are swiftly brought home to the criminal are effective justice.

Nick Herbert, Speech to PSA, 14.09.11, p.3.

Yet, despite the 'informed' commentary and assertions espoused within the national and local media, there was, and still remains, little information about those who have been processed though the CJS as a consequence of their 'involvement' in the riots. Arguably, the social, political and media reactions impeded a clear exploration of the rioters characteristics and previous experiences with the CJS and what may have contributed to their involvement.

This chapter develops upon a previous paper published in January 2012 which described an emerging profile of 79 individuals convicted and sentenced for their actions in the riots in Greater Manchester. This chapter aims to provide a more detailed discussion of the 'rioter' profile, by considering the personal and social circumstances of these men and women, and their previous involvement in the CJS. I acknowledge the efforts made by *The Guardian* and LSE to understand and profile the motivations of the rioters but my chapter is more focussed on a selection of four case studies, which highlight their circumstances, how they came to be involved in the riots and how the CJS processed them. I base this all on data from probation records, interviews with probation colleagues who case manage these people and from discussions with the participants themselves.

How We 'View' the Rioters

In the months following the riots there have been attempts to describe who the rioters were, explain their motivations, and how the CJS should respond to their behaviour.

The Criminal Justice System lens

The Ministry of Justice (MOJ) published two statistical bulletins in the months following the disturbances. The first (published in August 2011) focussed on the emerging outcomes for those individuals who had appeared in court as a result of the riots (MOJ, 2011a). The second (published in October 2011) included some basic profiles: demographics; previous convictions;

and information on socioeconomic indices, achieved through the merging of justice data with that from Department for Education, and Department for Work and Pensions (MOJ, 2011b). However, the reporting was deliberately 'risk factor'-oriented and gave no detail on social or structural problems of discrimination, racism, community tensions and the like. This transparency is relatively unprecedented, and the information provided has been used to inform much of the debate in the media. The key findings widely debated in the media included the criminal histories of those arrested, their age, ethnicity and socio-economic position, and the proportionality of sentencing.

Whilst this step has undoubtedly facilitated a more informed discussion regarding the immediate response of the police and courts to the disturbances, there remain some challenges in using this information to underpin a reliable understanding and effective response. However, these datasets are flawed for a number of reasons. Firstly, any profile which includes individuals who have not yet been charged and convicted may change. For example, 17 per cent of cases initially included by the MOJ have since been removed from the data because charges have been dropped, or the individual has been acquitted or the charge withdrawn (MOJ, 2011b). This information has not been updated and shared publicly since October 2011. Secondly, those arrested and charged are unlikely to represent those who took part in the riots. The application of police intelligence strategies such as reviewing vast amounts of CCTV footage or undertaking house visits to known offenders, is likely to mean that the 'usual suspects' were targeted, thereby confirming political associations of the 'criminal underclass'. More nuanced understandings have come from obtaining personal testimonies.

Personal testimonies

The Guardian newspaper and London School of Economics (LSE) were commissioned to undertake a research project examining the motivations, attitudes and experiences of those who rioted (*Guardian* and LSE, 2011). This research was a large self-report study and while some of their participants were contacted via personal details held on court listings others had identified themselves as being involved in the riots and became involved in the research via local networks, rather than via criminal justice agency identification. This group were young (83 per cent aged 24 and under) and ethnically diverse (with 26 per cent white British), 16 per cent of their sample (of 270) came from Manchester or Salford. Interestingly, although the sample was not generated via the CJS lens, and the majority of these individuals hadn't been arrested for their involvement it was found '68 per cent admit to having previously received a caution or conviction' (*Guardian* and LSE, 2011: 14).

Broadly speaking the research drew on a range of sociological explanations for the individuals' motivation to riot, and issues of poverty, unemployment, inequality and policing were consistently referenced as reasons. However, when compared to a public *Guardian*/ICM Poll, the rioters' views differed from the public in relation to the influence of greed, criminality and moral decline, where the public were more likely view these as key contributory factors.

The Greater Manchester profile

In Greater Manchester, the number of individuals being convicted for their involvement has substantially slowed—only five cases were sentenced in December 2011. We also have a greater appreciation of who these individuals are, with more assessments and information captured in the local case management systems, which can assist us to explore what may have influenced their involvement. Importantly, and in contrast to the MOJ information and personal testimonies, the data used to inform this chapter is constructed entirely of individuals who have concluded the justice process from arrest to conviction to sentence. As a result the number of individuals included in the analysis is reduced, but importantly they have been convicted and sentenced, and therefore represent those with whom agencies such as the Probation Service will supervise post-sentence or post-release from custody. The data was developed using the local probation case management and assessment information systems. These data systems offer a wide range of information.

There were 110 individuals convicted and sentenced for involvement in the riots in Greater Manchester (AGMA, 2011).[1] Collectively, this sample represented three different trajectories. Forty four (40 per cent) have no previous

---

1.   It is difficult to estimate the actual number of individuals who rioted in the local area. The best estimates suggest that the number involved but not yet arrested or charged in Greater Manchester may be a further 700 individuals.

convictions (or no 'event'[2] recorded on the local adult probation system) in the last five years. This does not necessarily mean they have no previous convictions as some may have served previous sentences prior to 2006. Forty (37 per cent) of these individuals are commencing a new sentence, having served at least one sentence with Greater Manchester probation in the last five years. The remaining twenty five (23 per cent) were already on an active order or licence with the Probation Service at the time of the riots. Let us now look more closely at the demographics.

Demographics

The information presented in the table below shows comparative demographics of those individuals convicted and sentenced against the broader probation caseload in the Manchester area.

Women are represented at a slightly higher rate in this sample than the wider offender population, which is made up of nine per cent women. This over-representation is exaggerated when considering those who were previously unknown on the adult offender caseload, here 20 per cent of the 44 unknown individuals were women and just two per cent of the 25 who were on current orders or licences were women. The age profile is similar to that of the MOJ dataset, that the individuals involved in the disturbances were younger than the general probation caseload. Importantly, there is a concentration of young adults (60 per cent of the 18-25 years olds) who have not previously been present on adult criminal justice caseloads.

Of those convicted of riot-related offences, 32 per cent were identified as non-white British, excluding 26 cases where the data was missing. This is higher than expected when comparing to the caseload data. However, the proportion of individuals on the caseload who are from a black minority ethnic background fluctuates in different localities across Greater Manchester; in Manchester City and Salford, this is 38 per cent and 13 per cent respectively. However, further caution must be taken as these comparative profiles are not age adjusted. A conclusion which can be tentatively drawn from this is that

---

2. A court sentence which has either required the preparation of a court report or supervision, either a community order or post custody licence, by the Probation Service.

the ethnicity of individuals convicted in Greater Manchester broadly reflects the ethnic profile of the wider offender group in the local areas affected.[3]

Figure 1: Key demographic characteristics of the 110 rioters included within the analysis alongside the demographic profile of the general offender population in Greater Manchester.

GENDER	Male	Female
Riots	87%	13 %
General Profile	91 %	9 %

AGE (years)	18 – 21	22 – 25	26 – 34	35 +
Riots	43 %	17 %	20 %	20 %
General Profile	15 %	18 %	31 %	37 %

RACE & ETHNICITY	White British	Mixed Race	Black or Black British	White Irish	Other Ethnic Group
Riots * 10 % missing data	62 %	12 %	16 %	4 %	6 %
General Profile * 3 % missing data * GMPT not key riot locations	76 %	3 %	6 %	2 %	11 %

---

3. However, it should be noted that this is generally much higher than the proportion of black minority ethnic individuals in the general population in these areas.

Offences

Information taken from local partner documents, and presented in media depictions of the riots in Greater Manchester, suggests that the riots began in Salford and were initially a series of violent exchanges between the police and groups of locals, prior to developing into the mass systematic looting which then took place in the city centre. The nature of the crimes recorded in Greater Manchester reflected national data. The majority of individuals were convicted of some form of acquisitive offence including burglary (61 per cent); handling stolen goods (8 per cent); theft (5 per cent) or 'stealing from shops' (5 per cent). Given the majority of offences were acquisitive, and that we know the majority of offending by women is acquisitive in its nature, it is perhaps unsurprising that a higher proportion of women appear in both this profile and at a higher level again in the 'Reading the Riots' profile (*Guardian* and LSE, 2011). Offences involving criminal damage and public order made up almost one fifth, including: 'offences against public order' (seven per cent); 'going equipped' (two per cent); 'breach of the peace' (two per cent); 'obstruction or failure to comply with an officer' (two per cent); 'putting people in fear of violence' (two per cent); and 'threatening behaviour' (two per cent). Finally there were a small number of individuals convicted for violent disorder (seven per cent). The second publication by the MOJ indicated that Salford had the largest proportion of arrests for violent offences — 26 per cent versus on average six per cent in other locations.[4]

Court disposals

The greater use of custody and comparatively longer sentence lengths demonstrated in the MOJ data seemed to indicate that an increase in the severity of sentences has become the norm, contrary to what Nick Herbert suggested. In Manchester, far few individuals received a non-custodial disposal, and in this dataset none received community orders. However, almost one fifth will remain in the community on a suspended (custodial) sentence order (SSO). The majority (82 per cent) received immediate custodial sentences, with 21 per cent of these individuals receiving tariffs of less than 12 months (on average just over five months). Because they are regarded as 'non statutory'

---

4. This includes 'causing an affray'; 'threatening behaviour'; 'assaulting a police constable' and 'violent disorder'.

prisoners, most will receive very little intervention. At the other end of the spectrum, a significant number received sentences of two years or more in custody. However, we have seen some cases appealed in court, and consequently, sentences reduced (Keegan, 2011).

Criminal justice histories prior to the riots

For those individuals in this group who have previous events recorded on the system the majority of their previous offences are for a series of breaches (29 per cent) or shoplifting (23 per cent). The breaches include breach of community orders, curfew and restraining orders, and anti-social behaviour orders (ASBOs). There were very few burglary or violent offences linked to the 348 events, with just 16 of the latter. The remaining offence types included various summary and indictable offences such as public order, possession of cannabis, driving offences and one offence of 'begging'. This group had experienced the full range of court disposals, with over a quarter previously serving custodial sentences.

Socio-economic and personal factors related to offending

There has been regular debate about those involved in the August 2011 UK riots and their experience of poverty and deprivation. The government data indicates that just over a third of the adults arrested for rioting were claiming benefits. The juveniles involved were characterised by poor educational attainment, and significant numbers had special educational needs status and registered as claiming free school meals (Department for Work and Pensions, 2011; *Guardian* and LSE, 2011; Singleton, 2011). Newburn reflected that many of the 'risk factors' associated with future criminal involvement were present in this group of young people. However, we must be cautious in drawing any conclusions as such descriptives don't necessarily reveal the complete picture; it's to say, the fact that they are 'claiming benefits' or have 'poor educational attainment' did not propel them to riot.

The detailed assessment information from Manchester indicates that, at the time of sentence, almost one quarter of these individuals had no fixed abode and another quarter were 'at risk' of becoming homeless. Almost two-thirds are currently unemployed (not including those classed as 'unavailable for work') and three quarters have 'some' or 'significant' problems with their employment history, often having little or no work history Some also have significant debt and finance issues. In half of these cases there is evidence that they experienced significant problems in childhood. This may encompass poor relationships with parents and other family members, absent parents (for some as a result of imprisonment), experiences in care, and experiences of neglect and poverty in childhood — or a combination of these factors. For many, such negative experiences have affected their adult lives; for example over one third (42 per cent) of those convicted of involvement in the riots said they had a recent history of domestic violence as either perpetrator or victim.

The assessment of lifestyle indicates that most (85 per cent) are easily influenced by their peers, while this does not lead to conclusion that these individuals have any greater lack of social control than other people it does reflect that any response must address the individual's involvement in the wider social context. Over three quarters reported drug use (78 per cent) and a third of these this relates to drugs such as heroin and crack cocaine. This drug use is likely to be associated to the difficulties coping and social isolation, which for nearly one third has led to episodes of self-harm and in one quarter of cases, regular support on medication for diagnosed mental health issues.

The results of this analysis confirm the conclusions drawn from analysis of the MOJ data, as Newburn reported, these findings 'look less remarkable, however, if we begin to look at them in the context of social deprivation, or what in recent years might have been referred to as social exclusion' (Newburn, 2011: 1). The offending of the rioters profiled here, whether part of a history of offending or not, is exacerbated by the wider social and personal factors at play. David Cameron's conclusion that the riots were 'not about poverty' is disputed by this evidence, which demonstrates that many of the convicted individuals had multiple and entrenched issues around housing, employment, finances, substance use and mental health.

Individual Case Studies — Understanding Personal Motivations and Influences

This section is concerned with exploring the inter-relationship between the sample's personal histories, their socio-economic position, previous offences, experiences of the criminal justice system, and their subsequent involvement in the riots. For that reason the remainder of the chapter focuses on four case studies, selected from the 110 individuals. The case studies have all had a history of contact with probation, which means that there is much more known about them. The selection represent different ages, backgrounds, movements prior and during the riots and consider how they were processed through the CJS.

The way in which information was collated for the case studies relied on qualitative sources held on probation IT systems, including the pre-sentence report, sentencing documents, the OASys assessment and the case file records (with particular focus on the 'contacts log'[5]). Following content analysis of this documentation, I interviewed a number of practitioners who had supervised them on prior orders (sometimes immediately prior to the riots) or who were engaged in preparing the report for sentencing the riot offence. In one case, where one was serving a suspended sentence in the community, I was able to meet with them and discuss directly their involvement in the riots.

Case Study 1: Salma

Leading up to the riots

Salma is 22-years-old and has served one previous community sentence, over a year prior to the riots. On this occasion, she completed all her requirements successfully, including a lengthy period of community payback. The previous offence was 'burglary' — the motivation, Salma says, was to instigate revenge against a man who she believed had been harassing her sister. Salma completed school and college gaining a range of qualifications including GCSE's and a BTEC, and was looking for employment in the summer of 2011. Although her accommodation was relatively tenuous, she told me that she had no significant issues or 'stresses' at the time of the riots.

---

5. This record reflects a wide range of information including engagement with previous and current sentence of the court, various contacts with the probation officer and other staff, key decisions about the case, etc.

The night of the riots

Salma said she had to walk through Manchester City Centre to get home from a friend's (due to all transport being suspended) and that she found a bag containing alcohol and an electrical shop scanner. When the police stopped her and her sister she said she was just looking at the bag and hadn't decided whether to take it. However, she did recognise the potential consequences, but said she 'didn't think taking something you know in the street that isn't yours — that doesn't belong to anyone — I never knew that was a crime.' Her personal gain from the property in the bag seems inconsequential. The bottles of wine were of little value and no use to her as she doesn't drink for religious reasons, and the scanner, she asked herself: 'What would I do with that?' She said she didn't know what she would have done with the goods had she been able to walk away with it without being apprehended. Fitting with the broader implementation of harsh punishments for rioters, she was originally charged with burglary. However, following further review of CCTV and other evidence, the offence was reduced to 'theft by finding'. Salma, however, had already spent four weeks on remand in HMP Styal and this was her first experience of prison. In the end, she served 34 weeks in custody which had been suspended for 12 months, the requirements of this order included regular supervision with her probation officer and 80 hours unpaid work.

Since the riots

Salma has already completed over half her required hours of unpaid work and talks positively about probation. She seems to have taken the opportunities on offer to get support with access to employment and housing advice. When I met her she had just seen her supervisor and was setting up further appointments with a skills adviser. Perhaps the contagion of seeing others doing similar things was some influence: 'there were lots of people, you know getting away with free stuff' she reflected but also perhaps some naivety that her actions would not be connected with the rioting in the city centre. She didn't consider that her actions were criminal.

There is a clear question regarding whether Salma posed such a threat that she needed to be remanded in custody, a potentially damaging experience for this young woman. The delivery of her suspended sentence order

(SSO) requirements have been relatively flexible to ensure that while Salma completes her order it doesn't directly impact on her ability to sustain employment. She was able to request a change to her curfew requirement to allow her to take up a new job, and her unpaid work placements had been arranged so that they would not interfere with work. Overall, she has complied with all that has been asked. Reflecting on the longer-term consequences of her involvement in the riots last summer and her subsequent conviction, she worries that it could be an obstacle to her ambitions for the future, in particular as she strives for a vocation in care work. She said:

> I want to get into [the] care [sector], I don't want to you know just work in shops.
> I worked in a nursery before it shut a while ago and yeah I liked it.

Case Study 2: 'Lucy'

Prior to the riots

Lucy has lived a very difficult life in the margins of society. She is from a large family and both her and her siblings have experienced violence and neglect over many years, both in their family home and in the care system into which they been on numerous occasions during childhood. Lucy has suffered violence and abuse as a child and this has continued into her adult life, as she is victimised from serious assaults on a regular basis by a long-term partner with whom she has struggled to separate. Although she has had children, both were taken into care as young infants and these events have triggered episodes of self-harm and severe depression. On one occasion, following the birth of her second child, set herself on fire. She has used drugs and alcohol for many years, including heroin for a substantial period from her mid-teens until very recently, and at 31-years-old continues to drink heavily and use benzodiazepines and other prescribed drugs alongside a methadone prescription.

Her file indicates that she has been regularly involved in crime for the majority of her life, and that her offences (mainly low level and acquisitive) are inextricably linked to funding her substance misuse, and that this in turn may be a coping mechanism for dealing with her experiences of abuse.

Her convictions are for largely low-level acquisitive crime and anti-social behaviour but the persistence of offending and her lack of engagement with all the sentencing options, has led to several prison sentences. She has resisted engaging with most community based sanctions, both those aimed at punishment or rehabilitation. This includes opportunity to engage with women's specific services in the local community. I have spoken with three practitioners who have supervised her over the years and they all reflect that sadly, on occasions, Lucy has stated a clear preference to go to prison. One Supervisor suggested that this offers Lucy the opportunity to 'be medicated, be fed and be looked after'. Perhaps this is unsurprising given the difficult life she has had to navigate. It seems also likely that Lucy would see a short period in custody as preferable to engaging with statutory agencies such as probation. This is perhaps a result of her experience of other statutory agencies such as the police or social services, having experience of the latter both as a child in and out of the care system and the removal of her own children.

Prior to the riots, she had just been released from custody and upon release Lucy had missed a GP appointment to collect her medication. She disclosed in the interview for her court report that she had started to drink more alcohol in order to self-medicate her symptoms, often drinking a litre of vodka a day. She was required to attend appointments related to an existing suspended sentence order but had recently missed appointments and, by August 2011, the police were actively seeking to serve her with an anti-social behaviour order.

The night of the riots

Lucy was drinking 'socially' in her regular spot in a park area of the city. She had no means of knowing what was going on through the media but was drawn to the disturbances when she started seeing people running through the streets with their faces covered. Like Salma, she too was found by police with a large bag; hers contained bottles of spirits and cigarettes. Her court report indicates that she knew she was handling stolen goods. For Lucy, it seemed a risk worth taking, as she was a heavy drinker and a smoker. In her court report interview she acknowledged that she knew she was handling stolen goods. As a woman with nothing to lose (in terms of a job or fixed address) and someone who wasn't a stranger to coping with the consequences of the criminal justice system, those who knew her suggested that (and many others in a similar situation) events seemed quite 'exciting' for her in the city that night.

Lucy was arrested and remanded in custody. She was later sentenced to a 40 week custodial sentence but this was suspended for 18 months with a requirement that she attended a group work programme for women, delivered by a local charitable organization with a 'one-stop shop' on site for women offenders. The sentencing judge stated that Lucy had 'succeeded in getting yourself off heroin in the last year, your next task is to get yourself off alcohol'.

Since the riots

Lucy has not engaged with any of the requirements of the suspended sentence order, having missed appointments with her probation officer and planned times to attend the women's centre. As a result of this breach, Lucy was arrested and re-sentenced. In court, once again, she expressed a desire for prison, however, the judge attempted to encourage Lucy to engage with the programme sentencing her to a further suspended sentence. A sentence of seven weeks was passed, on this occasion suspending the prison sentence for 24 months providing a longer period to prepare for and complete the requirement to attend the women's programme. Due to a breach of an ASBO condition, Lucy had since been arrested and the suspended sentence was activated. She has begun the original ten month sentence in custody. According to one probation supervisor, prison may offer a 'mixed blessing' for Lucy:

Prison sometimes offers an opportunity to break the cycle, maybe give her a rest, but often they're just doped up and held, nothings addressed or moved forward. So they come out and are back on it just like before. The sentencing Judge wanted to offer Lucy the opportunity to engage with services that may help her make changes in relation to her alcohol use and personal circumstances. Those who had worked with Lucy considered what it would take to make a difference.

There are so many people like Lucy in the system … how can we solve their problems? It's not easy, there's no quick fix. We haven't got the resources to work with them as they need and so they stop coming. Because she didn't attend nobody really got to the bottom of her issues.

Supervising Probation Officer 1

We need to be more accessible to them, go out into the community and find the Lucys and gain some trust. It is so hard to break down that barrier initially, get them to the initial appointment where they engage.

Supervising Probation Officer 2

Two of the practitioners with whom I spoke talked about how they had also supervised her family members reflecting on the importance of working with the family network of people caught up in this lifestyle:

Dealing with [people like Lucy] as individuals … I'm not sure how much success we can ever have. I supervised her sister Anna and her partner, they were doing really well at one stage, but they got sucked back in [to the drugs]. It's almost impossible when that's the pull and the people around them are their support no matter how messed up it is.

Probation Officer

Case Study 3: 'Marlon'

Prior to the riots

Marlon is 41-years-old and has two previous criminal convictions. Twenty years ago he assaulted his then partner's father, for which he served a short period in custody. More recently, in 2011, he was convicted of a public order offence, where he verbally abused a police officer while drunk. He received a short community order with a requirement to attend a very short group work programme which aimed to improve problem solving skills. At the time of the riots, he was half way into this order and had attended a number of appointments with a probation officer. This low-intensity order was appropriate due to the low (10 per cent) likelihood of reoffending, measured using the 'offender group reconviction score' (OGRS) tool. However, it meant that

Marlon would be afforded only a very minimum level of intervention from the Probation Service. As such, his practitioner struggled to make any clear statements about Marlon, his lifestyle or his attitudes. He had also seen a 'Community Links worker', whose aim was to signpost Marlon to relevant mainstream support services, he was pursuing an in further education.

The night of the riots

Marlon had attended an appointment at probation on the morning of the riots and his probation officer had indicated that if he attended the six planned group sessions, he could complete his order within a few months. Later that day, he had been socialising and smoking cannabis at a friend's house on the other side of Manchester but later went through the city on his route home. Marlon had tried to find a shop to buy some cigarettes but all premises had been closed due to the riots. He said he entered a shop and took a box of 200 cigarettes. He spoke at length to both the police and probation, during the interview for his court report about being shocked by the events he witnessed in the city. He articulated how angry he felt about the damage done to the city he loves. However, he became involved himself stealing £70 of cigarettes, importantly for him though this was from a shop which had already been heavily looted.

Since the riots

Marlon was convicted of burglary and is serving a 14 month prison sentence. The probation practitioner supervising Marlon indicated that this level of punishment reflected that judges were 'making an example of people'. However, the probation officer who wrote his court report advocated the sentence, indicating that this should mean that Marlon would have sufficient time to complete some offence focused work in prison. However, there is no indication that any such work has begun. At the time of writing in February 2011, he was eligible for release in a few weeks, at the seven month stage. Upon release he may likely face further pressures of unstable housing and considering education avenues. Any ambition for these will likely be countered by the prison sentence he has now received to his criminal record.

Case Study 4: 'James'

Prior to the riots

By comparison, James has had a different experience. He finished school with five GCSEs and went into various training and work placements for the next few years. Life changed in his teens when James's brother died suddenly of a brain haemorrhage related to persistent alcohol consumption. James's began drinking heavily and lost his job. Relations with his parents became strained, in particular, with his father. By the age of 23, James had been diagnosed with chronic liver disease as a result of alcohol use and was drinking heavily most days.

In this period, he was convicted of a series of petty crimes such as driving-related offences, possession of cannabis, drunk and disorderly behaviour, and theft—invariably receiving fines and low level community orders. Most recently, in 2005, he was convicted of possession of an offensive weapon (a kitchen knife); he said he was carrying it in anger after arguing with his father about his drinking and had been told to leave the house. After he was sentenced, James had fairly sporadic attendance at probation due to the serious ill health of his mum: she had a stroke and following hospitalisation, came home with James assuming full-time care responsibilities. His order was revoked early on the grounds of these circumstances, before he had the chance to address his alcohol-consumption.

The night of the riots

At the time of the riots, James felt that he had his drinking under control and had been prescribed medication to support his abstinence from alcohol. In the two weeks prior to the riots, he had taken on some temporary work on the railways and was working most days but had started to drink in the evening. On August 9th he had not gone in work and had been drinking for the majority of the day but also taken cocaine. He said he couldn't remember the events of the night but there was CCTV evidence which identified him throwing stones at the police with a large group of people of varying ages. Despite this, James did not express any anti-police attitudes. Furthermore, there was no evidence from the CCTV (as reported in the police report) of him interacting with other rioters, or having been in contact via his phone or other forms of social media about the riots prior to his involvement. To the outsider, James's involvement in the riots appears to have been fuelled by alcohol and drugs but there are likely to be more complex reasons. His sister suggests that he 'got caught up, encouraged by a woman he knows well from the estate, that she egged him on and he was in no fit state'.

Since the riots

James received a 20 month prison sentence and one family member has said that 'this prison sentence has really shocked him'. His probation officer is now in regular contact with his sister and early release on home detention curfew has been granted to her address. His family want to support him, and believe that James can make progress:

> Working together with the family, it feels like we have a real opportunity when he comes out.
>
> *Probation Officer*

His probation officer recognised that James's drinking and offending appeared to be related to the emotional loss of his brother. The challenge now is to find professional support to address this, and encourage James to explore the option of counselling:

> Yes we need to try and get at the root of the problem, if he's ready to do that. I will encourage him to request bereavement counselling with his GP. I hope he'll think about it, its hard though for a man you know his age talking about things isn't easy.
>
> *Probation Officer*

When he is released, it may be more difficult for James to find work and establish access visits with his daughter.

Discussion

'Rioters': individuals versus the collective

This chapter illustrates that the rioters cannot be defined as one homogeneous group, nor can their motivations and behaviour be understood through the application of one theoretical paradigm. Some politicians and media have attempted to individualise the behaviour of the rioters, suggesting it reflects some sort of psychological defect or that the people who were involved were 'feral rats'. Other commentators refer to social dynamics such as poverty and the illegitimate use of power by the police as being the significant triggers to the events. The case studies reflected here represent the interaction of a diverse set of personal and social experiences leading up to riots. While there are undeniably some common themes which could be drawn out, they equally demonstrate that there is a need to look beyond the immediacy of the riots, and the need to explain these events at a macro level to place the individual's behaviour in their personal, social and structural context—the everyday lived realities of the individuals who became involved (Young, 2011).

As such, the aggregate datasets developed by MOJ and here as the broader Greater Manchester profile, can only go so far in explaining and understanding the riots. There remains the illusive gap between those involved and those caught and convicted for their involvement, it is almost impossible to establish the extent to which such profiles represent the wider group. The lens of the criminal justice system can distort the picture and the conclusions regarding who the rioters were and their motivations. Where attempts have been made to engage individuals through local networks, such as in the 'Reading the Riots' project, sampling relied heavily on court lists—reflected in the proportion of their interviewees who have previous convictions. As with the data based profiles such survey approaches cannot account for the representativeness of the sample of respondents, or wholly understand the variety of reasons why self-report versions may be distorted by the individual. We therefore need to continue to draw from other methodological approaches.

Whilst the application of case studies will not enable broad conclusions to be drawn about why the riots occurred, those in this chapter offer is an insight into the broader trajectories for adults already caught up in the CJS—how they say their involvement in the riots occurred and importantly the potential consequences. The evidence illustrates a need to move beyond the all-encompassing label of the 'rioter' which now seems to carry similar labelling powers as 'gang member' or 'single mother' (indeed, politicians have tried to attribute the disorder to both these social groups evident in their rhetoric). That the search for a 'collective' definition will inevitably ignore the critical interplay between the personal and social, and in some cases situational pressures which contributed to each individual's involvement in the disturbances.

In some cases the pathways into the disorder did not necessarily hinge on 'background' risk factors, for Salma or Marlon, participation was quite situational. This opportunistic response to the circumstances presented by the riots was also reflected in the 'Reading the Riots' responses.

> Many rioters conceded their involvement in looting was simply down to opportunism, saying that a perceived suspension of normal rules presented an opportunity to acquire goods and luxury items they could not ordinarily afford.
>
> *Guardian and LSE, 2011: 5*

While none of the individuals included in the case studies can be described as 'shopping for free' (as some younger looters from *The Guardian* and LSE research defined it) the fact that they were drawn to the riots, the plastic bags or the bootleg cigarettes, may be indicative of their position in society—struggling to find employment and/or financial footing. In particular in the case of Lucy her struggle with daily life on the margins of society, drinking on the streets and coping with a history of abuse, make the riots a somewhat unremarkable event. For Lucy the riots came and went, and her circumstances generally remain unchanged. In this context David Cameron's statement that the riots were 'not about poverty' are difficult to acknowledge, when individual's like Lucy face such economic hardship and lack a stake in society:

> They expressed it in different ways, but at heart what the rioters talked about was a pervasive sense of injustice. For some this was economic—lack of a job, money or

opportunity. For others it was more broadly social, not just the absence of material things, but how they felt they were treated compared with others.

Guardian and LSE, 2011: 24

The justice system goes back to the 'day job'

Deterrent and retributive sentencing, which was the overwhelming response, means the CJS will likely now compound the problems faced by the individuals in the case studies. It isn't necessarily the offence, but arguably the symbolic expressive punishments and the barriers now erected in front of the rioters that pose the greater problems and the challenge for the future. In considering the future for these individuals, it is evident that, regardless of action, most received heavy tariffs which may not necessarily benefit them in the future. Now the retributive dust is settling, we must carefully consider what the riots and the response to the riots means for the future.

In the cases of James and Marlon, they will leave custody having served a sentence which allowed them to do little constructive while held in overcrowded prisons. For James the experience will have been his first of prison, and as a result of the custodial sentence he lost his job. Positively though the keen expression of support by his family, and the ability to be released to his sister's address will at least buffer the challenge of resettling into society. In Marlon's case his accommodation has now been lost and so he will leave prison with the most significant obstacle many of those released face — securing a place to live.

So whilst speed and severity have been lauded as the key tenets of effective justice, in the context of containing the events and deterring immediate further disturbances, the consequences of such a response for the individuals and wider society in the longer term are less clear. The issues presented in this chapter raise questions about the political response to the riots to engage with and address both the causes of the initial disturbances in Tottenham and the speed with which they spread. There are valid reasons why the process of justice requires time — in order to ensure the key factors and consequences of decisions can be appropriately considered, and to avoid creating problems for the future.

From a probation perspective — these are precisely the individuals who practitioners are working with on a daily basis; people who reside within a 'cycle of disadvantage' where the social impacts upon the personal. For a variety of reasons, ranging from individual tragedy to wider structural factors, establishing a stake in society is a significant challenge for some individuals. Importantly, without this 'stake' the potential for individuals to take the risk of getting involved in such riots may increase. What the case studies begin to demonstrate is that for some the riots are not the most significant event — rather, it is the experiences and events which led up to the riots which have greater meaning in terms of how we understand and respond to those involved in the riots. Intervening with these individuals then becomes more than 'reacting' to the riots, it prompts wider questions of rehabilitation and effective sentencing, the role of wider social policies in creating a context within which such individuals can position themselves 'in' society.

References

AGMA Team Manchester Public Protection Officers meeting 23rd November 2011: 'The August 2011 Civil Disturbances: Compilation of Partner Reflections'.

Herbert , N. (14th September 2011) Speech to the Police Superintendents Association of England and Wales: www.justice.gov.uk/.../speeches/nick-herbert-justice-should-be-swift-sure

Guardian and LSE (2011) 'Reading the Riots: Investigating England's Summer of Disorder'. The research was supported by the Joseph Rowntree Foundation and Open Society Foundations.

Keegan, M. (14th October 2011) 'Manchester Riots: Four Youths Locked By Courts Have Sentences Reduced on Appeal': http://menmedia.co.uk/manchestereveningnews/news/s/1461927_manchester-riots-four-youths-locked-by-courts-have-sentences-reduced-on-appeal

Ministry of Justice (2011a) *Statistical Bulletin on the Public Disorder of 6th to 9th August 2011.* 15th September 2011.

Ministry of Justice (2011b) *Statistical Bulletin on the Public Disorder of 6th to 9th August 2011.* October update. 24th October 2011.

Newburn, N. (25th October 2011) 'A RiotBorn in Deprivation': www.guardian.co.uk/ms/p/gnm/op/smJrB_uC_bdfnu-gq4P-KHg/view.m?id=15&gid=commentisfree/2011/oct/25/uk-riot-born-in-deprivation&cat=uk

Young, J. (2011) *The Criminological Imagination*, Cambridge: Polity Books.

Steve Briggs is a Bachelor of Laws, Kings College London with an MSc in Social Work Studies from Chelsea College. He then worked as a Qualified Social Worker undertaking the full range of duties involving state intervention in family life, particularly in adult and child protection and concerning looked-after children. Between 1988 and 2004, Steve Briggs worked in local and national government managing teams of health and social care inspectors to register, inspect and take enforcement action to safeguard adults and children in all kinds of regulated settings. He retired in 2010 as Her Majesty's Inspector, Social Care in Ofsted, having carried out numerous Children's Services and CAFCASS inspections, Serious Case Review Evaluations, and Ministerial Briefings on serious child care incidents. He has always fought for vulnerable people and advocated non-urban perspectives in policy formulation.

15

RURALITY AND THE RIOTS:
FROM THE PANEL TO THE VILLAGE PUB

Steve Briggs

Introduction

Most, if not all, of the commentary on the riots has been in the context of urban areas—despite some references to 'less urban' and 'rural' areas being affected by the disturbances. Therefore, I would like to take forward the theme of 'rurality' which arises in several forms in this chapter. The first is through an understanding about how policing urban riots and other large scale public order events also affect rural areas, because the urban police forces managing those events inevitably borrow our police to do so. Known as 'mutual aid', I will explore its impact in August 2011. I cannot quantify the adverse effect on prevention and detection of rural crime by major urban policing events, because further research is needed, but I show that there is an impact. The second area which receives attention is the apparent back-tracking the House of Commons Home Affairs Committee and the Riot Communities and Victims Panel ('the Panel' hereafter) Interim Report in their investigations into the riots. Initially they had identified that the riots affected some 'less urban' or even 'rural' areas. However, having identified those areas, they gave what happened there no further scrutiny. This section challenges the uncritical way in which whatever went on in those areas may have been interpreted as part of the August 2011 riots.

The last section is based on a study of last summer's riots which takes opinions from ordinary people living in a rural village near Norwich, far from the scene of trouble. The study is small but significant, as it is the first to look at rural perceptions of urban riots in the social media age. Rural populations with no direct contact with the riots are likely to have informed their understanding of the disorder from news media. I will consider whether the opinions of the villagers in this study follow or escape from the 'presumed reality' of crime and disorder as constructed by media institutions (Yanich, 2005). Here I show how the 2011 English riots seem to have shattered the public's normal messaging pattern received from the media and made people really think.

How Rural Police Forces Were Affected by the Riots

Police forces often rely on borrowing from other constabularies to regulate major events. Seven force areas requested mutual aid from their neighbours in August 2011 at a significant cost which may or may not be recouped by the 'donor forces'.[1] In addition, leave may be cancelled, shift planning for the whole force may go out of the window, and special constables might be called up to police in 'donor' areas. For example, Hertfordshire Constabulary (2011) reported that while the force was deploying trained teams of officers to support the Metropolitan Police Service (MPS), the Special Constabulary was asked to respond rapidly to a request to provide additional high-visibility reassurance patrols between Tuesday August 3 and Sunday August 14.' During this period, it was noted how special constables performed 3,098 duty hours on dedicated town centre patrols and a further 1,555 duty hours on other high-visibility patrols—a staggering 4,653 hours in just six days! Intriguingly, this unusual deployment began the day before Mark Duggan was shot and suggests that the force was already short-handed or some significant problems were expected.

Officers may also be called away for long periods at short notice. The House of Commons Home Affairs Committee[2] heard that Cambridgeshire

---

1. Home Affairs Committee Paragraph 51 'Mutual Aid'. Cambridgeshire Constabulary website Freedom of Information request 0520/11 shows the force actually deployed 406 officers to the MPS in the first phase and 27 officers over three subsequent weekends for 4-5 days at a time, a huge chunk of resources.

2. Home Affairs Committee—16th Report—'Policing Large Scale Disorder: Lessons from the Disturbances of August 2011' Paragraph 31 Acting commissioner Tim Godwin stated: 'The thin blue line is quite thin on occasion. The August disturbances were one of these occasions'.

Constabulary deployed 120 officers per day to the MPS for a considerable time during the riots when the force only had 240 trained officers in the Police Support Unit (PSU).[3] It was admitted that Cambridgeshire police resilience was stretched and this illustrates how large scale urban disorder affects rural policing. What is not clear, and I suggest there is no official will to evaluate it, is the actual extent to which mutual aid force donations to our big cities lead to any occurrence or increase of crime and disorder in rural areas, and the extent to which time and opportunity is lost on pre-existing crime detection.

There is also a specific problem with mutual aid in riot situations in that constabularies are liable to pay compensation to uninsured claimants who suffer loss or damage during a riot. So if a police force is lending officers elsewhere and riot occurs in its own area, the donor constabulary is faced with liability it might not have incurred at full strength. A dilemma probably occurred in August 2011 for rural forces lending officers but also facing some disorder on their patch, between recording and reporting a sufficient volume of such crimes in the hope of recouping central funds, but not defining the disorder as a riot[4] to avoid civil liability for loss and damage. This may well account for what happened in Hertfordshire, as I will show.

The issue of force capacity and training is also dealt with authoritatively by HM Inspector of Constabulary: 'The Rules of Engagement: A Review of the August 2011 Disorders', HMIC (2011). In a further review of public order policing HMIC describes the August disorder as 'game changing'.

3. PSU trained officers would be likely to be more suitable for deployment in major public order events. A freedom of information request to Cambridgeshire Police (website, FOI reference 0520/11) shows that 406 officers were initially deployed to the MPS, with 27 officers being deployed over three subsequent weekends for four to five days each. The force was therefore averaging out in its evidence to the Home Affairs Committee.

4. The criminal law definition of riot is—twelve or more persons who are present together use or threaten unlawful violence for a common purpose and the conduct of them (taken together) is such as would cause a person of reasonable firmness present at the scene to fear for his personal safety. The offence of violent disorder is the same but with three or more such people. Coincidentally or not, very few charges of riot have been laid, most are for theft, burglary, criminal damage, affray and violent disorder which attract no civil liability to the police.

What the 'Inquiry' into the Riots Tells Us About Peripheral/Rural Areas

The Panel was the Prime Minister's flagship body exploring last summer's riots. In the context that her regarded the riots as 'criminality, pure and simple', the Panel's Interim Report set out 'the facts', outlining what happened where and who was involved using the following definition of riots:

> We have chosen for the sake of simplicity and consistency to use the term 'riot' in its broadest sense....to apply to all the criminal activity that could be regarded as part of the large scale public disorder which took place between 6 - 10 August.
>
> *The Panel, 2011: 24*

Here, the Panel departed significantly from Home Office definitions upon whose data it relied:

> There is no full account available of the large numbers of people who participated in the disorder. The closest there is are details of those who were arrested, and in some cases sent on to court, for the part they allegedly played. This will not necessarily be representative of all those who took part, and unless or until a person is convicted or cautioned, their participation is not proven.
>
> *Home Office, 2011: 4*

'All the criminal activity that could be regarded as part of ... ' is a rather loose definition. Without proper rigor in its investigation, the Panel risked vacuuming up any relevant-looking crime in the riot week without adequate contextual data. The risk of failing to neither distinguish between assertion and fact nor find proper links between cause and effect is inbuilt. This may be a secondary issue: concentrated disorder clearly occurred in the main urban locations where most of the damage was done. However last summer's outbreaks were a prime-time demonstration to the criminal class, to disaffected opportunists, and to 'joyriders', that when there are large scale policing operations in some areas, other areas are open to crime and disorder. What happened on the periphery in August 2011 ought to have been important to the Panel: a victim is a victim wherever they are.

The Panel's Interim Report included a timeline that identified 'affected areas' as the trouble spread (see also *Guardian* and LSE, 2011; HMIC, 2011). The locations included Cambridge, Milton Keynes, Medway, Gloucester and Oxford. These are provincial locations and arguably not the main riot affected areas, but now forever have riot-related history by virtue of the Panel's say so. Canvey Island in Essex, and Cheshunt and Waltham Cross in Hertfordshire were also identified by the Panel as 'affected areas'. Whether these are rural areas is debatable, and indeed what 'rural' means in the context of crime is often contested (Stenson, 2005). However, they are not densely-populated urban areas. *The Guardian* also finds 'validated incidents' of rioting also occurred in Slough, Chatham and High Wycombe. *Figure 1* shows the general pattern of street level crimes in summer 2011 in all these areas, including the types of crime that were selected as relevant by those police forces who reported to the Home Office on 'riot-related incidents'.[5]

It would be facetious to argue that the riots were on balance a good thing in most of these so-called 'affected areas': less recorded crime in August 2011 than in most other months in that summer. Acknowledging that these are the headline figures only, nevertheless they include all the types of crimes likely to have been deemed 'riot-related' and reported to the Home Office from that one week in August. The data points to numerous issues that have been overlooked. In the Panel's reports there is no description or investigation of any incident at any locations in *Figure 1*. Nor is there exploration of how crime related to 'rioting' in these peripheral and rural areas could be interpreted. There is also no investigation in the context of which crimes might normally occur in these time periods. Nor has it been considered

---

5. A one-off data request was sent to 22 forces via the Association of Chief Police Officers (ACPO) asking for detail on all crimes recorded, as well as the characteristics of those arrested, *that the forces considered to be related to the public disorder*. Forces were asked to supply data that were readily available to them; they were not asked to collect new data. This meant that some forces were unable to provide all data requested and there is some inconsistency between forces in the data provided, e.g. on the definitions of previous contact with police and gang membership. Two forces were initially identified as having some disorder and were approached as part of the data collection process but stated that they did not record any crimes related to the wider disorder during the period. One force did not provide any data. Home Office 2011, *Op cit*.

whether 'riot crimes' are everyday crimes that have been serendipitously sexed-up by some police forces.

Month	Slough	Chatham	H. Wycombe	Camb	Milton Keynes	Medway*	Glouc	Oxford	Canvey Island	Cheshunt	Waltham Cross
April	433	550	259	769	183	0	753	313	150	161	225
May	536	497	290	831	148	0	798	408	127	203	235
June	404	433	242	856	148	0	732	331	132	227	235
July	463	578	233	783	160	0	724	316	151	242	251
August	373	558	390	800	134	0	691	284	135	200	254
Sept	590	631	359	701	216	0	853	628	137	280	313

Figure 1: Police Crime Maps (PCM) statistics: reported street-level and ASB crimes by six month period April-September 2011, excluding 'other crime' (fraud, forgery, etc., and in September drug offences are recorded separately).

* PCM does not recognise Medway as a location.

Hertfordshire is recorded as one of the 'most affected areas' in the country (Home Office, 2011)[6] yet North Hertfordshire, St Albans, East Hertfordshire, Welwyn/Hatfield, and Hartismere experienced only 'isolated incidents'. No incidents were detailed in Broxbourne, Stevenage, Waltham Cross and Watford. Indeed, specific crimes and arrest are not recorded. Nor is any incident explained by any information that I can trace from Hertfordshire Constabulary or government departments, except at Waltham Cross. A search of news

---

6. Home Office 2011 *Op cit* p.3: The most affected areas are defined as 20 or more disorder-related crimes recorded. Also note that this report states that statistics will change as more arrests/convictions are secured. There were 62 people arrested in Hertfordshire, but it is not clear that they were all arrested in connection with disorder in Hertfordshire.

reports reveals some information[7] but suggests general downplaying by the police of any disorder relevant to the riots:

- A BBC news report on 9th August stated 'Hertfordshire and Bedfordshire police also said there was no truth in stories of disturbances in the two counties' (BBC, 2011);

- No relevant crime occurred in Cheshunt until 12th August (after riots ended), described by a police spokesperson as 'not believed to be connected to the recent disorder' (*Cheshunt Mercury*, 2011);

- Nothing much seems to have happened in Watford except a motley crowd gathered and dispersed (*Watford Observer*, 2011);

- A 17-year-old from Broxourne was arrested in Waltham Cross but there is no reports of massive disorder in Broxbourne (*Hertfordshire Mercury*, 2011);

- Three cars were set on fire in Stevenage but the local paper reported that 'A spokesman for Herts Police said there was no evidence that the arson attacks were linked to the rioting in London and elsewhere' (*The Comet*, 2011).

A policy of blandness seemed also to have been set as a response to the one quantifiable serious incident in the county at Waltham Cross, but this disguises a total contrast between official assertion and actual fact, and hides the cause and effect. Look:

Police are reassuring residents in Waltham Cross and Cheshunt following disturbances last night (August 7). The Force Communications Room received numerous calls from members of the public from 9.50 pm to report groups of youths in the area. Officers in high visibility clothing were deployed to the area and the situation was closely monitored with a command structure being set up. During the course

---

7. The Home Office also relied on press reports to help compile its data on crimes and arrests, suggesting a lack of faith in formal information channels.

of the night, a specialist public order unit was deployed along with officers from the Bedfordshire and Hertfordshire Dog Unit. Officers made use of a section 60 order and any groups of people were dispersed and the public disorder resolved peacefully. A burglary occurred at a jewellers in the High Street in Waltham Cross and criminal damage was caused to another jewellers in the same road. Two police cars were also damaged. No officers or members of the public were injured. Assistant chief constable Alison Roome-Gifford said: 'The disturbances seen in Waltham Cross and Cheshunt are being linked to disturbances in London'.

Hertfordshire Constabulary, 2011

But the truth was told beyond reasonable doubt when an offender appeared in court in January 2012; surely this would confirm the police were on top of the situation and that this was not as a consequence of the deployments 'high visibility public reassurance' from the Special Constabulary … or maybe not:

Prosecutor Alison Ginn told the jury that on the night (7 August) the police withdrew from the town centre (Waltham Cross) after a mob of young men in hoodies with scarves around their faces ran at them. The manager of Ozcan, Mrs Tugba Temel and her husband, who had been called out to the shop after the burglar alarm went off, were left on their own as a mob stole £20,000 worth of jewellery.[8]

So perhaps the rural/peripheral forces were stretched. But any visitor to small cities and town centres in both suburban and rural areas on Friday or Saturday night at any time of year can expect to see numerous youth groups: some paralytic or stoned, some hooded, some not, singly and in sizeable groups, behaving anti-socially with police attending. Perhaps a loosely-defined riot? Gladly, the rioting didn't reach Norwich. Here, the last riot

---

8. 'Looter jailed' Hertfordshire Constabulary Latest News, 21/02/2012. I also found that a claim for compensation under the Riot Damages Act by a Waltham Cross business was refused by the Police Authority on 9 September 2011 as follows: 'The rejection was on the grounds that "business interruption due to closure" is not covered by the Act and should therefore be by the insurers if appropriate. It was therefore not necessary to take a view on whether the events in Waltham Cross had constituted "riot" as set out in law. However, our initial view is that the necessary thresholds for constituting riot were not met'.

was in 1887 in an era of working-class discontent and shortly after a riot in West London.⁹

Why Not Norwich?

The Panel's terms of reference included finding out why the 2011 riots happened in some places and not others. Under the heading 'UK riots latest: why not Norfolk?' the local newspaper *Eastern Daily Press* (EDP) reported on 12 August 2011:

> Twitter pinpointed locations across Norwich in which the disaffected and angry would meet to emulate the disturbing scenes taking place across the country, and potentially cause chaos in the process. Except they didn't. Aside from a few extra policemen on the beat, the city remained calm and trouble-free. Over recent days, scenes of anarchy have been broadcast to an often stunned public, as what began as a peaceful protest against the shooting of a man turned into something more dangerous, leading to deaths itself. Starting in Tottenham, then Hackney and then boroughs across the capital, it has extended beyond the M25 to places like Manchester, Birmingham and even Gloucester, often fuelled by modern means of communication. So why has this happened and what likelihood Norwich is next?

The EDP then lists good community/police relations, on-the-ground social welfare projects in the more deprived parts of the city making an impact, and the relative isolation of the city as possible reasons for keeping the peace.

---

9.   'As if to underline the fear of the authorities, and respectable classes, on Friday January 14 the unemployed rioted in Norwich. The riot broke out after the unemployed had marched from a meeting addressed by Mowbray and Henderson of the local Socialist League branch to demand help. Here the insulting tone of the mayor, the unconcealed contempt from the councillors and the aldermen angered the crowd and they broke away. The mansions of the wealthy had their windows smashed and the shops in the centre of Norwich were looted. The riot if anything made the league more popular and there were large demonstrations to welcome Mowbray and Henderson on their release (from prison). The situation improved somewhat over the summer but as the winter approached unemployment again increased. A placard posted in Norwich in October "by unknown hands" threatened "Notice to all concerned: the unemployed do not intend to starve for any longer. If employment is not found for them, they will soon make some". As a result 200 special constables were sworn in. More sensibly the local authorities decided to temper their show of force by providing public works'. Extract from *The Slow Burning Fuse. The Lost History of British Anarchists*, John Quail, Paladin Books, 1978, p.69.

But although as the EDP hints, Gloucester—where rioting and looting took place—is rather like Norwich in terms of size and demography, so we cannot really judge the cause of a non-event here. But what for considering the views of a rural population totally separate from the disturbances. The last section in my discussion of 'rurality' is devoted to this area and is based on my small study in a rural village.

All About the Village and the Pub

Our village, Blafelda, is about three miles from the edge of the city of Norwich. Blafelda's population of 3,250 has grown steadily. High-density private housing fills the fields between the larger residences, older bungalows, and former council housing. The primary school was recently graded 'outstanding'. Two of the three community centres have recreation grounds attached. The two church communities are vibrant. There is a doctor's surgery and a care home for older people, a library, seven assorted small shops, a garage and two pubs. Public transport links by bus are good with a rail station in the neighbouring village. Blafelda is a busy village, distinctly rural with a sense of community, despite being cut in two by a large and busy bypass.

Despite this, employment is hard to find. Most people work in nearby Norwich (population 386,000 including suburbs), where the business and finance sector accounts for 31 per cent of employment, the public sector 24 per cent, and manufacturing just eight per cent. In the summer of 2011 the number of vacancies advertised on the local 'Jobs 24' website offering jobs in Norwich averaged around 180, mostly requiring skills and qualifications. The jobless total in the city alone averaged 4,400 with the rate for 18-24 year olds rising proportionately more quickly. In Blafelda, these days the large farms are run by just two or three people. Only four village employers have more than ten staff. Postcards in shop windows advertise more men than two years ago offering to garden or do minor building works, and women offering garment repairs, dog-walking, etc. Now twice the number of CRB-checked baby sitters advertise in the free monthly local magazine.

The Police Crime Map (PCM) of the area suggests that Blafelda is a pretty safe place, and indeed being a long-term resident, I can say it is. A typical month would record a single criminal damage; a burglary; a theft usually from property; a couple of incidents of domestic violence.[10] (DV is sadly consistent). Anti-social behaviour (ASB) is sporadic and not prominent. However, the dataset distorts the good name of the village because the crime map for Blafelda catches some high-density private housing in the next village, 'Allburnd', a mile away. Considering that Allburnd is also a comfortable community with similar demographics, its monthly crime rate is generally three or four times higher than Blafelda; in particular, with higher levels of burglary and theft from property. *Figure 2* shows the contrast between the two similar neighbouring communities in the summer of the riots:

Month 2011	Street level/ ASB Crime Allburnd	% total Allburnd crime	Street level/ ASB Crime Blafelda	% total Blafelda crime
April	36	70	11	65
May	28	66	10	95
June	28	58	2	20
July	21	68	5	75
August	16	75	2	40
September	8	50	2	66

Figure 2 — PCM statistics for crime in the two villages, April-September 2011.

(The original contains some extra notes of explanation)

---

10. This information comes from a free monthly magazine posted through our letterboxes with information about local crime from the police community support officer and is more detailed than the PCM data.

My small study of pub quiz attendees in Blafelda reveals they were very aware of the riots over 100 miles away, but were completely unaware of the 'higher crime rates' across the fields in Allburnd, despite the greater probability of being burgled by a person from Allburnd than becoming a victim in a riot. This may contradict other findings about perceptions of rural crime in that when it does occur it may receive disproportionate attention (Mingay, 1989), and that rural residents view ASB as more serious than it really is (Cloke, 1993; Marshall and Johnson, 2005; Williams, 1999). Although Cloke (1993) suggested that fear of crime in rural areas could be attributed more to a perceived threat to the rural 'idyll', the real impact of rural crime perhaps requires further and more discerning investigation.[11]

Although the recession has hit business in the Queen's Arms hard, pub quiz night is popular. Most attendees are locals and predominantly white British.[12] The teams mostly comprise of couples and families members mixed with friends, or groups of friends. New teams occasionally turn up to try it out. Few parents attend because it runs from 8.30 pm to 10.30 pm The quiz is a comradely affair, with much politically incorrect innuendo and laughter. It always includes some pictures and questions about current affairs, politics and history, so participants tend to have some knowledge about the body politic, and seemed keen to facilitate this research.

Methodology

I had to balance having sufficient material, and respecting my own part in the village where I have lived for 28 years (I would call this low-key, high-visibility). It was not likely that any manageable means of research would provide large enough numbers of good enough responses to be statistically significant. Therefore some tools used in ethnographic methods such as

11. Perhaps the issue is that research has been centred around rural business crime as outlined in the helpful report by the Crime Reduction Unit: www.crimereductionunit.org.uk/sections-detail.php?s=195&subs=81&id=5&tableID=269, which tends to source data from people with a lot to lose.

12. County Demographic Update 2010, released March 2011 states seven per cent of the population are of ethnic minorities (i.e. not white British/white Irish). It is an area of net migration, primarily older people, however there has been a significant number of migrant workers entering the county, the most significant nationalities in the latest figures being Lithuanian, Latvian, Polish and Bulgarian. In our district council area only 2.4 per cent of the population are not white.

qualitative interviewing proved useful. The number of possible respondents at the pub quiz and the ability to pop back for supplementary discussions gave me the best target group. Social class was not investigated, but this is not a posh pub, and not really a class-conscious village. The landlord allowed me to interrupt the quiz routine and roam around asking people questions. I asked for written replies to open questions and then followed up with interviews and informal discussions based on those responses. This all took place on four Monday evenings from 15 February 2012. I spoke with 46 people, with 23 written returns completed (12 female, 11 male). Ages ranged from under 26 (n=8); 27 to 50 (n=1); and over 50 (n=14). This is fairly typical for the pub demographic. Those that I to spoke in more detail included two pharmacists, two nurses, a bookmaker, a Post Office manager, an engineering worker, two teachers, a home-maker, two students, and two care staff. I have known some of these people for years. Firstly I consider how and why the disorder occurred, as seen by villagers; secondly, their views on the media reporting; thirdly what they thought of the rioters; finally what the criminal justice response should be.

How and Why the Riots Started

Most respondents gave several causes for the riots with wider explanations mixing the how and why, with distant reference to the shooting of Mark Duggan. No one referred to him in person and in subsequent discussion only one person did so. Four people gave a fairly accurate view of how things started, although perspectives differed:

> The demonstrators needed an excuse for civil disobedience which happened when it was deemed that an underdog in society was shot by authority. R14

> Began as a legitimate protest to a police shooting. Escalated and got out of hand like many protests do when a minority take advantage of the situation to cause havoc. R21

However, the immediate cause seemed less important than the major social issues. In the main, this was attributed to deprivation and unemployment as highlighted by these two respondents:

315

Social deprivation, unemployment and plain boredom of how they had seen their lives and the lack of prospects for them. Some people jumped on the bandwagon seeing shops being looted giving themselves the chance to get something for nothing especially goods they wouldn't have the funds to buy. For this to happen great organization would be needed, created by social networking internet sites. Without these it would have been impossible to organize and the carnage would have much less. R16

I don't know how they started, but I think they happened because a lot of people feel hard done by, without work, little money to live on. R19

As R16 hints, there was a clear perception of escalating events. In addition, R15 said it was 'young people taking advantage of a bad situation' while R20 thought that despite a 'small protest march at the death of a man, several other people joined just to cause disruption'. As R3 indicates:

I believe it was due to an event that happened with the police and a gang. This then acted as a domino effect and caused more and more people to join forces and create criminal activities such as stealing, violence and anger against the police and Parliament.

In contrast to the prominence given in the Panel's Final Report, only two people mentioned poor parenting as potential a causal factor. The words 'copy-cat'; 'breakdown in (social) responsibility'; 'something for nothing'; 'no/lack of respect' cropped up in numerous replies. Several people also suggested that an element of organized criminality was at play, and some suggested that this was encouraged by a criminal justice system that had not delivered or was not effective enough in deterring offenders. Ten respondents thought the media and social media such as Twitter were a major cause of the disorder and that it led to the escalation of the unrest in other cities. This view was typified by R23, a hospital theatre nurse saying: 'Coverage of the shooting of one young boy hit all the papers plus television, with facebook/ twitter etc. A lot of attention was stirred up for the wrong reasons, helping to promote the riots'. Significant emphasis was placed by some on the inadequacies of the police, either for not being better prepared, or preventing the riots getting out of hand.[13]

The word 'greed' was used by three people as a motivator for the rioters. In direct contrast, 'greedy bankers/greedy wealthy' were cited by others. R14 mentioned 'the unfair distribution of wealth, the greed of capitalist bankers, utility companies'. By contrast, R6 said:

> There are a lot of ordinary people in this country, Steve, who feel and who are treated badly. The rich are getting richer, they flaunt it in your face, and they don't give a toss and never will.

Views of News Media Reporting

Most respondents' knowledge about the events came from television (n=21). Other sources were newspaper (n=8); radio (n=3); internet (n=1); Twitter/Facebook (n=3). Some had gleaned their knowledge by taking to friends and family (n=4). One couple knew someone who was directly affected, their daughter was trapped in a friend's house for 48 hours by the complete breakdown of law and order in central Croydon. Of interest is the high level of criticism the villagers made about the media coverage of the riots. For example, R2 said it represented 'enforced panic and negative coverage which was construed around violence'. The villagers also recognised that the 'over the top' reporting 'fuelled' further unrest (R7, R1) because 'people came out to hang around' (R22) in the absence of the police, which R3 believed 'advertised it to gangs and criminals allowing them to organise other riots and criminal activity'. In discussion with five people one evening, they referred to the constant necessity for news media to fill space, sell their product and 'the need to fill time by wheeling out the experts for everything' as R10 said, and find news in August 'the silly season' (R8, R12).

---

13. This was a view expressed by several over-50s who had seen the impact of the Brixton riots in 1981 and Broadwater Farm, etc. They believed that the police should expect more trouble in August, described by one couple as 'the riot month'. This perspective is an echo of the evidence submitted to the Home Affairs Committee by the Black Police Officers Association who said that the police service had not retained its 'collective memory'.

Positive responses about media coverage were fewer and briefer. R16 a betting shop manager being the most positive, 'Excellent news coverage giving full details and reasons for the riots giving fair assessments for both sides — the protesters, the rights of ordinary people and the businesses involved'. However what surprised me most was the emotional impact months later from people with no proximity to events and no connections except through the media:

> Shocked and ashamed that such a thing could take place in this country. R9.

> It certainly showed us what was happening, and was quite frightening to watch. R18.

> It was horrible seeing these people reacting, the way they were causing so much damage to their own towns they should be ashamed of themselves. R19.

> They seemed in some way to almost feel this sense of shame. Graphic images of loss of civil control and destructiveness on our city streets had therefore scorched the rural viewer. However, in conversations there was also an unsolicited sense of despair/disgust about politicians, with shock and horror about the devastation.

Opinions About the Rioters and Looters

The understanding that respondents had expressed about the causes did not extend to tolerance for the actions taken. The most common words used to describe the people directly involved in rioting and looting were 'morons', 'scum', 'thugs', 'just thieves' and 'opportunists'. Surprisingly, only one person, (R4, a young person himself), wanted to 'bring back capital punishment'. Several explained their view of those involved in the context of a place in society, but any mitigation was qualified:

> They have no moral conscience or genuine desire for social change. It was driven by greed — food was not stolen so they are not trying to feed their families. It shows a complete lack of respect for others, property and goods. R12.[14]

---

14. R12's father had retired at very senior rank in the MPS. She was the most critical of all the respondents at the preparedness and reaction of the police which she thought was a leadership issue.

Morons, greedy, just as bad as those they thought they were attacking [police, state]. The Capitalists were unscathed and the innocent law-abiding citizens became the victim. R14.

There was also a view from some respondents that those who got caught up in the 'social media/ Twitter-type' excitement—who turned up for no apparent motive other than to be there but may have got involved in any case—were of a different order of social problem: something new and different which had not been seen before.

What the criminal justice system should do

It was no surprise to hear the words 'harsh', 'severe', 'heavily' and 'stiffer' used for punishments. But responses were not without reason. R22 is a Post Office manager in Norwich and sees a lot of day to day hassle. He graded his response accordingly:

[They should be treated] harshly. These are not minor incidents. Not like 'Occupy London'. They are major incidents. If dealt with lightly they will only encourage more people to join next time.

What might be termed a 'hard line' response came from nine people. Despite my challenging their assertions about prison being the answer in the light of the fact of the UK's already high prison population, they put cogent arguments for a sentence being a sentence in full with no remission and therefore a proper deterrent, which they asserted most offenders did not get:

Word soon gets round with the criminal fraternity that the most you will get is two years, so if you come out and you have made £50k out of it in the bank, it's a good return. R16.

It is difficult to counter this view since the Ministry of Justice itself admits that comparing effectiveness of custodial versus community service based sentencing is beyond its current data competence (MOJ, 2011). It is therefore similarly difficult to support the number of respondents who thought that there should be community sentencing or restorative justice, not imprisonment, and that this ought to be a cheaper and more effective result. R17 wrote:

> Make the people who did if they are caught go and clean all the graffiti off walls and paint over things they can't clean as it will be more effective than a fine or prison.

R17 has multiple sclerosis, life is quite a struggle, but she makes the best of things. Her further insight was to recall that:

> [In] the old days when they had stocks, you was put in the stocks so everyone could see what you done and no argument. You'd feel a prat. If they go to prison, no one sees them and they can come out saying they are the 'big I am'. No one can say not and they just go and do it again.

Maybe this is homespun philosophy, but maybe there is something to learn about swift and locally visible restorative punishment too.

Discussion

The underlying theme of my chapter is rurality in the context of the August riots. I have examined it in three ways. Firstly, how 'rural policing' may be affected by large scale urban riots, secondly, how 'peripheral/rural' disturbances were constructed as part of the August unrest and lastly what rural people, insulated in location and daily routines from the disorder, had to say about the events they watched on TV. Here I summarise the main themes in more detail.

I have examined constabulary and police authority and Police Federation websites, and local press reports for all the 'affected areas' identified in *Figure 1*. I found that the incidents in Waltham Cross and Chatham included or were prompted not by local 'rioters' but by people who travelled out from London, I suspect specifically for crime.[15] In Gloucester and Cambridge they were locals milling around the town centre, possibly not uniquely so. The aetiology of the crowd and its psychology will be different and therefore, as

---

15. This adds to the picture being created by *The Guardian* and is probably a further distance of travel than they have noted to date.

Reicher and Stott (2011) would indicate, the route to prevention will probably be different. Gloucester is the only location in which it seems to me there was a large scale, clearly abnormal incident. In all the other rural/peripheral locations, from such information as is visible, the notion that they ought to be classed as 'riot-affected areas', as are Tottenham, Croydon or Birmingham just does not follow. I have no doubt that with the reality of expenditure cuts for years to come the prospect of more serious sporadic or rapidly spreading disorder is real. If the measures outlined in the robust and focused recommendations of HMIC's reports into the riots are put into effect, it may be that the 'tipping element' of loss of control by the police and consequent gain of power by the crowd will not occur, but this requires major re-resourcing when all the police websites are also prominently debating the cuts.

Despite all the effort of the various the inquiries so far, we perhaps are none the wiser what really happened in those areas that I have called 'peripheral/ rural'. There was great contradiction between the Panel's reporting and Home Office documentation, which define these areas as 'riot affected', and police statements made at the time that most incidents that reached their or media and social media attention were 'unconnected to the riots'. As I have shown in Hertfordshire, deemed to be one of the most affected areas, some of this is positively misleading. Sadly, while Lord Scarman was appointed by a 'liberal' Conservative Home Secretary to document the reasons for the riots of 1981, I very much doubt that the current Liberal/ Conservative Coalition, populated by comfortable people who seem to want power at the expense of most things, wished to be so forensic.

In their persuasive summary of crowd behaviours, *Mad Mobs and Englishmen*, Steve Reicher and Clifford Stott note that media values mean we will look at the 'exciting and transgressional elements' of the riots. They find that 'proper' riots involve specific kinds of triggers, such as that in Tottenham and some of the affected areas. Accompanied by a loss of control by police, this re-enforces the feeling of power in the crowd, but more generally, individuals in crowd situations are strongly influenced by the psyche of that crowd at that time, criminal, political, casual and so on. To overlook the makeup of those crowds in seeking future solutions to public disorder is 'to throw away gold dust' (Reich and Stott, 2011). I suggest that this is what has happened with the 'peripheral/rural' riot affected areas, because no proper inquiry has been made. I am sorry to say that despite a lot of well-intentioned energy and some useful work, I believe the Panel failed to find the facts as they set out to do. Unfortunately their work will be misapplied for political capital, and value will be lost in their veritable flood of recommendations.

My interpretation of findings from the 46 pub quizzers is that, given the chance to express their views, ordinary people living in a seemingly comfortable and far-removed rural area welcomed the opportunity to speak about the riots. They were not necessarily giving me political or media stereotyped opinions but had reflected on the events and articulated specific views. There was a strong sense of shock and upset. Perhaps when an event is so emotive, people escaped the constructs of media institutions (assuming that the media themselves have time to apply any filters to disaster events). Most saw through the sensational and transgressional elements of media broadcasting (Jewkes, 2004; Yanich, 2005; Reicher and Stott, 2011). They ignored any attempt to guide them away from criticism of state institutions (Chomsky, 1989). In the rawness of the event they formed quite independent views.

Villagers had a much clearer opinion about the underlying reasons than the actual cause, which seemed less important than the major issues. Poor policing was identified as an aggravator to the situation: management unpreparedness in the peak riot month, and ineffective on the ground once it kicked off (*Guardian* and LSE, 2011). Graphic constant media coverage and social media was also identified as a catalyst to the disorder. Overall, the two strongest causal themes were firstly: copy-cat/domino opportunism coupled with criminality. Secondly inequality/deprivation/unemployment/austerity programme.

However, the theme of greed across the social spectrum: rioters wanting something for nothing and ostentatious wealth or bankers activities. These ideas were not detached from each other and suggested that most respondents had a more balanced view of the causes than expected. This was not thought to be about 'criminality, pure and simple' nor to do with 'poor parenting' — a feature which the Panel suggested was one main feature.

Sympathy for participants in the disorder was absent. They were regarded as opportunist criminal thugs, with a few acknowledgements about disenfranchisement or differential treatment by the authorities. Many felt that the lack of prospects for many young people was no excuse for criminality.

Half the respondents thought punishments were not long enough, but half thought community sentencing or restorative justice was the best sanction. But for most of us, like 9/11 and 7/7, it was witnessing an unprecedented event and it wasn't outsiders and terrorists, it was thousands of British people trashing what could have been the retail park up the road ... but luckily for Blafelda, it wasn't.

References

BBC News (2011) 'Police from east of England sent to help', 9th August 2011.

Cheshunt Mercury (2011) 'Gang of yobs attack Cheshunt flats', 19th August 2011.

Chomsky, N. (1989) *Necessary Illusions: Thought Control in Democratic Societies*, Boston: South End Press.

Cloke, P. (1993) 'On "Problems and Solutions": The Reproduction of Problems for the Rural Communities in Britain During the 1980s' in *Journal of Rural Studies*, 9: 113-121.

Guardian and LSE (2011) 'Reading The Riots: Investigating England's Summer of Disorder', London: *Guardian* LSE.

Hertfordshire Constabulary (2011) *Special Constable News*, August 2011.

Hertfordshire Mercury (2011) 'Arrests after Waltham Cross riots' 8th August 2011.

Home Office (2011) *An Overview of Recorded Crimes and Arrests Resulting From Disorder Events in August 2011*, London: Home Office.

HMIC (2011) *The Rules of Engagement: A Review of the 2011 Disorder*, London: HMIC.

Jewkes, Y. (2004) *Media and Crime*, London: Sage.

Reicher, S. and Stott, C. (2011) *Mad Mobs and Englishmen: Myths and Realities of the 2011 Riots*, London: Constable and Robinson.

Riots Victims and Communities Panel (2011) *Five Days in August: An Interim Report on the 2011 English Riots*, London: Riots Victims and Communities Panel.

Marshall, B. and Johnson, S. (2005) *Crime in Rural Areas: A Review of the Literature for the Rural Evidence Research Centre*, London: Rural Research Centre.

Ministry of Justice (MOJ) (2011) *Compendium of Re-offending Statistics and Analysis*, London: MOJ.

Stenson, K. (2005) 'Sovereignty, Biopolitics and the Local Government of Crime in Britain' in *Theoretical Criminology*, Vol. 9(3): 265-287.

The Comet (2011) 'Fear that riots have spread to Stevenage after triple arson attack' 10th August 2011.

Watford Observer (2011) 'Undercover reporting of the Watford 'riot', 10th August 2011.

Williams, B. (1999) *Rural Victims of Crime in Dingwall*, G. and Moody, S. R. (eds.) (1999), *Crime and Conflict in the Countryside*, Cardiff: University of Wales Press.

Yanich, D. (2005) 'Kids, Crime and Local Television News' in *Crime and Delinquency*, Vol. 51(1):103-132.

Part IV

THE WIDER PICTURE: SOCIAL CHANGE
AND GLOBAL DISCONTENT

John Strawson is Reader in Law at the University of East London and Director of the Centre on Human Rights in Conflict. He works in the areas of International Law and Middle East Studies with particular interests in Postcolonialism and Colonial Legal History. His publications include: *Partitioning Palestine: Legal Fundamentalism in the Palestinian-Israeli Conflict* (2010).

16

STATE-SPONSORED RIOT:
TALES OF REVOLT AND CRIME IN EGYPT 2011

John Strawson

We are the Youth
Who opened the Door
And threw out Hosni
With the Dogs[1]

Introduction

Revolutions are destructive events. They tear down those in powers and
unleash a profound disorder that cuts deep into society. All that was once
legal becomes illegitimate. Police stations are attacked, centres of power set
on fire and the streets become the site of slogans that were once sedition.
As Trotsky writes 'at those crucial moments when the old order becomes no
longer endurable to the masses, they break over the barriers excluding them
from the political arena, sweep aside their political representatives and create by their own interference the initial ground work for the a new regime'
(Trotsky 1965: 17). This was all true in Egypt during the 18-day uprising
against the 30-year rule of Hosni Mubarak in January and February 2011.
The colourful chant of the youth in Tahrir Square confirms Trotsky's view
of the active manner by which the masses made sense of the events in which
they participated. This chapter will argue that the manner in which the
Mubarak leadership sought to retain power revealed much about the specific

---

1. Slogan used by a group of young people in Tahrir Square in April 2011, in notes retained by
    the author.

character of the Egyptian state.[2] Under pressure, the regime was not only prepared to use the official state apparatus against the popular movement but also a layer of criminal 'thugs' which had previously been recruited to police, the ruling party and the business class. This adds a new dimension to Engels observation that in the last analysis, the state is 'but armed bodies of men' (Engels 1968: 586-589), and while he was aware that these were supplemented by 'material adjuncts, prisons and institutions of coercion of all kind,' he could not have imagined how degenerate a state could become which would allow convicts to escape prisons to cause havoc while mobilising thousands of hired 'thugs' against an uprising in order to cling to power. New special armed bodies indeed.

Mubarak's Regime

Mubarak presided over a regime that was in effectively run by his family and cronies. Political power was monopolized by the ruling National Democratic Party (NDP) and economic wealth was dependent on access to those in power. While Hosni Mubarak was President, one son Gamal ran the party and another Alaa, had a vast stake in the free enterprise sector of the economy. Beneath the family was a network of powerful people linking together political power, the free enterprise economy and the military. The formal institutions of the state, such as Parliament, therefore became the plaything of those in power. Elections were rigged to ensure that the ruling party remained dominant and the 2010 elections had seen a particularly ruthless application of this policy with only a handful of opposition candidates being 'allowed' seats (Al-Aswany 2011: 39-42). The role of the state institutions by and large was to rubber stamp the decisions of the governing elite. At its disposal were the central security forces and the police under the control of the Ministry of the Interior who were charged with keeping order.

Throughout his 30 year rule, Mubarak had relied on laws under the state of emergency that had been declared in the wake of the assassination off his predecessor, Anwar Sadat. The regime ensured that political activity was carefully monitored by the powerful and pervasive intelligence service and

---

2. I would like to acknowledge the influence of the papers by Charlotte Peevers. Yoriko Otomo and Stephen Humphries presented at the 'International Law and the Periphery Conference', held in Cairo, February 17-19, 2012.

many opposition movements were banned such as the Muslim Brotherhood. Activists who were seen as particularly dangerous were detained or possibly tried (but usually in military courts). Prisons were notorious for their appalling conditions and torture was commonplace (Amnesty International, 2010). Egyptians were as much excluded from political influence as they were also the victims of social exclusion, with some 50 million of its 84 million national population living in poverty. Neither politics nor economics brought benefits for the average Egyptian. As Amin has observed Egypt was a good example of Gunnar Myrdal's concept of a 'soft state' (Amin 2011: 7-19). While all the trappings of the state were excessively on display, decision making at all levels of society took place outside of it. The Egyptian regime protected the elite through political manipulation, the repression of opponents and safeguarded the interests of the rich at the expense of the poor. It was for all these reason that the most popular slogan during the demonstrations that began on January 25 was 'Bread, Elections and Social Justice' (see: Ghonim 2012: 169; El-Menawy 2012: 72).

The Regime's Historical Origins

Mubarak headed a regime that had its origins in the 1952 revolution (Cook 2011: 39-63). The decay that was evident in 2011 was the result of the way in which this regime had been formed and developed. When the Free Officers Movement overthrew King Farouq and removed the pro-British government in 1952, it had set out to create a new dispensation for a free Egypt. However, as the result of a political struggle in the Revolution Command Council in 1954, Gamal Abdul Nasser became the dominant figure and the fateful decision was taken to reject holding democratic elections (El-Din 1995: 177-187). In place of democracy, the revolutionaries opted for a Soviet-style regime that would combine the leadership of a single party with central economic planning, nationalization of industry and the collectivisation of land while ensuring a central role for the military.

In the 1970s, Nasser's successor Anwar Sadat changed course with the economy and announced the period of opening — the infitah — which saw de-nationalisation of industry and return of land to private enterprise (Fahmy 1989). However, there was a military sector of the economy that was controlled by the Ministry of Military Industries which remained firmly under control of the armed forces. While freeing up a large sector of the economy from state ownership, the government remained under the monopoly control of the ruling party renamed the National Democratic Party. The disbursement of the nationalised sector and collectivized land saw the emergence of a powerful business class that had become entrepreneurs through their connections with the ruling party, rather than their own endeavours. The nationalised assets were disposed of by state officials who sought out potential entrepreneurs who would be compliant with the monopoly of political power by the party. At the same time those who wanted to buy assets and stock needed to ingratiate themselves with the officials.

From the mid-1970s, this class rapidly grew rich and their ability to do so was dependent on maintaining their close proximity to power. In addition, it was the state that gave them access to the international market. When Mubarak assumed power in the wake of the assassination of Sadat, he inherited a state quite different to that which Nasser had established (see, generally, Baker 1990). On the outside the state looked strong with its large military and security forces and the constitutional niceties ensured that there was an elected President and Parliament and distinct judiciary (see, generally, Mustafa (2007). However, economic liberalisation had eaten its way through this edifice and undermined the formal process of decision-making meaning that corruption and graft were commonplace. The relationship between politicians and business at all societal levels was based on an exchange between political patronage and economic gain. Through these interactions politicians, officials and business people created a cosy strata which held sway over national and local developments. Whether it was obtaining planning permission, getting promotion or gaining concessions, it was this layer in society that was decisive. The military meanwhile had maintained and extended its sector in the economy. The Ministry of Military Industries was based on the model used by the Soviet Union, which the Nasser Government had copied. The original plan was that the military would be economically self-sufficient and so would be assured of equipment, munitions and ancillary supplies (e.g. housing, medical services, uniforms) without having to rely on civilian sources. Over the years the Ministry had overseen the growth of a parallel economy with a stake in pharmaceuticals, engineering, financial services, household goods and holiday resorts. Currently it is estimated that the military control between 30 per cent and 40 per cent of the whole economy. This sector has no public accountability for its financial situation and there is no record of tax paid (if any). As with the central military budget, security is the justification of completely secrecy. While the military appears as a state within a state, in reality, it has remained dominant within the government apparatus supplying all five heads of state in 60 years with many military personnel holding high political office including occupying the Ministry of Defence.

State Decline the Arab Spring and the Egyptian Uprising

By the beginning of 2011, Mubarak's future was much publicly discussed. Then in his early 80's the question of his successor much exercised the ruling clique. It was evident that some circles were planning that Mubarak's younger son Gamal would assume the Presidency in his father's place. Such hereditary Republics are not unknown in the Middle East where the Assads of Syria stand as exemplars. However, the attempt to impose Gamal Mubarak on the Presidency was so blatant that it drew attention to the character of the whole regime. There was a sense of public outrage and even some within the elite thought that this could be a step too far (El Menaway 2012: 98-99). The plan highlighted the manipulative and crony character of Egyptian politics and underscored the contempt that the regime held for democracy and equality. In the weeks before the beginning of 2011, a massive wave of protests had swept through Tunisia which had removed Zine El Abidine Ben Ali from power. This had created a frisson throughout the Arab world so long in the thrall of autocratic governments. The fall of a tyrant in the face of a popular upsurge where large sections of the population appeared to have lost their fear of the security forces introduced a new element into the politics of the Middle East; the 'Arab Spring' was born (Anderson, 2011). While Egyptian Ministers insisted that Tunisia was a unique case and that Egypt was stable opposition movements especially youth groups began to organize a demonstration against the government on January 25 2011. The mobilization for demonstration was aided by the use of social media including Facebook. In this, the page created by Wael Ghonim titled 'Kullena Khalid Said' (We Are All Khalid Said) protesting the brutal death of Khaled Said at the hands of police in Alexandria in 2008, was to play a pivotal role.

As protesters filled Tahrir Square on January 25 neither they nor the government they were challenging had any feel for the course of events. For the government which had seen protests come and go over the previous decades the question was whether or not the events could be contained or whether decisive action would be needed by the security services to disperse them. Tahrir Square is large space in the downtown Cairo which runs parallel to the Corniche along the Nile and is a major transport intersection. Perhaps most significant in this context, the largest buildings on the square are the Mogamma building — the Ministry of the Interior — and the NDP headquarters. It is also the home to the Egyptian Museum and the original campus of the American University in Cairo. Mass demonstrations in the square therefore cause tremendous disruption to the traffic and indeed to everyday life right at the heart of the city.

The demonstration took place on National Police Day; a holiday which commemorated a bloody clash between Egyptian police and British troops in Ismailia 1952 when 50 Egyptian officers died (Cook, 2011: 181). The holiday was relatively new and its purpose undoubtedly was an attempt to re-attach the corrupt and brutal police with a patriotic past. The irony of a mass demonstration demanding freedom under the shadow of the Ministry of the Interior building which controlled the police was not lost on the protesters. Nor was the challenge lost on the authorities. In a massive operation around 30,000 police (El-Menway, 2012: 64) were deployed to control the demonstrators. The police both in uniform and plain-clothes surrounded and infiltrated the protesters. As the crowds became more confident, they began to target symbols of the regime and massed outside the NDP building while the police responded with tear gas. Throughout the day, the police battled to keep control of the 100,000 or some demonstrators using their well-established tactics; snatching individuals seen as ring-leaders, and the liberal use of water cannons, tear gas, rocks and live bullets to try to disperse the people. On this occasion, however, the demonstrators would not leave the square. A deadline of midnight was declared for the masses to retreat yet the crowds stayed. Eventually massive and concentrated force succeeded in removing the people — although many re-grouped elsewhere in central Cairo. However, believing that the demonstrators had been crushed, the Minister of the Interior insisted on driving through the square to demonstrate that it has been brought back under his control (El-Menawy, 2012: 75). This victory drive was premature and as we know the square was never really reclaimed by the Mubarak forces again.

Tahrir was not the only site of contest and throughout Egyptian cities such as Alexandria, Suez and Port Said other oppositional actions were taking place. The police were the first line of defence for the regime and the Interior Ministry was used to dealing with limited protests, strikes and terrorism in the past. However, confronting a mass of citizens who has lost their fear of the security forces was a quite new experience. While January 25 apparently passed with the apparent restoration of order, it was in fact the day that a critical moment in the relationship between the people and the regime had been decisively broken. Over the next two days, it became apparent that January 25 had been a turning point in the mood of a broad section of the Egyptian public; like their Tunisian comrades they too had lost their fear of the security forces and indeed of the authorities in general. This time it was not that the security forces had ceased to act but quite the contrary. Despite the fact that large numbers of activist were detained and questioned, including Wael Ghonim,[3] the public attitude towards authority had changed and the police in particular no longer had legitimacy.

January 28 was to be the most decisive date of the 18-day uprising. A call had been put out for mass demonstrations across Egypt on what was to be a 'day of rage' in protest at the brutality of the police and security forces. The initial police reaction to demonstrators was so violent that hundreds were killed and thousands injured. There had also been hundreds of arrests. Instead, the tactics of the regime deepened the sense of injustice about government behaviour in general. At the same time, the Ministry of information had used its powers to ensure that none of this was to be broadcast on state television. Instead a concerted political attempt was made to portray January 25 as a foreign plot, Facebook was said to be owned the CIA and it was suggested that the planning for the protests had been organized abroad by powers that wanted to disrupt Egypt (Ghonim, 2012: 191-193). These positions were argued in all the state media including the newspapers. On the

---

3. Wael Ghonim was a pivotal figure in the uprising as it was his Facebook page 'We are all Khaled Said' that had attracted hundreds of thousands of Egyptians to the brutality of the regime and had been critical in publicising the 25 January demonstration.

one hand, they sought to downplay what had taken place while, at the same time, to characterize it as the act of a foreign hand. This media campaign did much to discredit the regime as Egyptians could use the social media or could tune into Al-Jazeera and the BBC where a quite different story was being told.

The January 28 demonstration took place on Friday which is the beginning of Egyptian weekend and for many Muslims that day's noontime prayers are a major communal as well as spiritual event. As tens of thousands of people attended Friday prayers they offered an occasion to mobilise for political events. The authorities knew that as people poured out of the mosques at the end of prayers many would join the demonstrations. The regime therefore put in place a number of steps aimed at diminishing these demonstrations. First, it adopted the drastic policy of interrupting the internet and cutting the mobile phone networks. Then it mobilised the police across Cairo at major intersections with the aim of stopping different marches from amalgamating. Police were stationed in large numbers in and around Tahrir Square. At the same time the NDP decided that the time had come for pro-Mubarak demonstrators and so deployed a mixture of genuine supporters and hired 'thugs' at various strategic points especially in the vicinity of Tahrir. It appears that the plan was to try to disrupt all kinds of communications between protesters and then to subject hard core demonstrators to attacks by the pro-Mubarak forces.

However, the people involved in the protests already knew the gathering points for the marches, and while the lack of mobile phones did cause some problems, activists on motorcycles maintained contact between the different contingents. While this has been described as 'Facebook Revolution' Egyptian political history is rich in protest movements and the productive use of all forms of popular communication, as Fahmy has so well documented in the 1919 revolt against the British (Fahmy 2011: 151-166). As the police sought to prevent different demonstrations from reaching Tahrir Square in Cairo, pitch battles took place. One example was on the Kasr El Nil Bridge that leads across the Nile to Tahrir, which links the southern neighbourhoods of the city and Giza to the downtown area. However the tidal wave of people now freed from their fear of the regime proved so resolute the even injury and death would not prevent them moving forward and the police were just pushed aside. As this tactic failed vast crowds—estimated to be hundreds of thousands—once again congregated in the square. It was then that the pro-regime forces came into their own and began violently confronting the protesters. Street fighting broke out as the pro-Mubarak supporters and 'thugs' hurled rocks, Molotov cocktails and other missiles at the demonstrators (Soueif, 2012: 28). However, the infinitely more numerous demonstrators held their ground and became more organized. Some of the protestors fought back others organizing security to ensure that their opponents did not infiltrate the crowds while some set up improvised clinics and still others insured that the demonstrators were supplied with food. As the tension heightened a section of the anti-government forces surrounded the headquarters of the NDP and before long those guarding the building were forced aside. Some protesters began to loot and ransack the building, before it was finally set on fire—a fire that lit up the night sky of the city. The symbolic significance of this act was profound as it meant that none of the regime's institutions were immune from the uprising.

State-Sponsored Riots: Commissioning the Lawless

On the night of January 28 crowds besieged police stations to protest about the brutality meted out to the demonstrators and across Egypt some 99 police were stations burnt. Members of the police were attacked and some 2,000 police vehicles destroyed. In a dramatic turn of events it was the police who now feared the public. But it was not only the police that were targets of the ire of the population. Shops, office and showrooms of the firms that were owned some of the most prominent business people were also attacked; ransacked, looted and set on fire. These were for the most spontaneous acts of anger and sometimes of opportunist criminals eager to take advantage of the situation. Amidst all this some 20,000 convicts were also set free. Although the circumstances are disputed, there are accounts of prisons being broken into by well organized groups who faced little resistance from the prison staff. This it has been suggested was made possible through the Minister of the Interior Habib Al Adly, who allegedly hired criminal thugs with the intention of sowing a crime wave and creating panic amongst the public that would lead to pleas for firm government to restore order. Incidentally, Al Adly is currently standing trial for charges arising out this incident along with other offenses. Whether this was a plan devised at the highest level we do not know but it was evident that the attacks on the prisons were organized, met little resistance and did not led to the release of any political prisoners but of those mostly convicted of theft, violent crime and extortion (El-Menawy, 2012: 24-26).

Among all this the discredited and fearful police began to remove their uniforms and slip away. Undoubtedly the ruling clique would have sought to mobilise the army. However, although the military were controlled by long-term Mubarak loyalist Field Marshall Tantawi, he appears to have opted to save the regime and sacrifice its head. The military refused to fire on the people and so would remain neutral and they even put out a public state-ment to that effect. With the police out of action and the military neutral, the question of how to attempt to recover the initiative from the protesters was sharply posed to the regime. The Central Security Forces were intact and doing their work with normal brutality as snatch squads went after known activists. However, it was evident that this method would not secure general order especially as plans for more protest demonstrations were well advanced. In the space created by the absence of the police the *Baltagiya*[4] — the 'thugs' on the pay roll of the security forces, the ruling party and the business com-munity — would come into their own.

The Baltagis had acquired a major reputation within the country — they were an ever present intimidating force who had the capacity to generate a general fear in society. While mired in criminality, the regime found them to be a useful pool of informal enforcers when the state needed to look clean. They were equally useful for business people who wanted to frighten com-petitors or break a strike. In addition, if the government wanted to disrupt an opposition meeting or frighten an opposition politician, the Baltagis were a convenient force that could pose as enraged members of the public. This was particular useful at election time. As they were not formally part of the state so therefore the state would not take responsibility for their actions. As such they provided useful excuses when fielding international questions about human right standards. At the end of January 2011 they were to be deployed again — only now the stakes were higher.

---

4.   I have used the Arabic plural of Baltagi for accuracy but I will from now on anglicise the term to Baltagis.

As Addul Latif El-Menawy the head of Egyptian Radio and Television commented at the time 'the state was dead. No government, no police, no Ministries, no Ministers, there was no one' (El-Menawy, 2012: 131). Mubarak's advisers and indeed the president himself had failed to grasp the reality of the situation. When some constitutional reforms were offered, Mubarak pledged not to stand for office again, and a vice-president was appointed. However, these were wisps in the wind. As El-Menawy says the 'state was dead'. It was precisely at this point that the freed convicts began to their work. Across the country and particularly in the affluent areas of Cairo groups of criminals began a burglary spree. Blocks of apartments were targeted and there were reports of the thieves going from apartment to apartment. Terrified residents could watch the gangs working through their neighbour's property while they attempted to secure their own homes. Phone calls to the police were of course unanswered and instead residents began to call televisions stations for help (El-Menawy, 2012: 127). Calls were also made to Al-Jazeera based in Doha which became the first channel to publish a helpline; so embarrassed were the Egyptian channels that they followed suit. In the absence of the police the only hope of help came from the army units that had been deployed. However, despite few cases of assistance, on the whole the people were very much in their own. The result was the formation of popular committees which organized a form of community self-defence. These groups were rudimentarily armed with household items but systematically checked Identity cards and generally only allowed honest people through their neighbourhoods. It was fitting that the popular response to the state-sponsored crime wave was the emergence of active civil society organizations (Soueif, 2012: 37-38). The committees were highly successful once established and provided a much needed sense of security.

The demonstrations continued after the January 28 and so too did the confrontations as the government remained convinced that it would be able to suppress the uprising by force. As a result the death toll had risen significantly by early February 2011. However each death — and there were to be some 850 — only reinforced the determination of the protesters. If anything the movement deepened and it was evident that the youth who had spearheaded the actions were now attracting much larger sections of the population. Nevertheless, the government persisted and threw their 'thugs' at the demonstrators. In one hideous moment of political theatre, a ramshackle force of some 3,000 led symbolically by camels and their owners normally working at the Pyramids of Giza, charged into the Square. In the wake of the camels and their riders wielding all manner of improvised weapons, came the Baltagis once more who were equipped with knives and bricks to set about the demonstrators (Alexander, 2011: 58-61).

Discussion

The authorities' attempts to seize the initiative were unsuccessful. Their approach had simultaneous functions. On the one hand, it was supposed to challenge the physical safety of the protesters while acting as a deterrent to those likely to join them. On the other hand, it tried to craft a narrative of a 'divided Egypt.' On one side therefore was the anti-government protests, organized by foreign powers while on the other were the loyal supporters of the government. This, Mubarak's Government hoped, would create the basis for decisive government intervention to restore order. Indeed this was expressed in Mubarak's first televised speech during the uprising, where he cast himself as the defender of order:

> The country is passing through difficult times and tough experiences which began with noble youths and citizens who practice their rights to peaceful demonstrations and protests, expressing their concerns and aspirations but were quickly exploited by those who sought to spread chaos and violence, confrontation and to violate constitutional legitimacy and to attack it…. Those protests were transformed from a noble and civilised phenomenon of practicing freedom of expression to unfortunate clashes, mobilised and controlled by political forces that wanted to escalate and worsen the situation. They targeted the nation's security and stability through acts of provocation theft and looting and setting fires and blocking roads and attacking vital installations and public and private properties and storming diplomatic missions.
>
> *Mubarak, 2011*

As we can see the transformation from the 'noble' protests to 'unfortunate clashes' are under the influence of unnamed political forces which are exploiting the good intentions of the citizens. The clashes are thus posed as a consequence of political manipulation which is seen as some foreign intervention because it attacks the constitution as well as the 'nation's security'. The discursive image of a president speaking on behalf of the attacked nation — a common one in such situations — has the aim of attempting to win over the viewers even if they support the 'noble aims' of the protesters. Indeed within this narrative Mubarak was attempting to cast himself as the protector of the demonstrators interests; it was he who could cleanse the movement from the anti-patriotic exploitation. This kind of political exercise goes to heart of the legitimacy crisis that hangs over all revolts: the authorities appeal to rule is no longer accepted by the masses and those in revolt claim the right to replace those in power. In Egypt's case this goes much deeper as large sections of society have come to see the Mubarak Government as an illegal regime because it was seen as usurping the rights of the citizens as well as illicitly benefiting from the economy. The manner in which the state responded to the uprising was also seen in criminal terms. As Wael Ghonim explained 'the regime had committed unforgiveable crimes over the many years of its rule, and particularly in the past few days' (Ghonim, 201: 258).

While the president was making his address, Ghonim was in jail where he was interrogated and abused about his alleged links with foreign powers and accused of being a traitor (Ghonim, 2012: 221-224). He was mistreated throughout his eleven day detention which included beatings by guards and highly dubious psychological pressure during repeated interrogations. However, when interviewed on television after his release, but before Mubarak's resignation, it was the pictures of those who had died, the martyrs of the revolution that brought him to tears. It was at this point that he said 'I would like to tell every father and mother who lost a child, I am sorry. I am sorry, but it is not our fault, it's the fault of everyone who clung on to power and would not let go' (Ghonim 2012: 260). Like Mubarak's speech, Ghomin's statement also contains a critical narrative of revolt from the side of those who are engaged in the uprising. Whereas Mubarak struggles to assert legitimacy of power Ghonim claims the legitimacy of those in revolt by blaming the deaths of the regime clinging to power. What we have here is a war of law against law. As the edifice of authority dissolves, so too does legitimacy. Each side vies for the high ground — it is not just a power struggle — this is not the will to power but the right to power.

If in the last analysis the state is armed bodies of men, in the case of Mubarak's Egypt the tawdry Baltagis were these. They were fitting representatives of regime that had degenerated under the weight of its own corruption. As the convicts went from street to street on the lookout for loot, they became metaphors for the way in which Egypt's economy had been ransacked over the years. When they threw bricks at demonstrators, this became the reminder of the daily violence meted out Islamist, liberals and leftist opponents of the regime in police stations and prisons across the country. They thought they could act with the same impunity as the state that used them.

After January 28 the regime was politically on the defensive. As the formal coercive instruments of the state either collapsed along with the police or remained neutral as the military the role of the Baltagis increased. However, as we have noted both the demonstrators and the people in the residential districts had found their way of dealing with them. Lethal though they could be, in reality, the power of the Baltagis was much greater when acting in stable conditions created by the state. Breaking up a strike, stuffing ballot boxes or intimidating an opposition politician depended on a passive public. What the mass demonstrations had done was to transform the social atmosphere. The 'thugs' remain in Egyptian society and there is suspicion hey have been deployed since the Supreme Council of the Armed Forces assumed control when Mubarak resigned on February 11 2011. Indeed, this should not be surprising as Mubarak's departure left the regime intact. While the military had been hailed as heroes during the uprising the slogan 'the people and the army are one hand' has turned sour when it became evident that the armed forces continued as the centre of power. However the 25 January Revolution did change Egypt. Free elections have taken place and the once illegal Muslim Brotherhood are now the leading force in both Houses of Parliament. Mubarak, however, was sentenced to life imprisonment for the deaths of the hundreds of protestors killed at the hands of the Baltagis, and his two sons were sentenced to time already served after being convicted on some but not all corruption charges they faced. But there is a more profound change. Although the revolt had unleashed disorder, at the same time its freed part the people from the control of the regime and political parties, youth groups, coalitions of all forms blossomed. Part of the destructive character of revolutions is the toppling old ways of thinking about power long with regimes and at the same releases a new spirit of empowerment that can prefigure a new social order. The young people who swept Mubarak from power will not forget 2011.

References

Al-Aswany, Alaa (2011) *On the State of Egypt: A Novelist's Provocative Reflections*, translated by Jonathan Wright. Cairo and New York: The American University in Cairo Press.

Alexander, Jeffrey C (2011) *Preformative Revolution in Egypt: An Essay in Cultural Power.* London and New York: Bloomsbury.

Amin, Galal (2011) *Egypt in the Era of Hosni Mubarak 1981-2011.* Cairo and New York: American University in Cairo Press.

Amnesty International (2010) 'Egypt: Amnesty International Report 2010: www.amnesty.org/en/region/egypt/report-2010 (Accessed February 27 2012).

Anderson, Lisa (2011) 'Demystifying the Arab Spring', *International Affairs*, Vol. 90, No. 3: 2-7.

Baker, Raymond William (1990), *Sadat and After: Struggles for Egypt's Political Soul.* London: I. B. Tauris.

Cook, Steven A (2012) *The Struggle For Egypt: From Nasser to Tahrir Square.* Oxford and New York: Oxford University Press.

El Din, Khaled Mohi (1995) *Memories of a Revolution: Egypt 1952.* Cairo: American University in Cairo Press.

El Menawy, Abdel Latif (2012) *Tahrir: The Last 18 Days of Mubarak.* London: Gilgamesh.

Engels, Frederick (1968) 'The Origins of the Family, Private Property and the State', in *Marx and Engels: Selected Works,* 455-595. London: Lawrence and Wishart.

Fahmy, Mahmoud Khaled (1989), *Legislating the Infitah: Investment, Currency and Foreign Trade Laws.* Cairo: American University in Cairo Press.

Fahmy, Ziad (2011) *Ordinary Egyptians: Creating the Modern Nations Through Popular Culture.* Stanford: Stanford University Press.

Ghonim Wael (2012) *Revolution 2.0: The Power of the People is Greater than the People in Power.* London: Fourth Estate.

Moustafa, Tamir (2007) *The Struggle for Constitutional Power: Law, Politics and Economic Development in Egypt.* Cambridge and New York: Cambridge University Press.

Mubarak, Hosni (2011) Hosni Mubarak's Speech: Full Text, *The Guardian* February 2 2011.

Soueif, Ahdaf (2012) *Cairo: My City, Our Revolution*. London, Berlin, New York, Sydney: Bloomsbury.

Trotsky, Leon (1965) *The History of the Russian Revolution*, translated by Max Eastman. London: Victor Gollanz.

Celia Díaz-Catalán has a BA in Sociology (Complutense University of Madrid), a post graduate qualification in Planification and Management of R&D Projects in the Social Science School (Latin American States Organization and CSIC) and is a PhD candidate in Sociology. She is a researcher in the Sociology and Political Sciences Association and Fundación Ideas. She works on topics such as Social Policy, R&D systems, University-Enterprise collaboration and Evaluation Research.

Professor Lorenzo Navarréte-Moreno has a BA in Sociology (Complutense University of Madrid), an MA in Political Sociology (Constitutional Studies Center) and PhD in Sociology (Complutense University of Madrid). He has been senior lecturer in the Department of Sociology V in Complutense University of Madrid since 1990 and is now Director of the research group GISOF and Dean of the Sociology and Political Sciences Association. His main areas of interest are Youth and Socialisation and he coordinated the 'Youth in Spain' report for the Spanish Youth Institute.

Ricardo Zúñiga has a BA in Psychology and an MA in Social Policies from ARCIS University. He is also a PhD candidate in Social Psychology in the Complutense University of Madrid and an Associate Professor in the Social Psychology Department. He teaches Secondary Socialization and Psycho-sociology of Negotiation and Conflict, and this main work is related to immigration, identity and youth.

17

'IF YOU WON'T LET US DREAM, THEN WE WON'T LET YOU SLEEP':[1]
DEMARCATION OF SPACES AND THE RISE OF THE SPANISH 15 M

Lorenzo Navarréte-Moreno, Celia Díaz-Catalán and Ricardo Zúñiga

Introduction

The 15M is a hybrid movement which seeks to convey alternative points of view on the social structure. On the one hand with regard to urban movements, 'mobilisations that influence structural social change and transform the urban meanings' (Castells 1983; Nicholls 2011), and those which characterise counter-globalisation[2] (Calle 2005). On the other hand, they are hybrid across spatial dimensions, combining both physical meetings and virtual tools (Candón Mena 2011). In this chapter, we try to explain the boundary-works (Gieryn 1983; Lamont & Molnar 2002) of the 15M from the beginning of the movement as a process which challenged the police force and were subsequently criminalised by some media. We focus the phenomena from a cultural approach, and consider the framing processes (Goffman 2006) in both their mobilisations and discourses, and how this emphasised their actions.

---

1. The statement refers to one popularised message during the 15M camps.
2. A counter movement also known as anti-globalisation movement, counter-globalisation movement, global justice movement, alter-globalisation movement or movement against neoliberal globalisation.

The 15M Movement

The so-called 15M movement originated from demonstrations in 58 Spanish cities on the 15th of May 2011. The call to demonstrate, organized by *Democracia Real Ya*[3] (Real Democracy Now), an organization independent from political parties and trade unions, was made through social media networks, and attracted more than 200 supporting associations (El País 2011). The purpose of the call was to protest against austerity measures taken by the Spanish Government in 2010 in an attempt to control the European financial crisis. On the one hand, the protests labelled the banks as the responsible actors for the crisis and denounced the way in which public funds were used to bail out their debt. Secondly, they were protesting against the budget cuts to the main pillars of the welfare state. One of the greatest milestones of these demonstrations was to gather a large number of heterogeneous citizens, with respect to their age, under the common demand for a real democracy while making the point of refusing to be treated as commodities at the hands of bankers and politicians.[4]

The protests started on the 15th May 2011 but their real significance evolved several hours later after the demonstrations when exchanges between police and protestors resulted in arrests for public disorder and criminal damage (Público 2011). From that moment onward, physical and virtual social networks began to merge. And within a few hours, thousands of citizens were watching images and videos of police repression circulating across the web.[5] This then led to the gathering of a group of about 40 people who spontaneously decided to camp out in Sol Square in Madrid (*Puerta del Sol*) as a protest against the violent police intervention (*Madrid Toma la Plaza* 2011).

This demonstration seems to reflect other movements such as the Arab Spring, or Greek, Portuguese and Icelandic uprisings, which have occurred since 2008. In these demonstrations, citizens were protesting against the cuts to both their decision-making power and social services as the global economic crisis deepened. In Spain, various organizations, such as *Jóvenes Sin Futuro* (JSF: Youth Without Future), *Plataforma Por Una Vivienda Digna* (Decent Home Platform) or Anonymous, had evolved to fight specific

---

3. See http://www.democraciarealya.es/
4. See News 17 May 2011 (http://www.democraciarealya.es/prensa/)
5. For example: http://www.youtube.com/watch?v=dQ1nLPA56as

problems. These groups were also involved in 15M together with those who were detached from any organizational commitment.

Hereafter, we will try to explain the phenomenon of 15M as a cartographic metaphor of boundary-works (Gieryn 1983). This is because the 15M provided a blueprint for citizenship by heading the protests and secondly reconfigured the democratic territory. This seems to represent boundary demarcations (see Lamont and Molnar, 2002) in the context of democracy.

We are the 99: Framing the Movement

15M is considered to be a heterogeneous hybrid movement. Firstly, with regard to its relationship to previous social movements which have sought to counteract financial policies through social mobilisation (Martínez and García 2011), the hybridisation is produced with urban social movements (Castells 1985) and those which constitute a counter-globalisation perspective (Calle 2005). On the other hand, it is hybrid in the sense that the participatory spaces where they take place involve physical and virtual meetings (Candón Mena 2011).

One of the most remarkable features of 15M is its internal diversity. The accessible and neutral characteristics of the movement have fostered a more appealing participation for citizens (Manje 2011). Previous movements, composed of activists and organizations, have been replaced by a new insurgency whose fundamental propelling force consists of ordinary people making their voices heard through informal networks (Lara 2012). Although we point at these features as its main strengths, we believe that it is not possible to understand 15M without first considering some of the organizations participating in its constitution as a movement.

These organizations are considered to be citizen platforms which articulate social issues on behalf of the majority. Some of them have taken part in drawing attention to specific social problems; for example, the international organization Anonymous, which claims freedom of expression and internet independence, played a prominent role in Spain for their actions against the so-called *Sinde* Act[6] (Similar to the American SOPA), by helping to regulate web sites and intellectual property protection. Another example, *No les votes*[7]

---

6. Named after a minister.
7. See http://www.nolesvotes.com/

(Do not vote for them) attracted public attention to the Spanish electoral system, highlighting the disparity and showing that it serves to benefit only the three main parties of the parliamentary arc: PP, PSOE and CiU.[8] In this sense, the interests of the majority were being ignored and this is why they tried to instigate campaigns against the aforementioned parties.

DRY and JSF[9] were the major drivers of the first call. Together with *Estado de Malestar*[10] (State of Unrest) and the National Unemployed Association[11] (*Adesorg*), they demanded change to the current economic and political situation. Adesorg has also contributed by drawing attention to unemployment policies, while JSF has mainly concentrated its activities on the precarious housing and education systems. While the *Plataforma Por Una Vivienda Digna*[12] (Decent Home Platform) also shares these standpoints, instead its activity has mainly been focused on the difficulties in accessing housing.

Each of these organizations has contributed to the 15M movement from traditional demonstrations to other more creative and innovative protests, such as the performance organized by *Estado de Malestar*.[13] The actions of these groups were distributed through social networks, which improved the way in which the groups were connected and the way in which they communicated. The convergence with the squatter movement also provided extensive mutual aid by facilitating social centres (Martínez and García 2011).

The greatest achievement of 15M has been to unite Spanish citizens in forms of collective protest concerning the social dissatisfaction across Spain in the context of the economic crisis, unemployment and disillusionment with the political class. It is possible to identify republican ideals, such as citizenship as a central narrative in the movement (Cerrillo Vidal 2012) and thereby rejecting its characterisation as delegitimised and reductionist. As such, the only response politicians can make is to discredit the whole mobilisations (Manje 2011).

Indeed, when people started to camp out in Sol, both right-wing media and some politicians tried to de-legitimise the gathering by associating

---

8. See the Popular Party, the Socialist Party and the Conservative Catalan Party.
9. See http://www.juventudsinfuturo.net/
10. See http://malestar.org/
11. See http://adesorg2009.magix.net/website/
12. See http://www.viviendadigna.org/
13. See http://malestar.org/2012/02/11/videos-edm/

participants with the terrorist group ETA, or even labelling them with delegitimised categories, such as 'anti-system' (Errejón Galván 2011). The movement's responses were to erect banners denying the labels and upload similar counter-claims on the internet. Examples of this are: 'We're the 99 per cent', 'We're not left-winged or right-winged, we're those below and we're coming for those above'. The social support for the 15M was at its peak in June 2011 when at that time, 70.3 per cent of the Spanish population regarded it as a positive move (CIS 2011).

I Love You, Democracy, But You Seem Absent. They Call it Democracy, But It's Not Democracy at All

The novelty and the multi-dimensionality of the 15M movement is expressed in the way it criticises the current political system and its respective democracy. In particular, it is the way in which technology and social networking sites have been used to make these criticisms which have enhanced the call's civic and media power. Yet the contents of these criticisms do not differ substantially from those made by traditional parties, trade unions or other previous movements against the political system for a number of years. The fundamental differences are, on the one hand, that none of the traditional critics have been mobilised in this way before and, on the other, that 15M has established a boundary-work process in the demarcation of the democratic space.

The content of 15M's messages suggest that they are primarily critics of the system, rather than offering an alternative. The movement tries to diagnose the main problems Spain faces and disseminate it via online means: citizenship in the web, or what has been called 'the digital fifth column'[14] (Alonso and Arzoz 2005) because the movement seeks to instigate change from within Spanish society (Abellán Bordallo 2011; Alonso and Arzoz 2011). Among other causes, the movement blamed bipartisanship, claiming it was responsible of the current Spanish political system, because it made possible the austerity measures implementation without public approval.

15M also point to specific problems in the distribution of rights and social benefits. Another part of the movement's ideology was to denounce

---

14. This term originated with the Spanish Civil war, and is used to refer to the 'enemy within'.

the limited space for citizens' political participation, especially for young people. Statements such as 'Youth without future', 'Real democracy now' or 'Mortgage affected platform', linked the movement to criticisms of the political system, and how it perpetuates 'active minorities' rather than majorities (Moscovici *et al.* 1996). Thus, they argue for a democratic society on the grounds of equality, labour and housing.

The current Spanish democratic system is also delegitimised by its internal corruption. The level of denial, lack of coherent answers and a perceived inability to represent social collective demands have been believed to have aggravated the current economic crisis. One clear example is: 'Do not vote for them'. But in the same line, we find: 'They call it democracy, but it is not', 'They do not represent us', 'PSOE and PP are the same thing!' We therefore see significant popular disillusionment between the Left and Right parties because the public now recognise that essentially their politics and policies are the same.

The criticism of the system also affects both national and local structures: 'What does a deputation serve for?', 'For what do we have the Senate?' In addition, 15M is also critical of European structures and the way in which decision-making occurs through supranational governance which provokes the loss of state sovereignty: 'People Europe, not merchants Europe', 'Yes: Europe for all. No: Euro for few', 'We want to regain our sovereignty', 'They are not bailouts, but blackmail', 'We don't pay you crisis'.

Criticisms from 15M are made directly against the politicians and other actors of political and economic power, such as bankers and media. This criticism is made in a moral tone, as shown in the following examples: 'Corrupt politicians, solution now!', 'There's not enough bread for all the *chorizo*',[15] 'It's no crisis, it's a scam', 'Your Botín, my crisis'[16]. The powerful are therefore seen as part of the system that sustains a democracy that 'isn't'. In this respect, criticism appears to be directed at the Spanish political system. During the democratic transition post-Franco, a system, which guaranteed civil liberties was envisaged for a generation, but now, 15M has exposed it as

---

15. A popular Spanish sausage, Chorizo can be eaten with bread and at the same time means 'a vulgar thief'.

16. Botín means 'to rob' but it is also the name of the president of the main Spanish private bank: Emilio Botín, Santander Bank.

for being oppressive and opaque. Exemplifications of this are: 'Everything that is not evolved is extinguished', *'It's not a* good health symptom to be adapted to a sick system', 'It's time to wake up!', and 'Our dreams won't fit in the ballot box!' or 'Market Dictatorship Out!'

In a context marked by regional and local elections[17] held on 22nd of May 2011, the movement made claims against the austerity measures captained by the PSOE, but also criticised the PP because they were perceived as the only alternative for change. The day before elections and despite the highest electoral authority prohibiting any stay in Sol Square, more than 20,000 people gathered in the city centre. Not only did they congregate in Sol Square, but in other Spanish city squares throughout that night, giving rise to a form of civil disobedience which received significant support from Spanish people (Martínez and García 2011). Here the movement took part in a new form of boundary-work, by demarcating the organizational and participatory activities in the squares as a 'true' democratic exercise; unlike the elections. One poster expressed this active attitude for beneficial change for the majority by proclaiming that the square be renamed *Plaza Solución* (Solution Square). Similarly, 'If you won't let us dream, we won't let you sleep' indicates the consciousness of adopting disobedient conduct, which is, at the same time, justified as a response to an oppressive system.

Popular depictions of 15M reflect a democratic governance, that sees the current system as oppressive and without spaces and processes for decision-making. However, as we have already stated, the 15M movement is heterogeneous and the idea of a corrupt and distant political system derives from two fundamental positions. On one side is the vision from within the system which refers to the need for changes in the current policies of the Spanish state and the need for space in the system for those who feel excluded from it, as reflected in discourses such as: 'We are not anti-system, the system is anti-us', 'More education, less corruption', 'Violence is to earn 600 Euros', 'Thousands of well-formed unemployed youth', 'Worth work now!', 'Worth wages now!', 'Violence is not enough to live on' or 'Stop evictions'. The second vision is more ground-breaking and envisages the movement as the beginning of something new, seeking to align with other similar global

---

17. Thirteen of the 17 Spanish regional governments were elected.

movements with similar interests and values. Some examples are: 'It's time to wake up'; 'We will change the world', 'If not we go out in the newspapers, we will go in the history books'; 'Decreasing now!' 'Fight in the street, create another world!' and 'Joined for a global change'.

The former view appeals to improve the democratic functioning, expel the corrupt actors and implement policies that citizens' would support under referendum or any other means of political participation. People who vote for the traditional political parties, but feel betrayed by them, encompass this vision. The conflict here is therefore with the inconsistency of the political class, and that's what generates the public outrage.

The second vision, on the other hand, is revolutionary. At its foundation, it seeks to push for revolution. This movement is located against the traditional political parties and other structures of the traditional Spanish system, such as trade unions and the media. This alternative view is, to a great extent, responsible for the movement's internal organization, and supports the establishment of sovereignty in the Assembly, without spokespersons or representatives (Alonso and Arzoz 2011). Some messages in this respect are: 'Trade unions: thanks for coming', 'The politicians and media piss on us and they say it rains', 'Human rights are unable asking, please fight!', 'First, they ignore you. Then they laugh at you. Then they attack you. Then, you win: Gandhi.'

The conflict between these two visions comes from searching for a change in the whole system. Indeed, the fracture between both discourses was exhibited in one landmark event at which members of the movement attended. 'World Youth Day', with the presence of Pope Benedict XVI, enjoyed significant government funding. It was held in Madrid during the summer of 2011. This event provoked the protests of several groups linked to 15M, although the turnout was significantly lower than in other demonstrations. Although the various internal visions co-exist harmoniously, it was possible to see these differences in the debates at this event.

Despite these difficulties of organization, the resource has resulted in both legitimised internal decisions and a high volume of member identification with the movement. These elements of coexistence are those, which demonstrate two key issues of the movement: the conviction of the right and the belief to form the basis for Spanish citizenship. These elements appear to be enough to form common identification with the movement, which seeks to have future influence towards change.

This revolutionary vision comes from the collective momentum of other causes and global movements present such places as Iceland, Egypt, Tunisia and Greece. This highlights a global common ground (Alba Rico 2011) and is found in the following examples: 'Yes, we camp'; 'Tahrir equals Sol Square'; 'The spirit of Iceland goes out'; 'Global revolution'; or 'In Iceland bankers in search and capture, here Botín is free'. The global dimension of the movement crystallised on October 15th 2011 with one of the largest attendances of a demonstration with the statement: 'Joined for a global change'. These elements of 15M have been imprinted on the current social representations of Spain as a movement of solidarity.

The current status of the movement, although it has lost coverage from daily news front pages, is one of retreat and reflection. The 'City Square' occupation has since moved to smaller neighbourhoods. The current direction is focussed mainly on two axes: housing and the evasion of payment on modes of transport, with the campaign *Yo no pago* (I don't pay). Both these approaches are civil actions with a high level of 'disobedience'. Housing actions to support evicted people have been supported through social networks (with accounts of squatting as a means of accommodating evicted families). Evasion of payment for public transport, as in Greece, sees people entering the subway without paying as a means of protest against successive austerity cuts.[18]

The current status quo sees a new central government increasing cuts, freshly formulated labour reform and widespread discontent stemming from corruption. Consequently, demonstrations are becoming more frequent. Although the number of demonstrators has decreased, the violence undertaken by the state security bodies has grown, as is evident in media footage and YouTube clips. The number of detainees of 15M is also increasing and the movement faces legal action.

---

18. More than a dozen were arrested.

Discussion

15M had a home, it was brilliant and its topicality or latency was more discrete in the toughest moments in which Spanish society lives as a result of the crisis today. More than two-thirds of 15M were young people, but there were other age groups involved. Its diminishment arrived with the holiday in August 2011 and the withdrawal from the most emblematic squares. Which is why, in the same month, when we saw the violence and disorder of the English riots, we wondered whether the beautiful 15M would be the only purely peaceful movement. The main difference between the two sets of protest is therefore about the conflictive dimension of 15M. Compared to the English riots and other clashes like those of Athens in Greece, Italy or the Arab countries, it had lower intensity-conflict. Another observation is that, unlike disorder in other countries such as England, 15M contained very few situations of violence against policemen or material goods.

From the outset, the peaceful approach dominated the protest, giving rise to a similar consensus among the members of the body of the 15M. Although one could expect that some groups had more violent behaviour, everybody adapted to the general non-violent attitude. Due to the public support which was achieved so quickly, the majority decided to continue participating in the movement which grew in the early stages with each day. Thousands of visitors went consistently to the squares, showing their solidarity and collaboration to the movement.

The movement produced a political speech which encapsulated political grievances and citizens' aspirations. The physical, material and symbolic space of the movement itself was manifested in the city camps. *Sol Camp* in Madrid was replicated in other Spanish cities. This sedentary feature was essential to consolidate the non-violent nature of the movement. The largest violent expression took place in Barcelona where the Catalan police evicted the campers on the pretext of avoiding incidents with football supporters as the world's media watched the destruction of the *micro-polis*. Some episodes of resistance were transformed by the media, in an attempt to end up with something that belonged to all: a new city under construction.

At the time of writing this chapter, nine months have passed since 15M was conceived. However, it continues to be a non-violent movement and has been incorporated as a social and political response in the current climate of the economic crisis and high levels of unemployment that plague Spanish society, especially among its youth. In this context it has made significant progress with some of its most genuine claims. Nine months on, it seems that political parties have incorporated the ideas of openness towards citizenship in their programmes. They launch messages and statements about the need to be more participatory, and relay messages that they have 'understood 15M demands'. The efforts to maintain a certain level of tolerance to the claims in the street are also evident. However, the most pressing questions must be what will happen if the crisis deepens in Spain and whether 15M has a role to play in response.

References

Abellán Bordallo, J., 2011. De la red a la calle: un estudio del proceso moviliza-dor que condujo a las manifestaciones del 15 de mayo de 2011. — Google Académico. En AECPA. Murcia, p.32: http://scholar.google.es/scholar?q=De+la+red+a+la+calle per cent3A+un+estudio+del+proceso+mo vilizador+que+condujo+a+las+manifestaciones+del+15+de+mayo+de+2011. &hl=es&btnG=Buscar&lr= (Accessed February 7, 2012).

Alba Rico, S., 2011. 'La qasbah en Madrid'. *Rebelión*, p.4.

Alonso, A. and Arzoz, I., 2011. El 15M y la quintacolumna digital; comentarios para un laboratorio estratégico. Teknokultura. Revista de Cultura Digital y Movimientos Sociales, 8(2).

Alonso, A. and Arzoz, I., 2005. La quinta columna digital La quinta columna digital La Quinta Columna Digital. Antitratado comunal de hiperpolítica, España.

Calle, A., 2005. Nuevos movimientos globales: hacia la radicalidad democrática, ELE, Editorial Laboratorio Educativo.

Candón Mena, J., 2011. La dimensión híbrida del movimiento del 15M: Entre lo físico y lo virtual: http://es.hybrid-days.com/sites/default/files/31. Comunicacion_La_dimensi per centC3 per centB3n_h per centC3 per centADbrida_del_movimiento_del_15M_Entre_lo_f per centC3 per centADsico_y_lo_virtual.pdf

Castells, M., 1985. *The City and the Grassroots: A Cross-cultural Theory of Urban Social Movements*, University of California Press

Castells, M., 1983. *The City and the Grassroots: A Cross-Cultural Theory of Urban Social Movements.* Berkeley, CA: University of California Press.

Cerrillo Vidal, J. A., 2012. 'The 2011 Uprisings and the Republican Democratic Tradition'. Conference, Feb 9-10, Bizkaia Aretoa, Bilbao, Spain.

CIS, 2011. Barómetro de Junio. Informe de resultados., Madrid: CIS: http://imagenes.publico.es/resources/archivos/2011/7/6/1309953070828Barometro per cent20junio per cent202011.pdf

El País, 2011. Movimiento 15-M: los ciudadanos exigen reconstruir la política: http://politica.elpais.com/politica/2011/05/16/actuali-dad/1305578500_751064.html (Accessed February 6, 2012).

Errejón Galván, I., 2011. El 15-M como discurso contrahegemónico. Encrucijadas: Revista Crítica de Ciencias Sociales, (2), pp.120–145.

Gieryn, T.F., 1983. 'Boundary-work and the Demarcation of Science from Non-Science — Strains and Interests inProfessional Ideologies of Scientists'. *American Sociological Review*, 48(6), pp.781-795.

Goffman, E., 2006. Frame Analysis. Los marcos de la experiencia, Madrid: CIS.

Lamont, M. and Molnar, V., 2002. 'The Study of Boundaries in Social Sciences'. *Annual Review of Sociology*, 28, p.29.

Lara, Á. L., 2012. Los nuevos movimientos y el déficit de amor. madrid15M, p.10.

Madrid Toma la Plaza, 2011. Día 1, por la mañana. 16 de mayo. Madrid Toma la Plaza: http://madrid.tomalaplaza.net/2011/05/17/dia-1-por-la-manana-16-de-mayo/ (Accessed February 7, 2012].

Manje, M., 2011. 15M-Internet y la movilización global. Teknokultura. Revista de Cultura Digital y Movimientos Sociales, 8(2).

Martínez, M. A. and García, Á., 2011. Ocupar las plazas, liberar los edificios: http://www.miguelangelmartinez.net/IMG/pdf/articulo_ACME_8000_v1_doc.pdf

Moscovici, S., Olasagasti, M. and Barriga, S., 1996. Psicología de las minorías activas, Ediciones Morata.

Nicholls, W. J., 2011. 'The Los Angeles School: Difference, Politics, City'. *International Journal of Urban and Regional Research*.

Websites

http://adesorg2009.magix.net/website/
http://legal15m.wordpress.com/
      documentos-para-la-defensa-de-los-derechos-ciudadanos-2/
http://malestar.org/
http://malestar.org/2012/02/11/videos-edm/
https://www.facebook.com/yonopago
http://www.juventudsinfuturo.net/
http://www.nolesvotes.com/
http://www.viviendadigna.org/
https://twitter.com/#!/yo_no_pago

Details for Dr. Daniel Briggs appear under *About the Editor* at the start of this book

18

POST-MODERN GREEK TRAGEDY:
WALKING IN THE STEPS OF THUCYDIDES IN ATHENS

Daniel Briggs

Some legislators only wish to seek vengeance against a particular enemy. Others only look out for themselves. They devote very little time on the consideration of any public issue. They think that no harm will come from their neglect. They act as if it is always the business of somebody else to look after this or that. When this selfish notion is entertained by all, the commonwealth slowly begins to decay.

Thucydides

Introduction

What Thucydides describes here seems very fitting to the precarious social and economic climate of contemporary Greece. Public and private debt cannot realistically be repaid in full and the effect of possible 'disorderly default' would exacerbate a European and worldwide financial system in chaos with slow and uncertain outcomes. However, neither the European Union (EU) nor global processes are the sole culprit of Greece's current financial instability. After 30 years of democratic governance, both corruption and financial mismanagement have led to a never-ending austerity horizon, rising unemployment, and episodes of violence and social unrest; the impact of which have been aggravated by police treatment of the public at protests but also the militaristic policing of particular social groups. Unlike the riots in England in 2011, the episodes of public disorder and violence across Athens and other Greek cities has been more politically focussed. Compared with London, for example, the looting and targeting of retail establishments in Athens has been minimal, and instead anger, frustration and violence predominantly seems to be symbolically directed at state institutions — in particular the Constitution Building in Syntagma Square.

In this chapter, I would like to contextualise these events by reverting to the Classical Period in Ancient Greek history: a time when democratic and social progress in Athens and Greece were perhaps at their zenith. Though not perfect, the Classical Period was a time of investment in public works, political and social reform and rights, and employment. I briefly chart how Greece arrived at this 'Golden Age', by describing the emergence of democracy, philosophy and theatre. I show that one forum through which politics and philosophy circulated was Greek tragedy, and it was through this arena the everyday public engaged with narratives of politics, conflict and social life. In contemporary Greece, however, corrupt politics have exposed the country's socio-economic position. In fact, politics, and any effort to usurp the government, seem to have been far removed from public ownership. Using the theoretical framework of 'performative violence', I suggest that the social unrest and violence in places like Syntagma Square in Athens, in effect become the stage on which the players of this real life Greek tragedy act out their respective roles and the audience observe this all through the lens of the media. I present this as though Thucydides, the doyen of ancient Greek political historians who reported politics and conflict during the classical era of Athens, was there observing events, 'as they happened' when I was witness to social disorder in Athens in June 2011.

The Journey to Democracy in Ancient Greece

Ancient Greece is considered to be the 'birthplace' of Western democracy, and although various organized civilisations flourished from 3000 to 1200 BC,[1] it wasn't until around 600 BC that signs of democracy started to flourish. Democracy gained its first step in 594 BC when Solon, an Athenian aristocrat, was given complete authority to rule the city state of Athens. Solon

---

1.   Such as Minoan and Mycenaean civilisations.

ended the practice of enslaving debtors, and decreed that all debts be written off. He also divided citizens into classes by wealth, defining the rights and duties of each class, limited the amount of land that individuals could own and made laws ensuring locally elected magistrates held office for only one year. He reformed the unjust and arbitrary laws of his predecessor, Draco, and codified the law, achieving a stable government and social cohesion. Sadly, when he retired to travel, civil war broke out. However, democracy took another step forward when Cleisthenes, another Athenian statesman, proposed a constitution be drawn up in Athens. In 508 BC, he dismantled power from the nobility, instead extending voting rights in the assembly to all free adult men and established a council of 500 members, which was open to any adult male citizen. His reforms thus gave many more citizens a chance to serve in the government. However, this early democracy was not perfect as many poor citizens, all women and slaves were excluded from political participation.

Greece then entered a phase of political and philosophical development interspersed with war and autocratic rule, known as the Classical Period (from 500 BC to 323 BC), achieving its greatest political and cultural heights with the full development of the democratic system of government under the Athenian statesman, Pericles. As well as being in charge of the military during the Peloponnesian Wars with Sparta, Pericles was industrious and worked hard to improve Athens for its people. For example, some of the laws he passed allowed the poor to attend theatrical performances for free and jury service became a paid duty. He also used money from the treasury to fund the reconstruction of Athens in 448 BC, which saw the rebuilding of the Acropolis and its centrepiece, the Parthenon. Indeed, throughout the 430s, public works and prosperity continued under Pericles which not only displayed the city's beauty and power but also gave work to Athenians. The Classical Period was therefore one of prosperity and new democracy; where public life flourished around mythology, philosophy and theatre.

The Politics of Greek Tragedy

Greeks living in this classical era benefitted from a range of public theatrical performances. They included the tragedies of Sophocles, Aeschylus, and Euripides, as well as the comedies of Aristophanes; the genres structured around themes concerning the gods, mythology and politics (Sullivan, 1998; Cotterell, 2000; Kershaw, 2006). Aristophanes, in particular, was renowned for his political satires highlighting some of the troubles in Athens during the Classical Period, in particular during the Peloponnesian War. His second surviving play, 'The Knights' (424 BC), was directed at the Athenian states-man Cleon; his tyrannical leadership but also for his alcoholic tendencies. While Athenian leaders tended to endorse triumphal accounts of the city's military history and army courage and avoiding mention of war's human costs, three of Aristophanes' tragedies advocated peace. Other writers such as Euripides also made anti-war references. In 'Trojan Women', which focussed on the aftermath of the Trojan War, Euripides emphasised the suffering of the defeated and the war crimes of the victors (Pritchard, 2010). Tragedy was therefore a resource for the ancient Greek public to engage in current ethical and political dilemmas (Euben, 2007). Democracy and tragedy were therefore intrinsically linked during the time of the Athenian city-state — in a form of symbiosis. However, the often contradictory plots that formed the basis for tragedies remind us — as they did the Greeks — that no social order is ever free from of contradiction; that democracy is not about com-plete control but about recognising political limitations and dealing with the forces of chaos and change (Chou and Bleiker, 2009). Such forces certainly seem to be evident in contemporary Greece.

Contemporary Greece

In recent years, Greece has witnessed immense social, political and economic instability which have resulted in significant expenditure cuts and austerity measures, growing unemployment and episodes of social unrest and violent rioting. The overt nature of public violence represents anger towards gov-ernment and state institutions; a level of public dissatisfaction with public administration, corruption, mistreatment by militaristic law enforcement and unsuccessful democratic governance which has, for many years, lacked an effective means of expression due to Greece's weak civil society (Hugh-Jones *et al*, 2009). The context for 'change' reflects a failure of civil government despite recent shifts towards a 'democratic' society. Let us briefly consider these areas in a bit more detail.

Greece experienced difficulty making the transition from exclusivist parliamentarism regime (pre 1974) to democratic government (Pridham, 1990); predominantly because the old tradition countered the democratisation of politics (Mouzelis 1979; Samatas, 1986). Over the last 20 years, disillusionment with political parties has increased and many Greeks, particularly the younger generation, consider their political system as elitist, corrupt and inflexible, instead operating for its own survival instead of the country's interests (Karamichas, 2009). There is substantial anger and frustration over the economic state of the country. When Greece joined the Euro in 2001, the government completely disguised its financial position in order to qualify for Eurozone membership. Furthermore, the 'Olympic Legacy' post-2004 failed to improve transport and housing (Matasaganis, 2011). In the same year, the authorities conceded they lied about the financial position to qualify for the Euro. Although there was some economic recovery, the global financial crash of 2007/8 led to a re-consideration of the true strength and value of public and private assets versus public liabilities, and Greece became exposed.

In October 2009, a new government announced that earlier fiscal data had been misreported, and financial deficits and public debt estimates were radically revised (Monastitiriotis, 2011). At the end of 2009, national debt reached 262 billion Euros and Greece was advised by EU partner countries and the International Monetary Fund (IMF) to cut public sector pay and raise taxes (Featherstone, 2011). In May 2010, the government negotiated an unprecedented €110 billion rescue package with the EU, the European Central Bank (ECB) and the IMF, committing the Greek Government to sweeping spending cuts and revenue increases (IMF 2010). At the same time, a second round of austerity measures was also announced (Matasaganis, 2011). Under the terms of the measures, public sector pay and pension benefits were cut which increased inequality and sharpened the experience of poverty (Matasaganis, and Leventi, 2011). This created wider public dissatisfaction with the governing party, especially so when Prime Minister Papandreou's indecision was seen to block progress for a bailout resolution. At the time of writing this chapter in July 2012, Greece was 200 billion Euros in debt after having secured another billion-Euro bailout.

These issues have lead to public sector strikes and protests but there have been further triggers for recent outbreaks of violence. One significant trigger was the killing of 15-year-old Alexandros Grigoropoulous by the police in December 2008. Alexandros' death resulted in a series of demonstrations, which swiftly turned to violent riots in Athens but also broke out in many Greek cities. But mistrust in the Greek police force runs deep (Mouzelis, 1979; Hugh-Jones *et al*, 2009), and this has also been consistently reinforced by the police's inability to provide good services, and because they are seen as the shield of the two established major political parties. Spells of unrest have also evolved on the anniversaries of Alexandros' death, in December 2009 and December 2011 respectively. These spells of social unrest were also fuelled by feelings of outrage toward political mistreatment of protestors, unwelcome social reform, economic stagnation and government corruption. One way of capturing such anti-state feeling, public hostility and disorder is through the theoretical perspective of performative violence.

Performative Violence

Performative violence is a form of meaningful interaction through which social agents construct reality based on available cultural templates (Juris, 2005). It is 'performative' in the sense that it is symbolically expressive because it seeks to communicate and dramatise important messages and ideas through violence (Riches, 1986). This theoretical framework discounts violence as 'pathological' or 'senseless' but rather as a changing form of communicative interaction which has developed throughout history as a cultural form of meaningful action (Blok, 2000). Such a perspective has been used by other commentators in the context of political activism through social protest and disorder (Juris, 2005, 2008; Rhodes, 2001). These performances are also often captured by news media which acts as a lens through which the actions gain further meaning and receive additional discursive analysis (Bauman and Briggs, 1990; Juris, 2005). And although there is the risk for manipulation and distortion, the media, who desperately seek out such sensational stories, images and clips, happily oblige because symbolic images of burning cars and protestor/police clashes often immediately attract national and international networks (Juris, 2008). It is thus the purposive and symbolic nature of violence in Athens and other Greek cities which seems to relate closely to this theoretical framework. It was at one such episode of summer rioting and violence that these performances were played out, when I walked around parts of Athens, documenting 'what happened' in a similar fashion to the historian, Thucydides.

Walking in the Steps of Thucydides in Athens

Thucydides was an Athenian aristocrat born around 460 BC and lived at the height of the Classical Period. A Greek historian, he was mostly renowned for his first-hand observations and documentation of the Peloponnesian War between Athens and Sparta in the 5th Century BC. Some say his gritty accounts represent early forms of 'political realism' (Donnelly, 2000), and although some disagree (Betts, 2007), it is difficult to ignore his ability to document 'what happens'. He interviewed both Athenians and Spartans, researched records, and provided eye-witness accounts on events:

> And with regard to my factual reporting of the events of the war I have made it a principle not to write down the first story that came my way, and not even to be guided by my own general impressions; either I was present myself at the events which I have described or else I heard of them from eye-witnesses whose reports I have checked with as much thoroughness as possible.[2]

I tried to adopt a similar approach in the two days I was in Athens at the height of violent protests against government austerity measures in June 2011.

From Monastiraki to Mitropoleos

In June 2011, the Foreign and Commonwealth Office had issued statements indicating that there were no restrictions on travel to the Greek capital or any part of the country but warned that visitors should avoid the 'student protests' in Syntagma Square.[3] However, this area in Athens was difficult for me to avoid since the conference for which I was attending was very close to the square. To save money, I booked a cheap hotel in the centre of the Plaka district — located in the centre of Athens among a labyrinth of small streets and alleyways. Plaka sits under the watchful eye of the Acropolis, and is the

---

2. Thucydides, *History of the Peloponnesian War*, Book 1:1, 20, 21, 22.
3. Syntagma in Greek means 'Constitution'. This square is home to the Parliament Building.

ancient district that Thucydides would have known as 'Agora'. These days thousands of tourists amble up and down these streets, purchasing modern memorabilia of Greek history, ranging from mini statues of Caryatids[4] to tragic comedy masks.

The first thing one sees, walking out of Monastiraki metro, is the Acropolis — the pride of Classical Athens and living proof of the age of Pericles and early democracy. It was late afternoon when I stepped out from station on to a busy street, only to breath in a deluge of lorry fumes. The pavements overflowed with a mixture of busy locals and loitering tourists looking at maps then pointing around. I strode to my right, wheeling my travel bag behind me and lifting it over oil-stained puddles and large potholes. As I crossed, I glanced back on boarded-up and dilapidated shops near to the station. Abandoned carts which would normally sell dried nuts or sesame bread rolls lay broken by the roadside. This was not the Plaka I had come to know over the last 12 years.

As I left the main road and walked into a pedestrian area, I tripped over several bricks which stuck out from the ground. Piles of uncollected rubbish bags stacked the roadside and the street demographic became one of scattered young Athenians, small tourist groups, local homeless people, and stray dogs. Ten years, ago it would have been difficult to move in these small streets because of the summer tourist invasion and the overflowing popularity of the shops. Now, the only active business seemed to be semi-thriving tourist shops and restaurants; the shop owners standing solemnly outside either smoking cigarettes and discarding them in the drains or looking bored of the pick-up-then-put-back interest most tourists showed in their goods.

Even in this tourist zone, there were signs of social unease; the police patrolling this pedestrian area on large, technologically-adorned Honda bikes, stopping only to make assessments of potential troublemakers. In the small local cafes, a few customers stared at the TV screen which showed revolving images of the social unrest. After only about 50m or so, I passed a group of local young men smoking what smelt like cannabis; they were dressed in jeans, trainers and one had a t-shirt of Ché Guevara. Their group presence seemed to attract the attention from one of the mobile police officers and

---

4.   These are sculpted female figures from the Temple of Athena Nike on the Acropolis.

there were tense visual exchanges while the policeman sat there on his bike for several minutes, without moving his head while he spoke into his radio.

I turned right in to a small, dirty alleyway where I had booked my hotel. In the street, behind their sunglasses, the locals drank strong Greek coffee and smoked cigarettes. With each step I looked up as the Acropolis towered over me. As I entered the hotel, I saw a few designer shops standing vacant opposite, but I was quickly reminded of where I was by the air-conditioning back-draft. As I checked in, I was told of the glorious tourist sites available to me and it felt like I was being pushed into a tourist bubble. The hotel's main attribute in this respect was a roof terrace which overlooked views of Athens and the Aegean Sea. As the assistant gave me the check-in forms, he slipped out of polite-hotel mode and side stepped to look beyond me at the flat-screen TV, assuming some sort of concerned look. I finished my forms earlier than he expected and turned to look at what he was immersed in. He was looking up at the local news channel showing events from the previous night's violence in Syntagma Square, just round the corner. He took my check-in form, reassumed his customer service role, and gave me my key saying 'have a nice stay'.

When I got to my room, I couldn't help but switch on the news; after all, the unrest had been unfolding just up the road from my hotel. I flicked through BBC News, MTV, ABC and CNN (American), RTE (Italian) and TVE (Spain) and eventually found ERT—the Greek news channel. The violent images were relentless, and although I couldn't make much sense of the language, I was drawn to the graphic pictures of the protestor surges on the parliament building in Syntagma Square and the violent responses from the police. In one shot, a reporter proudly stood within feet of periodic rushes by the crowd on the Constitutional Building in Syntagma. I realised that I'd probably have to pass this somehow when I attended my conference the following day because it was located beyond Syntagma Square, on the corner of Orimou and Solonos. I unpacked, and found my way to the hotel roof balcony for a Greek salad and a couple of Mythos beers. The seats and chairs on the hotel roof were placed so tourists could gain the best vantage point of either the Acropolis or the sunset over the Aegean. Most of the tourists with me had claimed the most aesthetic viewpoints while I sat at the back of the rooftop space. Between my reveries at the glowing Acropolis as dusk set in, I heard distant noises. While the tourists remained mesmerised by the history in front of them, I was increasingly drawn to the history unfolding behind them — likely to be another night of rioting in Syntagma.

From Ermou to Orimou (and Then to a Deserted Acropolis)

The next morning, I got up early to watch the news on ETR, which reported another night of violence in Syntagma. I was curious about what the aftermath looked like. It was around 8.30 am when I walked out of the hotel; a street sweeper was taking his wide-reaching broom between the public seating on which numerous homeless men were lying. Between them all, stray dogs wove in and out, searching for discarded food in the streets. Walking past Mitropoleos, I continued past an Orthodox church to Ermou — a street which leads to Syntagma. Ermou is a boutique shopping street but a good proportion of the shops I walked past were empty; some of which littered with naked plastic dummies posing lifeless behind the windows.

When I arrived at the end of Ermou, I was confronted with Syntagma Square on which stood the Constitution Building. It could have been any normal workday in any urban European capital city. The few roads which were open were busy but the clean-up from last night's events had begun on those which were closed. I stopped to absorb this as people walked busily past me with their sunglasses on. I called in to a local café to pick up a take-away frappe and crossed the road into the square. As I walked on to the paved marble slabs, either side of the trees were permanent protestor camps. Some were two-man tents while others seemed to be improvised constructions made up of materials draped between lampposts and public seats. Some tents were tattooed with text and drawings. Hanging above the camps were banners, mostly in Greek but the few in English proclaimed 'We want democracy' and 'No more lies'. There was a subdued feeling but a few people had emerged from their camp. I drifted over to talk to one man who must have been in his mid-20s. In his broken English, he told me he had been staying with a friend who was camping there. He had been unemployed for nearly two years and had vowed to stay in Syntagma until he saw change. He was critical of the 'corrupt government' he said and angry at the police. 'This city founded democracy, what do you call it now?' he added. Shrugging his shoulders, he disappeared to receive a phone call and light another cigarette.

I hurried away as I was already late for my conference. My paper on the risk behaviours of young British people on holiday seemed to be received well and, between the sessions, I talked with the conference organisers who had lived in Athens all their lives. Aside from bemoaning how speakers had cancelled because of the political instability, they too expressed outrage at the police treatment of Greeks in the process of protesting: 'They treat us like they do the dogs' Georgios, the conference convenor told me, adding 'the people will never get democracy unless it changes'. I was eager to get back to Syntagma and decided to skip the afternoon sessions. When I returned to Syntagma, five hours had passed and there was a murmuring hubbub about the place. A few helicopters circulated above and the TV cameras had set up. Small groups of people lined either side of the main pathway through the square where I had talked earlier with the young man. Not only students but men and women of all ages dressed in everyday clothing — they looked to be Athenian people, not the 'students' of which the Foreign Office had warned. As I passed through the square, I stepped over bulky camera wires and tried to overhear conversations. Although disadvantaged with my limited Greek vocabulary, I got talking to a couple of local women who had made banners in Greek. They told me it said 'Papandreou step down'. When they spoke of their anger of their country's economic and social demise, it was directed at the government and the police. Each time they said politicians' names or described particular events, they started pointing at the Constitution Building as if was the origin of all sin.

It was mid-afternoon when I left Syntagma Square, vowing to myself to return in the evening. I left because I was eager to walk up to the Acropolis before leaving for the UK in the morning. I returned to the hotel to change from academic attire to tourist outfit. I left the hotel again late in the afternoon and, once again, was again among my tourist contemporaries in Plaka: swathes of American and Japanese tourist groups perusing the gift shops. They picked and fiddled while most of the shop owners I passed smoked cigarettes or/and watched TV news channels which were reporting on, what looked to be, the previous night's violence. I walked down Kalamiotou, turning right at Adrianou and then left on Panos, and followed what becomes a marble pathway lined with pine trees. As I ascended, the sight of the white-crested buildings scattered across Attica came into view. However, more tourists seemed to be descending than ascending—and I found out why as I approached the main entrance. There was a large sign at the ticket office stating that the Acropolis was closed because of public strikes against government austerity cuts. As tourists approached, they tut-tutted, shaking their heads as if to suggest they were unsympathetic to the real reasons for the strike. Instead I climbed to Choris Ornoma, a vantage point opposite the Acropolis which offers a decent view of the structure. By the time I returned to my hotel, it was early evening. I was ready to return to Syntagma.

The stronghold of Syntagma

By now, I was completely captivated by what was going on. I had come to learn about the riots in Athens in 2008, stemming from the police killing of a teenager and had learned of the country's economic problems which had since deteriorated, but to be among potential unrest felt almost unreal, perhaps mythical. It was about 7 pm as once again I walked up Ermou. Loudspeakers boomed out and a crowd-like drone hit my senses as I walked swiftly to Syntagma. As I walked, a few others overtook me while pre-paring to tie handkerchiefs over their face. When I arrived at the foot of the square, people were scattered intermittently around the streets and the square. It was a difficult sight to absorb. There must have been about 800-900 people (the main group) near the main Constitution Building which was guarded by the police while several hundred others scattered around in small groups or as individuals. Most were men and had their face covered. For some reason, some were half naked. There was no visible main group near me and the roads were completely littered with rubbish, broken bottles and paper. People stood on public seats, bus shelters, and hung half way up lamp-posts, chanting and shouting at the Constitution Building. I was one of the few people there who had their face uncovered and felt pretty vulnerable. It struck me as almost impossible to establish conversations in these moments, even though I was used to undertaking very tense research in conflict situations. Instead I remained and watched from the corner of the street. As a neutral, I couldn't work out whether it was better to be by oneself or with a group, whether to stand still or be mobile, or how to act should trouble come my way.

Then a protest march appeared from my left from a road running parallel to Ermou—and emptied into Syntagma. It was led by hooded protestors with large banners, some of whom held sticks and small broken-building debris. They were all chanting. This march was about 100 strong. However, they were cautiously pursued behind by the police as they marched into the square. They turned around to face the police who were following in pursuit.

Meanwhile, on the other side of the square, near to the Constitution Building, the crowds made explosive surges towards the police who stood defensively, fending off the protestors with large swipes of their batons. The banners bobbed up and down between the many Greek national flags which were being waved by the protestors. Drums were beating and new chants emerged. While people walked in and out of the main group near the Constitution Building, tear gas was fired about 150m to the right of me and I retreated 20m back to the edge of Ermou. I didn't even know where the tear gas came from but it seemed strange it was fired at the patchy gatherings while the masses continued to surge against the Constitution Building. As the tear gas arrived, most of the small crowd to my right showed their ingenuity and put on gas masks.

Then, to my left, I saw more police with batons and riot uniform engage in another attempt to enter into the lower half of the square the parallel road. They walked like a human wall, ten wide and 15 or 20 so long, single file behind each other. The crowd threw stones, bricks, whatever they could find at them while the stray dogs aimlessly jogged around, somehow keeping out of the line of fire. There seemed to be no clear pattern to the rioters' attacks; only that they were in response to the tear gas. Even then, most protestors were ready, either having their own homemade face protection or gas masks. The protesters then cleverly contrived to push back the police marching from the parallel road by instigating their own form of riot shield, by sliding large plant boxes forward, and intermittently hiding behind them as they lobbed various makeshift bombs in the general direction of the police.

After they had succeeded in blocking further police entry to the square from the parallel road, they then retreated having set their roadblock and dispersed somewhat. After five minutes, they started to re-form as a group.

Word seemed to have got round that the police were attempting to re-enter the square from the parallel road. They stood inactive, waiting for the police to make the next move but the police held back. With no sign of police advance, the crowd, which had gathered behind their improvised road-block, again started to dissipate. A few young-looking men cycled around while another couple circulated on mopeds. It looked like the police had retreated until a huge wave of tear gas was launched from the parallel road which shifted the remaining protesters from the area. As I remained stood at the top corner of Ermou, a few resolute protestors lingered there, seemingly invincible in their gas masks and handkerchiefs. They stood with their arms outstretched, inviting some sort of police response. They continued to look directly at the police, aggressively gesticulating and thrusting their arms in the air and shouting as if they would die for their cause. Then a few retreated to where I was standing and looked on at the Constitution Building.

The main crowd at the Constitution Building then launched petrol bombs at the parliament grounds which had been resolutely guarded by the police. Feeling a little more confident, I moved forward between people loitering and running around to get a closer look. As I moved closer, the jeering and boo-ing of the crowd became more formidable. The petrol bombs were replaced by bricks. I moved closer out of curiosity to within about 100 metres of the Constitution Building and saw the main group retreat as tear gas was fired into them. The police then moved their barricades and fortified their line in front of the Constitution Building. There were visible violent exchanges as the crowd surged in small groups; some individuals breaking off to make their own independent attacks only to receive personal repercussions when the police rushed back at them, applying swipes to their legs with long batons. Bells started to ring as another group managed to penetrate the police line and started shaking another police barricade, which divided the square from the Constitution Building. Suddenly, a batch of tear gas was fired on them and they also retreated. To my right, about 50m away, there was a commo-tion between protestors and some started to beat each other with sticks and throw rocks at each other. This fight started to move my way and this was when I decided I had seen enough. I swiftly backed down Ermou and to the relative safety of my hotel room.

Discussion

This chapter captures the experience of contemporary Greek socio-economic problems against a historical consideration of the 'democratisation' of Ancient Greece and through the observational style of Thucydides who was one of the first to make use of a political realism (observation, documentation of eye witness accounts) to understand politics and social life in the context of conflict (Peloponnesian War). Through these observations, the chapter shows that a form of performative violence liberates the Greek peoples' discontent, and the violence and unrest which ensues, in my view, embodies a post-modern Greek tragedy which was played out on the stage of Syntagma Square. I concede to my tourist status and the language barriers but I have come to know Athens and its people reasonably well, having visited the city almost every year for the last twelve years. It seems clear to me that what I witnessed in Athens, and what has been written about these violent outbursts across Greek cities (Matasaganis, and Leventi, 2011; Monastitiriotis, 2011), seems far more politically focused than the unrest that took place in England weeks later in August 2011 because the public anger was primarily directed at the state institutions and faltering democracy.

Indeed, despite steps towards democracy in contemporary Greece, the recent Greek politic ideology is one of lies and deceit of its people (Alivizatos 1990; Mouzelis 1979; Samatas, 1986). The assurances of fiscal stability when Greece entered the Euro, embellished by the elite's promise of glory in the 2004 Olympic Games, post-Olympic economic prosperity and resulting growth. However, 'stories' that 'Greece is 'stable', it could 'enter the Euro' and 'didn't need financial support' despite the billion Euro deficit, masked the realities of a floundering national economic system which had misled the EU when joining the Euro and continually been accused of government corruption (Karamichas, 2009; Matasaganis, 2011; Monastitiriotis, 2011). The Greek public were asked to foot the bill for the blunders of the powerful who continued to retain positions of power (Matasaganis, and Leventi, 2011) under police protection (Mouzelis, 1979; Hugh-Jones *et al,* 2009).

The way in which public action against Greece's economic decline and public treatment by the authorities (Karamichas, 2009) took form seems to be through a form of performative violence (Juris, 2005, 2008; Rhodes, 2001). This theoretical lens is useful because it treats violence as a method of communication and dramatisation to convey particular messages (Riches, 1986). The violence and disorder in Athens and across Greek cities had meaning, a political significance which, as Juris (2005: 427) argues, counters any question of its senselessness in the context of such political protests:

> Performative violence is neither random nor senseless, but rather responds to a specific economy of signification. The resulting mass media images helped bring a great deal of public visibility to anti-corporate globalization movements, and even to many of their political demands.

As Greek political representation decreased and public anger and frustration increased (Hugh-Jones *et al*, 2009), and the forum by which public expression was manifested was through a form of Greek tragedy. In Ancient Greece, the public performance of tragedies created by poets and playwrights was one means by which the public were able to engage in ethical and political dilemmas (Euben, 2007). One parallel to make with contemporary Greece is that of the theatre itself. From what I observed, the stage for the contemporary social unrest and violence was Syntagma Square and the set was the backdrop of the Constitution Building. Secondly, the 'rioters' and police became the players of the tragedy, acting out the issues of concern; the 'rioters' protesting and fighting in opposition to oppressive governance (Karamichas, 2009; Pritchard, 2010) and the police on behalf of the higher powers who sought to maintain power and advantage (Mouzelis, 1979; Hugh-Jones *et al*, 2009). Thirdly, the media became the lens by which Greeks in their shops, in hotels, and at home saw the tragedy and took part as the audience. When walking round Athens, it seemed to me that some of the audience certainly critical of the current political system and its players (Hugh-Jones *et al*, 2009), and this was evident in some of the testimonies of those with whom I spoke. In this way, the tragedy was played out so that knowledge of the country's suffering could extend beyond the confines of political deliberations in the Constitution Building on Syntagma Square (Euben, 2007) — a key dictum of performative violence — so that the message attracts discussion (Bauman and Briggs, 1990; Juris, 2005) and the national and international news networks (Juris, 2008).

Steps toward political change and economic stability in contemporary Greece (Chou and Bleiker, 2009) are undoubtedly thwarted by fragile public trust in the competence of political institutions. Indeed, these spells of social unrest have been for some years now ever present in places like Syntagma and evidence of increasing austerity was everywhere I looked (Matasaganis, and Leventi, 2011), even within the tourist showpiece of Plaka and around the symbolic glory of the Acropolis. To me, it seems difficult to ignore the social advances of the Classical period when Greeks still refer to ancient splendour of Greece and its democratic roots, evident in the words of one protestor with whom I spoke: 'This city founded democracy, what do you call it now?' Perhaps some lessons could be learnt from the Ancient Greek democratic forefathers; in Classical Greece, Solon wrote off debt, Cleisthenes dismantled political control from the powerful and Pericles invested in public works. Nevertheless, it difficult to see if, how and when Greece will emerge from the political and economic doldrums and, like Thucydides thousands of years ago, we are left asking questions:

> When will there be justice in Athens? There will be justice in Athens when those who are not injured are as outraged as those who are.
>
> *Thucydides*

References

Bauman, R. and Briggs, C. (1990) 'Poetics and Performance as Critical Perspectives on Language and Social Life', in *Annual Review of Anthropology* 19:59-88.

Betts, R. (2007) 'Not With My Thucydides, You Don't', in *The American Interest*, Spring Edition: 140143.

Blok, A. (2000) 'The Enigma of Senseless Violence', in Goran Aijmer and Jon Abbink (eds.) *Meanings of Violence*, pp. 23-38. Oxford: Berg.

Chou, M. and Bleiker, R. (2009) 'The Symbiosis of Democracy and Tragedy: Lost Lessons from Ancient Greece' in *Journal of International Studies*, Vol. 37(3):659-682.

Clark, S. (1993) 'Ancient Philosophy' in A. Kenny (ed.) *The Oxford History of Western Philosophy*, Oxford: Oxford University Press.

Cotterell, A. (2000) *Classical Mythology*, Singapore: Anness Publishing Limited Hermes House.

Cutrofello, A. (2005) 'Foucault On Tragedy' in *Philosophy and Social Criticism*, Vol. 31(5-6): 573-584.

Donnelly, J. (2000) *Realism and International relations*, Cambridge: Cambridge University Press.

Euben, J. (2011) 'The Tragedy of Tragedy' in *International Relations*, Vol 21(1):15-22.

Featherstone K. (2011) 'The Greek Sovereign Debt Crisis and EMU: A Failing State in a Skewed Regime', *Journal of Common Market Studies*, Vol 49(2): 193-217.

Hugh-Jones, D., Katsanidou, A. and Riender, G. (2009) *Political Discrimination in the Aftermath of Violence: The Case of the Greek riots*, London: Hellenic Observatory Papers on Greece and Southeast Europe.

IMF (2010) *Greece: Staff Report on Request for Stand-by Arrangement*. Country Report No. 10/110. Washington DC: International Monetary Fund.

Juris, J. (2005) 'Violence Performed and Imagined: Militant Action, The Black Bloc and the Mass Media in Genoa' in *Critique of Athropology*, Vol. 25(4):413-432.

Juris, J. (2008) 'Performing Politics: Image, Embodiment, and Affective Solidarity During Anti-corporate Globalisation Protests' in *Ethnography*, Vol. 12(4):61-97.

Karamichas, J. (2009) 'The December 2008 Riots in Greece' in *Social Movement Studies* 3(8), 289-293.

Kershaw, S. (2006) *The Greek Myths: Gods, Monsters, Heroes and the Origins of Storytelling*, London: HarperCollins.

Matasaganis, M. (2011) 'The Geographical Dimension of Austerity' in V. Monastiriotis, (Ed) (2011) *The Greek Crisis in Focus: Austerity, Recession and Paths to Recovery*, London: Hellenic Observatory European Institute.

Matasaganis, M. and Leventi, C. (2011) 'The Distributional Impact of the Crisis in Greece' V. Monastiriotis, (ed.) (2011) *The Greek Crisis in Focus: Austerity, Recession and Paths to Recovery*, London: Hellenic Observatory European Institute.

Meghir C., Vayanos D. and Vettas N. (2010) 'The economic crisis in Greece: a time of reform and opportunity (mimeo)' Version published as 'Greek reforms can yet stave off default' *Financial Times* (23 August 2010).

Monastiriotis, V. (2011) *The Greek Crisis in Focus: Austerity, Recession and Paths to Recovery*, London: Hellenic Observatory European Institute.

Mouzelis, N. (1979) *Modern Greece: Facets of Underdevelopment.* Basingstoke: Macmillan.

Pridham, G. (1990) 'Political Actors, Linkages and Interactions: Democratic Consolidation in Southern Europe', *West European Politics,* Vol. 13(4), 103-117.

Pritchard, D. (2010) 'The Symbiosis Between Democracy and War: The Case of Ancient Athens' in D. Pritchard (ed.) in *War, Democracy and Culture in Classical Athens*, Cambridge: Cambridge University Press. 1-76.

Rhodes, J. (2001) *The Voice of Violence.* Westport, CT: Praeger.

Riches, D. (ed.) (1986) *The Anthropology of Violence.* Oxford: Blackwell.

Samatas, M. (1986) 'Greek McCarthyism: A Comparative Assessment of Greek Post-Civil War Repressive Anticommunism and the US Truman-McCarthy Era, *Journal of the Hellenic Diaspora,* Vol 13(3-4):5-75.

Sullivan, K. (1998) *Greek Myths and Legends*, London: Brockhampton Press.

19

CONCLUDING THOUGHTS

Daniel Briggs

Introduction

The chapters in this book have reflected on different aspects of the English riots of 2011: how and why they occurred, the motivations of who took part and why, and what was the state response. The book has also examined similar forms of unrest in other areas of the world because what we witnessed that year was representative of both global social change as well as national and local social challenges. Undoubtedly, there will be further contributions to these discussions by the time this work is published but in a world which shifts so rapidly, we—as people who think and write about it—shouldn't stay still for too long without responding. Therefore in this final chapter, I would like to draw together the main themes of the book and offer some concluding thoughts.

Looking Back But Thinking Forward: Contextualising the English Riots

In a television interview for RAI2[1] in February 2012, I was probed on whether I thought the riots were something historically attributable to the English; whether this form of disorder was in 'our blood.' And if we examine our past, England has been marked by violent rioting in different periods, so what happened in the summer of 2011 was therefore just another chapter of

---

1.   The Italian television equivalent of BBC2.

disorder in our national history. However, history tells us that, regardless of motivation, disorganized behaviour such as rioting enables politicians and moral entrepreneurs to close their eyes, reach in the usual suspects cupboard and pull out a straw man at which they can attribute the disorder. First out was some sort of feral, underclass youth; 'a lost generation' in the words of Kenneth Clarke.

As Geoffrey Pearson points out, it may be easy to blame the immoral youth for this sudden break from the social status quo because attribution to social change has always been directed, to some degree, at the 'youth problem'. So therefore moralising youth behaviour is historically endemic; the concerns embedded in the generational anxiety which seems to surface once in a while when people say that 'the country has gone to the dogs'. While the Riots Communities and Victims Panel lambasted 'poor parenting' as the locus of the disorder, it is clear that concerns about absent or substandard parenting have been commonplace throughout history (*Chapter 3*). State and parental concerns about behaviour 'getting worse' as time passing is therefore a red herring because as generations mature, they reconstruct their lives around the innocent and 'better times' in which they grew up before the degenerative processes of social change invaded and changed their experience of the world. No doubt one day people will be saying 'in the good old days of BB messenger and Facebook' and the like!

In the same cupboard, the politicians and moral entrepreneurs pulled out the 'immigrant' or 'alien other'—the person/people from the 'outside' somewhere; people who had somehow intentionally arrived to invade our idyllic English communities while simultaneously sucking on the nipple of the welfare state, failing to engage with 'our way of life' and assimilate to our culture, and getting involved in crime. Unfortunately, it seems that these days immigration and the 'alien other' have started to receive increased attention as the crisis in democracy across the West fuels national insecurity and an increasing support for fringe far-right parties. This has resulted in the rise in anti-Semitism and anti-multiculturalist rhetoric—perhaps most visibly apparent in the recent elections in France 2012 at which the far-right party, *Front National*, gained no less than 19 per cent in the first round of the country's vote. However, as *Chapter 4* shows, history tells us that anti-immigration and anti 'other' discourse, and the legislation which consequently ensues, is generally unhelpful when it comes to: (a) explaining how and why social disorder takes place in urban minority communities and (b) aiding the integration of those groups. Just look at what happened in the Banlieues of Paris in 2005. If anything, it tends to aggravate minority ethnic urban community relations, the social exclusion they experience and the generic reaction towards them from the aggressive right-wing media and others local to the same area. However, like 1958 and 1981, we are witnessing further anti-immigration and anti-multiculturalist attitudes as countries across the Eurozone also start to impugn this 'other' group for the perpetual downfall of their constituency and violation of national identity.

An investment in this ideology frames the English rioters as people who aren't representative of our 'national character' (see *Chapter 5*) — they do not symbolise the dated, stereotypical post-war-daydream-like England and its constructions of bunny rabbits, green meadows and country picnics. To me, this resistance against typical Englishness signals a broader level of denial of the changes which this country has experienced and is still experiencing. Does the Coalition Government not know how much we rely on foreign labour just to sustain this country economy? If it is not evident in the construction metal heap of the Olympic Stadium in Stratford, London where a crude mix of Russian and Eastern Europeans plug away on a daily basis then it is obvious in the GP surgeries where Pakistani and Indian doctors fill in where English medics have left to open private practices. Our economy survives on the 'non-English' person. Thus a careful ideological balancing act ensues as government rhetoric tries to paint a picture of our country as somewhat 'untainted' by the globalised tidal wave of the 1970s which somehow retains its quaint, quintessential English personality.

Then 'gangs' were pulled out of the cupboard — in the main, blamed for causing the disorder (*Chapter 10*). Although gangs were reportedly involved, it was not as central government or some independent studies predicted (Briggs, 2012) because they, as well as those attached to that lifestyle or at least familiar to it in some form (*Chapter 10*), came together to fight the police and state oppression. Yet their pull to consumerism seemed ever present in the narratives (*Chapter 2*) and this meant many used the riots to siphon off as much cash/consumer goods as possible while making clear their hate for the authorities. However, while gang rivalries were suspended as, what it seems was an opportunity to payback against the police and claim as many freebies as possible, when the rivalries resumed, so too did volatile relations. So can gangs co-exist more peacefully? Are strained police relations with urban youth the main barrier to reducing youth violence? Lastly, new social media was plucked from the cupboard—because it represented a new form of *social politick* which transgressed geographical spaces through virtual networks (see *Chapter 16*). Harbouring the potential for a fresh moral panic, new social media was lambasted as the 'driver' for the disorder when, as discussed, it was merely the vehicle in some capacity and its benefits of riot resistance and riot clean-up were forgotten (*Chapter 9*).

Just as times past, anger and sour feeling about the police and state institutions quickly came to the surface. The continual problems of discrimination and structural violence which have played a part in historical rioting episodes (in particular recent episodes of 1981 and 1985) can't be ignored and the evidence that things haven't changed shouldn't be discounted (*Guardian* and LSE, 2011). Nearly 20 years ago, it was Stephen Lawrence but in recent months fresh questions of police legitimacy emerge; still the police hassle urban, working-class groups and minority ethnic populations on a daily basis, often for little apparent reason. Therefore the subjective nature of what it feels like to experience discrimination, lived oppression and racism on a daily basis plays some part in what we saw in 2011 (see *Chapter 6*). Maybe some people see history repeating itself; in that, it has to take the death of a black man at the hands of the police to once again remind us of the deficiencies in policing urban communities.

The first thing to note is that riots—as a form of disorder in this country—are nothing new; and perhaps like the dormant volcano they erupt every now and then, reminding us of the power and influence they can generate, only to drift from our consciousness as the collective magma from the social caldera cools, forming another layer in our violent history. It is evident that, despite one-sided political framing in news media, riots are often attributable to 'feral youth', the 'immigrant' or some 'other' group or symbolisms of change (in this case new social media). But we have seen that there are more to these disturbances and, in looking back, we need to think forward and consider correctly what the riots represented.

What the English Riots Represented

It is unanimously evident that the 'riots' represented more than just one explanation. Despite the shallow political attempts to mark it as behaviour of the 'criminal classes' and the narrow 'background factor' conjectures made by the Ministry of Justice, academic commentators tended to favour explanations which highlighted: (a) growing social inequality, discrimination and racism; and (b) the vibrancy and social significance of life in consumer society (*Chapter 1*). The empirical data provided in *Chapters 2*, and that collected by *The Guardian* and LSE (2011), indicate that these elements likely interplayed in August 2011. Evidence in this book seems to suggest that while there was some initial motivation to get back at police/state, generally these demands masked a commitment to secure as many consumer items as possible while the law and order levies were down (see *Chapters 8, 11*).

Indeed, historical evidence would suggest that periods of economic hardship often lay foundations for such social responses and this period of austerity may have had some bearing on collective social feeling. But it was the killing of Mark Duggan which seemed to stimulate fragile community relations — the similarities of the death of Cynthia Jarrett in 1985 on Broadwater Farm (Solomos, 2011) and Brixton 1981 are likely to be still fresh for some (*Chapter 6*) — and this became the moment which led to protests, resulting in the first episode of disorder (*Chapters 2, 6*). The failings of the police in numerous ways also seem familiar: a lack of intervention and failure to follow procedures correctly allowed for a protest to turn ugly and for a stagnant crowd to look for ways in which to express their frustration and anger (*Chapter 7*).

Just because all this went on in a 'black neighbourhood', it didn't mean the riots were all about 'race' — although the UK has witnessed its fair share of urban unrest in the context of race relations, inequality and unemployment in 1981, 1985, and 2001 (*Chapters 4, 6*). Although the riots in London were multi-ethnic, they were framed discursively as black, working-class and nihilistic — the view presented by David Starkey on 'Newsnight' who said that the 'whites had become black' but it was not only 'blacks' turning out on the streets of England (*Chapter 4*) because Manchester, Birmingham and Nottingham saw 'Asians' (*Chapter 1*) and 'whites' (*Chapter 14*). So, as *Chapter 12* shows, 'race' became politicised in the context of both 'black' and 'white' constructions of the protagonists. Some linked the unrest to 'battle for public space' (*Chapter 11*; Lea, 2011) by hypothesising that the rioters responses represented aggressive statements against increasing criminalisation of young people and the urban spaces in which they interacted. Indeed, some YouTube clips recorded prior to the riots seemed to confirm that they many urban youth had little choice but to 'hang around' on the streets—an idle population seeking activity but instead attracting continual police attention—because school was out and so was youth provision (Angel, 2012).

But it is evident that Slavoj Žižek (2011) is right to some extent because the rioters were not completely destitute like some who live in other parts of the world; they had means, homes, clothes, etc. Nor did they have a political message such as the students who walked on Whitehall in London in December 2010. Moreover, Žižek argues, the rioters and looters were raging disorder in their own communities, reflecting what he calls, 'society against society'; a discord 'between those with everything, and those with nothing to lose'. Different areas experienced different levels of crime and disorder, and in some places the targets were symbolisms of the police and state (*Chapter 1*) while, in the main, the targets were just designer boutique shops, retail stores and shopping malls (Briggs, 2012). Indeed, despite all the political waffle and the relentless news media interviews, the most absent accusation for the disorder was that it reflected a shallow dependence on consumption. Without discounting the hassle that some of these people experience from the authorities, could some of the subjectivities about negative police treatment have been talked up to researchers (*Guardian* and LSE, 2011)? It was evident that the real disorder—highlighted by the extensive looting—was downplayed in some interviews (*Chapters 2, 8*) and this points to the centrality of a consumerist way of life and its grip on contemporary English society; an ugly reflection to concede to if indeed we are honest enough to hold a mirror against what happened.

Over a hundred years ago, Thorstein Veblen (1994) introduced the concept of 'conspicuous consumption'; that is, whether rich or poor, we seek to present our social position through the self-adornment of commodities. Today, with more choice than ever, the higher up the social ladder we can climb if we are seen to display how much we can consume. A 'consumer society' breeds a constant need for something new in an effort to escape boredom and existential disuse. These feelings are neutralised through shopping malls, trendy cafes, designer outlets, cinemas, the leisure industry and the night-time economy. The pressure for satisfaction (or maybe to counter dissatisfaction) is never-ending, non-stop (see *Figure 2*). Indeed, Hall *et al* (2008: 87) note:

> Rather the constant waves of consumer symbolism and the partial democratisation of opulence in the consumer/service economy renew their desire to acquire, to go out and be seen to successfully wrestling significance from a harsh world.

Maybe this was what last summer represented; maybe some protagonists of the riots were seeking to create 'experience' in real terms rather than in the unreal world of consumer culture. Because it seems to me that living in an everyday vortex of ontological insecurity, social exclusion, perpetual

---

Figure 2 — Consumer race: Everyone wants to run (and look nice when they do so)

From a young age, we are socialised into running a consumer race; we are told it is healthy and good-citizenesque to be a successful runner in this race. Even through the finishing line moves with the horizon, being a winner means being someone who can 'look like a winner', have people envious of their pace and spunk away cash without even being bothered it has been spent. However, once we start to walk, we discover there are many others in this race; and participation becomes infectious in that, the momentum to participate motivates us to walk faster thinking we need to keep up. As we look around wondering what this is all about, we move from jogging to running because: (a) we don't want to be left behind; and (b) we want to be 'winners'. However, to run, we realise that we need all the gear, the trainers, the joggers — we need to look like the other runners otherwise they won't think we are serious about the race. Not all can keep up but, on inspection, we are envious of those who have 'nice stuff' and seem to be walking or who have reduced their sprint to a canter. But because running is such a public affair, the pressure to look good and continue looking good never ceases; the more miles we pass, the more ground we cover, the more difficult we find it is to take a break (or even stop).

unemployment, boredom and in a general day-to-day attitude of 'lets see what happens' unfortunately generates a populace quite passive to virtual invitations to loot and claim as much as possible — especially for those who have no access to a life of consumption. Indeed, Zygmunt Bauman (2005: 78) says 'it is precisely the inaccessibility of consumer lifestyle that the consumer society trains it members to experience as the most painful of deprivations'. For some, the riots presented a chance to transcend all the (social, individual and moral) boundaries under which one is measured and generate credibility (*Chapter 10*) — without perhaps being caught; a way to cheat the consumer game at its own rules.

For me, the irony was that while politicians were pointing the finger at those lower down the class structure for their 'take-what-they-can-get' attitudes, those looking up must have been equally bemused given that the elite had been doing similar things such as fiddling MPs expenses, the irregularities in FIFA, the phone hacking scandal and the risks which were taken which led to the banking crisis of 2008. It didn't seem to me that there was much gained by attacking the police or the state because a form of symbolic accumulation seemed to come more from the freebies on offer in the shops (*Chapter 2*).

Closing Time at the Shops and the State Homecoming

While the disorder and looting spread throughout London on Sunday 7th and Monday 8th August, other areas such as Birmingham, Liverpool, Manchester and Nottingham also started to experience similar forms of unrest. Indeed, while the Brixton riots raged for a few weeks in 1981, by comparison, the 2011 riots were short lived. Flooding the cities with police seemed to deter disorder from continuing in London but in areas such as Birmingham, it took the death of some community members before pleading that the disorder stop — and the next evening it did. But perhaps it couldn't have lasted longer because there seemed to be little coherent political message to the disorder (*Chapter 8*); people seemed to have some idea that this was temporal and that they needed to take advantage of the moment (*Chapter 2*). There was severe criticism against the police for being too timid, evident in the revolving media images of the disorder. Yet we can see now that they were in an awkward position, with little strategic leadership, low morale because

of impending austerity cuts to the force, and worried about accountability should they act improperly under the lens of the media (*Chapter 7*). To
account for this, there needed to be a central ideological theme which could
excuse the social issues which were at play below the surface.

The 'Riot' Rhetoric

I have come to learn that, the greater the distance from the essence of a
social problem, the more authoritative the label on what the problem is
and what it represents, while at the same time, the more inaccurate the
diagnosis of it. This was reflected in the riot discourse during and after the
disturbances. Predictably, the political and police riot rhetoric was painful
and distant, reflecting no real sense of what the violence and disorder represented. In the main, David Cameron has confined it to some 'simple' form
of criminality—an absence of 'morality' and 'community' among the urban
underclass—probably as a means to distance the Coalition from their social
policies (Solomos, 2011). People like David Lammy stayed close to a discourse
around poor parenting probably just so it could be conveniently confirmed
by the Riots Communities and Victims Panel (*Chapter 15*). Kenneth Clarke
said it was the 'criminal classes' who were responsible. Perhaps this was true:
only inferences from my contacts in the youth justice industry indicated that
police procedures seemed to be along the lines of 'who do we know who we
can nick [arrest]'—thereby skewing who was caught in the criminal justice
net. Indeed, the police were under immense political pressure to 'get the
baddies'. I remember watching a TV interview with one senior Met officer
who said how they hoped to make '3,000 arrests by Saturday' (a week after
the riots began): as if there was a satisfactory threshold which they had to
reach to justify the authority of their efforts. No wonder they banged up
any old Tom, Dick or Harry who took a bottle of water or stole a sandwich
(*Chapter 13*). This meant the supposed 'law abiders' who took part were not
represented in the police figures which probably bolstered an argument that
it was 'criminality, pure and simple' because the 'pure criminals' were the
ones arrested and charged for the disorder (*Chapter 14*).

There was further confusion. It seemed as if the riots provided a political
arena by which contemporary social division could be played out by using
existing social feeling about particular groups to either talk up their deviance

_ ratchet up political attention towards them—such as the accusations made against 'gangs' and the EDL (*Chapters 2, 10, 12*). In fact, I don't think the public ever got a clear picture of who was doing this and why. Perhaps there was an easy way out—to draw up a social blueprint of the classic social dropout; you know, the one who failed school, didn't get qualifications, can't get a job, takes drugs and the like (see *Figure 1* in *Chapter 1*). People like that surely deserve to be treated harshly for their meritocratic failure and participation in the disorder.

Harsh punishments

Within a few days, the state was able to restore its power and the way it did this raised significant questions about established criminal justice processes and procedures. Promises of 'feeling the full force of the law' seemed to represent typical neo-classicist blame attribution on the faulty moral compass, the decline of civility and the deterioration of family values and discipline among 'feral' youth. When the green light was given to licence 24-hour courts to process offenders, my contacts indicated it was mostly professionally-trained district judges rather than lay magistrates who took the stand. Youth offending team (YOT) workers, youth workers and probation officers told me the people (both young and old) who came before the court were being denied bail; that there was little, if any, consideration of their welfare or background circumstances, or even seriousness of the offence with which they were charged. 'But what else could happen?' explained one probation worker: 'some social control needed to be exercised' he said (see Body-Gendrot, 2011).

A paradox of opportunity arose: while on one hand the rioters and looters were taking advantage of the moment to enable their subjective frustrations and/or claim the goods available to them, the state similarly took the opportunity to ratchet up already-agreed social policies on them and enable severe punishments on the culprits in the name of deterrence. However, because the 'rioters' actions came under the banner of the disorder, blanket sentencing measures were orchestrated by the Justice Secretary (*Chapter 14*). There was also evidence to suggest that magistrates' court personnel were urged to disregard normal sentencing procedures and that prison term sentences were 25 per cent longer than normal. Is a tariff of six months in prison for throwing a bottle appropriate for someone with no previous convictions? How helpful is it to issue heavy sentences for people already well known to the criminal justice system or who are quite vulnerable in society in any case?

The 'Inquiry', Policy Responses, and Research Endeavours

In 1981, Lord Scarman reported on the oppressive policing culture in Brixton and the widespread grievance attached to protest and rioting (Scarman, 1981; Benyon, 1984). In my view, the only 'official' response to the English riots of 2011 was to get a small bunch of smartly-dressed people of varying ages together who look as if they represent urban communities (because they are ethnically diverse), film them walking around talking to victims and ask them to write something which Whitehall was dictating to them over the phone (*Chapter 15*). I mean let's be honest: how could any serious investigation be undertaken which did not even consider the views of those who participated in the riots? After all, who would want to fund a study/investigation into something which would only reflect badly on the governing party? Better yet, who would want to find out about something which may involve significant thought to resolve and likely, at the first hurdle, produce more questions than answers?

To me, it feels like denying the structural significance of a large crack in the front of a stately house and this seems to be the default response when social problems arise. At the moment, the way of dealing with the unsightly crack is to just apply a fresh coat of paint but the problem is the crack doesn't go away because it seems to keep reappearing; as the social elements permeate the paint peals away again. Funny that. Each time it reappears, it is that little bit larger, having attracted the damp and exposing new areas of concern. But the stately house owners are not concerned with actually resolving the structural issue which may threaten the foundations of the building and the welfare of the residents. Instead they get more fretful when the aesthetics of the house deteriorate and fool themselves into thinking that a little DIY 'here and there' will resolve the problems. They quickly paint over the crack so the other residents and neighbours won't know/talk about it, lying to themselves in the process about the significance of the fault.

This is precisely what happens in the event of major social disturbances like rioting—the coat of fresh paint being the Riots Communities and Victims

Panel. The riot-affected areas seemed to have been exaggerated and there was no clear means of determining what crimes were considered to be 'riot-related' nor any breakdown of their classifications of the crimes included in the disorder (*Chapter 15*). Both the Interim and Final Report regurgitated many things which were already known about discriminative police practices in urban areas and deprivation but quickly started to condemn parenting practices, and recommend more social support and that people develop greater personal resilience. We have heard it all before. Gone are the Keynesian days of welfare state (Lea, 2011). We need a new, radical response to these issues which does not recite a predictable realisation of same problems only to advocate the same solutions, and then, only to sound surprised when the same issues resurface some years down the line.

The Coalition's policy responses were to enable already-established social policy plans on 'gangs', 'problem families' and immigration. Aside from downgrading 'gang member' to 'gang affiliate' (well in most urban deprived neighbourhoods, who doesn't know someone in a gang?), the accusation against gangs acted as a rationale to pass through premature 'gangbo' policies (*Chapter 13*) — which were in the pilot stages prior to the riots. Suddenly, they were elevated to national rollout status. In fact, 'ending gang violence' became one popular headline from the riots. Another was 'problem families' which received new financial and policy backing. The government also used the riots to take forward new legislation to restrict immigration to the UK, when the country's workforce and student body relies so much on these groups: we start to strangle ourselves while simultaneously calling for more rope with which to tighten the grip. But all this, if anything, reflects the meagre difference there is between the main political parties and their approach to dealing with social issues. As *Chapter 13* showed, contract governance, which was a feature of the Labour government, was adopted as a policy response to the riots from the Coalition. All they did was change the name. No one would be any the wiser.

Research endeavours have come in the void of any 'official' inquiry. Some commentators seem to be churning out the same sort of material, harking out the familiar defects of the 'rioters' as people who failed at school, couldn't get it together to get a job and have criminal records (Morrell *et al*, 2011). The most commendable efforts are probably being made by *The Guardian* and

LSE but this research risks missing a key feature of the riots—one which has emerged in this book: that while the riots were constructed as political, they were also apolitical. Indeed, at some post-riot meetings and symposiums, and as we saw in *Chapter 8*, some left liberal academics seem to be anchoring themselves in quite familiar theoretical constructions of riots. Should we pursue this pathway, we will be just as guilty as the Riots Panel, the government and the media because we are also undermining our position and the opportunity we have to document what is really taking place here. The book has shown that narrative constructions of the riots have been quite opposing and almost contradictory. In hindsight something more apparent seems to be coming to light—the 'rioters' were as much victims as they were perpetrators, talking up their anti-police/state grievances but at the same time revealing a default setting to loot and indulge in free shopping.

And perhaps the public, to some extent, also recognise this; maybe they know more than we think—despite their confused initial reactions (*Chapter 1*). Look at the way in which some seem critical of the government and media's ideological framing of the riots and, to some extent, seemed to see something into the rioters' motivations (*Chapter 15*). In the words of one village pub quiz attendee, 'the rioters were just as bad as those they thought they were attacking' leaving the 'capitalists unscathed'. But there are also some other clues in this short narrative; some sense that we at least have some idea to the systemic deficiencies which plague the world's social and economic engine while, at the same time, recognising how easily it can be brought to its knees.

Neo-liberalism and the Dark Clouds of Global Discontent

Global capitalism: A default setting of profit and consumption

The world has entered a new phase. We face new economic, social and ecological catastrophes which don't seem to be taken that seriously by our world leaders—perhaps evident in the continual failure to balance the 'Eurozone' markets; make the banking sector more 'ethical and accountable'; rebalance the rich/poor divide; and protect the planet from its impending demise. The state points the finger at the market only for the market to point the finger back at the state and, in the end, it is the 'irresponsible citizen' who finds themselves at the centre of all the problems for their moral, social and financial lacking. While some peaceful protests have tried to draw attention to these issues, such as the Occupy Wall Street and Occupy London movements, there is little sign of change. Yet the crises continue and efforts to resolve these problems have not really materialised. Instead they become familiar soundbites on the news and part of the accepted social fabric of 'that's just how things are' — a normalisation of insecurity. We become so used to hearing it that its authenticity fades, safe in the knowledge that, although the problems do actually exist, we aren't doing enough to solve them and it isn't our responsibility in any case; there is always the fake tan to look forward to at the weekend or summer Coldplay gig.

What is perhaps most disturbing about the neoliberal order is the eternal obsession to ensure that each year there is continual growth which can be churned into sizable bonuses. Surely there is not much more room to grow, if anything! Yes there is — it just comes at the expense of powerful, corporate CEOs who are applauded when they streamline business by severing thousands of jobs, offloading labour to unregulated sites in developing countries where a blind-eye can be turned to human rights and working conditions, and generally raping the environment in the name of mineral pursuit — basically whatever the cost to squeeze out some more growth, some more profit. Still no one seems to be in control and we are left asking questions while the bonuses continue — just where exactly is this growth coming from as countries and their economies retract? How many zeros can be added to the debt which is incestuously being repackaged and miscellaneously misplaced only to be placed on the taxpayer's tab? Just how 'real' is the money? How 'real' is the problem? The situation feels like the old Warner Brothers roadrunner cartoons where the coyote runs off the cliff but keeps running… then he looks at the camera and realises that there is nothing underneath him before dropping into the canyon. It's to say, we have already exhausted the precipice, already run over the cliff edge yet somehow we are still running… but only on very thin air; in fact, there is little, if any, substance to our movement. The moment of realisation being the glance at the camera when we see the extent of the problem. When, then, will we drop into the canyon?

The only way there can be growth is at the expense of the Third World countries and/or if we, the West, can politically bully other countries into making use of their resources while, at the same time, perpetuating their domestic fragility by taking advantage of their enthusiastic workforces. We don't know much about people in these countries but we see a few stories on the news or, if we are that interested, some half-an-hour documentary about a few poor kids making Nike jumpers or beaten-out women slaving over sewing machines in India for 18 hours a day. Nevertheless, it is a world away from our leisure lives of takeaways, whole weekends watching box-set DVDs and getting pissed on holiday in Ibiza. And these days very few cultures are exempt from this default setting of profit and consumption: from the ancient retreats of the temples in Bali where hundreds of tourist sellers descend to sell different Balinese cultural paraphernalia to the Andaman Islands where only recently a tribe has come into contact with the Western world in the late-1990s. Tourists flock there to pay them to dance by giving them food and money; it is essentially illegal but the police turn a blind-eye and also cash in as well by doing so. Global capitalism touches everyone and affects everything. Thus, we (the consumers) consume their misery (the producers). It is structurally embedded.

So what's this got to do with the English riots? In an insecure world where all we see on the news is the economic fragility of the world, war, famine, ecological crises, thank god for the comfort of our leisure lives. All we need to do is turn off the TV and it disappears and we can indulge in a bit of shopping to further escape all these catastrophes. Best make the most of this world and take as much advantage of it as possible. After all its what everyone else seems to be doing—regardless of the level of their responsibility. And when global capitalism throws more people into the margins, while at the same time, offering them a way to seek a sense of self through consumption, a familiar strain occurs (Young, 2007). People become less concerned about their class position and instead seek self-actualisation through participation in consumption practices and the symbolism of social envy which is consequently generated (Hall *et al*, 2008). They are the 'Consumtariat' as Žižek (2011: 236) argues:

> The 'Consumtariat' (the idea that, in developed societies, the lower class is no longer a proletariat but a class of consumers kept satisfied with cheap, mass produced commodities, from genetically modified food to digitalised mass culture) becomes

a reality with basic income: those excluded from the production process are paid the basic income not only for reasons of solidarity, but also so that their demand will fuel production and thus prevent crises.

They essentially become docile to the market, powerless to their own demands and redundant to political action. This is how it might work on a daily basis (see *Figure 3*). People in these positions seek inclusion through the market rather than through collective political representation so when the opportunity arises to take such a stance, it is seized. This is what happened in the summer of 2011 when the 'flawed consumers', as Zygmunt Bauman describes, came forth to claim what was rightfully theirs when the law enforcement levies were suspended. The book shows that while some had clear grievances, it was the default setting of consumption was disguised somewhat beneath these subjectivities of police treatment, inequality, anti-state feelings, etc — most poignantly highlighted in *Chapter 2* in the discussions between Will, Craig and Steve (*Chapter 8*; Moxon, 2011). An odd duality of power and powerlessness therefore arises: for those who took part in the English riots last summer, who have very little to show for their participation, might now be thinking that they were in control — that they exhibited power. Yet if anything it revealed their powerlessness and subordination to consumerism.

A new age of rioting and social discord?

The use of new social media has been a recurrent theme in anti-globalisation protests in recent years (Solomos, 2011) as well as remonstrations across southern Europe, Northern Africa and the Middle East. It has changed the way in which social issues in these countries come to light while simultaneously impacting on how people form a collective response (*Chapter 17*). In addition, like many other episodes of violence and disorder in recent years, what happened across English cities in 2011 seemed to be triggered by police injustice/maltreatment of particular minority ethnic social groups (*Chapter 7*). In this respect, it is evident that this has something in common with what took place in places like France in 2005, Greece in 2008, and Tunisia and Egypt in 2011. There seems to be something resolutely similar in the way in which these events have also been orchestrated with the use of social media

Figure 3—A typical Consumtariat family day

It is a typical day in the Consumtariat household. Mum and Dad must work and the kids have school; its their GCSE year so best they try as hard as possible. The two girls skip breakfast, spending more time in the mirror on their make-up and scruffy school-girl image while Mum offers to take them to school in the new BMW — she loves driving around in it especially with her sunglasses on. The girls leave the car glued to their BlackBerry screens and don't even say goodbye. However, the school drop leaves Mum almost out of petrol and she has to stop. Bizarrely, the petrol prices seem to rise as Mum fills the tank of the car. She shrugs her shoulders *'what can I do?'* she thinks. On the radio, the government issues a statement blaming the markets which had to increase oil prices because of some political tensions in some far away country. But there is no time to think about that. Meanwhile, Dad arrives at the train station where he learns the private train company, ScamRail, has increased the weekly season ticket for the third time this year. He shrugs his shoulders, shakes his head and automatically hands over his credit card (which reminds him to pay off the £400 on the card which he still owes after a lads weekend in Eastern Europe). At work, Mum flicks the computer screen between her excel spreadsheet loaded with figures to some online discount deals at BHS. At lunch, she heads out to Starbucks for her Grande Latte and miniscule sandwich which is drastically overpriced. Tasty but sadly its the only thing available in the area—such a relief that the companies devote a proportion of their profit to ethical trading and sustainable communities she thinks *'at least they're doing their bit.'* Dad is busy, snacks on crisps and chocolate for lunch, and under pressure to find a cheap holiday, books a five-star hotel in Spain—slightly concerned that it is more than he budgeted. *'Nevermind'* he reasons and remembers the 'priceless' nature of the memories he will retain. *'Good old credit card'* is his Facebook status. Meanwhile, the girls slip out of school an hour early for lunch with some friends and sneak into KFC. On arriving home, Mum and Dad open the post to find the gas, water and electricity bills have increased, switch on the news to find taxes are going up, and see that there are fresh terrorism threats and that more 'illegal immigrants' are claiming benefits and welfare off the NHS. As the frustration starts to build, it desists as a Britain's Got Talent blooper special comes on and Dad cracks open a bottle of wine. As the family reconvene between glances at their mobile phones, there is little time to eat and Dad suggests a take-away pizza. Happy days.

as a means of communicating between different social groups (*Chapter 9*). Take the way in which, for example, social media was used as a means of communication and organisation when traditional media was shut down in Egypt (*Chapter 16*) and the importance of mediums such as YouTube in communicating messages where regimes were reluctant to reveal the extent of the violence they waged on their own people in Libya, Tunisia, and Syria. Paradoxically, in England, people were arrested when boasting about their disorder on Twitter or by uploading images and clips of their booty on Facebook and YouTube. There seems to be clear differences in how we used social media in England in the riots in comparison to how it is was used to galvanise real collective effort to fight for democracy in Europe, Northern Africa and the Middle East.

The crisis of contemporary political systems: The failure of democracy (and the stuttering steps towards it)

In contemporary times, democracy seems to be stuttering. In countries across Europe such as Spain and Greece, an electorate of all ages have protested and rioted against a restrictive political system, austerity measures, fiscal mismanagement and police treatment. The resulting violence exemplified a resistance to the political power structures and was also manifested in other ways through, for example, *Yo no pago* (I don't pay) in Spain and Greece whereby people refused to contribute to the system — perhaps as a more individualised means of power resistance (*Chapter 17*). In Northern Africa such as Tunisia, Libya and Egypt, and in the Middle East such as Syria and Yemen, there is a general feeling among a predominantly internet-savvy, educated youth cohort that politics do not represent the majority—that the public are generally excluded from political representation (*Chapters 16, 17, 18*). In particular, there exists a real passion for the cause reflected in the way in which thousands of lives have been lost to protest and violence across North Africa and the Middle East. In interview after interview, the people reiterate their commitment to the cause because they say they would die for it. In these countries where the people are pushing for some sort of democracy against quite stagnant, autocratic militaristic regimes, there has been a long and bloody road to convey the message. In episodes of violence and disorder, the manifestations of protest and anger have come directly against the symbols of the political regimes, which in response, often wage all out violence on those who campaign against them. It is difficult to fathom the extent to which some of these regimes are polluted and corrupt, and the measures by which they will take to cling to power by instigating all out violence on their own populace. Take for example how Mubarak hired 'thugs' and set criminals free from prison to try and quell the Egypt uprising (*Chapter 16*). Yet despite death, injury and continual suffering, still the people take to the streets, still they protest.

In England, despite widespread awareness of the inconsistency of the political classes and their obscene behaviour, still we vote. We know the extent to which they fiddle the books, claim second or third homes at our expense, have incestuous relations with the police and media, and increasingly appear in more and more farcical predicaments only to step down from one parliament position and assume another. No one notices a reshuffle and still we vote. As in Spain and Greece, we also experience a similar disorientation with our politics; there is very little difference between our centre left (conservative) and centre right (labour) parties. They say they offer different policies but their approaches are not dissimilar to their rivals (*Chapter 8*). Fittingly, as I write, one of David Cameron's own constituents accuses him of being 'an out of touch arrogant posh boy' who has no understanding of ordinary voters. So where is our sustained protest? Why do we not display a similar level of passion against our crooked political regime? Why is there very little politically-driven protest in England?

Firstly, as discussed, it is to do with the way in which the working classes—who would normally lead such a charge—have been made docile through consumerism. Secondly, it seems to be the case in this country that if protest is not 'done properly' (i.e. in a civilised manner, peacefully and the like) then it is not a democratic form of expression—it somehow represents a savage way of conveying dissatisfaction and one which should not be tolerated. This was certainly the case in the post-riot constructions of the student protests in London in 2010. The very ideology which circulated around the protests depoliticised it; that is, anything which may have happened as a result of genuine frustration was then attributed to 'outsiders' or some senseless minority who came along with the intention to cause trouble and therefore didn't represent core protestor values. Consequently, we don't tend to have sustained protests; there are more important issues in our lives to consider such as our leisure commitments and the time it may take out of our precious lives. I feel that we are an individualised and atomised populace, too accepting of the status quo while too sceptical that we can instigate change.

We return to the analogy of the structural crack in the front of the stately house because these days the residents don't seem to be bothered that the wealthy house owners have plastered another coat of paint over the fault of their English dwelling. They are told instead to be more concerned about the structural faults which exist among others on the same street (Europe) and in other neighbourhoods (North Africa and Middle East) because they might affect the mortgage payments and living standards. For just down the road, the neighbours (Europe) have similar problems with cracks—some more severe than others. At the neighbourhood meetings, the other rich house owners gloss over the significance of the fractures in their buildings, and talk up the stability of their residence even though there is obvious subsidence in some houses (Greece, Spain, Italy and Portugal). In some districts, there is concern that the house owners can't manage their tenancies (Iraq, Afghanistan) so some intervene but end up leaving more structural uncertainty. While other neighbourhoods (Egypt, Syria, Tunisia, Libya) are left to their own devices in the hope that they will summon the means to patch up the structural faults themselves. Maybe it's time to address the faults before the residents take to the streets again; either to make political statements or to go shopping.

References

Angel, H. (2012) 'Were The Riots Political?' in *Safer Communities Special Edition on the Riots*, Vol 11(1):24-32.

Bauman, Z. (2005) *Work, Consumerism and the New Poor*, New York: Open University Press.

Benyon, J. (1984) *Scarman and After: Essays Reflecting on Lord Scarman's Report, The Riots and Their Aftermath*, London: Pergamon Press.

Body-Gendrot, S. (2011) 'Disorder in world cities: Comparing Britain and France' cited online 1st March 2012: www.opendemocracy.net/ourkingdom/ sophie-body-gendrot/disorder-in-world-cities-comparing-britain-and-france?utm_source=feedblitz&utm_medium=FeedBlitzEmail&utm_ content=201210&utm_campaign=Nightly_2011-08-16 per cent2005:30.

Briggs, D. (2012) 'What We Did When It Happened: A Timeline Analysis of the Social Disorder in London' in *Safer Communities Special Edition on the riots*, Vol 11(1): 6-16.

Guardian and LSE (2011) *Reading the Riots: Investigating England's Summer of Disorder'*, London: *Guardian* and LSE.

Hall, S., Winlow, S. and Ancrum, C. (2008) *Criminal Identities and Consumer Culture: Crime, Exclusion and the New Culture of Narcissism*, Cullompton: Willan.

Morrell, G., Scott, S., McNeish, D., and Webster, S. (2011) *The August Riots in England: Understanding the Involvement of Young People*, London: National Centre for Social Research.

Moxon, D. (2011) 'Consumer Culture and the Riots of 2011', *Sociological Research Online*, Vol 16(4): No page numbers.

Solomos, J. (2011) 'Race, Rumours and Riots: Past, Present and Future' *Sociological Research Online*, Vol 16(4):20.

Lea, J. (2011) 'Shock Horror: Rioters Cause Riots! Criminals Cause Crime', *British Society of Criminology Newsletter*, No.69, Winter 2011.

Scarman, Lord. J. (1981) *The Brixton Disorders, 10 - 12th April (1981)*, London: HMSO.

Veblen, T. (1994) *The Theory of the Leisure Class*, Harmondsworth: Penguin.

Žižek, S. (2011) *Living in the End Times*, London: Verso Books.

INDEX

Symbols

15M Movement *347, 356*

A

Abbott, Diane *122*

academics *195, 196, 208, 385*

acceptable behaviour contracts *260*

accountability *127, 333, 389*

acquisitive offences *15, 285*

Action for Children *265*

activism *178, 214, 238, 239, 349*

actualities *45*

Adesorg 350

adrenaline junkies *206*

Africa *396*

　North Africa *21, 398, 400*

age *194, 281*

agency

　criminal justice agencies *127*

　spontaneous agencies *47*

aggression *93, 197, 198*

agitation *98, 129*

alcohol *139, 290, 295*

aliens *70, 71, 382*

　'alien criminals' *75*

Al-Jazeera *336, 339*

Allburnd *313*

Alliot-Marie, Michele *129*

ambiguity *140*

ambition *294*

Americanisation *49*

anarchy *98*

anger *20, 114, 135, 137, 200, 221, 311, 337, 365, 385*

　pent up anger *92*

Anonymous *348*

anti-Semitism *382*

anti-social behaviour *140, 154, 258, 291, 313*

　Anti-Social Behaviour Act 2003 *260*

　anti-social behaviour order *260, 286*

anxiety *45, 58, 71*

　generational anxiety *382*

apology *135*

Arabia *21, 138, 356*

　Arab Spring *128, 129, 164, 172, 333, 348*

Argos *36*

arrest *131, 136, 194*

　'3,000 arrests by Saturday' *389*

arson *14, 16, 30, 207, 210, 309*

Asians *220, 385*

aspiration *18*

assassination *101, 330*

assault *136*

　assault on police *53*

Astor, Viscountess *69*

Athens *22, 356, 361, 367, 377*

Atkinson, Rowland *22*

austerity *12, 102, 127, 132, 322, 348, 355,*

361, 385

authorities *31, 37, 95, 98, 134, 140, 193*

   secondary authority *202*

B

Babylon *120*

background *19*

   background risk factors *17, 20*

Baden-Powell, Robert *51*

bail *390*

Bailey, Michael *81*

balance *27*

Baltagis *338*

bankers/banks *196, 317, 322, 348, 352*

   bailout *352, 365*

   banking crisis *261*

   bonuses *35*

   venal bankers *154*

Barcelona *356*

Barking and Dagenham Youth Offending
     Service *vii*

Barnet *238*

Barnett, Mary *52*

Bateman, Tim *22*

batons *239*

BBC *12, 60, 94, 309, 336*

Bedford *96*

'beefs' *34, 198*

   'postcode beefs' *198*

begging *286*

Benedict XVI (Pope Benedict) *354*

benefits *286*

Berlin *129*

Besant, Walter *57*

Bethnal Green *81*

Bexleyheath *243*

Big Society *13, 128, 263*

birch *50*

Birkenhead *15*

Birmingham *13, 14, 71, 81, 95, 96, 101,*
     118, 133, 200, 321, 385, 388

BlackBerry *12, 28, 38, 171, 174, 177, 201,*
     202, 382, 396

black issues *28, 31, 79, 99, 103, 111, 114,*
     138

   black community *100*

   'black neighbourhoods' *385*

   black solidarity *105*

   'Black War on Police' *74*

   invasive 'black' culture *70*

   'whites have become black' *60, 65*

Blafelda *312*

blame *10, 13, 98, 173*

   blame attribution *390*

blandness *309*

boarding up *14*

Bolton *96*

boredom *155, 316, 387*

Bosanquet, Helen *52*

Bouazizi, Mohamed *138*

boundary demarcations *349*

Bourdieu, Pierre *196*

Bow *182*

Bradford *75*

bragging rights *197*

branding *vii*

Bratton, Bill *194*

breach of court orders *286*

bread riots, demonstrations, etc. *331*

Bristol

  St Pauls *95, 100, 103, 118*

British

  British identity *76*

  British Medical Association *46*

  British Nationality Act 1981 *80*

  British Sociological Association *21*

  'British way of life' *65*

Brixton *14, 23, 66, 95, 100, 110, 117, 122, 385*

  Angel Park Estate *119*

  Brixton black community *115*

  Brixton riots/uprising *21, 66, 74, 79, 91, 97, 104, 111, 118, 122, 317, 388*

Broadwater Farm *28, 29, 97, 99, 179, 200, 317, 385*

Broken Britain *66, 67, 266*

Broxbourne *308*

'Bullet Boy' *113*

bullying *67*

burglary *14, 15, 16, 49, 285, 313*

Burney, Elizabeth *258*

Burnley *75*

business *10, 14*

Butler, R A *78, 82*

Butterworth, James *48*

C

Cable Street *246*

Cairo *138, 334, 336*

Calvert, Roy and Theodora *48*

Cambridge *49, 307, 320*

Cameron, David *vii, 13, 18, 27, 65, 66, 80,* *92, 96, 129, 131, 153, 170, 194, 224, 247, 251, 263, 266, 287, 389, 399*

Campbell, Bea *227*

cannabis *286, 368*

Canvey Island *307*

capitalism *158, 162*

  global capitalism *393, 395*

Cardiff *72*

carnival *38, 57, 197, 201*

  carnivalesque triumph *154*

case studies *280, 287, 288*

  case management systems *282*

Casey, Louise *266*

Castells, Manuel *201*

catalysts *150, 187*

causes

  root causes *151*

cautions *18*

CCTV *281, 289*

  CCTV evidence *295*

censorship

  social media *131*

Centre for Social Justice *194*

change *47, 54, 59, 61*

  'Everything changes, nothing moves' *61*

chaos *14*

Chapletown *118*

Chatham *307, 320*

chavs *46*

Chelsea Boys *54, 56*

Cheshunt *307*

Children and Young Persons Act 1933 *50*

'child soldiers of the third world' *71*

China *131*

church *47, 119*

CIA *335*

cigarettes *294, 298*

citizens *154*

    birthright citizenship *80*

    blueprint for citizenship *349*

    British citizenship *80*

    citizen platforms *349*

    citizenship *349, 350*

    'real' citizens *71, 80, 82*

    white British citizens *81*

city types *53*

civil

    civil discord *75*

    civil disobedience *353*

    civil liberties *352*

civility *390*

Clapham *14*

    Clapham Common *117*

    Clapham Junction *65, 181, 182*

Clarke, Kenneth *12, 45, 96, 279, 382, 389*

class *20, 138, 395*

    'class making' *224*

    class narrative *161*

    class politics *258*

    'criminal classes' *389*

    'dangerous classes' *59, 139*

    lower class *395*

    On the Treatment of the Dangerous and
        Perishing Classes of Society *59*

    poorer classes *35*

    ruling class *35*

    working-class *48, 53, 56, 69, 154, 161,*
        224, 385

clean-up/cleansing *10, 13, 182, 183*

Clegg, Nick *267*

closed shops *130*

Coalition *80, 96, 102, 257, 259, 261, 262,*
    270, 321, 383, 389, 392

coat of fresh paint *391*

Coe, Lord *121*

coercion *96*

Cohen, Stanley *46, 170*

collectivism

    collective action *172*

    collective life *160*

    collective magma *384*

    collective social feeling *385*

Commonwealth Immigration Act 1962 *78*

community

    black community *135*

    community building *230*

    community cohesion *45*

    Community Links *294*

    community orders *285*

    community relations *136*

    community safety/partnerships *192,*
        262

    community self-defence *339*

    community sentencing *323*

    erosion of community *45*

    family and community *19*

    minority ethnic communities *100, 111,*
        214, 383

compensation *13*

condemnation *93*

confidence *13*

conflict *134, 196*

    conflict management *126*

    neutralising conflict *136*

conformity *31*

confrontation *93, 221*

Connexions *103*

consequences *126*

   'consequence of actions' *17*

   unanticipated consequences *133*

consumerism *12, 13, 20, 22, 23, 34, 155,*
     222, 385

   consumer race *387*

   consumption *36*

      'conspicuous consumption' *386,*
        395

      'Consumtariat' *395*

      default setting of profit and consump-
        tion *395*

control *38, 82, 132, 201, 202, 238, 244,*
     287, 321

   controlling the young *128*

   control of the streets *16*

   feeling in control *225*

   military control *333*

   social control *260*

      gangs by *193*

conviction *123*

   previous convictions *18, 391*

coping skills *287*

Cornwallis, C F *59*

corruption *35, 154, 352, 353, 355, 361,*
     364, 370

costs *10*

   cost of living *102*

counselling *296*

courts *220*

   24-hour courts *390*

   court disposals *285*

crack down *194, 195*

crime

   Criminal Justice Matters *21*

crime/criminality *12, 31, 171, 282, 322*

   acquisitive crime *291*

   casual criminality *12*

   causes of crime *216*

   copy-cat crimes *50, 61, 200, 316, 322*

   Crime and Disorder Act 1998 *260, 262*

   Crime and Security Act 2010 *260, 264*

   'crime drop' *258*

   crime prevention/reduction *16, 192,*
     272

   criminal damage *14, 16, 27, 285, 348*

   criminal histories *194, 279, 286*

   criminalisation *347*

   'criminality, pure and simple' *vii, 12, 27,*
     37, 131, 165, 306, 322, 389

   criminal justice net *389*

   criminal justice system *16, 21, 131, 139,*
     258, 279, 288, 297, 319

      'broken CJS' *279*

   criminal people *12*

   expressive crime *197*

   'native' criminals *76*

   opportunist criminals *337*

   'presumed reality' *304*

   processing by CJS *23, 280*

   protest as crime *131*

cronyism *130*

crowds *92, 94, 97, 104, 134, 320, 385*

   dispersal of crowds *238*

   double-reflexive crowd *177*

   mediated crowd *172, 173, 186*

   power in the crowd *321*

   role of the 'crowd' *20*

virtual crowd *177*

Croydon *10, 14, 200, 317, 321*

culprits *17*

culture *49, 169, 347, 395*

British culture *114*

celebrity self-obsessed culture *80*

cultural diversity *65*

cultural dynamics *172*

cultural segregation *81*

'gang' culture *132, 263*

popular media culture *65*

urban street culture *193*

curfew *10, 286, 290*

Currys *36, 202, 207*

custody *16, 285, 299*

deaths in custody *135*

cutbacks *101, 127*

cyber circuits *137*

cynicism *153, 158*

dark cloud of cynicism *154*

D

Dalston *237*

damage *93, 137, 141, 219*

damage to property *10*

danger *10, 12, 50, 59, 139, 311, 331*

dangerous classes *139*

data *209*

explanations of *208*

Davies, Andrew *54*

deaths *10*

debasement *59*

debt *287, 348*

Decent Home Platform *348*

defiance *48*

democracy *157, 348, 351, 362, 370, 398*

Democracia Real Ya *348*

democratisation movements *128*

global democracy *129*

demographics *20, 283*

demonisation *138, 139*

demonstrations *200, 336*

Department for Communities and Local Government *265*

depravity *50*

depression *290*

Great Depression *48*

deprivation *18, 104, 112, 133, 193, 216, 286, 322*

despair *97*

destructiveness *318*

deterrence *17, 132, 226, 299*

Detroit *138, 227*

deviancy *140, 258*

'defining deviancy down/up' *258*

dialogue *127*

'difficult to manage' areas *201*

digital fifth column *351*

dilemmas *45*

direct action *141*

disadvantage *138*

'cycle of disadvantage' *300*

disaffection *311*

disapproval *258*

discipline *51, 96, 202, 267*

disconnect *179*

discontent *81, 355*

'Winter of Discontent' *102*

discord *81, 396*

discrimination *12, 37, 97, 100, 163, 281, 385*

    discriminatory practices *20*

    reverse discrimination *65*

disease *97*

disenfranchisement *322*

disillusion *350, 352*

disobedience *315, 353, 355*

disorder *14, 16, 76, 92, 171, 216, 239, 329, 348, 381, 390, 396*

    social disorder *15, 196*

    violent disorder *285*

dispersal

    dispersal of stolen goods *209*

    dispersal orders *221, 260*

dissatisfaction *163*

dissent *92, 94, 102, 133*

dissonance *131*

distinction *197*

district judges *390*

disturbances *91, 95, 133, 136, 193, 281*

diversity *349*

Do not vote for them *350*

dress *55*

driving offences *286*

drugs *31, 126, 139, 198, 201, 286, 287, 290, 295*

Drury Lane Boys *54*

Duggan, Mark *9, 14, 28, 34, 81, 122, 135, 137, 150, 175, 200, 227, 304, 315, 385*

    ballistics report *135*

Duncan Smith, Iain *67, 71, 80, 264, 269*

E

Ealing *14, 96, 200*

Eastern Daily Press *311*

East Ham *14*

economics *101, 104, 128, 130, 134, 139, 142, 149, 159, 197, 314, 350*

    economic contraction *127, 130, 133*

    economic fragility *395*

    economic hardship *298*

    economic stagnation *132*

        Greece *366*

    economic turmoil *153*

    economic uncertainty *81*

    financial instability *361*

    fiscal retrenchment *101*

    market economies *131*

    market uncertainty *22*

    socio-economics *92, 281, 286*

        Greek socio-economics *375*

edgy anticipation *9*

education *18, 45, 102, 122, 139, 194, 263, 350, 353*

    Department for Education *265*

    education maintenance allowance *35, 104*

    special educational needs *18, 286*

Efford, Clive *245, 246, 251*

Egypt *23, 128, 138, 329, 333, 396*

elites

    educated elites *160*

    feral elites *154*

    gang elites *199*

Eltham *237, 239, 241, 249, 250*

empowerment *202, 207, 225*

Enfield *14, 237, 241*

Engels *330*

English Defence League *23, 70, 236, 237*

    EDL activists *239*

Englishness *381, 383*

    'English Hottentots' *61*

Enlightenment *129*

envy *395*

equality/inequality *12, 22, 36, 160, 187,*
    282, 322, 352, 385

Estado de Malestar *350*

ETA *351*

ethnicity *194, 220, 281, 396*

ethnography *21*

Europe *128, 132, 352, 398*

    Euro 2004 *94*

    European Central Bank *365*

    European Convention on Human
        Rights *65, 80*

    European Union *21, 361*

    Eurozone *365, 383, 393*

    social disorder in *101*

evidence *195*

excitement *37, 222, 224, 292, 319*

exclusion *287*

excuses *315, 322*

existential disuse *387*

experiential adventure *153*

exuberance *206*

F

Facebook *16, 28, 32, 36, 38, 174, 237, 317,*
    335, 382, 396

    'Facebook Revolution' *336*

    viral accelerator *61*

failure *18*

fairness *160*

family *47, 296, 302*

    'chaotic families' *224*

    dysfunctional families *10*

    family and community factors *19*

    family breakdown *45*

    family discipline *96*

    family dysfunction *45*

    family networks *293*

    family values *390*

    foreign families *65*

    'problem' families *265, 392*

    right to family life *80*

    'stable families' *67*

    troubled families *265*

        Troubled Families Team *265, 270*

    weakening of family life *51*

fear *244*

fecklessness *154*

femininity *216*

    emphasised femininities *224, 229*

    feminism *215*

    resistant femininities *229*

'feral' youth, rats, etc. *13, 23, 297*

films *49*

Finsbury Park *96*

firearms *28, 57, 201*

firebomb *16*

flash point *138*

Flickr *270*

football firms, hooligans *46, 237*

Footlocker *210*

force *201*

Ford, Richard *49*

foreign *79*

    'dark' foreign interloper *71*

    foreign labour *383*

    foreignness *61, 76*

    Foreign Office *371*

Fortnum and Masons *94*

Foucault *185*

Fox, Chris *22*

fragility *31, 246, 385, 395*

France *176, 396*

freedom *48, 207*

    freedom of expression *349*

'free-for-all' *20*

frustration *20, 28, 104, 130, 163, 365, 385*

Fukuyama, Francis *129*

Fulham Boys *54*

fun *37*

funding *127*

G

Gaddafi, Colonel *129*

gangs *10, 19, 31, 45, 99, 114, 383*

    'Belt and Pistol' gangs *57*

    branding *197*

    Clerkenwell Pistol Gang *54*

    Dick Turpin Gang *54*

    evolution *211*

    fluidity *195*

    'gang-affiliates' *195, 199, 264, 392*

    gangbo *194, 260, 392*

    'gang'/gangster culture *60, 132, 263*

    gang injunction *194, 260, 264*

    gang life *122*

    gang mythology *197*

    'gang' neighbourhoods *197*

    gangs programme *122*

    'gangsta rap' *45*

    Gangs Task Force *194*

    gang strategy *99*

    gang violence *123*

    Girdle Gang *54*

    hierarchy of gangs *197*

    Pinus Gang *54*

    police as a gang *198*

    recruitment *266*

    rival gangs *31*

    rowdy gangs *54*

    'social field' *203*

    'threat of gangs' *17*

    truce *19, 137, 193, 204*

    urban street gang *193*

    Velvet Cap Gang *54, 56*

    Waterloo Road Gang *54*

    white gangsters *118*

gas masks *373*

gender *20, 23, 194, 215, 228*

    'male universalism' *217*

    race and gender *227*

General Strike *48*

geography

    social geography *225*

'get the baddies' *389*

'getting high' *207*

girls *228*

    'girls gone wild' *222*

Glasgow *72*

globalisation *196*

    counter-globalisation *347, 349*

411

global change 355

global social change 21, 381

Gloucester 307, 312, 320

'going off the rails' 267

Golden Age 66, 69, 161

Greece 362

Goliath 227, 230

Goodwin, Matthew 70

Gorst, Sir John 52

Gove, Michael 266

governance vacuum 201, 202

government 31, 36

Grant, Bernie 99, 110, 112, 123

Great Depression 48

Greater Manchester 15

Greater Manchester Police 184

Greece 23, 130, 348, 356, 361, 396

Greek tragedy 363

greed 222, 282, 317, 318

Green, Damian 80

Greenwich 174

Grey, Charles 72

grievances 105, 137, 187, 196, 221

H

habit 196

habitual discourses 250

Hacking, Douglas 69

Hackney 32, 96, 121, 137, 182, 200, 201

Hallsworth, Simon 22

handling stolen goods 15, 285

Handsworth 118

harassment 31, 100, 135, 138, 199

Harringay 237

Hastings, Max 67

hate/hatred 31, 70, 112, 117, 118, 139, 199

Hatfield 308

health 17

Heathcote, C G 51

Heath, Edward 79

hedonism 91, 154, 164

Hegel 98

help 13

Herbert, Nick 93, 279, 280, 285

Hewitt, Roger 250

High Wycombe 307

hindsight 91, 92

historical amnesia 45, 59

Hoggart, Richard 46

Home Affairs Committee 194, 303, 304

home invasions 207

homelessness 286, 368, 370

Decent Home Platform 348

Home Office 82, 99, 195, 239, 262, 306, 321

Home Secretary 99, 123, 171, 194, 208, 262, 263

homespun philosophy 320

homogeneity 76

hoodies 12, 46, 310

hooligans 51, 52, 54, 57

hope

suffocation of hope 162

hostility 113, 139, 238

hotspots 10

housing 17, 350, 355

Howard League for Penal Reform 270

Howard, Michael 269

Hull 96

human rights *131, 354*

    'corrosive influence' *76*

    European Convention on Human

        Rights *65*

    right to family life *80*

    'twisting and misrepresenting' *80*

humiliation *162, 163, 199*

I

Iceland *348, 355*

idealism *160*

identity

    social identity *161*

ideology *23, 94, 102, 157, 383*

    ideological uniformity *153*

    ideology of conservatism *81*

    liberal capitalist ideology *149*

'I don't pay' *355*

ignorance *97*

images *348*

imitation *50*

immigration/immigrants *23, 65, 72, 79,*
    196, 247, 249, 382, 392

    Commonwealth immigration *77*

    Immigration Act 1971 *79*

    Immigration and Asylum Act 1999 *80*

imposters *82*

incitement *131, 137, 185*

Independent Police Complaints Commis-
    sion *135*

indignation *13, 151*

individualism *161*

Industrial Revolution *69*

'initial moments' *30*

injustice *97, 104, 135, 149, 224, 298, 396*

'insanity' *10*

insecurity *394, 395*

insight

    crude insight *19*

instinct *134*

Institute for Fiscal Studies *103*

instrumentality *161*

insurance *10*

insurrection *98*

intelligence *281*

    intelligence failures *185*

International Monetary Fund *131*

internet *348, 351, 398*

    internet independence *349*

    interrupting the internet *336*

intervention *17, 141, 286, 294, 302, 385*

    counter-productive *140*

    well-intended intervention *126*

interviews *19, 32, 288, 294, 297, 315*

intimidation *128, 197*

investment *265*

invincibility *202*

Iran *131*

Irish Republican Army *115*

Islam

    'militant Islam' *239, 241*

Italy *130, 400*

J

'Jack England' *238, 252*

Jackson, Jesse *112, 123*

Jamaica *115*

    Jamaican patois *60, 116*

Jarrett, Cynthia *179, 385*

J D Sports *36*

Jefferson, Tony *22, 153*

joblessness *103, 154, 196, 298*

    Job Centre *31*

Johnson, Boris *132*

Johnson, Marilynn *226*

Johnson, President Lyndon *97*

Jóvenes Sin Futuro *348*

joyless joyfulness *154*

justice *36, 160*

    Justice Secretary *390*

    retributive justice *50*

juveniles *19*

K

Keytie *120*

King, Mervyn *261*

Klein, Axel *207*

L

labelling *140, 351*

labour

    Labour Government *79, 102*

    labour market *128*

    Labour party *257*

    New Labour *140, 258*

lack

    sense of lack *154*

Lambeth *119*

Lammy, David *97, 136, 171, 226, 389*

'larrikins' *54*

law

law and order *13, 20, 79, 80, 92, 93, 96,*
    127, 141

law enforcement *137*

    overzealous *128*

'laws as tactics' *80*

suspension of normal rules *298*

Lawrence, Stephen *111, 245, 250, 384*

Lea, John *22, 96*

Leavis, F R *49*

Leeds *96, 118*

left

    decline of the organized left *105*

    far left *98*

    left liberal intelligentsia *151*

legitimacy *141, 180, 201, 259, 329, 335,*
    350

    cover of legitimacy *137*

leniency *50, 140*

Lewisham *14, 115, 200, 202, 207, 244*

Libya *129, 135, 398*

lifestyle *287, 293*

    consumer lifestyle *388*

Lion Boys *54*

Liverpool *13, 15, 72, 101, 118, 388*

Livingston, Ken *121*

London *13, 14, 30, 72, 101, 102, 111, 138*

    London councils *17*

    London School of Economics *99*

looking good *387*

looting *10, 12, 14, 15, 30, 34, 36, 97, 104,*
    142, 149, 150, 153, 193, 207, 210,
    219, 237, 279

    'Catch A Looter' *185*

Los Angeles *138, 176*

loss *13*

lost generation *45, 382*

Lunar Society *133*

Luton *96*

M

Macleod, Iain *79*

Mad Mobs and Englishmen *321*

Madrid *348, 354*

magistrates' courts *50, 269, 390*

mainstream *13*

making people think *304*

Males, Michael *139*

Manchester *13, 15, 23, 71, 81, 95, 101, 200,*
    279, 385, 388

    Greater Manchester *279, 282*

    Manchester Boys *58*

marginality *31, 37, 81, 82, 149, 150, 154,*
    196, 216, 258, 395

Marley, Bob *91, 92, 104*

martyrs *341*

masculinity *216*

    consumerism and gender *222*

Mason, Maurice *184*

Masterman, Charles *52*

materialism *19, 96*

May, Theresa *65, 99, 132, 171, 262, 263*

McLuhan, Marshall *176, 180*

McPherson Report *111*

Mead, George Herbert *176*

media/press *10, 12, 92, 128, 196, 206, 207,*
    239, 252, 259, 304, 317, 339, 347,
    350, 352, 356, 366, 369, 376, 389

    media and popular representations *139,*
        285

media values *321*

new/social media *17, 19, 23, 135, 137,*
    169, 170, 186, 237, 296, 396

    pernicious effect *131*

'old' media *174*

right-wing media *151*

social media networks *348*

state media *335*

medication *287, 290*

    self-medication *291*

Medway *307*

memory

    collective memory *30*

mental health issues *287*

meritocracy *36, 390*

Merkel, Angela *247*

Metropolitan Police Interim Report
    (2011) *170, 184*

Middle East *128, 133, 396*

military *338*

    militaristic policing *361*

    refusing to fire *338*

Millbank Tower *94*

Millwall *237, 243*

Milton Keynes *307*

Ministry of Justice *18, 194, 220, 269, 319,*
    385

minorities

    'active minorities' *352*

misperceptions *13*

missiles *337*

mistreatment *37, 101*

mitigation *318*

mob *94, 96, 104, 105, 133, 310*

    mob rule *153*

mobile telephone *12, 201*

    cutting networks *336*

mods and rockers *46*

Molotov cocktail *337*

money *34*

mood

    dark mood *203*

morality *9, 49, 128, 131*

    breakdown in *91*

    children's morals *59*

    human rights and *76*

    'moral alignment' *203*

    moral boundaries *388*

    moral certainty *51*

    moral collapse *65*

    moral compass *134*

        faulty moral compass *390*

    moral conscience *318*

    moral crisis *49*

    moral dodo-ism *61*

    moral economy *133*

    moral entrepreneurs *259, 382*

    'moral landslide' *60*

    moral levelling *258*

    moral nihilism *141*

    moral outrage *92*

    moral panic *45, 46, 151, 169, 186, 259,*
        384

    'slow-motion moral collapse' *66*

Morgan, A E *50*

'morons' *318*

Moscow *129*

Moss Side *95, 100*

motive *17, 18, 319*

    motivation *16, 19, 32, 93, 137, 173,*

        187, 281, 287, 297, 381, 385

motor-bandits *49*

MPs' expenses fiddles *35*

Mubarak, Hosni *329, 399*

muggers *46*

multiculturalism *65, 75, 76, 99, 247, 248*

    anti-multiculturalist rhetoric *382*

music halls *58*

Muslims *239, 246, 251, 336*

    Muslim Brotherhood *331, 342*

Myrdal, Gunnar *331*

mythology *197, 363*

N

---

naming and shaming *269*

narratives *19, 27, 32, 206, 225, 237, 247,*
    383, 393

    alternative narratives *216*

    anti-police narratives *200*

    class narrative *161*

    contradictory narratives *149*

    'gang' narrative *196*

    political narratives *154, 362*

    racialisation and resentment *237*

national

    national character/identity *75, 76, 383*

    National Citizen Service *267, 268*

    National Front *115, 116, 119, 123*

neglect *287*

Newburn, Tim *150, 287*

Newham *121*

nihilism *149, 154, 385*

no fixed abode *286*

no quick fix *292*

normality *258*

norms

    shared norms *225*

North Africa *128, 132, 133, 138* – *See also* Egypt

Norwich *303, 310, 312*

No les votes 349

nostalgia *259*

nothing to lose *119, 291, 386*

Nottingham *13, 15, 65, 71, 79, 81, 101, 385, 388*

    Nottingham University *70*

Notting Hill *65, 68, 71, 79*

nuisance behaviours *258*

O

OASys *288*

obligation *134*

'observing' *219*

Occupy

    Occupy London *319, 394*

    Occupy Wall Street *394*

offenders

    'known offenders' *12*

    'offender group reconviction score' *293*

off licences *15*

Ofsted *267, 302*

Oldham *75*

Olympics *121, 122*

openness *357*

Operation Swamp 81 *119*

Operation Trident *136*

Operation Withern *269*

opportunity *114, 121, 299, 318*

    domino opportunism *322*

    lack of opportunity *81*

    opportunism *20, 222*

oppression *36, 98, 353*

    oppressive state governance *22*

ordinary people *349*

Orwell, George *48*

otherness *12, 73, 75, 382*

    othering *98*

outrage *10, 134*

    moral outrage *92*

outsiders *71, 91, 92, 98, 99, 132, 323*

    criminal-outsider *75*

Oxford *307*

    Oxford Circus *14*

P

parents

    parental authority/discipline *48, 226*

    poor parenting/relationships *17, 19, 113, 287, 322, 382*

Paris *138*

participants/perpetrators *19, 30, 36, 37, 136, 196, 210, 280, 391*

    profile *194*

payment by results *266*

Pearson, Geoffrey *68, 382*

'pecking order' *225*

peers

    influence by *287*

Pembury Estate *201*

permissiveness *66*

personal histories *196*

perversity *160*

pessimism *45*

petrol bombs *95*

Phillips, Melanie *67*

philosophy *363*

phone hacking scandal *35*

pickpockets *49*

pilfering *202*

Pitts, John *93*

Plataforma Por Una Vivienda Digna *348,*
    350

plunder *30, 37*

police *36, 53, 127, 140, 239, 262, 348*

    aggressive policing *12*

    assault on police *53*

    'bad apples' *138*

    Cambridgeshire Constabulary *304*

    common enemy *137, 138*

    'donor forces' *304*

    effective policing *10*

    Essex Police *184*

    excessive policing *141*

    failings of the police *385*

    firm policing *96*

    greater police funding *132*

    'hard' policing methods *100*

    heavy investment in *141*

    Hertfordshire Constabulary *304*

    hostility to the police *53*

    known to the police *16*

    lack of decisive action *32*

    Metropolitan Police Service *184, 194,*
        304

    militaristic policing *201, 361*

    mistrust *135*

    mutual aid *303*

oppressive policing culture *391*

perceived police brutality *100*

Police and Crime Act 2009 *260*

police and crime commissioners *262*

police brutality *81*

Police Crime Maps *312*

police distrust *81*

Police Federation *320*

police harassment *31*

police presence *13*

Police Reform and Social Responsibility
    Act 2011 *262*

police repression *348*

policing as a causal factor *127*

policing public order *16*

poor relationships with *221*

purpose of policing *141*

Report of the Metropolitan Police
    Commissioner 1899 *53*

Royal Commission on the Metropolitan
    Police *53*

rural policing *304, 320*

self-policing *13*

'service of last resort' *141*

Special Constabulary *304, 310*

structural policing deficits *127*

sympathy with *10*

tactical errors *127*

policy

    policy-makers *140*

    policy perversities *126*

politics *20, 92, 97, 104, 114, 127, 159, 196,*
    210, 257

    apolitics *149, 153*

    over-politicising *21*

political capital *322*

political correctness *258*

political disenfranchisement *196*

political elites *21, 98, 129*

political manipulation *341*

political protest *128*

'political realism' *367*

political rhetoric *13*

political symbolism *94*

political theatre *340*

politicians *12, 13, 348*

politicians 'cooking the books' *131*

politics of distraction *151*

sub-political struggle *253*

popular

popular entertainment *45*

popular revolt *132*

Portugal *130, 348, 400*

poverty *18, 73, 97, 116, 196, 282, 286*

absolute poverty *103*

child poverty *261*

Powell, Enoch *65, 73, 79, 81*

power *185, 199, 321, 329, 348, 390, 396*

illegitimate use of power *297*

power imbalance *35*

pragmatism *160*

Prague *129*

predators

'super predators' *139*

preoccupations *45*

prescriptions *76*

Priestley riots *133*

prison

overcrowded prisons *299*

'prison works' *269*

probation

probation officers *390*

Probation Service *282, 294*

problems *121*

embedded social problems *20*

Proctor, Harvey *79*

profiling *279, 282*

profiteering *35*

proportionality *270, 281*

protest *9, 30, 37, 80, 92, 129, 138, 219, 336, 348*

collective protest *350*

'noble' protest *340*

political protest *128*

protest as crime *131*

street protests *131*

provocation *30, 135, 163*

psychology *216*

public

public disapproval *10*

public opinion *10*

public order *136, 238*

public outrage *354*

public safety *127, 132, 140, 141*

public space *93, 228, 386*

punishment *10, 17, 80, 263*

capital punishment *318*

firm punishment *50*

harsh punishment *13, 289, 319, 390*

penal-laden statements *269*

'proper' punishment *269*

punks *46*

purposefulness *225*

Q

Qatar *128*

R

'rabble' *98*
race-course roughs *49*
racism *12, 20, 100, 250, 281, 385*
    'institutional racism' *81*
    latent racist assumptions *97*
    'race riots' *72, 138*
    'racial dimensions' *81*
    racial discourse
        resistance to *249*
    'racialisation' *244*
    racial tensions *74, 81*
    racial violence *239*
    systemic racism *141*
radicalisation *98*
rage *115, 386*
    collective rage *149*
    'day of rage' *335*
    inarticulate rage *163*
    'rage capital' *163*
    unconscious, etc. rage *154*
raids *31, 55*
rampage *207, 279*
ransacking *30*
rap music *70*
ratcheting-up *13, 38*
Reading, Berkshire *96*
'Reading the Riots' *194, 198, 215, 221,*
    285, 297
realism *153*

reality TV *155*
reasons *17, 30, 122*
rebuilding *17*
recession *101*
    permanent recession *150*
recompense *13*
recruitment *174, 183*
redemption *110*
Redwood, Hugh *49*
reggae music *118*
regime change *129*
regulation *17, 257*
Reicher, Steve *321*
relational boundaries *196*
religion *45*
    religiously-aggravated crimes *239*
remorse *222*
renunciation *13*
repatriation *79*
Report of the Metropolitan Police Com-
    missioner, etc. 1899 *53*
repression *348*
republicanism *350*
reputation *197, 207*
    building self-reputation *197*
    'reputational extravaganza' *207, 210*
research *18, 20, 31, 207, 216, 392*
resentment *100*
residents *237*
resilience
    personal resilience *392*
resistance *92, 180*
resources *127, 132*
respect *52, 80, 197, 207, 248, 318*
    Respect Action Plan *265*

Respect Agenda *265*

respect for authority *45*

response *16, 22, 98, 263*

    academic responses *150*

    default response *391*

    heavy-handed response *165*

responsibility *395*

    social responsibility *263, 266*

restorative justice *319, 323*

restraining order *286*

restrictive practices *130*

retribution *93, 203, 299*

revenge *201, 203*

revolution *127, 128, 133, 329, 354*

    'Facebook Revolution' *336*

rhetoric *195, 226, 257, 389*

    populist rhetoric *257*

right

    far right *239*

    right-wing media *151, 383*

    right-wing punishment policies *269*

rights *134– See also* human rights

ringleaders *133*

riots/rioting *52, 237, 306*

    aftermath *23, 263*

    'August Riots in London, The' *215*

    bread riot *134*

    British custom *93*

    causes *132*

    contested involvement of gangs *193*

    exceptional nature *92*

    gender and the riots *215*

    not all the same *93*

    poll tax riots *95, 200*

    race riots *138*

'Reading the Riots' *194, 285, 297, 298*

'riot-affected areas' *307, 321*

Riot Cleanup *181, 182, 384*

Riot Communities and Victims Panel
    266, 303

riot discourse *389*

rioting examined *10, 91*

riot prevention *270*

'riot-related incidents' *307*

Riots Communities and Victims Panel
    16, 18, 216, 382, 389

riot tactics *10, 16*

'Rotis not Riots' *222*

speed and scale *169, 186*

state-sponsored riots *329, 337*

'student' riots *94*

temporal riots *388*

unpredictability *91*

USA *100*

risk

    risk factors *286*

'Rivers of Blood' *73*

roadblocks *373*

robbery *35, 97*

    'daylight robbery of the poor' *35*

    street robbery *119, 197*

Rock, Paul *46*

'Romans' *81*

'Roots' *115, 116, 119*

Routledge, Paul *70*

rubber bullets *10*

Rudé, George *93*

Rule of Law *141*

rurality *303, 312*

    rural perspectives *23*

Russell, Charles *58*

S

Sadat, Anwar *330*

Safer Communities *vii, 22*

safety *127, 140, 141*

    public safety *132*

    safe space *205*

Sainsbury's *32*

Salford *15, 101, 279, 285*

Sarkozy, Nicolas *129*

Saudi Arabia *131*

scandals *261*

scapegoating *132*

Scarman, Lord *21, 67, 74, 97, 98, 111, 228,*
    321, 391

school

    exclusion from *18*

    truancy *18*

scrutiny *127*

    'Scrutiny' Group *49*

'scum' *318*

Scuttlers *54, 55*

Second Life *206*

self-actualisation *395*

self-adornment of commodities *386*

self-defence *135*

self-harm *287, 290*

self-protection *217*

senselessness *32*

sentencing *10, 151, 226, 281, 285, 286,*
    299, 390

    community sentencing *323*

    disproportionate sentencing *16*

    tough sentences *131*

seriousness *390*

severity *299*

shaming *31*

shared perception *138*

shootings *45, 46*

shopkeepers *237*

shopping *395, 400*

    'shopping for free' *221, 298*

'sick' acts *12*

Sikh community *237*

silly season *10*

Silverman, John *184*

Sinde Act *349*

skinheads *46, 116, 117*

slavery *116*

Slough *307*

slums *97*

smokescreen *36*

social

    new social media *186, 396*

    social anxiety *23, 45*

    social change *22*

    social conditions *81, 259*

    social contract *77, 129*

    social control *260*

    social disorder *15*

    social division *82*

    social envy *395*

    social exclusion *287*

    'social field' *196*

    social inclusion *76, 154*

    social inequality *37*

    social isolation *287*

    social ladder *386*

social media *19, 131, 135, 137, 169, 237, 296*

  new social media *170*

  pernicious effect *131*

  social media networks *348*

social mobility *12, 31*

social networking *185, 197, 201*

social policy frameworks *257, 260*

social politick *384*

social problems *13*

social responsibility *263, 266*

social symptoms *16*

social tragedy *168, 176*

social unrest *9*

Socialist Worker *98*

Socialist Workers Party *98*

society

  civilised society *263*

  sick society *251*

  societal factors *19*

  societal imbalances *261*

  'society against society' *386*

  stake in society *298*

Sociological Research Online *21*

solidarity *137, 138, 355, 396*

Sol Square *348, 353*

Somers Town Boys *54*

Southall *95, 237*

Southampton *96*

Soweto *120*

Spain *23, 130, 348, 398*

Special Crime Directorate *136*

speed of events *299*

spontaneity *183, 337*

squatting *350, 355*

stabbings *45, 46*

stability/instability *102, 129*

stake *19*

St Albans *308*

standards *48*

standoff *14*

Starkey, David *60, 65, 385*

state *36, 37, 127, 390*

  'hyper active state' *140*

  multicultural state *82*

  redefinition of the state *131*

  role of the state *141*

  security state *139*

  state authority

    threats to *75*

  state retrenchment *201*

  state-society relations *126*

  state-sponsored riots *329, 337*

State of Unrest *350*

statistics *20, 68, 74, 208, 280*

  gender statistics *220*

  statistical profiling *17*

status *197*

stereotypes *17, 222*

Stevenage *308*

stocks *320*

'stolid, pipe-sucking manhood' *51*

stone-throwers *131*

stonewalling *135*

stop and search *20, 31, 100, 114, 119, 140, 199, 221*

strangeness *76*

street *206*

  'Code of the Streets' *203*

  'street Arabs' *61*

street capital *197, 207*

'street'-centred constructions *229*

Street Codes *198*

street government *193, 202*

street robbery *197*

strikes

public sector strikes *132*

struggle

'arena of struggle' *197*

stupidity *179*

substance use *287*

supermarkets *15*

surveillance *184, 201*

suspended sentence *285, 289*

symbolism *104, 175, 183, 199, 253, 337,
362, 366, 384, 386, 395*

Syntagma Square *367, 369, 372*

Syria *128, 398*

T

Tahrir Square *329, 334, 336*

Tameside *15, 279*

targeting *194*

unfair targeting *140*

'usual suspects' *281*

young people *229*

tariff *285, 299, 390*

Taylor, Charlie *267*

tear gas *373*

Tebbit, Norman *96*

technology

technological determinism *169, 172*

'Teddy Boys' *68*

Teds Under the Beds *46*

temptation *30, 37*

tensions *121, 122, 201, 281*

defusing tension *136*

territory *198*

testimonies *196, 281*

Thatcher, Margaret *96, 102, 119*

'The Adolescent' *46*

theatre *363*

theft *14, 15, 97, 285, 313*

'theft by finding' *289*

therapy *116*

Third World *394*

Thompson, E P *133*

threats *285*

Thucydides *361, 367, 375*

thugs *99, 269, 318, 322, 330, 399*

hired thugs *336, 337, 399*

'tipping element' *321*

tokenism *122*

tolerance *99, 258, 357*

'Top Boy' *113*

Tory party *47, 114*

Central Women's Advisory Committee
of the Conservative Party *49*

Tottenham *14, 28, 29, 65, 81, 97, 100, 135,
137, 173, 181, 193, 200, 210, 237,
321*

toughness *10, 93, 131, 267*

tourism *10*

Tower Hamlets *242, 246*

Toxteth *95, 100, 118*

trade unions *102, 354*

Trade Union Congress' March *94*

tradition

local traditions *196*

Trafford *15, 279*

transparency *29*

treatment *37*

    differential treatment *322*

    maltreatment *396*

triggers *28, 37, 141, 200, 297*

Trotsky *329*

troublemakers *92*

truancy *18*

truce *206*

trust *127, 135, 139, 293*

    police distrust *81*

truth

    truth events *164*

tuition fees *94, 104, 132*

Tumblr *174, 185*

Tunisia *128, 138, 335, 396*

turbulence *133*

Twitter *28, 38, 171, 174, 180, 184, 237,*
    311, 317, 398

Tyneside *72*

typologies *19*

U

underclass *10, 96*

    criminal underclass *281*

    educational underclass *267*

    feral underclass *60*

unemployment *81, 96, 101, 121, 122, 282,*
    286, 322, 350, 364

    work ethic *96*

unpredictability *92*

unrest *9, 21, 23, 81, 91, 127, 133, 169, 364,*
    381

urban unrest *149*

unruliness *67*

UN Security Council *131*

uprising *137*

up to no good *12*

urban areas *303*

    'less urban areas' *303*

    urban cities *13*

    urban street gangs *193*

    urban unrest *27*

'usual suspects' *10, 27, 140, 281, 382*

V

vacuum of authority *210*

values

    alternative value system *99*

vandalism *30*

Veblen, Thorstein *386*

victims *13, 27, 287, 307, 319*

    identification with *138*

    victimisation *198, 217, 239*

    victim testimonies *10*

video *348*

    CCTV, YouTube, etc. *238, 243, 348*

    video nasties *49, 58, 61*

vigilantes *202, 237*

violence *9, 12, 14, 16, 19, 27, 45, 66, 93, 97,*
    113, 123, 134, 135, 137, 169, 171,
    197, 203, 210, 216, 263, 279, 317,
    348, 396

    collective violence *227*

    domestic violence *287*

    'ending gang violence' *392*

    glorifying violence *60*

mindless violence *154*
non-violence *356*
'performative violence' *362, 366, 376*
plotting violence, etc. *132*
racial violence *239*
state violence *201*
violent disorder *14, 285*
virtual networks/tools *347, 384*
voyeurism *206*
vulnerable people *302, 391*

W

Waltham Cross *307, 308, 320*
Walthamstow *96, 248*
Wanstead *96*
Warsaw *129*
wartime
after-war conditions *48*
First World War aftermath *48*
inter-war years *48*
'post-war blues' *48*
post-war perspectives *47*
post-war social change *49*
pre-First World War *72*
pre-Second World War *69*
pre-war conventions *48, 70*
water cannon *10*
Watford *308, 309*
Watts, Los Angeles *138*
wealth *317*
material wealth *157*
ostentatious wealth *150, 164, 322*
weapons *295*
welfare *128, 390*

welfare dependency *96*
welfare model *50*
welfare state *139, 348, 382, 392*
Welwyn *308*
white defendants *101*
Whitehall *237, 252, 386*
Whitehall-driven initiatives *262*
Whitelaw, William *96*
Wilson, Harold *79*
windows
breaking windows *15*
Winlow, Simon *22*
'winners' *387*
Winterton, Earl *68*
women *14, 215, 228, 283, 292*
'acting like men' *228*
female Scuttlers *54*
women's centre *292*
Wood Green *96*
Woolwich *14*
World Bank *131*

Y

Yardies *118*
Yemen *128, 398*
yobs/yobbery *67, 137*
Yo no pago *355*
York University *21*
Young, Jock *96*
young people *102, 142*
criminalisation of young people *386*
gender and *221*
'lost generation' *45*
political representation *141*

urban young *141*

young people 'at risk' *268*

youth *357*

black youth *122, 123*

cuts to youth services *103*

decimated youth services *196*

demonisation of youth *138*

feral underclass youth *382, 384*

World Youth Day *354*

youth justice industry *389*

youth offending team *390*

youth provision *35*

Youth Without Future *348*

youth workers *17, 194*

YouTube *174, 238, 355, 386, 398*

Z

Žižek, Slavoj *98, 386*